icens and Conversion

Studies in Old Germanic Languages and Literatures

edited by Professor Irmengard Rauch

VOL. 6

PETER LANG

Oxford · Bern · Berlin · Bruxelles · Frankfurt am Main · New York · Wien

Saracens and Conversion

Chivalric Ideals in *Aliscans* and Wolfram's *Willehalm*

STEPHANIE L. HATHAWAY

PETER LANG

Oxford · Bern · Berlin · Bruxelles · Frankfurt am Main · New York · Wien

Bibliographic information published by Die Deutsche Nationalbibliothek
Die Deutsche Nationalbibliothek lists this publication in the Deutsche Nationalbibliografie;
detailed bibliographic data is available on the Internet at http://dnb.d-nb.de.

A catalogue record for this book is available from the British Library.

Library of Congress Cataloging-in-Publication Data:

Hathaway, Stephanie L.
  Saracens and conversion : chivalric ideals in Aliscans and Wolfram's
Willehalm / Stephanie L. Hathaway.
     p. cm. -- (Studies in Old Germanic languages and literatures ;
6)
  Includes bibliographical references and index.
  ISBN 978-3-0343-0781-9 (alk. paper)
  1. Wolfram, von Eschenbach, 12th cent. Willehalm. 2. Chivalry in
literature. 3. German literature--Middle High German,
1050-1500--History and criticism. I. Title.
  PT1682.W8H37 2012
  831'.21--dc23
                        2012012400

Cover images: Codex Vindobonensis 2670 fol. 56r: Pope Leo marries Duke William and
Queen Arabel/Gyburg (Ulrich von dem Türlin: *Arabel*) and Codex Vindobonensis 2670
fol. 66r: Duke William in battle, defending Orange against the Saracens on the field of
Aliscans (Wolfram von Eschenbach: *Willehalm*). Reproduced with permission from the
Österreichische Nationalbibliothek, Vienna.

ISSN 899-9872
ISBN 978-3-0343-0781-9

Peter Lang AG, International Academic Publishers, Bern 2012
Hochfeldstrasse 32, CH-3012 Bern, Switzerland
info@peterlang.com, www.peterlang.com, www.peterlang.net

Contents

Acknowledgements

I would like to express my gratitude and appreciation to Andrea Williams, Andrea Bandhauer, Max Walkley, Brian Taylor, Ahmad Shboul, Elizabeth Rechniewski, Annette Volfing, Anthony Hunt, Megan Kerr and Laurel Plapp.

Introduction

Ever since medieval literary scholarship began in earnest in the late eighteenth century, the study of it has been encumbered by the obstacle of genre categorization. This leads to attempts to slot certain works together, encompassing their themes, source material, characters and plots. When the cosmopolitan court at Thüringen in medieval Germany saw the composition of *Willehalm*, it was no doubt familiar with its subject matter: the deeds of Charlemagne's princes, forbidden love, Saracen adversaries, tested loyalties and valour in battle. It is unlikely, however, that they would have classified this work as 'epic' and thereby formed a framework of expectations about its themes or its source material. The myriad influences of the author and the *jongleurs* [travelling musicians] who composed the sources of his inspiration were drawn from materials with genres and backgrounds that infiltrated medieval society on many levels.

The legend of Guillaume d'Orange was possibly the most popular and prolific epic material in early twelfth-century Europe. The Old French *chansons de geste* [Old French songs of the deeds of heroes] of the *Cycle de Guillaume d'Orange* tell of Guillaume's knighthood and service to Charlemagne, his conquest of Nîmes and Orange, his acquisition of a fiefdom, his winning the hand of a Saracen queen and his later retirement to a monastery. *La Bataille d'Aliscans*, relating the two battles against Saracens intent on taking back their land and their queen from Guillaume, was most widely known and enjoyed, and survives in thirteen complete manuscripts and two fragments, more than any other in the *Cycle de Guillaume*.[1]

Guillaume was the quintessential epic hero: brave, indomitable, energetic, pious, a formidable warrior, a nephew of Charlemagne and a future saint. The battles around which *Aliscans* centres show Guillaume in his

---

[1] Bumke, Joachim, *Wolfram von Eschenbach*, 8th edn, vol. 36, Sammlung Metzler (Stuttgart: Verlag J.B. Metzler, 2004) 382.

prime, fighting against forces both earthly and heavenly to save his lands, his family and Christianity itself. 'Pour triompher, la chrétienté a besoin d'une famille solide, unie, ouverte aux hommes de bonne volonté et aux prosélytes d'ardente foi'[2] [In order to prevail, Christianity requires a strong, unified family, open to men of enthusiasm and disciples of ardent faith] and Guillaume's kinsmen, Christian and convert, come together under his command to save the realm. The text of *Aliscans* itself illustrates a carefully composed *chanson de geste*, attesting to its immense popularity and proliferation.

Building on this epic material, Wolfram von Eschenbach composed *Willehalm* during the golden age of Middle High German, some decades after the *chansons de geste* were written down. Wolfram made several innovations to the epic, such as incorporating material from other *chansons de geste* in the cycle, rendering it in couplets that characterize the forms of courtly romance and relating the story in his distinctive narrative style. In doing so, Wolfram established *Willehalm* not only as a work unique in genre, but also as one that surpassed the popularity of his earlier *Parzival* during the European Middle Ages. It survives in twelve complete manuscripts (some with scores of illustrations), some ninety fragments and numerous excerpts, more than any other courtly narrative of its time.[3]

During the nineteenth and twentieth centuries, after Lachmann's edition, *Willehalm* was viewed as a less significant work than *Parzival*. The last twenty years have seen a resurgence of interest in *Willehalm*, with many studies addressing themes such as poetic structure, narrative and genre,[4]

---

2   Lachet, Claude, 'Echos signifiants dans la composition d'Aliscans' in J. Claude Faucon, Alain Labbé and Danielle Quéruel, eds, *Miscellanea Mediævalia: Mélanges offerts à Philippe Ménard* (Paris: Honoré Champion, 1998), 783–97, 797.

3   Bumke, *Wolfram von Eschenbach*, 390–1.

4   See, for example: Volfing, Annette, '*Parzival* and *Willehalm*: Narrative Continuity?' in Martin H. Jones and Timothy McFarland, eds, *Wolfram's 'Willehalm': Fifteen Essays* (Rochester, NY: Camden House, 2002) 45–59; Wessel-Fleinghaus, Franziska, 'Gotes hantgetat. Zur Deutung von Wolframs Willehalm unter dem Aspekt der Gattungsfrage', *Literaturwissenschaftliches Jahrbuch* 33 (1992), 29–100.

the role of love and *Minnedienst*[5] [courtly love-service], the treatment of heathens and religion,[6] and the reception of the text in its historical environment.[7] *Aliscans* and its cyclic material, however, have seen a more steady stream of scholarly interest, the more recent addressing issues such as genre,[8] the development of the hero Guillaume,[9] the role of the Saracen

5 See, for example: Miklautsch, Lydia, 'Minne-flust: zur Rolle des Minnerittertums in Wolframs *Willehalm*', *Beiträge zur Geschichte der deutschen Sprache und Literatur (PBB)* 117 (1995), 218–34; Ortmann, Christa, 'Der utopische Gehalt der Minne. Strukturelle Bedingungen der Gattungsreflexion in Wolframs *Willehalm*', *Beiträge zur Geschichte der deutschen Sprache und Literatur (PBB)* 115 (1993), 86–117.

6 Much scholarship has concentrated on these elements in *Willehalm*. For example: Martin, John D., 'Christen und Andersgläubige in Wolframs "Willehalm"', *ZfdA* 133/1 (2004), 45–8; McFarland, Timothy, 'Giburc's Dilemma: Parents and Children, Baptism and Salvation' in Martin H. Jones and Timothy McFarland, eds, *Wolfram's 'Willehalm:' Fifteen Essays* (Rochester, NY: Camden House, 2002) 121–42; Gerok-Reiter, Annette, 'Die Hölle auf Erden: Überlegungen zum Verhältnis von Weltlichem und Geistlichem in Wolframs "Willehalm"' in Burghart Wachinger, Hans-Joachim Ziegeler and Christoph Huber, eds, *Geistliches in weltlicher und Weltliches in geistlicher Literatur des Mittelalters* (Tübingen: Niemeyer, 2000) 171–94; Fasbender, Christoph, 'Willehalm als Programmschrift gegen die "Kreuzzugsideologie" und "Dokumen der Menschlichkeit"', *Zeitschrift für deutsche Philologie* 116 (1997), 16–31.

7 Studies on textual environment also address illustrations in manuscripts and narrative descriptions of characters and their actions. See, for example: Chinca, Mark, 'Willehalm at Laon' in Martin H. Jones and Timothy McFarland, eds, *Wolfram's 'Willehalm': Fifteen Essays* (Rochester, NY: Camden House, 2002) 75–94; Starkey, Kathryn, 'Die Androhung der Unordnung: Inszenierung, Macht und Verhandlung in Wolframs Willehalm', *Zeitschrift für Deutsche Philologie* 121/3 (2002), 321–41; Pérennec, René, 'Histoire, géographie et écriture dans le Willehalm de Wolfram von Eschenbach', *Littérales/14 'La Chanson de geste. Écriture, intertextualités, translations. Textes présentés par François Suard'* (1994), 173–201.

8 See, for example, Kay, Sarah, *The Chansons de geste in the Age of Romance: Political Fictions* (Oxford: Clarendon Press, 1995).

9 See, for example: Bennett, Philip E., 'Heroism and Sanctity in the Cycle de Guillaume' in Martin H. Jones and Timothy McFarland, eds, *Wolfram's 'Willehalm': Fifteen Essays* (Rochester, NY: Camden House, 2002) 1–19; Vallecalle, Jean-Claude, 'Aspects du héros dans Aliscans' in Jean Dufournet, ed., *Mourir aux Aliscans: Aliscans et la légende de Guillaume d'Orange* (Paris: Honoré Champion, 1993) 177–95.

princess, love, female figures and converts.[10] Too few critical comparisons between *Willehalm* and its source material have been made, despite the advantage that this renders in understanding *both* texts in their geographical and historical environments. Some critics have, however, looked at *Willehalm* and *Aliscans*, discussing Wolfram's novel treatment of Saracens,[11] the application of a chivalric code to the epic material,[12] and the generic problems encountered by retransmitting a *chanson de geste* for the German audience.[13] Nevertheless, their focus confines itself to the alterations that Wolfram made to the source material. Though there was an effort in the Société Rencesvals of the late 1980s to initiate more comparison scholarship between Wolfram's work and the *chanson de geste*, few papers really addressed in-depth the relation of *Willehalm* to its source material. This

10   Saracens, especially female, have been a recent focus for many scholars of the *chansons de geste*. See, for example: Besnardeau, Wilfrid, *Représentations littéraires de l'étranger au XIIe siècle: des chansons de geste aux premières mises en roman*, Jean Dufournet, ed., Nouvelle Bibliothèque du Moyen Âge (Paris: Honoré Champion, 2007), esp. 303–488; Ramey, Lynne Tarte, 'Role Models? Saracen Women in Medieval French Epic', *Romance Notes* 41/2 (2001), 131–41; De Weever, Jacqueline, *Sheba's Daughters: Whitening and Demonizing the Saracen Woman in Medieval French Epic* (New York: Garland, 1998); Kinoshita, Sharon, 'The Politics of Courtly Love: "La Prise d'Orange" and the Conversion of the Saracen Queen', *Romanic Review* 86/2 (1995), 265–87; Kay, Sarah, 'La représentation de la féminité dans les chansons de geste' in *Charlemagne in the North: Proceedings of the Twelfth International Conference of the Société Rencesvals Edinburgh 4th to 11th August 1991* (Edinburgh: Société Rencesvals British Branch, 1993) 223–40.

11   See, for example, Pastré, Jean-Marc, 'Un avatar courtois de la Bataille d'Aliscans, le Willehalm de Wolfram von Eschenbach' in *Essor et fortune de la chanson de geste dans l'Europe et l'Orient latin: actes du IXe congrès international de la Société Rencesvals pour l'étude des épopées romanes, Padoue-Venise, 29 août–4 septembre 1982* (Modena: Mucchi, 1983) 333–47.

12   See, for example, Huby-Marly, Marie-Noël, 'Willehalm de Wolfram von Eschenbach et la chanson des Aliscans', *Études germaniques* 39 (1984), 388–411.

13   See, for example: Wolf, Alois, 'Rewriting Chansons de geste for a Middle High German public' in Douglas Kelly, ed., *The Medieval Opus: Imitation, Rewriting, and Transmission in the French Tradition* (Amsterdam: Rodopi, 1996), 369–86; Buschinger, Danielle, 'Rezeption der Chanson de Geste im Spätmittelalter', *Wolfram-Studien* 11 (1988), 86–106.

yielded not altogether exhaustive studies and certainly not all concerned themselves with Wolfram or *Willehalm*, but it represents an attempt to include Germanic studies. In general, these studies have not taken into account the elements that were present in other *chansons de geste* in the cycle, in addition to *Aliscans*, that did serve as a source for *Willehalm*. These elements include the Saracen princess and the role of Saracens, together with the concept of rewriting and authorship that has been investigated in relation to other medieval texts.[14] Bumke writes of the state of *Willehalm* scholarship:

> Von einem Konsens darüber, wie der Willehalm zu lesen ist, sind wir jedoch weit entfernt. Der Willehalm ist ein sperriger und schwieriger Text, der einerseits die Interpreten anzieht, sich ihnen andererseits immer wieder verweigert. In Wolframs Dichtung wird mehr in Frage gestellt als gesichert.[15]

> [We remain far from forming a consensus about how *Willehalm* is to be read. *Willehalm* is a cumbersome and complex text that on the one hand draws critics and on the other closes itself to them. With Wolfram's poetry, more is called into question than is answered.]

That, however, should be seen as precisely what Wolfram intended: to put ideals, philosophies, themes, characters and even language into question. *Willehalm* should be seen more in terms of rewriting: retelling a story for the purpose of exploring concepts in the context of its own historical environment. Alois Wolf, in his study on medieval authorship pertaining to the *chansons de geste*, asserts that 'rewriting seems to have been an essential feature of medieval literature in general and deeply rooted in the medieval mind,'[16] and he shows how the retelling of stories and the ownership of material were not the same thing. Moreover, there seems to have been a deeper purpose to retelling stories and rewriting texts, which engaged the audience in the investigation of ideals, morals, characters and behaviour

---

14   See, for example, Minnis, Alastair J., *Medieval Theory of Authorship: Scholastic literary attitudes in the later Middle Ages*, 2nd edn (Aldershot: Scolar Press, 1988).

15   Bumke, *Wolfram von Eschenbach*, 320.

16   Wolf, *Rewriting Chansons de geste*, 382.

using characters, plots and themes with which they were familiar. Wolf concludes that 'permeating all this rewriting is the monastic idea of spiritual rumination aiming at coming ever closer to the heart of the Biblical message,'[17] and also that, having been composed in the vernacular, the *chansons de geste* 'are to be understood as products of a continuous process of rewriting, similar to the rumination of the medieval monk, aiming at revealing more and more of the secrets of *minne* and *fin'amors*,' rendering each *chanson de geste* 'an element of a more comprehensive poetical process directed towards gaining ever-increasing insights into what *fin'amors* might be.'[18]

This process of retelling a story and reworking a text must have been conventional for Wolfram, too, when he rendered his *Parzival*, modelled on Chrétien de Troyes's unfinished work, as well as his *Willehalm* for which several *chanson-de-geste* sources can be distinguished. That Saracens, chivalry and *fin'amors*, or *Minnedienst*, were not only popular themes, but that Saracens were also pivotal characters exhibiting these ideals, was already evident in the *Cycle de Guillaume*, and this becomes clearer when investigating Wolfram's *Willehalm* as a rewriting of the *Aliscans* material (itself a product of rewriting), rather than merely as a German adaptation of a French epic.

Throughout this story in its many versions, Saracens feature centrally and their functions are varied. Their actions, motivations and relationships are important mirrors of how authors and audience perceived them.[19] It is essential to study both the *chanson-de-geste* sources and *Willehalm* in terms of narrative exploration of prevalent themes, especially chivalry and love-service, and no more powerful medium can be distinguished in these texts than the portrayal of the Saracen. Chivalry, with its spiritual cornerstones and motives in love-service, had already begun to be included in the *chansons de geste*, as had these ideals in terms of the Saracen adversary

---

17   Wolf, *Rewriting Chansons de geste*, 382–3.
18   Wolf, *Rewriting Chansons de geste*, 386.
19   See: Ramey, Lynn Tarte, *Christian, Saracen and Genre in Medieval French Literature*. Francis G. Gentry, ed., Medieval History and Culture (New York: Routledge, 2001).

and the Saracen princess. Wolfram engaged these elements and furthered the process of rumination through rewriting, progressing, together with *Aliscans* and *La Prise d'Orange* [*The Conquest of Orange*], further towards understanding loyalty, conquest, love-service and chivalry.

This volume also seeks to investigate *Willehalm* as a work in its own right, in viewing the themes surrounding Wolfram's portrayal of Saracens and above all to address these elements in terms of rewriting. We will consider *Willehalm* alongside its models rather than as an isolated work, presenting a valuable new perspective on both it and its source material.

The retelling / rewriting aspect allows a view of the *chansons de geste*, especially *La Prise d'Orange* and *Aliscans*, as the result of rewritten or retold stories, built upon by Wolfram to further explore certain themes as a mode of entertainment for the audience and narrator alike. It can then be said that, thematically, *Willehalm* has as much if not more in common with *La Prise d'Orange* as with *Aliscans*, and both works will be considered as sources for Wolfram's retelling of the story.

The Saracens in these texts are instrumental in the exploration of prevalent themes and they serve as links between the interrelated and key elements: conquest, loyalty and vassalage; the spiritual integration of chivalry and love-service; and the direction and practice of chivalry. Interwoven throughout these stories are depictions of Saracen warriors and knights who exemplify one or more of these important elements. Some remain formidable adversaries while some render assistance to the Christian Narbonnais; some are worthy of conversion and communion with the Christian God while some are fit only to be killed in battle. Rising above all of the protagonists, Christian and heathen alike, is the Saracen queen whose conversion out of love for her Christian husband sets her apart and whose faith, determination and influence in love-service are exemplary. It is through the Saracens that the Christian characters as well as the audience are able to learn about and explore their own behaviour and ideals: service and loyalty, love and spirituality. In many ways, the Saracens in these works are able to convey messages that a Christian protagonist cannot because of his or her position in the feudal order and in medieval society.

This perspective poses certain important questions: why, if the Saracens in the texts exemplify chivalry, loyalty, honour, respect for kinship, knightly prowess and dedication in service for love, is it not acceptable for them to be the victors? How does Christian chivalry benefit from contact with the exemplary Saracen knights in these stories? What trend do these themes of loyalty, kinship, vassalage, conquest and legitimacy follow from the *chansons de geste* through to *Willehalm*, and what influences the evolution and examination of these themes in the texts? What is learnt from the Saracens in these texts through the process of retelling and does the retelling of this story further our understanding of these themes and values because of their portrayal through Saracen characters? Most significantly, what questions are the *jongleurs* and Wolfram trying to answer through their retelling of the same thread?

Two main sections frame this investigation: the first comprises three chapters and focuses on historical background, authors, audience and themes; and the second comprises two chapters and presents a detailed study of the Saracen figures compared between texts. The first chapter will look at the motives and motivations behind the prominent themes of conquest, legitimacy, loyalty and conversion in the historical environment of the texts, providing a basis from which the ideals of chivalry develop and are explored. The problems posed to medieval society by Church doctrine, spiritual beliefs and contradictions in directives are reflected in the examination of chivalric ideals and this is achieved by more detailed depictions of Saracens in the texts. The ideal of chivalry is one that permeates these texts and the following two chapters will investigate how it is developed by both the *jongleurs* and Wolfram, who seek to show how chivalry should be directed and practised, and the figures who most exemplify its virtues. The study of how Saracens are depicted in both texts and of the common themes important to the *jongleurs* and later to Wolfram and to their audiences leads us to the complex characters themselves. The third chapter contends that the motifs, themes, character traits and attitudes towards Saracens present in *Willehalm* suggest that Wolfram was far more familiar with the *chansons de geste* than has previously been supposed. A closer look at the Saracen knights and kings in the fourth chapter, and how their portrayal changes from the *chansons de geste* to *Willehalm*, reveals a new perspective on chivalry and its purpose in the story.

Ultimately, Christianization must be seen as a moral imperative in these texts. The dilemmas this poses are personified in the Saracen queen and her duties as convert and Narbonnais liege-lady, alongside her desire to protect her city, its palace and her husband's claim to them. It is she, and through her, her brother Rennewart, who demonstrate the integration of chivalry and spirituality, exemplifying the practice of the ideals demanded of a knight and lady. In the fifth and final chapter, through investigation of her role from the perspective of rewriting and integrated sources, much more can be understood of her function in the story and of Wolfram's intentions in *Willehalm*. Certain elements will challenge the views of some critics on the objective and content of the queen's speech at the war council in *Willehalm*, and show how it was derived from the prominent figure of the queen in the *chansons de geste* to suit Wolfram's purpose. The queen stands as an example for the Saracens; conversion becomes a gateway to the proper practice of chivalry, for the advantage of God's judgement can only await a knight who has converted to Christianity.

The complexity of interpreting Wolfram's *Willehalm* can be seen to lie in the audience's familiarity with his source material. This intertextual approach opens up innovative perceptions of Saracens in the *chansons de geste* and in *Willehalm*, and what their depiction tells us about the intention of the authors, composers and their texts. It suggests a more integrated reading of the *chansons de geste* and related texts, and a broader understanding of the reasons behind some of the enigmas in Wolfram's narrative.

Conversion and Conquest

Conquest is the story of how a hero overcomes physical, mental, emotional and sometimes spiritual obstacles, or even treachery against him, how he excels in single combat or in larger-scale battle, many times with the aid of loyal friends, family, or both and how he gains renown, riches and love. It is the stuff of legend and epic, and it forms the centre of the story of

Guillaume d'Orange in the *chanson-de-geste* material that Wolfram von Eschenbach would later fashion into his Middle High German *Willehalm*. The story of the battle at Aliscans begins when Guillaume conquers the city of Orange and wins for his wife its Saracen queen, Orable, who converts to Christianity, becoming Guiborc, Gyburg in the German text. The necessity for conquest was perhaps clearer to a medieval audience and is spurred both by Guillaume's disinheritance by his father, Aymeri, or Heimrich, of Narbonne, and by Guillaume's duty and destiny, as prince of the Christian French empire, to gain, hold and rule over his lands. This conquest and its subsequent protection is made possible by Guiborc and the young Saracen Rainouart's conversion to Christianity, for it is by this change of faith that they pledge their oaths to serve their celestial liege-lord and enter into feudal Christian society, becoming loyal wife and vassal respectively, in a vow sealed by the ceremony of baptism.

The Saracen element in these texts reveals how and why Saracens were a popular adversary for the medieval European protagonist in literature and how their interrelation with Europeans influenced their treatment in literature. It is also valuable to look at the interrelation of the themes of conversion and vassalage, with attention to how these themes came to be connected to those of love, service and spirituality.

The Texts

Wolfram was an author notorious for including in his works information he had gleaned from a myriad of sources, both historical and contemporary, both factual and fictional. It is the main themes themselves, however, rather than Wolfram's added details, that will serve as the focus for this comparative approach. *Willehalm* and its source, *Aliscans*, as well as *La Prise d'Orange*, will be discussed and the latter two presented as sources of themes influencing *Willehalm*. Some debate continues about which *Aliscans* manuscript Wolfram used, if indeed any, as a source for *Willehalm*.

It can be presumed from study of the texts that Wolfram worked from a manuscript no longer extant or from performances of *chansons de geste* at which he had been present.

The *Aliscans* manuscripts used here include the four 'A' manuscripts published in one edition by Claude Régnier,[20] the Oxford / Halle 'S' manuscript,[21] and 'M' from Venice.[22] For citations, Régnier's edition will be used because of its relative uniformity of orthography and ease of reading, but the other two editions are included where relevant to the material. All citations from *Willehalm* are taken from the Werner Schröder edition.[23] When characters are compared across the two primary texts, their names will reflect the language in the text. For instance, in the case of the Saracen queen, if she is referred to as Guiborc, it will indicate the character from *Aliscans*; if Gyburg, the character in *Willehalm*.

Reading *Aliscans*, *La Prise d'Orange* and *Willehalm* together makes possible a better understanding of the interrelation between themes, plots and subject matter of all three texts, and the important thematic drive that

20 Régnier, Claude, ed., *Aliscans*, 2 vols, Les Classiques français du Moyen Age (Paris: Honoré Champion, 1990). Though Régnier's edition is a composite of the four 'A' manuscripts, he notes differences with other manuscripts where they occur. This is a clear and well-documented edition, widely referred to in secondary literature and scholarship. Notable deviations and variants of this edition from that of the 'M' MS, which is fragmentary, occur mostly in the later *laisses* and are indicated where relevant in this work in brackets, with notes. *Laisses* from the similar but also incomplete MS, 'S', are also cited where relevant. For MS comparisons, see Régnier, *Aliscans*, 8–9 and 313; and Lofmark, Carl, *Rennewart in Wolfram's 'Willehalm' A Study of Wolfram von Eschenbach and his Sources* (Cambridge: Cambridge University Press, 1972), 51–71.

21 Wienbeck, E., Hartnacke, W., Rasch, P., eds, *Aliscans*. (Halle, 1903. Reprint, Geneva: Slatkine Reprints, 1974).

22 Holtus, Günter, ed., *La versione franco-italiana della 'Bataille d'Aliscans': Codex Marcianus fr. VIII[=252]*. Kurt Baldinger, series ed., vol. 205, Beihefte zur Zeitschrift für romanische Philologie (Tübingen: Max Niemeyer Verlag, 1985).

23 Wolfram von Eschenbach. *Willehalm*. Werner Schröder, ed. (Berlin: Walter de Gruyter, 1978). When an English translation is available, it is used below citations unless detail and discussion makes necessary the use of my own translations. All unattributed translations are my own.

the Saracens provide. Special attention should be given to the character of Guiborc / Gyburg, the converted Saracen queen, who forms the centre of the plot and motivation for all three texts and who is depicted as the quintessence of chivalry, service, love and solidarity.

Cycle de Guillaume

One of the groups[24] of *chansons de geste*, the *Geste de Garin de Monglane*, comprises a smaller group, the *Cycle de Guillaume d'Orange*,[25] most of which was composed in the latter half of the twelfth century. These *chansons de geste* relate the deeds of Charlemagne's nephew, Count William of Toulouse, who defeated the Arabs when they invaded the Spanish March in 793 at a legendary battle on the river Orbieu between Narbonne and Carcassonne: Count William is said to have sent the Arabs back into Spain and out of French imperial territory. In 801, the count besieged and captured Barcelona.[26] Legends of these battles, other events surrounding them and the lives of William and his family abound in accounts of William's bravery and courage in winning the Saracen princess, Orable, of his capture of the cities of Nîmes and Orange, and of his retreat into a monastery near the end of his life. His nephews Bertrand and Vivien are also major characters, exemplifying the bravery and vitality that marked the heroes of the *chansons de geste*.

The cycles, sequences of poems forming a continuous narrative, were composed and propagated by the *jongleurs* of Southern France. They made their way into the northern regions before spreading throughout Europe at

---

24 The *chansons de geste* as a body of work are divided into groups or *Gestes* (songs of deeds) – for example, *Geste du roi*, *Geste de Garin de Monglane* and *Geste de Doon de Mayence*, which in turn are divided into cycles, a group of stories or songs revolving around a particular hero within a *Geste*, such as the *Cycle de Guillaume d'Orange*.

25 See the introduction by Lynette Muir to Price, Glanville, ed., *William, Count of Orange: Four Old French Epics* (London: Dent, 1975), viii.

26 *Chronicon Moissiacense*, George Henry Pertz, ed., Vol. Scriptores I, *Monumenta Germaniae Historica* (Stuttgart: Anton Hiersemann, 1963, 308ff).

various times. How these legends initially came to be expressed in heroic poetry and whether the tradition was recitation or performed musical composition continues to be a matter of insoluble disagreement.[27] Two views have been generally accepted, both opposing one another. Jean Rychner upheld the view that the *chansons de geste* were orally composed, improvised and transmitted by the *jongleurs*, while Maurice Delbouille opposed this opinion in favour of a cleric who wrote as he composed. Both scholars supported their views by citing aspects of the *chansons de geste* such as *laisse* [verse] subdivision, refrain formulae, unity in form and variations in manuscripts, paving the road for further debate.[28] Other prominent

27 For an overview of the debate fronted on opposing sides by Jean Rychner and Maurice Delbouille, see Ménard, Philippe, 'Les Jongleurs et les chansons de geste', *La Chanson de geste et le mythe carolingien: mélanges René Louis publiés par ses collègues, ses amis et ses élèves à l'occasion de son 75e anniversaire* (Saint-Père-sous-Vézelay: Musée archéologique régional, 1982), 33–50. Also see Bumke, *Wolfram von Eschenbach*, 378. (Though no one has yet established a clear superiority of one school of thought over the other, Ménard suggests a compromise model of *jongleurs* who made modifications to composed verse as it was performed: 'Il faut, je crois, se tenir à égale distance de deux théories excessives et systématiques qui voudraient, l'une faire de tout auteur de chanson de geste un jongleur, l'autre exclure tout jongleur de la corporation des écrivains.' Ménard, 'Les Jongleurs', 45.) [It is necessary, I believe, to keep an equal distance from two excessive and systematic theories: one which which would make a *jongleur* of every *chanson de geste* author, and the other which would exclude every *jongleur* from the body of authors.]

28 The papers presented by Rychner and Delbouille were followed by more scholarship on the topic of the origin and composition of the chansons de geste. See: Bezzola, Reto R., 'A propos de la valeur littéraire des chansons féodales', *La Technique littéraire des chansons de geste: actes du colloque de Liège Septembre 1957* (Paris: Société d'édition les belles lettres, 1959) 183–95; Delbouille, Maurice, 'Les chansons de geste et le livre', *La technique littéraire des chansons de geste: Actes du colloque de Liège Septembre 1957* (Paris: Société d'Édition Les Belles Lettres, 1959), 295–407; De Riquer, Martín, 'Epopée jongleuresque à écouter et épopée romanesque à lire', *La technique littéraire des chansons de geste: Actes du colloque de Liège Septembre 1957* (Paris: Société d'Édition Les Belles Lettres, 1959), 75–84; Diaz, José Miguel Lamalfa, 'La Culture musicale dans les chansons de geste', *Essor et fortune de la chanson de geste dans l'Europe et l'Orient latin: actes du IXe congrès international de la société Rencesvals pour l'étude des épopées romanes Padoue-Venise, 29 août–4 septembre 1982,*

themes characterizing the *chansons de geste* are kinship, illustrious lineage, solidarity, the problems of a weak monarchy and disloyal vassals, and threats from traitors and pagan enemies, especially the Saracens in the South of France and in Spain.[29]

The figure of William of Toulouse presented a magnetic and enduring subject for the *jongleurs* as his popularity ensured the composition of an extensive cycle, encompassing his Narbonnais family and heirs, the Aymerides. The stories emphasize his heroic qualities of physical strength, courage and loyalty. It was prime material for a budding nationalistic French public disenchanted by the weaknesses of the Capetian monarchy and keen to recall the exploits of a bygone hero of French imperial lore. Probably an amalgamation of several historical Williams, Guillaume d'Orange became such a well-known figure through the proliferation of the *chansons de geste* that other texts were found to have been written about him later, some to indulge the public appetite for more of the material and some to legitimize his existence and to connect St William of Gellone to the epic hero.[30]

---

v. I (Modena: Mucchi, 1982) 111–30; Ménard, 'Les Jongleurs'; Monteverdi, Angelo, 'La laisse épique', *La Technique littéraire es chansons de geste: actes du colloque de Liège Septembre 1957* (Paris: Société d'Édition Les Belles Lettres, 1959) 127–40; Rychner, Jean, Mario Roques, ed., *La chanson de geste: essai sur l'art épique des jongleurs*, Vol. LIII, Société de publications romanes et françaises (Geneva: Librairie E. Droz, 1955); Wathelet-Willem, J., 'Les Refrains dans la chanson de Guillaume' in *La Technique littéraire des chansons de geste: Actes du colloque de Liège Septembre 1957* (Paris: Société d'Édition Les Belles Lettres, 1959) 457–83.

29   These various themes are summarized and explored with reference to other cycles as well as that of the Carolingian cycle, including the *Chanson de Roland* and cycles of *Gestes de Doon de Mayence* and *Garin de Monglane* in: Ferrante, Joan M., ed. and trans., *Guillaume d'Orange: Four Twelfth-Century Epics* (New York: Columbia University Press, 2001). For summaries of themes prominent in *chansons de geste* and *Aliscans* also see: Price, Glanville, ed., *William, Count of Orange: Four Old French Epics* (London: Dent, 1975); François Suard, *Chanson de geste et tradition épique en France au moyen âge* (Caen: Paradigme, 1994), and Huby-Marly, Marie-Noël, 'Willehalm de Wolfram von Eschenbach et la chanson des Aliscans', *Études germaniques* 39 (1984), 388–411.

30   William is mentioned in several places after the proliferation of the cyclic *chansons de geste*: in Dante's *Divine Comedy*, paragraph XVIII, 46; in the Italian *I Narbonesi*; in

Aliscans

More manuscripts of *Aliscans* are extant than of any other poem of the *Cycle de Guillaume*. *Aliscans*, composed, like *La Prise d'Orange*, in the mid- to late twelfth century,[31] survives in thirteen complete manuscripts of varying length, as well as numerous fragments, some comprising elements that might suggest an earlier, pre-cyclical version of the story.[32] Besides the general points of convergence and similarity between *Willehalm* and *Aliscans*, Wolfram's own words indicate that this was the source for his *Willehalm*: 'des manec getoufter man engalt, ze Alitschanz ûf den plân' [Many a Christian paid, on the battlefield of Aliscans] (*Wh.* 10, 16–17).[33] It is generally accepted that Wolfram's model for *Willehalm* was the 'M' manuscript of *Aliscans*,[34] though there are certain alternatives that must

the Norse *Karlamagnussaga*; and as a saint in Oderic Vitalis' *Historia ecclesiastica* and the *Acta Sanctorum, Vita Sancti Wilhelmi*. See references in Bennett, Philip E., 'The Storming of the Other World, the Enamoured Muslim Princess and the Evolution of the Legend of Guillaume d'Orange' in Philip E. Bennett, Alexander Kerr and Wolfgang van Emden, eds, *Guillaume d'Orange and the 'Chanson de Geste'*, Société Rencesvals (1984), 1–14. Also see Bumke, *Wolfram von Eschenbach*, 380; Ferrante, 1–8; and Price, *Chanson de geste*, ix–x.

31 See: Ferrante, 10; also see Régnier, *Aliscans*, vol. 1, 40.

32 See Bumke, Joachim, *Wolfram von Eschenbach*, 381–3; Ferrante, 9–22; and Régnier, *Aliscans*, vol. 1, 7–11.

33 It is worthy of mention that Wolfram seems to acknowledge his inaptitude for the French language, indicating that he was working from a written or oral French text: 'seht waz ich an den reche, den ich diz maere diuten sol [See how I treat those for whom I should narrate this story!]' (*Wh.* 237 8–9). Note that the Kartschoke / Schröder translation, as well as the Gibbs / Johnson translation renders 'diuten' as 'to translate.' See: Wolfram von Eschenbach, *Willehalm*, Werner Schröder, ed., Dieter Kartschoke, trans. (Berlin: Walter de Gruyter, 1989) and Wolfram von Eschenbach, *Willehalm*, Marion E. Gibbs and Sidney M. Johnson, trans.(London: Penguin, 1984).

34 The 'M' manuscript, believed to be the closest extant version to what Wolfram's source would have been, is dated from the fourteenth century and is at St Mark's in Venice: label Venise, Marciana fr. VIII, CIV, 5. See Pérennec, René, *Wolfram von Eschenbach* (Paris: Belin, 2005), 113–14; Régnier, *Aliscans*, 8; Gibbs and Johnson,

be considered, such as manuscripts no longer extant, or oral transmission with comparative variation.[35] Similarly, *Aliscans* is thought to have been modelled upon the *Chanson de Guillaume*, both recounting the same tale with some divergences.[36] While *Guillaume* concentrates on Vivïen, *Aliscans* sees Rainouart move into the foreground.

Aliscans opens during a battle in which Vivïen and his uncle Guillaume face the Saracens, who have invaded. Vivïen, who has vowed never to flee in the face of the enemy, is dealt a deathblow after a long and terrible fight and is mourned deeply by Guillaume. Guillaume's wife, Guiborc, encourages him to go to Montlaon to ask Louis for assistance and tells him that she will defend Orange with the ladies and knights that are left. The meanness of the royal couple (the queen, Blancheflor, is Guillaume's sister) is shown by their refusal to help him. Only his parents, Aymeri and Hermengart, are able to elicit the support of their peers for Guillaume. At court, Guillaume meets the young Saracen giant, Rainouart, who is given to him by Louis, who says he does not want Rainouart baptized and is glad to be rid of him. Rainouart provides humour for the story through his almost childlike actions and untested strength. He later develops into Guillaume's loyal companion, serving heroically to motivate unwilling sol-

---

232–3; and Holtus, Günter, ed., *La versione franco-italiana della 'Bataille d'Aliscans': Codex Marcianus fr. VIII [=252]*, Kurt Baldinger, series ed, vol. 205, Beihefte zur Zeitschrift für romanische Philologie (Tübingen: Max Niemeyer Verlag, 1985). Carl Lofmark reviewed comparisons of *Aliscans* mss in detail with the same conclusion. See Lofmark, Carl, *Rennewart*, 51–9.

35   Joachim Bumke summarized the scholarship forming the basis for this opinion by citing several kinds of similarities of *Willehalm* to various manuscripts of *Aliscans* and then to the 'M' manuscript. He then noted certain dissimilarities and concluded that the possibility of oral transmission of the French material could not be ruled out. See: Bumke, *Wolfram von Eschenbach*, 384–8. It should be mentioned that Bumke's eighth edition of this volume contains revision to and expansion of the section on *Willehalm* by the author, which was lacking in editions previous to 2004. This is corroborated in Pérennec's 2005 edition: Pérennec, René, *Wolfram von Eschenbach*, 113–14.

36   Joan Ferrante makes the observation that the *Chanson de Guillaume* and *Aliscans* 'tell essentially the same story, but with different emphases.' See Ferrante, 19.

diers in battle. The rest of the story seems to centre on Rainouart, seeing him though many individual victories in the course of the last battle. He is finally baptized and later married to Aélis (in most of the manuscripts), who is the daughter of Louis and who dies bearing his child.[37] The poem comes to an end on the opening of the *Bataille Loquifer*. The spontaneity, violence, humour, boldness and conviction with which actions are carried out by the characters were seen as a sign of honour and courage.[38]

La Prise d'Orange

La Prise d'Orange takes place before *Aliscans* and relates how Guillaume won Guiborc's heart and, with her help, conquered the city with its opulent palace, Gloriette. The story opens after Guillaume's conquest of Nîmes, where he and his nephew Bertrand are becoming restless in their luxurious surroundings. Guibert, a Christian knight who has escaped from Saracen captivity in Orange, tells them of the city and the beautiful and unattainable Saracen queen Orable, whose conversion to the Christian faith is the clinching challenge that motivates Guillaume's move to conquer both the city and the lady. Guillaume disguises himself as a Saracen, enters the city and wins the love of Guiborc, but is captured. Guiborc helps him, giving him armour and weapons, and setting him free so that he can conquer the city and win its queen. Her Saracen husband, Tiébaut, however, vows revenge for the city and queen he has lost. The theme of underlying

---

37 Most of the *Aliscans* manuscripts have Rainouart betrothed to Aélis, but others, including *Aliscans* 'M', have him betrothed to Ermentrut. This is one of the anomalies of Wolfram's *Willehalm*, as it generally follows 'M' closely. Another of these unexplained inconsistencies is the battle cry of '*Monschoie*' in *Willehalm*, Charlemagne's battle cry in *Roland* (CV, 1349–1350), a point Wolfram makes certain the audience recognizes in Book III when Willehalm rides into Orléans; in MS 'M' it is '*Orange*'. For a summary of diversions from the *Aliscans* 'M' MS in *Willehalm*, see Bumke, *Wolfram von Eschenbach*, 384ff.

38 Marie-Noël Huby-Marly wrote of the demonstrations of boldness in *Aliscans*: 'La violence des réactions est donc la marque même d'une incontestable grandeur, et non manifestation d'un manque de mesure ou de maturité dont il faudrait se guérir.' Huby-Marly, 'Willehalm', 393.

importance in *Willehalm*, that seems to originate directly from *La Prise d'Orange*, is that the character Willehalm's power and legitimacy as a feudal lord rests with Gyburg, her city and her conversion; her marriage to him seals the contract.

Willehalm

Wolfram von Eschenbach, author of *Parzival* and Middle High German verse, left an unfinished poem after the death of his patron Hermann of Thuringia in 1217: *Willehalm*, composed, not, like the *Parzival*, from the *matière de Bretagne*, but from the epic material of the *chansons de geste* and the story of *La Bataille d'Aliscans*.[39] It continues the story of Guillaume d'Orange, or Willehalm, who, having already won the city of Orange and its Saracen queen, Gyburg, must defend it against the retaliation of the defeated King Terramer, who has come with his son-in-law to reclaim his lost territory. *Willehalm* opens just as the hero loses the battle on the field. He returns to his fortress to consult with his wife, Gyburg, and they decide that in the face of the impending siege by the Saracen hordes, Willehalm must secure the help and support of the imperial forces of France under Louis the Pious. Accordingly, Willehalm makes his way to Montlaon. At court, he confronts Louis and the queen, Willehalm's sister, and his Narbonnais family, and is forced to threaten the withdrawal of his fealty when support is not forthcoming from the weak monarch. There he meets the young Saracen giant, Rennewart, who enters into his service and develops into a strong knight on Willehalm's side. Willehalm returns with

---

39   Lofmark surveys several opinions on whether *Willehalm* is a fragment, putting
       all other arguments to rest with his very convincing conclusion describing why it
       is incomplete. Lofmark, *Rennewart*, 215–43. Even Fritz Peter Knapp, who argued
       for *Willehalm* being a complete work in his thesis, 'Rennewart', was convinced
       otherwise when he compared his work to that of Carl Lofmark. See: Knapp, Fritz
       Peter, 'Heilsgewißheit oder Resignation? Rennewart's Schicksal und der Schluß des
       Willehalm', *Deutsches Vierteljahrsschrift für Literaturwissenschaft und Geistesgeschichte*
       57 (1983), 593–612.

support troops comprised of Louis's princes, mercenaries paid for by his mother and sister, and the armies of the Narbonnais princes, and defeats Terramer's forces, freeing besieged Orange and Gyburg. At the end of the battle, there is a departure from what would usually follow a victory scene. Willehalm bitterly laments the blood that has been shed. He provides for the fallen and defeated Saracens. It is here that the poem ceases. Permeating Wolfram's version of this story are themes associated with romance, but found also in *chansons de geste* such as *La Prise d'Orange*: service, chivalry, love, the influence of the exotic Saracen princess and the introspection of self, spirituality and how these factors are intertwined with those of honour and loyalty.

Though Wolfram's language is characteristically complex and his verse charged with suggestion, several important points can be distinguished in *Willehalm*, his only work on the *matière de France*. The importance of loyalty and the legitimization of conquest by conversion to Christianity is augmented in the interrelation of these themes with those of service, love, chivalry and spirituality. In this respect, Wolfram does not add any new themes to the *chanson-de-geste* material, but his presentation of these themes, and the introspection he allows, reminiscent of the spiritual development in *Parzival*, stand out. Wolfram's innovations on his source material include smaller details such as drawing together the epic and romance themes found in *Aliscans* and *La Prise d'Orange*, and changing the sequence of some events to underscore thematic importance. Most important in his retelling of this story, however, is his depiction of the Saracen characters, especially in relation to these themes, which, as we shall see, both conforms to the depictions in the *chansons de geste* and departs from them by the nuance of introspection.

Europe and the Saracens

The presence and importance of Saracen figures is consistent and prominent in the story of the battle of Aliscans in its French and German versions. As the texts themselves span a period of about 100 years, and their material more than 400 years, the popularity of the Saracen character in pivotal roles reflects the continuous interaction and confrontation of the Muslim world with a Europe whose political borders, expanding as well as under threat, shifted frequently. The ambiguous cultural and ethnic borders of Europe often did not correspond to those mapped out by its sovereigns, and the exchange of trade, information and culture with the Near East, Islam and the Mediterranean world traversed those political boundaries. Through territorial disputes, wars and confrontation, as well as through diplomatic mission and intellectual and philosophical exchange, Europe came into repeated contact with a wealthy, formidable and cultured 'other': the Saracen of the expanding Arab world, a world whose borders, in the first century of Islam, spanned 'most of the former Christian Roman Empire, from Syria to Spain [...] in a conquest of unprecedented proportions.'[1]

The identification of Saracens with the 'other' is evident in medieval literature, fiction and non-fiction, and proves complex, for the Saracen took on a somewhat varied identity, as enemy as well as fellow knight, as invader and as conquered, as ally and as traitor. This is because of the challenge presented by an impressive culture that did not hold the same religious beliefs as those of Christian Europe, and therefore was not subject to a Roman pontiff, and also because there were other differences that medieval Christian Europe faced when confronting the Muslim world, including a

---

1   Tolan, John V., *Saracens: Islam in the medieval European Imagination* (New York: Columbia University Press, 2002), xiv.

reacquaintance with ancient cultures and with new and foreign technologies. Areas with ancient cultures, such as Greece, Persia and Egypt, were conquered and subjected to Muslim rule. They became connected by the use of the Arabic language, the *lingua franca* of the medieval Mediterranean world, in which documents of various subjects were written, and into which older documents were translated and disseminated. It is therefore easy to see why the terms 'Saracen' and 'Arab' were used interchangeably in medieval European literature.[2]

An indication that little was understood about the Muslim religion itself, Islam, or the difference between the ethnicity and religion of the Saracens, is the mystery that surrounds their appearance and the exotic lands over which they rule in medieval literature. Jean-Paul Martin suggests that the mysterious zone of the sea, whence the invaders come into Europe and into which they disappear, where their lands remain unreachable to Europeans, demonstrates how little was understood of the geographic origins of the Saracens.[3] There are differences in the depictions of different Saracen characters, some being noble and some fierce, wild or untamed, with no capacity for nobility.[4] Similarly, the varied, and at times inaccurate depiction of Saracens and their religion in this literature influenced the Crusaders' first impressions of the Saracens that they encountered.[5] That the Saracen was a character of mysterious origins, from faraway and exotic lands unseen, and practising a religion about which Europeans understood little, is evident in vernacular literature. The first Crusaders had to reconcile these impressions with the actuality of what they encountered and

2   Tolan, *Saracens*, xix.
3   Martin, Jean-Pierre, 'D'où viennent les Sarrasins? A propos de l'imaginaire épique d'*Aliscans*' in Jean Dufournet, ed., *Mourir aux Aliscans: Aliscans et la légende de Guillaume d'Orange* (Paris: Honoré Champion, 1993) 121–36: 133, 135.
4   Naumann, Hans, 'Der Wilde und der Edle Heide: Versuch über die höfische Toleranz' in Paul Merker and Wolfgang Stammler, eds, *Vom Werden des deutschen Geistes, Festgabe Gustav Ehrismann zum 8. Oktober 1925* (Berlin: Walter de Gruyter, 1925), 80–101.
5   See Bennett, Matthew, 'First Crusaders' Images of Muslims: the Influence of Vernacular Poetry?', *Forum for Modern Language Studies* 22/2 (1986), 101–22.

this is evidenced in that later twelfth- and thirteenth-century literature reveals that the focus of the roles of the Saracen and interaction with them revolves around that of land acquisition and defence. The drive for more land was both the threat and the motivation for attack and defence, and for the depiction of the Saracen as both an enemy and an exotic 'other' from whom knowledge of both lost and modern cultures might be gleaned; the religion itself forms only a part of this focus.

Points of Contact

Contact between Europe and the Saracens encompassed more than the martial conflicts that drive many plots in medieval literature, especially the *chanson-de-geste* material. Besides conquests and raids in stories and history, points of contact between Saracens and Christian Europe over several hundred years are found in accounts of pilgrims, canon law, diplomatic documents and endeavours such as foreign policy, treaties and the profusion of embassies. Political frontiers were by no means clear and cultural borders did not represent a departure from this phenomenon.

Initial points of contact between Europeans and the Saracens of the Muslim world came in Spain, well before the Crusades.[6] The interaction between Christian Europe and Umayyad Spain was one of enlightenment for both civilizations, where the culture, knowledge and learning that was the inheritance of the conquering caliphates of the Arab world came together with the laws and social structure practised in post-Roman feudal Europe. A great advantage for scholars today is the libraries that were kept, such as those in Cordoba and Toledo, housing volumes on philosophy,

---

6   See Serper, Arié, 'Sarrasins et chansons de geste', *Essor et fortune de la chanson de geste dans l'Europe et l'Orient latin: actes du IXe congrès international de la Société Rencesvals pour l'étude des épopées romanes, Padoue-Venise, 29 août–4 septembre 1982* (Modena: Mucchi, 1983) 179–83, esp. 183.

science, architecture, astronomy, poetry and religion, and the volumes
that came by way of Umayyad Spain in translations, glosses and facsimile
to abbeys and monasteries such as Cluny, Fulda and Canterbury as well
as many others.

Many of the impressions of Saracens and their lands to the East were
conveyed in pilgrimage literature such as Herodotus, or Egeria's *Peregrinatio
ad terram sanctam* [*Pilgrimage to the Holy Land*] (c. late fourth century),
which recognized the foreignness of the East and predated Islam.[7] Other
books introduced the Saracen culture as a mysterious, sometimes even
grotesque 'other' beyond the known geographical parts of the world.
Wonders of the East,[8] predating Islam and the Arabic conquests, and later,
St Augustine's works, precursors to Mandeville and Marco Polo, conveyed
a sense of the ethnocentricity that was pervading a vulnerable medieval Europe and an inflexible relationship with cultures alien to those of
Christian Europe, as well as underscoring the suspicion of the unknown and
of distance.[9] Such texts showed a recognition of the differences between
the Saracen and the European, a general lack of knowledge about the other
culture, and a suspicion of that which was little known, but they also reveal
a fascination with this exotic 'other', giving rise to moral indicators, and the
question of the association of status with sanctity.[10] In general, such texts
demonstrate that the 'limit of geographical knowledge was a point com-
monly charged with moral significance [...] and divine dangerousness,'[11]
but one that intrigued and fascinated.

7   Campbell, Mary B., *The Witness and the Other World: Exotic European Travel Writing
     400–1600* (Ithaca, NY: Cornell University Press, 1988).
8   This book of marvels of the unknown parts of the world written around the year
     1000 is included in a codex with *Beowulf* and other works. (See: Nowell Codex,
     London, British Library, Cotton Vitellius A. xv.) Two other editions exist, all with
     illustrations.
9   See Campbell, esp. 63.
10   Daniel, Norman, *The Arabs and Mediaeval Europe*, M.N.A. Ziadeh, ed., Arab
     Background Series (London: Longman, 1975), 63.
11   Campbell, esp. 53.

In subsequent centuries, fuelling this fear of the 'other' (the non-Christian Saracen whose exotic culture and appearance must attest to his immorality) were, naturally, the raids, skirmishes and wars that occurred periodically in a Europe whose borders were far from stable and whose political situation was at best fraught with disputes, shifting alliances and challenges to ruler succession. Trade had been conducted between Europe and the Orient[12] since before Mohammed's birth, and this continued after Islam had extended around the coasts of the Mediterranean, alongside political and cultural exchanges and confrontations, disputes over land or prisoners taken in wars, and the conclusion of treaties.[13] This interaction was a business, practised by both East and West, of exploiting travellers and ransoming captured slaves.[14] It was a result of the desire for land and power, and impressed areas of unprotected Europe with the need for safety from the mysterious Easterners, their different religion forming part of how the Saracen was defined in the medieval mind.

Commerce, discourse and conversion

The business of slave trade resulting from conquest and raids was only one example of affairs that demanded attention due to the legal, religious and cultural implications that they imposed upon the stability of medieval society. There was also a contradiction between the theoretical positions and the actual conduct of the Church, which came into the spotlight with institutions such as chivalry and endeavours such as the Crusades, during which 'the lack of any legal treatise devoted exclusively to the status of the Crusader was a curious omission since the Crusade involved a number of legal issues.'[15] As a result, diplomatic and canon legal correspondences and documents had to be drawn up. Conversion of non-Christians to

---

12   The term *Orient* is used here in a medieval, cultural sense, rather than a geographic sense.

13   See Daniel, *The Arabs*.

14   Daniel, *The Arabs*, 61.

15   Muldoon, PLI 5.

Christianity became the most direct and least problematic way to deal with legalities as well as power struggles, results of conquest and securing of borders.

The necessity of dealing with non-Christians and conversion in canon law surfaced repeatedly in areas where Christians and Muslims occupied the same geographical and political territories, where wars and conquest had effected the ethnic integration of peoples and where slaves wished to convert to the religion of their masters. One recent study makes a survey of these circumstances, citing canon laws and decretals dealing with the conversion of slaves and of spouses in mixed-religion marriages, as well as looking at debates that were held surrounding these issues,[16] demonstrating the frequency and complications of interrelations between Christian Europe and Saracens. Spain and Sicily present two examples of Christian-conquered Muslim lands in which the issue of non-Christians had to be dealt with in legal matters. The incorporation of Muslims into the army of Roger I of Sicily, as well as the temporary unity with which the Christian and Islamic Spanish fought against the threat from the African continent under El Cid, show the unavoidable interaction of these two differing cultures in war. One of the obligations of the pontiff and of the temporal rulers of medieval Europe to secure and maintain power, consequently, was the issue of conversion of non-Christians. Incidences of spiritual and temporal relations with non-Christians became a matter of legal necessity,[17] and Muldoon deduces that Christianization was part of a 'long-term effort to pacify a threatened body' and the 'conversion of non-believers became a matter of foreign policy.'[18]

One of the debates surrounding the conversion of non-Christians centred on the question of conversion by force or by free will. In the conquest of territory, force was inevitable. In war, conversion to Christianity

---

16   See Kedar, Benjamin Z., 'Muslim Conversion in Canon Law' ed. Benjamin Z. Kedar, *The Franks in the Levant: 11th to 14th Centuries* (Brookfield, VT: Variorum, 1993).

17   See Muldoon, James, *Popes, Lawyers, and Infidels* (Philadelphia: University of Pennsylvania Press, 1979).

18   Muldoon, James, ed., *Varieties of Religious Conversion in the Middle Ages* (Gainesville: University Press of Florida, 1997), 5.

might be seen as a means of making a bargain. The use of force in conversion has been often debated and centred on the conversion of Clovis, the writings of St Augustine and the idea that in many cases the necessity of the divine sign of greater force was the key to demonstrating the superiority of Christianity.[19] Though force was endorsed for the acquisition of land, or, as the Church saw it, the reclaiming of the Holy Land, 'the consensus of canonist thought branded the forced Christianization of Saracens unlawful' and Pope Innocent IV stressed that 'the act of conversion must result from a free decision.'[20] In the preceding century, Pope Urban II urged Archbishop Bernard of Sahagun in Spain to convert Muslims by word and by example, 'dealing ethically with Muslims.'[21] Similarly, in a decretal published in 1140 by Gratian, 'one of the canons encouraged debates between Christians and heathens so that non-believers might be led to the true faith by the force of rational argument.'[22] The canonists' efforts to express the necessity of free will in conversion show that a certain amount of consideration was afforded Saracens as an ethnic group and also that the sustained survival and security of papal power were principal concerns.

Diplomatic relations such as correspondence and embassies proved yet another quarter in which the topic of conversion demanded address, for much the same reasons. Victory in diplomacy as in war was seen as the triumph of the Christian faith over the 'other' who was threatening the stability of land acquisition and power. Though canon law forbade such

---

19   See: Duggan, Lawrence G. 'For Force Is Not of God? Compulsion and Conversion from Yahweh to Charlemagne' in James Muldoon, ed., *Varieties of Religious Conversion in the Middle Ages* (Gainesville: University Press of Florida, 1997), 49–62. Rüdiger Schnell, however, cites a number of textual examples supporting free will in conversion: see Schnell, Rüdiger, 'Die Christen und die "Anderen": Mittelalterliche Positionen und germanische Perspektiven' in Peter Schreiner and Odilo Engles, eds, *Die Begegnung des Westens mit dem Osten. Kongreßakten des 4. Symposions des Mediävistenverbandes in Köln 1991 aus Anlaß des 1000. Todesjahres der Kaiserin Theophanu* (Cologne: Jan Thorbecke, 1991), 185–202.

20   Kedar, 321–32, 328ff.

21   Cutler, Allan, 'The First Crusade and the Idea of Conversion', *Muslim World* 58 (1968), 57–71, 155–64, 58.

22   Muldoon, *Popes, Lawyers, and Infidels*, 4.

interrelation, treaties were concluded at times between Constantinople and
Cairo, between Cyprus, and Crete, and between others by rulers of Sicily,
Spain, and Turkey.[23] Merovingian and Carolingian Europe boasted embassies from Spain and Persia to Pepin at Aachen, and between Charlemagne
and Harun ar-Rashid.[24] Diplomatic correspondence also continued into
the thirteenth century, when a letter from Pope Innocent III to the Sultan
Saphildin, dated 26 April 1213, in the aftermath of a battle, refers to points
of unity in the beliefs of Christians and Saracens, namely that they worship
the same God and respect the same virtues, and it goes on to express a due
regard for the Islamic ruler and his people by recognizing the situation of
fault on both sides:

> [...] detentionem praeatae terrae [...]
> ipsaque reddita, et dimissis
> utrinque captivis,
> quiescamus a mutuis
> impugnationum offensis;
> ita quod apud te
> non sit deterior
> conditio gentis nostrae
> quia apud nos
> non est
> conditio gentis tuae.[25]

> [After the return of that territory (that was conquered) and the return of captives
> from both sides, we rest from the sins of both sides during the war, so that the living
> conditions of our people are no longer diminished at your hands, nor those of your
> people at our hands.]

This letter forms part of a tradition of papal missives to Sultans that
found its origins with the letter of Pope Gregory VII (1073–85) to the

---

23   Gauss, Julia. 'Toleranz und Intoleranz zwischen Christen und Muslimen in der Zeit
      vor den Kreuzzügen', *Saeculum* 19 (1968), 362–89.
24   Daniel, *The Arabs*, 50.
25   Migne, Jacques-Paul, *Patrologia Latina 1844*, v.216: column 832A. <http://pld.
      chadwyck.co.uk/> accessed 3 February 2012.

Mauritanian King Anazir (al-Nasir).[26] Throughout this letter, there seems to be a desire for mutual understanding that can be said to go beyond that of etiquette in formal diplomatic exchange and it seeks an amicable and mutual recognition of the impact of wars on the populace as well as to follow a tradition of open exchange.

The philosophical climate of Europe in the Middle Ages was strongly influenced by classical thought, such as Greek cosmology, and Persian expansion upon concepts such as *contingentia mundi*, a theological reasoning to prove the existence of God, as well as innovative ideas about the relationship between nature, man and God.[27] This proved a forum for interrelation between Europe and the Muslim world, as did law and diplomacy. There was already a convergence of religious and philosophical principles in medieval Europe. Scholars have pointed out that the argument was usually classical philosophy vs Biblical dogma and can be seen in contemporary diplomatic correspondence between rulers during the era preceding the Crusades.[28] In the East, at the frontier where two large and cultural empires stood in opposition to one another, the Byzantine-Christian and the Arabo-Islamic, there was a desire to find a universal belief formula and many Byzantine texts make excellent examples of endeavours towards the peaceful coexistence of the Christian and Muslim worlds.[29] This can be seen as both a necessary step towards and a consequence of neutralizing threat, power struggles and facilitating ease of commerce. The attitude in the Eastern Empire was such that a classical dialectic method

---

26 Bertau, Karl, 'Das Recht des Andern. Über den Ursprung der Vorstellung von einer Schonung der Irrgläubigen bei Wolfram von Eschenbach' in *Wolfram von Eschenbach: neun Versuche über Subjektivität und Ursprünglichkeit in der Geschichte*, ed., Karl Bertau (Munich: C.H. Beck, 1983) 241–58, 246. Bertau quotes from Pope St Gregory VII's letter that reads in translation, 'we believe in and confess the same God, although by different modes [*licet diverso modo*], we praise and venerate each day the Creator of the ages and Master of this world.' See: St Gregory VII, Letter III, 21 to Anazir (Al-Nasir), King of Mauretania PL, 148. 451A.

27 See Gauss, 385.

28 Gauss, 385.

29 Gauss, 364.

was practised and Christians, Jews and Muslims had through it a forum for the debate of their beliefs and the re-examining of their texts.[30]

Through conflict, commerce, canon law, diplomacy and philosophical debate, interactions between Christian and non-Christian, European and Saracen continued, the goal being to secure power and to neutralize threats to power and land. The means that later became, through various devices, the cause, was the difference in religion, and the directive to convert non-Christians to Christianity facilitated both legal and diplomatic endeavours. Later it would come to represent victory over enemies and threats, and the legitimacy of Christian rule, be it papal or royal.

Depiction of Saracens in medieval literature

The way in which Saracens are portrayed in medieval literature and histories demonstrates some key and lasting elements of medieval Europe's image of the Saracen: conflict with them is at the centre of the plots. Their martial skill, knightly and chivalric virtues, and noble lineages were admired; their religion was not understood and often misrepresented.[31] These differences allowed them to play characters in unique positions of influence that often aid the Christian characters in their endeavours to regain or to retain land and power, overcome traitorous acts, and even to become better Christians. The conversion of main Saracen characters and figures enables the legitimization of the Christian protagonists' power, success, culture and religion, perpetuating and underscoring the medieval European world view.

This world view is represented in literature in terms of the ideologies of beauty and political ambition, and of Frankish and indeed Christian supe-

---

30   Gauss, 378ff.
31   Matthew Bennett compares the portrayal of the Saracens in literature and chronicles, mainly the *chansons de geste* and the *Gesta Francorum*, showing how the latter could influence the former in what was and was not understood about the Saracen culture. See Bennett.

riority over Saracens, non-believers and their pagan magic.[32] Christianity and the Christian God are also generally depicted as a force for unity over plurality and multiplicity, a reconciliation of opposites. However, there is an underlying contradiction in almost all of the stories and Wolfram's *Willehalm* is no exception, so that in the end 'conflicts remain unresolved, [often] ending with the marriage' of the Christian protagonist to a Saracen princess and 'a state of continuing disintegration, rather then resolution, appears as a subterranean current.'[33]

The mystique of the Saracen lay in the fact that relatively little was known about the culture and the religion, and those things that were known, those impressions gathered before the Crusades and during the first journeys of the Crusaders into the Mediterranean world, were capitalized upon, reinforcing the cultural imperatives of medieval Europe and the Christian world. Exoticism was almost synonymous with the Saracen character and the physical beauty and material riches with which they were depicted were a mark of refinement and admiration,[34] characteristics that are intensified in *Willehalm*, where the Saracens' 'brilliant external appearance is not [...] ' an indication of Luciferian sinfulness but a manifestation of generosity and a high courtly standard,' illustrating 'privileged representatives of a courtly love surpassing even that of their Christian fellow-knights.'[35]

The role of the Saracen character was complex in one of the main themes and obstacles to the victory of the Christian protagonist: treason. Frankish traitors such as Ganelon in the *Chanson de Roland* were depicted as reprehensible, a traitor from within who corrupts the relation between

---

32   See De Weever, Jacqueline, *Sheba's Daughters: Whitening and Demonizing the Saracen Woman in Medieval French Epic* (New York: Garland, 1998), 114.

33   De Weever, 192.

34   Pastré, Jean-Marc, 'Étranges Sarrasins: le luxe et l'exotisme dans le Willehalm de Wolfram' in *De l'Etranger à l'étrange ou la conjointure de la merveille. En hommage à Marguerite Rossi et Paul Bancourt* (Aix-en-Provence: Sénéfiance, 1988), 329–39, 335.

35   Wolf, Alois, 'Rewriting Chansons de geste for a Middle High German public' in Douglas Kelly, ed., *The Medieval Opus: Imitation, Rewriting, and Transmission in the French Tradition* (Amsterdam: Rodopi, 1996), 369–86, 373, 377.

lord and vassal, and the disloyalty of Louis's barons in the *Geste de Garin de Monglane* is portrayed as villainous. Even Louis himself can be seen as a traitor to the Empire when he spurns his duty and breaks his word to his vassals who protect the crown.[36] However, when the Saracen becomes traitor to his own kind, the results must be condoned if it facilitates or brings about a Christian victory. This is especially true for the characters of the Saracen women, princesses and queens, who use their beauty, sexuality, power and wealth to the benefit of an enamoured French baron who gains land and power from their treachery to their family. The complex role of the Saracen women, the 'heroines [who] stand between two cultures: the culture betrayed and the culture embraced,'[37] are often manifestations of how the action governing the plots, the hero's 'need to gain a kingdom through war, since he has no inheritance,'[38] always features the assistance of the Saracen heiress. She provides arms to the Christian protagonist to be used against her family, secures the release of prisoners in return for the promise of marriage to the Frankish baron and embraces the culture, religion and society of her new husband, the victor. The dual nature of the depiction of treason and traitors underscores the ambition driving the plot: the attainment and defence of land in conquest by a Christian knight, i.e., victory over the Saracen adversary.

Though almost always the adversary, the Saracen provided a rich cultural backdrop for stories that reinforced the superiority of European Christianity and the values, ideals and ambitions that signified medieval European culture as it had developed. What better adversary over whom to claim victory than an exotic Saracen from a mysterious and faraway land of material, intellectual and cultural wealth, whose chivalry was admirable, whose martial prowess was formidable, yet whose ultimate determinant of victory, divine favour, was lacking? These exotic adversaries were often cast as monsters, inhuman and unscrupulous enemies, and 'by demonizing the

36   See Kay, 'La représentation de la féminité', 179.
37   De Weever, 191.
38   De Weever, 112.

adversary, the texts affirm Frankish standards of civilization even as they color the foreigners with their own misdeeds.'[39]

Role of Conversion

Just as conversion of pagans to Christianity made possible the resolution of issues in canon law and diplomacy, the conversion of Saracen characters in literature demonstrates loyalty to the Christian lord over the vassal convert, neutralizing threats to land, resources and power and legitimizing conquest of territory. The ceremony of baptism represents just as much a rite of investiture and vow of fealty to the Christian lord as it does the exchange of one religion for another. Conversion also solves the problem of traitors and disloyal vassals, for if such are Saracens whose treachery results in a Christian French victory over the traitor's family or lord, then the Saracen's actions are legitimized by his baptism and acceptance of service to the Christian God, lord and king, and turned into honourable acts that secure the hero's victory and gain him title and power. Beneath the immediate need to neutralize threat and legitimize conquest is the undercurrent of unity through love, service and chivalry and the idea that conversion assimilates the 'other' to the 'same,'[40] for when the complicities of love themes are in play, there is a motivation and a means for the Saracen to convert to Christianity. Though conversion was one way in which the outsider became recognized and accepted into Christian society, it was not the only way. Baptism was one of a number of rites or rituals that allowed the Saracen to integrate into his new community and be accepted as part of it, alongside marriage and knighthood. Some Saracen figures were accepted into the Christian community without adapting, such as Corsuble in *Raoul de Cambrai*, or Rennewart in *Willehalm*, because of their military useful-

---

39   De Weever, 142.
40   See Kinoshita, 272–3.

ness and loyalty.[41] In a brief survey of these roles of conversion in oaths of loyalty, love and service, we will achieve a well-defined setting for the detailed investigation of Saracens and conversion in our texts.

Conquest, baptism and vassalage

In the texts of *Aliscans* and *La Prise d'Orange* as well as in *Willehalm*, the conflict at the centre of the plot is between the Christian French and the attacking Saracens. Though obstacles might impede the progress and become a focal point for the hero, such as weak kings and disloyal vassals, it is the victory of the hero over the Saracen adversary that wins the day, be it military victory or winning the heart of the beautiful Saracen heiress. There is only one way in which a complete victory can be achieved, and that is by the conversion of the Saracen adversary to the Christian faith, submitting to Frankish religion, lord and culture, and pledging service to the French baron, giving up his title. When this does not happen, it is oftentimes the Saracen princess, a queen or heiress who, by marriage to the baron, enables the defeat of the Saracen threat to Frankish ambitions. Because the *Aliscans* material, like most *chansons de geste*, centres on Willehalm's own claim to the march, the plot and motives are depicted on a more personal level than in the case of Crusade material. This makes the issue of conversion and the entailing loyalty and allegiance an important signal of the hero's success: conversion 'sets a seal on the change of loyalty when it is confirmed by the act of baptism.'[42]

The idea of conversion in the *chansons de geste* demonstrates that religion represented allegiance rather than merely spiritual practice, and the Saracen characters have their own reasons for undertaking it. Saracens convert to Christianity to achieve and enter into Western culture and society, to align themselves with a God perceived and shown to be more

---

41   See Besnardeau, *Représentations littéraires*.
42   Daniel, Norman, *Heroes and Saracens: An Interpretation of the Chansons de Geste* (Edinburgh: Edinburgh University Press, 1984), 91.

powerful than the Saracen gods as they are depicted in the stories, or even for payment and reward for changing sides.[43] As religion can be interpreted in terms of political allegiance, a Saracen might convert because he looks to Christianity for restitution of what he has lost in inheritance or war.[44] Those who convert or achieve a position from which they can convert to Christianity and to the allegiance of the Franks are almost always Saracens within a ruling family and their conversion shatters the structure by which Christian France can be threatened; it can be observed that the 'real revolution is the break-up of the Saracen ruling family.'[45] Conversely, the solidarity of the Narbonnais princes as a family, along with newly converted members, secures their victory and title over the land conquered, as well as over the authority of the French Empire, as Claude Lachet remarks:

> La victoire d'Aliscans ressortit à cette solidarité du lignage aidé, dynamisé par un nouveau converti. Pour triompher, la chrétienté a besoin d'une famille solide, unie, ouverte aux hommes de bonne volonté et aux prosélytes d'ardente foi.[46]

> [The victory at Aliscans stood out in the solidarity of the lineage of vassals, revitalized by a convert. In order to prevail, Christianity requires a strong, unified family, open to men of enthusiasm and disciples of ardent faith.]

Many examples of conversion and changing allegiance can be seen in the Saracen characters in *Roland*, but in the *Aliscans* material the only two Saracens considered for conversion are Guiborc, the queen of Orange who is won by Guillaume in *La Prise d'Orange*, married and converted, and her brother Rainouart, both children of Desramé / Terramer, the powerful king. It is because of their familial relation to the Saracen ruler that their change of allegiance is so effective in facilitating victory for Guillaume, for once they have converted, and have sworn allegiance to Christian France and to Count Guillaume, they are in his service and the Saracen power and leadership have been rendered ineffective. Moreover, the title of the lands

---

43   See Daniel, *Heroes and Saracens*, 180–1.
44   See Daniel, *Heroes and Saracens*, 188.
45   See Daniel, *Heroes and Saracens*, 91.
46   Lachet, 'Echos signifiants', 797.

over which Guiborc is queen transfers to her new husband Guillaume once she converts to Christianity and is married to him. Therefore, conversion, the oath of loyalty and fealty, is seen in a legal and political sense, and the ceremony of baptism seals the vow. This concept is reflected in literature of the First Crusade era when conversion is correlated to vassalage, is viewed as an oath that cannot be retracted, is binding and is treated the same as vows of fealty.[47] In addition, the Christianization of the adversary legitimizes the authority and conquest of the baron over his own land, and, in the case of Guillaume, his sovereignty over the authority of a weak emperor and king as well.

The role of conversion as an oath of fealty and loyalty, as well as the necessity for securing and maintaining land and sovereignty, remains present in Wolfram's *Willehalm*. Though his audience cannot be expected to have been intimately familiar with the story of how Willehalm conquered Orange and Gyburg, the importance of keeping the march secure from the vengeance-seeking Saracens remains the goal of the plot, for although the queen has been converted and has bestowed upon her new husband the title to her lands, the threat has far from vanished with the withdrawal of Tiébaut at the end of *La Prise d'Orange*. The problem of securing a decisive victory that establishes Willehalm as the sovereign lord of the march drives the plot of both *Aliscans* and *Willehalm*, and demonstrates that this is a continuation of events that have already taken place and a consequence of the course of action taken in *La Prise d'Orange* when Guillaume decided to win both Guiborc and Orange.[48] That the final confrontation with the Saracens from whom Willehalm has taken Orange has been an expected event is reinforced in *Willehalm* by the words of Bernart of Brabant, Willehalm's brother and the father of Bertrand, the nephew who accompanied Guillaume on his conquest of Orange in *Prise*:

---

47   Cutler, Allan, 'The First Crusade and the Idea of Conversion', *Muslim World* 58 (1968), 162–4.
48   *La Prise d'Orange* IX, 262–6. All citations from *La Prise d'Orange* are taken from Régnier, Claude, ed., *La prise d'Orange: Chanson de geste de la fin du XII siècle / Editée d'après la rédaction AB*. 4th edn (Paris: Klincksieck, 1972).

du selp sibende starker man,
an den sô hôher art ist schîn,
wir müezen landes hêrren sîn:
wer liez uns lant und lande hort
âne bluot und swertes ort?
Tybaldes lant und des wîp
du hâst; dar umbe manegen lîp
noch gein uns wâgen sol sîn vâr.
du weist wol, über sehs jâr
sprach al der heiden admirât
sîn samenunge, diu nu hât
unser verch hie niht gespart.
[...]
wir hân mit schaden disen sige
errungen gein der überkraft
an stolzer werden heidenschaft.
(*Wh.* 457, 12–23; 458, 8–10)

[We seven strong brothers of manifestly noble lineage have to be rulers of our lands! Who ever yielded us land or its treasure without bloodshed and sword's point? You have Tibalt's land and his wife, and many a man will yet risk his life for that. You know that the Admirat of the heathens took six years to assemble his men, and they did not spare our bodies here. [...] We have won this victory, albeit with losses, against the superior forces of proud, noble heathendom.][49]

Bernart acknowledges the importance of attaining and ruling over land, and of the necessity for its constant defence and the significance of kinship and solidarity in achieving this. He further emphasizes, as an example, that it took the Saracens six years to return to seek retribution in battle, and that Willehalm and his clan have defeated a greater force, noble and worthy opponents on the battlefield. The importance of kinship and solidarity is underscored by the background of Gyburg herself, who is a member of the Christian Narbonnais clan because of her conversion to Christianity and the marriage vow she took, effecting her position as Margravine, loyal to her new family, with all her land and power.

49　Wolfram von Eschenbach, *Willehalm*, trans. Marion E. Gibbs and Sidney M. Johnson (London: Penguin, 1984), 221.

Wolfram effects a major innovation to the *Aliscans* material before
the second battle in the form of a war council, which is attended by the
Narbonnais princes, Gyburg and the French troops sent by Loys (Louis
the Pious). The Narbonnais each take a turn to speak to those assembled,
emphasizing the questionable reliability of the loyalty of the French troops,
and Gyburg herself delivers a speech demonstrating her commitment to the
Christian victory at Orange. The issue here lies in the fact that the French
knights have not taken an oath of allegiance to Willehalm, but to King
Loys who is not present. Their loyalty to serve Narbonnais causes has not
been sealed with a vow, so they cannot be trusted to remain loyal in battle;
in fact, they attempt to flee at the first sight of the adversary. It is their
presence, however, that is needed to impress upon the Saracen attackers
that Imperial France is behind Orange, and this requirement is the reason
Willehalm must leave Orange and Gyburg under siege after the first battle
to secure Loys's support at all costs in Montlaon. Without an oath of fealty,
Christian or Saracen, loyalty is not forthcoming and conversion is a means
of obtaining such an oath.

Conversion, love and service

In *La Prise d'Orange*, Guiborc's love for Guillaume motivates her to help
him in his conquest of Orange and its palace and lands, to free him from
prison, to secure weapons for him and to become his wife, giving him title
to the Saracen domain he has won in a symbol of supreme service that
results in restitution for Guillaume's disinheritance, for his years of loyal
service to the French imperial crown and for what he has risked to win
Orange. This also enables him to fulfil his duty as Narbonnais prince to
rule over his own march. The importance and power of love in this story
is evident in *Aliscans* in the loyalty of Guiborc and the solidarity of the
Narbonnais kinsmen, and even to an extent in the union of Aélis and
Rainouart, the Saracen and the French princess who eventually marry.
In Wolfram's *Willehalm*, love is presented as an integral part of chiv-
alry and service, a symbol of the divine, and its role in the conversion to
Christianity is emphasized.

In *Parzival*, Wolfram is decided in his message that divine love is both the driving impulse and the goal towards which Christian knights strive in order to draw closer to God, and that human love is an extension of the divine. The love of the heathen Feirefiz, Parzival's half-brother, for Repanse the Grail bearer, results in his conversion to Christianity, which in turn gives him the gift of being able to see the Grail. This is the way towards God and the only way that Feirefiz can become capable of seeing the Grail, an embodiment of divine favour. However, Feirefiz forged friendships with Parzival and enjoyed relationships with other Christians without feeling any obligation to convert to Christianity. He does not ask to convert in order that he may see the Grail; rather, it is his love for the maiden, Repanse, that is the primary motivating force.[50] For Wolfram, emphasis is placed upon the journey towards the desire to convert and upon the motivation for that desire more than upon conversion as an obligation. In *Parzival*, significance lies in this love and its workings in the character of Feirefiz and not in the inevitable and certain triumph of Christianity. Love is seen as the proof of the existence of God. Feirefiz is spurred to convert to Christianity not through force, reason or debate, but through his own volition, the divinity of love, brotherhood, service and compassion having been powerfully demonstrated to him by the Christian knights around him, and it is love that underscores his eventual baptism. Conversion is the symbolic first step towards living harmoniously with God.

In *Willehalm*, however, there is no corresponding *Munsalvaesche* [Grail castle] at which a mystical unification with God can be achieved. Though this material is generically different from the *matière de Bretagne* with which Wolfram worked previously, he seems to find the points and themes in it that most exemplify the ideals of a spiritually directed chivalry and to develop them. In *Willehalm*, epic material takes place at a temporal level, presenting characters with an individuality and a humanity with which the audience can identify. Willehalm himself is the embodiment of the Christian knight from the very beginning of Wolfram's narrative, developed

---

50   Wolfram von Eschenbach, *Parzival*, ed. Albert Leitzmann, 7th edn, 3 vols (Tübingen: Altdeutsche Textbibliothek, 1961), 813, 9–819.

physically, mentally and spiritually, and having already achieved renown for heroic service. He is highly capable, as we see right away when the story opens during the first battle, and piety comes as effortlessly to him as his expressions of duty, of devotion to his kinsmen and of service to ladies. As a knight, Willehalm possesses these laudable qualities, but he is also fallible and not a stranger to grief. He laments the situation into which fate has cast him: he must go into battle against Gyburg's family, who have besieged Orange and defeated, killed or captured all of his knights. He knows that he will emerge victorious, but there will be no celebration, for he will be forced to kill Saracens who are unbaptized; they are his relations by marriage and also relations of his friend Rennewart, and his actions will consign their souls to eternal damnation. He knows that no matter what steps he takes, this result is inevitable and it will be a sin: 'diu lücke ist ungeheilet, die mir jâmer durchez herze schôz' [The gaping hole that misery shot through my heart is still unclosed] (*Wh.* 456, 4–5).[51] Willehalm is well aware of his goal to quash threats and to legitimize his claim over Orange and he regrets that it will come at a spiritual price. The only solution is the conversion of the Saracens to Christianity, but to the last lines of the fragment, Gyburg remains the only converted Saracen.

Only when the medieval world is unified in Christian chivalry can the goals of redemption and absolution be realized, for without redemption and unity a world of harmony can never be achieved. Though the story might seem one of underlying pessimism and grief, its overtones are those of hope. The challenges that face the hero are overcome with the help, devotion, love and service not of his imperial liege-lord or an enlightened Christian mentor, but of his converted Saracen wife, Gyburg, and his faithful companion, her brother, the young and yet unconverted Saracen, Rennewart. Although Rennewart is of Saracen origin, it is he who, through his own nobility and in fulfilment of his loyal duty to Willehalm, turns back the fleeing French forces and makes them present again on the battlefield, symbolizing the might and support of the Christian empire. The eventual result is victory for Willehalm. Willehalm's personal obstacles,

51   Gibbs and Johnson, 220.

however, must also be overcome and Wolfram indicates in the prologue that this will be a key challenge:

swenn er gediende dînen haz
mit sündehaften dingen,
dîn erbarme kunde in bringen
An diu werc daz sîn manheit
dînen hulden wandels was bereit.
dîn helfe in dicke brâhte ûz nôt.
(*Wh.* 2, 28 – 3, 3)[52]

[Even if he merited Thy displeasure by sinful action, Thy Mercy knew how to guide him to works of such a kind that, with manly courage at his disposal and by means of Thy Grace, he was capable of making amends.]

The exact nature of this sinful action has been debated and three suggestions have been proposed: that it is his treatment of his sister, the queen, at Montlaon;[53] that it is his killing of Arofel after the Saracen has surrendered;[54] or that it is his questioning of God's will after the second battle.[55] However, as Burghart Wachinger points out, questioning the Christian Crusade ideology here only activates the already strong imperial conscience of the public.[56] Additionally, Willehalm later regrets that he has slain Arofel in combat, recognizes that he was acting out of grief for Vivianz and accepts the punishment love has inflicted upon him – namely, that the costly shield he has taken from Arofel is destroyed in the monastery fire. Willehalm's violent treatment of his sister at Montlaon can be seen as entirely justified,

---

52 Gibbs and Johnson, 18.
53 See Starkey.
54 See Rushing, James A., 'Arofel's Death and the Question of Willehalm's Guilt', *Journal of English and Germanic Philology*, October (1995), 469–82.
55 See Greenfield, John T., 'Willehalm's Fall from Grace', *Neophilologus* 73/2 (1989), 243–53.
56 See Wachinger, Burghart, 'Schichten der Ethik in Wolframs Willehalm' in Michael S. Batts, ed., *Alte Welten, neue Welten: Akten des IX. Kongresses der Internationalen Vereinigung für Germanische Sprach- und Literaturwissenschaft* (Vancouver, BC/ Tübingen: Niemeyer, 1995), 49–59.

as she earns the harshest rebuke for refusing her duty as liege-lady and her responsibility to influence the king on behalf of her kinsmen, and Wolfram later allows her to redeem herself admirably.[57] Other actions can be suggested, such as the past conquest of Orange, the killing of Tybalt's sons, Willehalm's losing of his own nephews on the battlefield or even going into battle against Tybalt and Terramer. Whatever Willehalm's sinful actions might be, be they within the text of *Willehalm* or in its background, they can only be surmised. The significant theme is that of redemption and of loyalty in service. In the spirit of Roland, who offered up his right glove to God in a demonstration of service to his celestial liege-lord, Willehalm, a future saint, never falters as a Christian knight. In the end, his actions are exemplary: he shows mercy to the defeated and laments his losses; his love for the noble Gyburg inspires him to respect and care for her fallen kinsmen, making sure they receive embalming effects and safe passage to the Saracen ships. He takes no prisoners himself, but collects those that have been taken at the camps of his men to exchange them for the missing Rennewart (if he is found to be a prisoner of the Saracens). This action demonstrates mercy and largesse, in that prisoners were a commodity that could be held for a ransom of land, riches and power.

Gyburg is the magnetic character who, by the time *Willehalm* is written, defines the ideals of loyalty, duty, vassalage, conversion, service, love, legitimacy in conquest, unity in solidarity, salvation, redemption and perfect spiritual chivalry. Above all, she inspires Willehalm towards perfection in Christian knighthood and spiritual chivalry. Her speech at the war council is innovative and through it Wolfram reveals some idealist ambitions for this story: a strong woman, a convert who has ties on both sides, Saracen and Christian, offers the hope that there can be victory without the sin of killing kinsmen to stain the soul. Building the bridge becomes a matter of applying the ideal to actuality and employing all of what Christian chivalry means: mercy, respect for the adversary and conversion and baptism as an

---

57   See Hathaway, Stephanie, 'Women at Montlaon: The Influential Roles of the Female Characters in Court Negotiations in *Aliscans* and Wolfram's *Willehalm*', *Neophilologus* 93 (2009), 103–21.

oath of temporal and spiritual loyalty. Loyalty is the concept that has been seen as demonstrating the spiritual and religious[58] viewpoint from which Wolfram writes and it causes his audience to reflect upon harmony and unity between Saracen and Christian.[59] In Gyburg, there is a unity of opposing sides, but it comes at a cost: being at the very centre of the dispute, she also symbolizes the reason for battle and the resulting deaths.

Focusing upon the story of Guillaume d'Orange, it can be seen that *Willehalm* builds upon the key themes from both *Aliscans* and *La Prise d'Orange*: the themes of conquest, love and service. These are endeavours profoundly affected by the prospect of conversion to the Christian faith and the pledge of service and loyalty as a vassal. The conversion to Christianity of the formidable Saracen adversary is seen as the ultimate victory, for thereby is gained a loyal vassal from a rich culture, a culture that has interacted with medieval Europe not only through conflict but also through commerce, diplomacy and intellectual pursuits, fuelling the integration and borrowing that occurred on a wide scale between the Arabo-Islamic world and medieval Europe. The Saracen characters in all three texts demonstrate this influence, as well as Wolfram's philosophical anticipations, by their actions and impact upon the plot. It emerges that their conversion to Christianity or the prospect of such a conversion is a central achievement in the success of the protagonist, Guillaume / Willehalm, in the perpetuity and safety of his march, lands and his title to them and in the legitimacy of Christian victory and rule, as well as signalling salvation and redemption. Wolfram adds to these important themes the facets of spirituality and chivalry, and interrelates them in his intricately woven plot with love and service, ideals that culminate in the pivotal character of Gyburg, the Saracen Queen.

---

58   Spirituality, the more personal relationship between man and God, as opposed to religion, the presribed practice. See also 'Spiritual chivalry and Sufism' in Chapter 2.

59   Schnell, 186–7, 202.

Chivalry and Crusades

swes leben sich sô verendet,
daz got niht wirt gephendet
der sêle durch des lîbes schulde,
und der doch der werlde hulde
behalden kan mit werdekeit,
daz ist ein nütziu arbeit.

(*Parzival*: 827, 19–24)[1]

[When a man's life ends in such a way that God is not robbed of his soul because of
the body's sinning and who nevertheless succeeds in keeping his fellows' good will
and respect, this is useful toil.][2]

The last lines of Wolfram's *Parzival* resound as a lesson reached through
reflection, through exploration of life, its values and its problems, and
through searching for an answer to the inconsistencies and contradictions
resulting from courtly behaviour and its consequences, expressed here by the
author. The self-reflective quality in Wolfram's works gives us an impression
of the courtly mindset with regard to knighthood and chivalry in literature.
Parzival's terrestrial and spiritual journey to find the Grail enabled him
to realize that chivalry would, though love, bring humans closer together
and closer, ultimately, to God. These lines suggest that Wolfram proposed
chivalry as an answer: 'Here [in *Parzival*], expressed without falter, is the

1   All excerpts from *Parzival* are taken from Wolfram von Eschenbach, *Parzival*,
    ed., Albert Leitzmann. 7th edn, 3 vols. Heft: Parzival. (Tübingen: Altdeutsche
    Textbibliothek, 1959–1961).
2   Wolfram von Eschenbach. *Parzival*, trans. Arthur Thomas Hatto (London: Penguin,
    2004, 410–11).

answer of chivalry to that *Contemptus Mundi* by whose austere authority the ordinary layman was apt to be overawed.'[3]

The problem, however, is more in question than the answer. Is the problem a human inconsonance with a *contemptus mundi* philosophy or is it the search for the coexistence of certain values within the code of chivalry itself: service and love, motivation and reward, in which moral weaknesses are exposed and explored by Wolfram through a type of triangulation method, a trial and error, as in *Parzival*?[4] Wolfram does not disregard chivalry in *Willehalm*, but makes use of its conventions, its characteristics and its familiarity. In *Parzival*, he sharpens the perception of the code of chivalry, explores its strengths and weaknesses, and expands its spiritual significance, thus arriving at an answer that is not an end: that perfection cannot be attained and that there is only striving. This attitude exploits the inherent morals and values of chivalry in their spiritual sense and applies them to the fallible, human world of the thirteenth century with its contradictory philosophies and conflicting sense of propriety. Wolfram uses chivalry as a tool to convey a philosophical message that his thirteenth-century audience would have understood as being consistent with its medieval world view. However, the chivalry of the romance *Parzival* is not the same chivalry that we see in the epic material of *Willehalm*.

To understand Wolfram's chivalry, it is necessary to ask what defines knightly behaviour in *Willehalm* and its sources, taking into account the development of a concept of chivalry in Europe, its geopolitical environments, and its influences on and by the Church.[5] What is Wolfram's idea of knighthood and chivalry? How and why does he incorporate these ideals into *Willehalm*? We will look at the development of twelfth-century

3   Richey, Margaret Fitzgerald, *Studies of Wolfram von Eschenbach* (Edinburgh: Oliver and Boyd, 1957), 115.

4   See Clifton-Everest, John, 'Knights-Servitor and Rapist Knights: A Contribution to the Parzival/Gawan Question', *ZfdA* 119/3 (1990), 290–317.

5   Parts of this chapter apear in Hathaway, Stephanie, 'From Knight to Chevalier: Chivalry in the chanson de geste Material from Aquitaine to Germany' in Stephanie Hathaway and David W. Kim, eds, *Intercultural Transmission Throughout the Medieval Mediterranean* (London: Continuum, 2012).

chivalry and those philosophies that influenced its core to elucidate the connection between spirituality and chivalry.

Though *Willehalm* and *Aliscans* are not Crusading stories, the role of the Crusades in these texts should not be disregarded in their reading. The concept of a courtly code of ethics features strongly and can be seen with regard to Saracen and Christian relations. A uniqueness in the German depiction of chivalry and the Crusades in *Willehalm* can then be seen to be due to the chronological and geopolitical environment during the composition of the text, resulting in a difference in the depiction of Saracens, yet reflecting the same attitudes towards their conversion to Christianity as its sources.

Harmony and Spirituality

A marked characteristic of the Middle Ages was the far-reaching application of the concept of chivalry among the nobility, the new patrons of a culture which has been described as being 'characterized by definite rules of social behavior stressing the knightly virtues.'[6] The concept of chivalry has also been defined as the knightly system with its religious, moral and social code.[7] Chivalry is closely associated and indeed came of age with the emergence in Europe of a kind of courtly code that dictated commerce between the sexes and advocated the veneration of ladies. The practice of chivalry was already manifest in the poetry and songs of the troubadours that made their way from southern France and Spain into the rest of Europe. By the thirteenth century, almost every piece of secular literature and lyric concerned itself with a chivalry that included knightly and courtly codes. A

---

6   Reinhardt, Kurt F., *Germany: 2000 Years*, vol. 1 (New York: Continuum, 1990), 97.

7   *The Oxford Dictionary of English*. 2nd edition revised. (Oxford: Oxford University Press, 2005).

code of chivalry could also entail more than just communion between the sexes; it could dictate the order of a society, its classes and its legal aspects. Jesús Rodríguez-Velasco's work on the *Order of the Sash* in Alfonso X's Castile illuminates this aspect of chivalry. He characterizes chivalry eloquently as 'an integral principle of Western politics, society, and morality' that influenced interpersonal networks, vocabulary and civil life, and a code for it represented a strategy for transformation.[8]

Chivalry remains a difficult term to define within distinct parameters, its very meaning variable, complex and even ambiguous, its strictures elusive.[9] The benefit of more than a century of focused scholarship on chivalry and its nuances demonstrates this diversity in opinion of what chivalry can be said to have encompassed in the Middle Ages. Jeremy duQuesnay Adams surveyed literature on chivalry, deriving a definition of the English usage of the word in terms of three aspects: martial prowess, social groups and code.[10] Bumke's works on the term 'knighthood' explore the implications of service and nobility while other scholars like Georges Duby, Jean Flori and Margaret Switten have concentrated on the aspects of chivalry as an order or ethos which was influenced by and in turn influenced medieval

8   Rodríguez-Velasco, Jesús D., *Order and Chivalry: Knighthood and Citizenship in Late Medieval Castile*, Eunice Rodriguez Ferguson, transl., The Middle Ages (Philadelphia, University of Pennsylvania Press, 2010), 1.

9   Maurice Keen, in his 1984 volume on chivalry, notes that 'chivalry is an evocative word [...] a word elusive of definition, [...] a word used in the middle ages with different meanings and shades of meaning by different writers and in different contexts.' Keen, Maurice, *Chivalry* (New Haven, CT: Yale University Press, 1984), 1–2. Similarly, Margaret Switten opens her exploration of the term *chevalier* with the remark: 'Although at first glance the meaning of chevalier seems self-evident, the term is not easily defined.' See Switten, Margaret, 'Chevalier in Twelfth-Century French and Occitan Vernacular Literature' in Howell Chickering and Thomas H. Seiler, eds, *The Study of Chivalry: Resources and Approaches* (Kalamazoo, MI: Medieval Institute Publications, 1988), 403–47, 403.

10   Adams, Jeremy duQuesnay, 'Modern Views of Medieval Chivalry, 1884–1984' in Howell Chickering and Thomas H. Seiler, eds, *The Study of Chivalry: Resources and Approaches* (Kalamazoo, MI: Medieval Institute Publications, 1988), 41–89.

literature.[11] By the twelfth century, this ethos was manifest as an ideology, 'paralleling in a way a codification of aristocratic courtly life, [and] it is possible to speak of a development in the status and the inner being of the *chevalier*,'[12] which would come to mark the flourishing of the ideal in medieval literature.

That chivalry became more closely integrated with spirituality in the twelfth century is evident in that, for the first time in European history, the warrior, his accoutrements and his society were religiously consecrated, motivated and even directed by the Christian Church.[13] It can therefore be put forward that this is the point at which knighthood became chivalry. Wacyf Boutros Ghali defines chivalry in terms of its religious elements, writing that it is a combination of ideas, morals, sentiments and institutions that cannot be held to one formula and that has its beginnings as a religious institution.[14] Some origins of this spiritual element of chivalry can be observed in the influences from the Islamic Mediterranean, and its sentiments prevail in the romances composed in Europe throughout the Middle Ages. By following the transformations of chivalry in terms of knighthood, spirituality, philosophy and Europe's centres of culture, we can observe the emergence of a class of nobility requiring expression, refinement and endorsement. It is valuable at this point to consider the origins of European chivalry and its influences, thereby setting the parameters for the discussion of Saracens as they are represented in our texts.

---

11   See: Switten; Duby, Georges, *Les trois ordres: ou l'imaginaire du féodalisme* (Paris: Gallimard, 1978); Flori, Jean, *L'essor de la chevalerie XIᵉ–XIIᵉ siècles*, Travaux d'histoire éthico-politique XLVI (Geneva: Droz, 1986); and Bumke, Joachim, *Studien zum Ritterbegriff im 12. und 13. Jahrhundert*, trans. W.T.H. and Erika Jackson (New York: AMS Press Inc, 1977).

12   Switten, 434.

13   See Fahrner, Rudolf, *West-Östliches Rittertum: Das ritterliche Menschenbild in der Dichtung des europäischen Mittelalters und der islamischen Welt*, ed. Stefano Bianca (Graz: Akademische Druck- und Verlagsanstalt, 1994), 16.

14   Ghali, *La Tradition chevaleresque des Arabes* (Paris: Plon-Nourrit, 1919), 1. Although written during the earlier years of the twentieth century, this volume is valuable to the investigation of Oriental chivalry as the subject of Arabic knighthood has rarely since been treated with as much detail and thought from a European perspective.

Origins of the knight

If we take a retrospective view from *Willehalm*, the latest of our texts, on knighthood and chivalry as they appear in courtly literature, imbued with undertones of service, conscience, duality and spirituality coupled with suffering and fate, we find that the source of these concepts in a post-Roman Carolingian Europe becomes focal. The investigation of a source or an origin for the concept of chivalry in medieval Europe inevitably leads to France: 'Von dort kam mit der höfischen Kultur und den höfischen Romanen das Wort *chevalier*, in dem fast alles das vorgeprägt ist, was dann den adligen Ritterbegriff in Deutschland auszeichnet' [With the courtly culture and courtly romance that came from there, came also the word 'chevalier', which held all the connotations that would distinguish this noble knightly term in Germany].[15] France, and indeed all of Europe, already enjoyed the institution of knighthood as an order for warriors, with a place in the feudal system that depended upon loyalty and vassalage for its survival. This feudal system which evolved, rescuing Europe from the bitter times following the death of Charlemagne and his empire,[16] made use of the knights of warrior societies that had been a part of European culture since before the Roman conquest. As the use of the horse and mounted armies came into prominence, so too did the image and ideal of a knight.

It is known from the writings of Tacitus that Germanic tribes exhibited a certain code of warrior conduct that included honour gained in battle.[17] It has also been suggested that the influences of the mounted peoples invading Europe from the Eastern Gothic Kingdom to the Iberian

15   Bumke, *Ritterbegriff*, 94. Bumke also writes that 'die deutsche Rittervorstellung der Blütezeit ist nicht denkbar ohne den Impuls aus Frankreich' [the German image of knighthood in the Golden Age would be unthinkable without the impulse from France] (95).

16   See: Owen, D.D.R., *Noble Lovers* (London: Phaidon Press Limited, 1975), 13.

17   See a summary of the characteristics of Germanic warriors by Ghali, in which he cites Tacitus and Herder, among others, in Ghali, 7–9. See also: Fahrner, 29–33.

Peninsula had a profound effect on the ideal of the warrior-horseman.[18] There is even evidence from literature of classical antiquity that suggests a type of knighthood in the classical hero, augmented when these texts were translated into the German and French languages of the Franks.[19] Did this code of knighthood originate with the Germanic tribes of pre-Christianized Europe or with their neighbours to the south in the classical world on the Mediterranean rim? Did it originate with the energy of the Merovingians or the troubadours who wandered from Umayyad Spain into Aquitaine and Provence?[20] It seems to be generally accepted that a kind of chivalry, implying knighthood or a warrior code, striving towards nobility in character, was a universal occurrence that demonstrated itself in various cultures throughout the medieval world.[21]

18 Rudolf Fahrner gives an overview of the mounted peoples arriving in Europe and writes that the Huns were the first Asian horsemen in Europe circa AD 558. See Fahrner, 25–7.

19 Fritz Peter Knapp summarizes some of the texts of classical antiquity, using examples such as Achilles, Joshua, David, Judas Maccabeus, Caesar, Alexander and Hector embodying the perfect knight, in order to show that the once purely political contrast between the Orient and Occident of the Caesars became surpassed by a medieval war between religions. Knapp notes that there are differences between the French and German translations of these classical works and he concludes from this that the encounters can be seen to be less as conflicts between East and West, and more as the first test of European knighthood in battle. See Knapp, Fritz Peter, 'Die grosse Schlacht zwischen Orient und Okzident in der abendländischen Epik: Ein antikes Thema in mittelalterlichem Gewand', *Germanisch-romanische Monatsschrift* 24/2 (1974), 129–52, 130–42.

20 Among many references to the influence of Arabic poetry upon Europe is the treatment this subject receives by Wacyf Ghali in his 1919 volume. Ghali discusses loanwords into French and Spanish from Arabic, use of Arabic metre in French and Spanish poetry, and the employment of troubadours in European embassies. See Ghali, 15–19. John Jay Parry also discusses the Arabic metric forms and themes later used by troubadours of southern Europe: see Capellanus, Andreas, *The Art of Courtly Love*, trans. John Jay Parry, ed. W.T.H. Jackson, Records of Civilization, Sources and Studies (New York: W.W. Norton, 1969), 8.

21 Rudolf Fahrner gives examples of acts of chivalry and a recognized code of behaviour from literature from around the world to illustrate this phenomenon, including texts from Japan and Persia. See: Fahrner, 16–21; Ghali, 3–4.

Chivalry as it existed placed high value on characteristics such as humanity in combat, generosity after victory, the quest for moral perfection and a concept of love that became refined, exalted and mystical, the foremost motivator of manly action.[22] Ghali sees chivalry as an inherent tendency in the nature of humankind: the desire for glory, passion and love, and for rules and governances made according to moral refinements.[23] However, he discounts that either the Germanic tribes or classical antiquity could have initiated any such influence over the chivalry that was to become Europe's.[24] While a recognition of forms of warrior codes existed in Europe prior to the twelfth century, with importance placed upon loyalty and vassalage, the emergence of a refinement of these values came not from the world of classical antiquity or from the ethics inherent in the tribes of Europe, but rather developed there with the benefit of influences from the Islamic Mediterranean at an opportune time when the cultures of Europe were ripe for it.

From France, where chivalry can be seen to be firmly established in one form or another in the literature of the thirteenth century, and in Provence in the twelfth century, one looks back towards Spain and the Islamic World for the influences that further refined a code of chivalry already forming under the established feudal regime, a regime largely reserved for nobles, an institution with a uniform manner exalting the warrior, his horse and his moral perfection. The development of these virtues can be traced in the literature of the troubadours, the *chansons de geste* and later in the romances. The refining traits of this chivalry exposed themselves in the spiritual and religious significance of the duty to service, in expression through poetry and in a courtly code of love. Though France is accepted as the cradle of this kind of European chivalry, whence the concept proliferated throughout Europe, the influence of the centuries-old cultures from the Islamic

---

22 Ghali, 3.
23 Ghali, 13–14.
24 Ghali, 8–9. Ghali also quotes from a letter from El-Malek-el-Nacer (1080–1225) 'boire en l'honneur du kalife la coupe de Chevalerie,' (sic) [drink [from the cup of] chivalry to the honour of the caliph] that he says establishes that Occidental chivalry did not exist as either a concept in itself or an institution until the twelfth century (28).

Mediterranean upon France and the rest of Europe during the Middle Ages should not be overlooked.[25] Though it is not within the scope of this study to suggest that Wolfram or even the *jongleurs* and troubadours had any first-hand knowledge of the Arab world or Arabic texts, the significance of the interchange of stories and ideas influencing both author and audience must be considered.

Saracen knights

During a time of heightened contact and relations with the Islamic World, it is only logical to search for such influential elements that would merge with one another and it is perhaps practical to think of the Eastern influence on medieval European chivalry as a balancing blend of effective concepts, much the same way that George Makdisi showed the European university to have evolved:

> The University, at first, was strictly European; and the college, strictly Islamic. But as the university absorbed the functions of the college, it took on characteristics which had their origins in Islam. [...] In this fusion of the elements, the medieval West benefited greatly by marrying the corporation to the charitable trust [...] it was the combination of both concepts that gave the composite institution the stability and flexibility it needed. Its remarkable longevity is due in great measure to a marriage of the two concepts.[26]

Likewise, the institution of chivalry as it came to exist in medieval Europe was a synthesis of ideals, spiritual and ethical, from Europe's own

25 Some scholars discount the significance of any influences from the Islamic Mediterranean upon the chivalry of France, while others entertain the possibility that it was great. John Jay Parry presents one reason for the former view in a pert footnote: 'Opposition to the theory of Arabic influence seems to be due largely to the reluctance of the modern school of French scholars to admit that French literature is indebted to any source outside its own country and ancient Rome.' Parry, 7, n. 31.

26 Makdisi, George, 'On the Origin and Development of the College in Islam and the West' in Khalil I. Semaan, ed., *Islam and the Medieval West: Aspects of Intercultural Relations* (Albany: State University of New York Press, 1980), 26–49, 42.

history, the influences of classical Mediterranean literature and philosophy, and the refining concepts adopted from contact with the Islamic Mediterranean.

To illustrate the significance of the substantial Arabo-Islamic influence upon French and ultimately European knighthood, it is worth looking at the knights of Arabia and their values as they were at the time that chivalry began to flourish in southern France in the eleventh century. It was just before and during the Crusades that much of the interaction between Christian and Saracen knights took place, whether in battle or in peaceful relations, whether between kings and caliphs or the humble knights of religious orders.[27] However, to form a more complete picture of Eastern knighthood as it was when its values filtered into Europe, we must first look at Saracen knighthood and chivalry in their established forms.

When the nomadic Arabic tribes united to varying degrees under Islam, they became a formidable force – one that was to conquer lands from the Asian Subcontinent to the Iberian Peninsula, absorbing ancient cultures that had thrived for centuries, and spreading them throughout the Arabic world.[28] The legacy of ancient cultures from India, Persia and Greece were translated into Arabic and proliferated, studied and expanded upon under the caliphates of Arabia in the lands they conquered.[29] With this inheritance came works on philosophy, religion, science, medicine,

27   In showing that there was a great amount of communication between Christendom, Byzantium and the Arabic world, Lawrence Duggan presents several letters and correspondences between caliphs and kings and even popes. See Duggan, 49–62.

28   The progression of the Arabo-Islamic empire and its boundaries, as well as a concise summary of the conquests of Islam, can be found in Kinder, Hermann and Wilgemann, Werner, *The Anchor Atlas of World History*, vol. I, trans. Ernest A. Menze (New York: Anchor, 1974), 134–7.

29   Elisséeff remarks that the grand cities of Islam not only absorbed the ancient cultures that resided there but also had far-reaching systems of communication within the empire over land, river and sea routes. Elisséeff, Nikita, 'Les échanges culturels entre le monde musulman et les Croisés à l'époque de Nur ad-Din b. Zanki (m. 1174)' in Vladimir P. Goss, ed., *The Meeting of Two Worlds: Cultural Exchange between East and West during the Period of the Crusades* (Kalamazoo, MI: Medieval Institute Publications, 1986) 39–52, 41.

agriculture, architecture and, most popular of all, poetry, all of which were not only translated but copied and studied in the great libraries that would become legendary.[30] Closest in proximity to the European centres of culture was the Umayyad caliphate in Spain, with centres in Cordoba, Toledo and Granada. These were cities of great learning, boasting architectural and scientific accomplishments; they were also centres with a cosmopolitan society of Muslims, Christians and Jews. Into these centres of culture flocked not only scholars and diplomats from all over Europe, as well as noblemen and knights, but also slaves and captives who interacted with the peoples of Spain and absorbed those ancient inheritances proliferated via Arabia.

Arabic chivalry itself did not appear as an institution or order until the twelfth century, but it seems to have been a part of life that was closely tied to religion for the Arabic world before the Crusades and existed in Persia even before Islam.[31] The Arabs were a nomadic people when the Persian influences filtered into their culture through conquest and invasion. It was their nomadic life that served as an incubator for the morals of Arabic chivalry, family and armaments, and life's struggle demanded perfection of one's tools, horses, weapons and ultimately oneself. These values were firmly embedded in the nomadic culture by the time of Muhammad.[32] Though war was not a career, there were aspirations for glory and a sense of dignity in arms; during the months of the Truce of God, a harmony of perfection was also sought and virtues such as moral beauty and pursuits such as poetry were practised.[33]

These Saracen knights did not form into strict orders, however, until after contact with knights of the European Middle Ages. This came about in the twelfth century, when increased conflict and the exchange of ideas

30   Elisséeff, 40–1.
31   Ghali, 32–3.
32   Ghali, 34.
33   Ghali. 35. Samer Ali gives an account of how the performance and composition of poetry permeated Arabic society. See: Ali, Samer M., *Arabic Literary Salons in the Islamic Middle Ages: Poetry, Public Performance, and the Presentation of the Past* (Notre Dame, Indiana: University of Notre Dame, 2010).

and philosophies brought armaments and organization from Europe that sustained the noble traditions of the Arabs.[34] Similarly, Christian knightly orders first appeared at this time, as Mahmud Shelton writes, the first ones 'along the marches of the same Muslim-European frontier, bringing together religious inspiration and knightly vocation.'[35] Shelton also writes of the Mamluk knights, whose sultan restored the caliphate of Baghdad in Cairo: how they preserved the rituals of spiritual chivalry, including the investing of foreign princes, and that their public equestrian exercises and their heraldic blazons made profound impressions upon their Christian counterparts.[36]

An intriguing example of the military knights and their orders is the Rabites, a military-religious order of Muslim knights who guarded the borders in Andalusia; they predate the Christian military-religious orders of St John and the Templars.[37] These elite border guards were volunteers in the defence of their frontiers against the Christian forces, with such

---

34 Although Ghali writes that the Arabs gained armaments from the Europeans (33), he does not elaborate upon the military science and agricultural improvements in Europe that resulted from Eastern contact in the Middle Ages. Nikita Elisséeff discusses several influences of Arabic design upon the Franks in the Levant, such as baths, the windmill, the number zero, paper, military tactics and a mobile cavalry, siege engines, innovations to defences and fortifications like a keep and towers, parapets, walls and *lisses*, as well as innovations to armour that included helmets and the display of a coat of arms, and the noble exercise activity of the hunt, which originated in Persia (45–9). Elisséeff's scholarship on Nur ad-Din is extensive, and his three-volume work on the reign of Nur ad-Din is exhaustive and detailed, giving a comprehensive account of the Middle East, its population, geography and economic and political aspects under Nur ad-Din, including maps and charts. Elisséeff, Nikita, *Nur ad-Din: un grand prince musulman de Syrie au temps des Croisades (511–569h, / 1118–1174)*, 3 vols (Damascus: Institut Francais de Damas, 1967).

35 See Shelton, Mahmud, 'Introduction' to Kashifi Sabzawari, Husayn Wa'iz, *The Royal Book of Spiritual Chivalry (Futuwat Namah Yi Sultani)*, Jay R. Crook, trans., Seyyed Hossein Nasr, ed. (Chicago: J.P. Kazi Publications and Great Books of the Islamic World, 2000), xxiv.

36 See Shelton, xxiii–iv.

37 Ghali, 26. *Rabite* here refers to the adjective 'Arabic', from 'Arabite' from French and Medieval Latin. See OED.

ideals as never to flee in the face of the enemy, to fight intrepidly and to die rather than desert one's post.[38] There is a compelling resemblance of this order to that of the Hospitallers and the Templars, founded a century later (about the time that the Crusades began)[39] and exemplary as *Miles Christi* in the medieval world – especially the Templars, that high order of spiritual knighthood.[40] Ghali writes that the chivalric character of the Arabic knight was to fight heroically and to be generous to his adversary, traits which the Arabs exhibited with the elegance and refinement of an established culture, bringing about a more tolerant and humane attitude in knighthood.[41]

With these Arabo-Islamic military orders came the influence of Persian literature and philosophy, generating a synthesis of the pre-Islamic Arabic champion and the ethic of piety.[42] What is hardly surprising is the close relation of chivalry with spirituality, and this is especially so in the Arabo-Islamic world. Ghali writes that Arabic chivalry existed only as a religious order before the twelfth century.[43] This can be seen in the phenomenon of chivalric orders and their organization, which included guilds of artisans and came about in the ninth and tenth centuries.[44] Central to this chivalry was the investiture into the order by the grand master, a caliph, with the symbols of pre-eminence and the code of behaviour with its deep spiritual underpinning.

38　See the introduction to Dozy, Reinhart Pieter Anne, *Histoire des musulmans d'Espagne*, trans. Francis Griffin Stokes (London: Frank Cass, 1972). Ghali refers to this work as well when he elaborates the influence that the chivalry of these knights had upon the Christian counterparts, in Ghali, 26–7.

39　Kinder, Hermann, et al., 153.

40　See Reinhardt, 153.

41　Ghali, 21–2.

42　See Loewen, Arley, 'Proper Conduct (Adab) is Everything: The Futuwwat-namah-i Sultani of Husayn Wa'iz-i Kashifi', *Iranian Studies* 36/4 (2003), 543–70, 543.

43　Ghali, 32.

44　See Nasr, Seyyed Hossein, 'The Rise and Development of Persian Sufism' in Leonard Lewisohn, ed., *The Heritage of Sufism, Volume I: Classical Persian Sufism from its origins to Rumi (700–1300)* (Oxford: Oneworld, 1999), 1–18, 9.

Spiritual chivalry and Sufism

Several phenomena of the orders of chivalry that appear in both the medieval Orient and Occident indicate the influence of an established and refined
ideal of conduct with a spiritual foundation. The ritual and importance
of investiture, the ideal of service to God and a code of proper behaviour
including social and moral conduct (*adab* in Arabic) had all become cornerstones of European and Saracen chivalry by the twelfth century. The
prominence of these ideals and values seems to suggest convincingly that
the cornerstones of medieval chivalry parallel the influence and promulgation of Sufism.[45] This religious order has origins in Persia, is associated
with Islam and has a tradition of spiritual chivalry prescribed in prolific
writings in Arabic, including manuals of practice, genealogies, histories,
poetry and theological works.[46] Of interest to Western scholars is the
spreading of Sufi ideals throughout the Arab world at this time of contact
with the Occident.

One of the most famous Muslim theologians, Abu Hamid al-Ghazali
(1058–1111) was a prolific author of jurisprudence, theology, mysticism and
philosophy, much of this work being influenced by Sufism and known
throughout the Persian-Arabic world.[47] Al-Ghazali's brother, Ahmad
ibn Muhammad Ghazali (d. 1123 or 1126), wrote the first manual of Sufi
discipline in Arabic, *Adab al-muridin* [*The Etiquette of Disciples*].[48] A
disciple of Ahmad Ghazali was Diya' al-Din Abû' l-Najîb al-Suhrawardi

---

45 See Milani, Milad, *The Secret Persia*, Gnostica Series (London: Equinox Publishing:
2012), and Milani, Milad. 'Medieval Persian Chivalry and Mysticism' in Stephanie
L. Hathaway and David W. Kim, eds, *Intercultural Transmission Throughout the
Medieval Mediterranean* (London: Continuum, 2012).

46 For an overview of early Sufi works from the ninth to the thirteenth centuries, see
Nasr.

47 For references to al-Ghazali and his works, see: Ghali, 40; Nasr, 8, 16; Huda, Qamar-ul,
'The Light beyond the Shore in the Theology of Proper Sufi Moral Conduct (Adab)',
Journal of the American Academy of Religion 72/2 (2004), 461–84, 464; and Elisséeff,
'Les échanges culturels', 41.

48 Nasr, 8.

(1097–1168), who founded one of the first Sufi orders, the *Suhrawardiyya*.[49] Al-Suhrawardi's nephew was the Sufi master Shaykh 'Abu Hafs 'Umar al-Suhrawardi (b. 1145) who was also taught by the prominent Sufi teacher Shaykh 'Abdul Qâdir Jilânî (d. 1166).[50] It is through 'Umar al-Suhrawardi's influential work that Sufi ideals can be said to have penetrated the political and spiritual life of Islam to such a great extent.[51]

The influence of Sufism on the social fabric was the result of the wedding of economic activity with ethics, beauty and art, and it is during the ninth and tenth centuries that spiritual chivalry became closely associated with Sufism.[52] Sufi tradition boasts much literature addressing *adab*, which in the eighth- and ninth-century Abbasid dynasty 'referred to aristocratic manners, refined tastes, a cultivated knowledge of wisdom, manners relating to cosmopolitan life in urban centers, proper styles in conversation and in gentlemanly behavior, and, particularly, the general codes of conduct while appearing in the Abbasid court.'[53]

The earliest texts on spiritual chivalry, or *futuwwat*,[54] such as the *Risala al-futuwwa* [*Book of Ethics*] by Sulami (d. 1021), reveal that the promulgation of these ethics through the organization of orders and guilds was an

---

49 Nasr gives a brief history of early Sufi orders, mentioning al-Suhrawardi's year of death (8), while Huda discusses al-Suhrawardi's nephew, and gives his year of birth (464).

50 Huda, 463.

51 Huda's article makes a study of the effect of Suhrawardi's influence of Sufism upon the Islamic Abbasid caliphate.

52 Nasr, 9.

53 Huda, 462. Nasr writes that the Sufis had a fascination for writing histories and genealogy due to their desire to preserve spiritual authenticity, and also that, 'From its very beginnings, the whole field of ethics (*akhlaq*) in Islam was dominated by the Sufis. In fact, in both the Sunni and the Shi'ite sects of Islam, the major ethical works composed over the centuries were all indebted to the inspiration of the Sufis.' See Nasr, 7 and 5. Arley Loewen also shows that the Arabic heroic ideal was much influenced by the ethics of Sufism: 'a synthesis of ancient Persian and Arabo-Islamic ideals, the ethic of piety towards God, which was influenced by the increasing dominance of Sufism, shaped a second model of heroism.' (543)

54 *Futuwwat* is from the Arabic words *fêta*, meaning knight, and *fêtuua*, connoting service to God and to the weak. See Ghali, 27–9.

integral part of the Sufi religious experience.[55] It was even earlier that the work of Ali al-Makki (d. 996) categorized Sufi practices and Huda lists other works showing that from the eighth century, 'the whole of Sufism is entirely based on the ways of behavior.'[56] Thus it becomes evident that Sufism embodied an established and refined set of ethical and moral rules grounded in spirituality, regulated by orders and taking on the title of *futuwwat*, spiritual chivalry, and that this integration of chivalry and etiquette was a result of Persian Sufism.

The influence of Sufism did not confine itself to religion in the Arabic world. It was 'Umar al-Suhrawardi who was advisor to that most influential and industrious caliph, al-Nasir li-Din Allah (1181–1223), who is credited with restoring the unity of *futuwwat* through Sufism from disparate branches and reaffirming the caliph as the focus through investiture. This investiture became sought after throughout the Islamic world and included embassies headed by Sufi sheiks sent to invest nobility, resulting in an 'impressive list of the caliph's knights from Spain to China.'[57] In 1200 he designated 'Umar al-Suhrawardi, who was a trained jurist, scholar of law, reasoning, ethics, philosophy and literature, as *Shaykh al-Islam*, a position that administered religious affairs for the state.[58] In this position, 'Umar al-Suhrawardi could advocate Sufi-state cooperation, and he was successful in emphasizing 'his own Sufi order at [the] forefront of Islamic religious politics,' connecting *adab* firmly with law and justice.[59] The promulgation of these orders and their values was part of the establishment of a tradition of knighthood and chivalry that was rooted in spirituality, ethics and duty, with a specific code of behaviour governed by the ideals of chivalry.

Investiture was to play a key role not only in centralizing the power of the caliphate, but in the relations between Saracen and Christian nobility during the period of the Crusades, influencing Christian knightly orders and their values. It was the Abbasid caliphate of Baghdad after al-Nasir

55   Nasr, 9.
56   Huda, 463.
57   See Shelton, xxiii.
58   Huda, 464.
59   Huda, 464, 468.

that invested Malek al-Adel Nur ad-Din Mahmûd (1117–73),[60] who in 1145 succeeded his father as ruler of northern Syria and defeated the Crusaders, capturing Tripoli, Antioch and Damascus. He was later defeated by his nephew Saladin, his successor, who completed the conquest of Egypt. It is Saladin who is remembered as 'that paragon of medieval chivalry'[61] and who himself, it is said, was dubbed a knight in Alexandria in 1174 by Humphrey of Toron, also a Templar master.[62]

The ritual symbols of investiture were linked to Islam, by way of God and Muhammad, by Hamid al-Ghazali in a story about the Sufi white woollen vest.[63] This item of clothing was the *soufis* that was given to Muhammad by God as a symbol of investiture. It symbolizes humility and poverty, the treasures of a chest that can only be opened by embracing the concept of love. The story in itself has many parallels in medieval Western chivalry

60   Huda mentions Nur ad-Din's successors and adds Zangi to his name (464). Dates and biographical information on Nur ad-Din are from *Chambers Biographical Dictionary*, eds J.O. Thorne and T.C. Collcott (Cambridge: Cambridge University Press, 1984). Nikita Elisséeff makes extensive studies of Nur ad-Din's reign and administration (Elisséeff, *Nur ad-Din*) and goes into some detail about the institution of the Abbasid caliphate and the powers and duties of the office of iman as jurist and spiritual counsellor. See Elisséeff, Nikita, *L'Orient musulman au Moyen Age 622–1260* (Paris: Armand Colin, 1977), 150–61.

61   See Shelton, xxiii. Saladin's nobility in word and deed is illustrated in several charming stories. In one, his brother is invested by Richard Lionheart during a battle of the Third Crusade; in another, he sent two new horses to Richard when he learnt that the king's horse had died in the midst of battle. (Fahrner, 18, 88)

62   Fahrner, 88. Though Fahrner gives no reference to the source of this story, it is referred to in other works, many of them citing the following: Lane-Poole, Stanley, *The Story of Cairo*, 3rd ed (London: J.M. Dent, 1918), 193; and Lane-Poole, Stanley, *Saladin and the Fall of Jerusalem* (New York: G.P. Putnam's Sons, 1898), 354. This is where Fahrner appears to have found his information, including the exchange of fruit and horses (above). See Lane-Poole, *Saladin*, 387ff. See also: Newby, P.H., *Saladin in His Time* (London: Faber and Faber, 1983), 50; and Hindley, Geoffrey, *Saladin* (London: Constable, 1976), 55. Although both are plausible and probable, the stories are not entirely substantiated.

63   This story is related by Ghali, who recognizes it as a legend that was probably applied to create a chivalric order amongst confusion and organise a grand master (30–1).

in both literature (such as Grail romances) and in knightly orders (such as the Templars, the Knights of St John and the Order of the Garter).[64] It then becomes apparent how tenuous would be the assertion that either culture had exclusive influence over the other. When the rituals and rules of the etiquette of Sufi spiritual chivalry were written down in the fifteenth century by Husayn Wa'iz Kashifi Sabzawari, it became evident that these established ideals had long since become a part of the chivalric orders of the Christian West.[65]

Girding and its significance in Western knightly orders might be seen to originate with *futuwwat* traditions of spiritual chivalry. A girded or belted waist was a symbol of that man's service to his patron, a 'statement of spiritual reality and a public commitment by the initiated individual to practice that reality through proper conduct.'[66] This is a concept that would have integrated easily into feudal vassalage. The idea of knightly virtue emanated through the symbols of investiture, too. Shelton writes of the Grail-Templar knighthood being replaced by a new formulation of chivalry in *Sir Gawain and the Green Knight*, one that was 'symbolized by

64 Shelton draws several parallels between Christian orders and legends and the *futuw-wat*. Among many examples, he mentions that the Holy Grail as a cup has its origins in the investiture outlined in Sabzawari's *futuwwat*; Wolfram's *Parzival* depicts the grail as a miraculous stone akin to the Islamic Black Stone. He mentions that the Templar Order's rule calls for the restoration of a spiritual chivalry and the number of its articles, seventy-two, 'recalls the importance of seventy-two in *futuwat* doctrine.' Likewise, this order's centres are built in the image of the dome of the Rock Mosque. See Shelton, xxiv–xxvi.

65 See Kashifi Sabzawari, Husayn Wa'iz, *The Royal Book of Spiritual Chivalry (Futuwat Namah Yi Sultani)*, Jay R. Crook, trans., Seyyed Hossein Nasr, ed. (Chicago: J.P. Kazi Publications and Great Books of the Islamic World, 2000). Loewen also writes of the *Futuwwat* as an institution that incorporates regulations and customs, dress and insignia, initiation rites and codes of behaviour, showing that it is a compilation with a wide range of Sufi references within the text, which in turn suggests that it 'represents a codification of the literature on the subject of the institution of futuw-wat,' and that these customs and rituals had been recorded in earlier works (Loewen, 543–5).

66 Loewen, 557.

a belt and delivered by an axe-bearing figure not derived from legend.'[67] He also sees this figure as none other than al-Kadir, literally 'the Green', who was a spiritual guide especially associated with chivalry, and the axe and belt as an 'explicit reference to *futuwat* traditions.'[68]

Another story is related in Fahrner's work about a green knight exemplifying ethics of chivalry.[69] This seems to suggest that the idea of a knight in green was either common or originated in an earlier source. Saladin had made no progress at Tyre against Christian forces under a Spanish knight in green armour whom the Turks called 'the Green Knight' and he then fell back on and besieged Tripoli. William of Sicily arrived in Tyre with his fleet and two hundred knights, allowing the Margrave Konrad to send reinforcements to Tripoli with his ships, aboard one of which was the Green Knight who led the attack against the besiegers with the reinforcements. The Saracens took him for one of their own and Saladin invited him into the city, offering him hospitality. Instead of treacherous behaviour, the knight refused the hospitality, explained that he was indeed the enemy, and left the city. Which story influenced which is difficult to determine, although there seems to be a recognition of the values that were *futuwwat* in all cases.

It was not only the symbols and code of etiquette required in investiture that were so important but also who the patron was. By the thirteenth century, the activity of the Crusades and the enthusiasm for following chivalric ideals saw the caliphs of the Arab world and the Seljuks of the Anatolian frontier invested by the nobility of the Christian West, demonstrating a common respect for a knightly code and an importance placed upon loyalty to a liege lord or to an ideal.[70]

It is not extraordinary that such ideas originating in Persia and the Arab world became so influential in Arabo-Islamic culture and filtered into Europe with literature, with translations into Arabic, the *lingua franca* of

---

67   See Shelton, xxvi.
68   Shelton, xxvi.
69   See Fahrner, 19.
70   See: Fahrner, 83–9, for examples of investiture between Saracen caliphs and Christian nobility.

the twelfth century, and with personal contact between combatants and diplomats. Baghdad had become a centre for translations of a number of texts on philosophy and science in the eleventh and twelfth centuries and budding Arabo-Islamic philosophies had a large following, incorporating Greek traditional thought with Iranian and Indian influences.[71] Even the Abbey of Cluny in the twelfth century under Peter the Venerable boasts the first translation of the Qu'ran into a European language as well as an analysis of the Muslim religion and an intensified study of Islam.[72] This work was preceded by translations of Eastern religious texts by the Eastern Orthodox Niketas of Byzantium in the tenth century and again in the twelfth century by the Cluniac translators Marcus of Toledo and the Scotsman Robert of Ketton after the Crusades had begun.[73] At an abbey in Hereford, England held the first Arabic–Latin gloss and Toledo in Spain remained a great cosmopolitan centre of Arabic translation,[74] indicating that the Arabic language, philosophies and texts were far from unseen in Europe and the British Isles.

It was already evident that philosophies had travelled around the Mediterranean rim and beyond in the Hellenic and Roman eras, and mysticism, being a universal element in all major religions, had proliferated with them.[75] It might be said that the mystical elements found in both Christianity and Islam were influenced by the same early philosophies and were taken up in turn, as development allowed, with the writings of Plato and Ovid, the founding fathers of the Church, and later with St Augustine, St Bernard of Clairvaux and Meister Eckhart.[76] Mysticism was

---

71   Elisséeff, 'Les échanges culturels', 39–41.

72   Elisséeff, 'Les échanges culturels', 44.

73   Gauss, Julia, 'Toleranz und Intoleranz zwischen Christen und Muslimen in der Zeit vor den Kreuzzügen', *Saeculum* 19 (1968), 362–89, 382.

74   Gauss.

75   F.C. Happold writes of mysticism that it is 'a manifestation of something which is at the root of all religion and all the higher religions have their mystical expressions.' Happold, F.C., *Mysticism: A Study and an Anthology*, 3rd revised ed. (London: Penguin, 1990), 16.

76   Happold defines the role of mysticism thus: 'In that syncretism of Greek and Oriental philosophy which occurred in the centuries immediately preceding the birth of Christ,

a prominent feature of Christianity in medieval Europe, just as it was for Islam and Sufism in Arabia. It encompassed intellectual as well as perceptive realms to explore the world of the unseen, resulting in a spirituality that did not have to be linked to religion but often was. Happold writes that mysticism was 'the inspiration of much philosophy, poetry, art, and music,'[77] and that, in the religious experience, there was 'a direct experience of the presence of God.'[78] If a case were to be made *against* Christian and Sufi mysticism being mutually influential to some degree during the Middle Ages, it would have to be a particularly strong one. Texts provided just one of the vehicles by which these ideas travelled.

The far-reaching ideals of ethics and spirituality that were the Sufi legacy in prolific writings, in practice and in the law and politics of the Arabic world emerge in all of the cultures that had contact with Arabia in the twelfth century, including European Christendom.[79] Nasr writes that 'many people are not aware that the ethical works that they are reading come in fact from Sufi sources, even if, outwardly, they have nothing to do with Sufism.'[80] The many diplomatic correspondences show that the desire was present to find a universal belief formula or to come to a diplomatic agreement, such as was sought between rulers exemplifying chivalric ethics, such as Richard the Lionheart, Saladin, Emperor Frederick II and Al Kamil.[81] If it was not in fact pursued relentlessly, the sentiment of respect for peers in

---

known as Neoplatonism, [mysticism] came to mean a particular sort of approach to the whole problem of reality, in which the intellectual, and especially the intuitive, faculties came into play. As a result of Christian and Neoplatonist ideas in the early centuries of the Christian era, a system of so-called mystical theology came into existence, which was one of the main foundations of Christian mysticism.' Happold 18.

77   Happold.
78   Happold, 19.
79   Shelton writes that 'the concern of Sufism, the power of spiritual chivalry reached beyond the borders of the Islamic world.' (xxi)
80   Nasr, 5.
81   See Fahrner, 83–9, in which examples of poetry as diplomatic relations are given. Ghali also gives examples of embassies and treaties concluded between Arabic caliphs and European kings. (19)

the institution of knighthood and chivalry was certainly present among its practitioners. What is more, it is known that Christianity adopted some of its religious philosophy from Persia, such as the contingency theory, a Persian variant on a classical argument for the proof of God's and the universe's existence that is the foundation for all other existence, which became an essential element of medieval metaphysics.[82]

Included in Sufi ideology was the search for unity. Perhaps it was Caliph al-Nasir li-Din Allah and his minister al-Suhrawardi that appealed to Christian knights by employing Sufi *adab*, the aristocratic code of conduct, as a means of strengthening the caliph's power by enforcing behavioural practice and investiture. Shelton writes that 'not surprisingly, the Christian West found in the spiritual chivalry of Islam a model in its efforts to establish this "true power"' of a united head of spiritual authority and temporal power.[83] However, as the Arabic world contended with its enemies by employing spiritual chivalry, it sought the same answers for unity and harmony that the European West aspired to in a post-Roman Feudal Age in which the rift between Byzantium and Rome was felt profoundly, politically as well as religiously. Oleg Grabar writes that 'similar concerns and similar needs lead to an almost automatic transfer of information. [...] The Christian West turned to Islamic ideas and interpretations because the same issues of faith and reason had been posed, not because of a precise influence of Islamic thought on the West.'[84] It was timely for both cultures in the twelfth century to gain a deeper sense of spirituality in moral code and a more ethically defined chivalry from their contact with each other, resulting in, among many things, a spiritual and ethically grounded code for chivalric orders, both religious and military, as well as the influence that is apparent in literature.

It bears mentioning that Sufi and Arabic writing exemplified a form of courtly love that was new to Europe in the eleventh century. The Arabic

---

82   See Gauss, 385.

83   See Shelton, xxiv.

84   Grabar, Oleg, 'Patterns and Ways of Cultural Exchange' in Vladimir P. Goss, ed., *The Meeting of Two Worlds: Cultural Exchange between East and West during the Period of the Crusades* (Kalamazoo, MI: Medieval Institute Publications, 1986) 441–6, 443.

influence on Sufism can be seen in that the vocabulary of Persian became enriched with Arabic words from about the ninth century. Words with a strong religious orientation that were deeply influenced by the Qu'ran were borrowed and poetic forms embellished, though Persian Sufism had been inextricably linked with poetry from its inception.[85] Sufi poetry was known far beyond the borders of the Arabic world and comprised characteristic Sufi concepts such as a contemplative intellect, divine love, selflessness, service and a deep yet ambiguous sentiment that required inner reflection. The ability to compose poetry was as important a component of chivalry in the Arabo-Islamic world as it was to become in the courts of Europe.

It is this spiritual chivalry that the Crusaders met in their campaigns in the Holy Land and that so intrigued nobles of Spain and the southern French marches through its poetry, inspiring knightly orders and a code of behaviour. Although they might not have been the only influence upon European knighthood, the Arabs were a beneficial influence on the spirit and sentiments of chivalry through the example set by their refinement and elegance in thought, word and deed, characterized by moderation, soft-spokenness, and generosity.[86]

From knighthood to chivalry in Europe

The infusion of a spiritual and ethical code into the elite warrior image transformed knights into *chevaliers*, with a shift from a professional to a social emphasis.[87] The source for many of these sentiments lies in the Arabo-Islamic world and there were many interactions and points of contact with Europe before the tenth century, including Spain, Sicily, Provence

85 Nasr, 9.
86 Ghali, 21.
87 Helen Cooper notes this shift in describing the change in the meaning of the word knighthood. Cooper, Helen, *The English Romance in Time; Transforming motifs from Geoffrey of Monmouth to the death of Shakespeare* (Oxford: Oxford University Press, 2004), 41–3.

and Aquitaine.[88] There existed certain diplomatic and cultural exchanges between Europe and the Islamic world, such as the embassies that the Carolingians boasted about receiving at Aachen from Spain and Persia,[89] but relations were not always peaceful. A vulnerable Europe in its early Feudal Age was the stage for invasions and attacks from Vikings, Magyars, and Arabs. During the eighth and ninth centuries, the breakdown of the unity and power of the caliphate of Cordoba led to raiding and pillaging by Saracen pirates up and along rivers, burning monasteries and ambushing pilgrims to sell in the thriving slave trade.[90] In Spain, however, in the caliphate itself, emirs, caliphs and small Christian kingdoms existed, sometimes united, sometimes divided, in and out of which trickled the ideas and culture from the East that would make a permanent mark on the chivalry of Europe.[91]

Journey from the Orient to the Occident

Spain can be seen as an example of an intercultural environment in which the richness of the cultures of the Orient were shared and combined with the institutions, industriousness, curiosity and values of the Occident. The Umayyad Caliphate introduced many Arabo-Islamic concepts into Spain, including centres for learning and great libraries where texts from the far corners of the Arab world were collected and translated on topics as broad as medicine, theology, philosophy, poetry, botany and music,

88   Elisséeff writes that the direct influence of the Mediterranean Orient permitted a prodigious cultural enrichment of the Occident, to which the role of the Crusades is only secondary. Elisséeff, 'Les échanges culturels', 43.

89   Daniel mentions several sources relating embassies received by Carolingian kings, including a meeting between Charlemagne and Harun ar-Rashid. See Daniel, *The Arabs*, 50–1.

90   Marc Bloch summarizes the Arab threat to Europe to explain the development of feudalism in Europe, mentioning the Garde-Freinet, who used the Camargue as their base for mountainous and river raids. See Bloch, Marc, *La société féodale*, vol. 1 (Paris: Albin Michel, 1939), 13–16. This raiding syndicate is also discussed in: Daniel, *The Arabs*, 51.

91   See Bloch, *Société féodale*, 12–13.

among many.[92] The Caliphate of Cordoba fell in 1031 and until about 1086 'the period was one of pleasure and luxury, wine and love, but it was also a period of culture.'[93] The eleventh and twelfth centuries are seen as a period of 'French involvement, militarily and politically, in Spanish affairs,'[94] and into and out of this cultural centre came diplomats, poets, knights, captives, slaves, pilgrims and clergymen. It is not difficult to imagine the relative ease with which contact between France and Spain could be made in the twelfth century; one has but to follow the pilgrimage route back from Compostela.

That the influence of this Hispano-Arabic culture reached far into Europe is apparent in things as various as the use and stock of horses, clothing, hairstyles, music and musical instruments, spices and even the games

---

92   Juan Vernet presents a study of the Abbasid caliphate in Spain and of the Arabo-Islamic influence there, showing that both the advanced civilization that was the inheritance of the Arabs and the cosmopolitan and diverse ethnic population in Spain resulted in an impressive centre of cultural exchange. Vernet, Juan, *La Cultura Hispanoárabe en Oriente y Occidente* (Barcelona: Ariel, 1978), 15–37. Armand Maurer outlines some Islamic philosophers influential to the development of scholasticism in Europe, noting that the translation of Greek philosophical texts in the Abbasid Caliphate from Persia to Spain was of great importance to European thought and that 'the Moslems' knowledge of Greek science, mathematics and philosophy, and their original creations in these areas, were far in advance of the Christian West.' See Maurer, Armand A., *Medieval Philosophy*, ed. Etienne Gilson, 2nd edn, Etienne Gilson Series 4 (Toronto: Pontifical Institute of Medieval Studies, 1982), 94. That Umayyad Spain played a prominent role in the distribution of Arabic translations is evident when it is mentioned in Alison Weir's biography of Eleanor of Aquitaine: 'Thanks to the rediscovery of the works of Aristotle, and Greek and Roman writers [...] hitherto preserved by Arabs and disseminated through wider contact with Moorish Spain and the Orient, scholars became reacquainted with classical learning.' Weir, Alison, *Eleanor of Aquitaine: by the Wrath of God, Queen of England* (London: Jonathan Cape, 1999), 28. See also Reinhardt, 109–10, in which he describes the same influences from the Arab world on Germany, pointing out that the influences were strengthened after the Crusades.

93   See John Jay Parry's introduction to Capellanus, 7.

94   Ferrante, Joan M., *Guillaume d'Orange: Four Twelfth-Century Epics*, trans. and ed. Joan M. Ferrante, Records of Western Civilization (New York: Columbia University Press, 2001). 25.

that became popular in Europe, such as polo, hunting, cards and chess.[95] Wolfram made mention of the game of chess in *Willehalm*, demonstrating not only his familiarity with it but that of the audience as well.[96] There has been speculation on how much of Spain's multicultural atmosphere influenced Wolfram, but scholars are in agreement that Wolfram's portrayal of Islamic people and culture is remarkably intuitive. Though Wolfram was not a 'book-learned' poet, his insightfulness and the detail in *Willehalm* suggests that some cursory knowledge of Islam must have sifted through to him.[97]

---

95   Boyd makes many references to the influences from the Arabic world that were already apparent in Aquitaine in the tenth, eleventh and twelfth centuries, including fashion, architecture, poetry, music and games in his biography of Eleanor of Aquitaine. See Boyd, Douglas, *Eleanor April Queen of Aquitaine* (Stroud: Sutton, 2004), 9–35. Also see Elisséeff, 'Les échanges culturels', 49. Chess is said to have travelled from India to Europe via Persia and the Arab conquests and to have become popular among Europe's nobility in the twelfth century; see Gamer, Helena M., 'The Earliest Evidence of Chess in Western Literature: The Einsiedeln Verses', *Speculum* 29/4 (1954), 734–50, 744. It is also noteworthy that a team of British archaeologists recently excavated an ivory chess piece dating to the sixth century in a palace in the Byzantine city of Butrint, now in Albania. See 'Ancient Chess History Unearthed', BBC News World Edition: Europe, Saturday, 27 July 2002, <http://news.bbc.co.uk/1/hi/world/europe/2155916. stm>, accessed 9 February 2012. Willehalm and Gyburg can be seen playing chess in an illumination from the Vienna MS, cod. Ser. nova 2643.

96   'Ir hers mich bevilte, der zende ûz zwispilte, ame schâchzabel ieslîch velt, mit car-damôm, den, mit dem prüeven waere gezalt, Terramêr und Tybalt, heten mangern rîter dâ' (*Wh.* 151, 1–7). All excerpts from *Willehalm* are taken from Wolfram von Eschenbach, *Willehalm*, ed. Werner Schröder (Berlin: Walter de Gruyter, 1978). [Their army was too much for me. If one placed cardamon seeds on the squares of a chess-board and doubled their number each time on each square, counting all the way to the end, then Terramer and Tibalt had more knights than that] (Gibbs and Johnson, 84). It bears mentioning that this reference does not occur in any of the extant manuscripts of Wolfram's French sources, though *Ruodlieb* is noteworthy among chess historians for being one of the earlier European documents to mention it. See Gamer.

97   See: Knapp, Fritz Peter, '*Leien munt nie baz gesprach.* Zur angeblichen lateinischen Buchgelehrsamkeit und zum Islambild Wolframs von Eschenbach', *ZfdA* 138 (2009), 173–84.

Even if Europe had little immediate knowledge of Arabo-Islamic culture before the conquest of Jerusalem in the twelfth century,[98] it had, through trade and relations in Spain and the Mediterranean Rim, and especially the French participation in the *Reconquista*[99] been influenced by it.[100] The influence upon the actions of women in Aquitaine was already apparent in that they had inheritance rights as well as a right to autonomous rule over lands owned, due to the melding of Visigothic law and Umayyad culture. The women also participated in social affairs alongside men and were 'renowned for their elegance in dress, yet censured by the Church for their painted cheeks, their charcoal-rimmed eyes and their oriental perfumes,' as well as for a lax attitude towards morality and adultery.[101]

Games, fashion and text translation were not the only Oriental influences from Muslim Spain. Literature and poetry were among the farthest-reaching and most popular influences of the Orient via Spain. The encouragement of literature among Arabs 'was one of the traditional manifestations of royal power' and consequently, each of the petty kings arising in Spain after the fall of Cordoba had his court poets. These were all trained in the classical Arabic tradition[102] and one of the more prolific

---

98   Elisséeff, 'Les échanges culturels', 39–40.

99   See Rossi, Marguerite, 'Rapport introductif: épopée française et épopée non française' in *Essor et fortune de la chanson de geste dans l'Europe et l'Orient latin: actes du IXe congrès international de la Société Rencesvals pour l'étude des épopées romanes, Padoue-Venise, 29 août–4 septembre 1982* (Modena: Mucchi, 1983) 247–65, 250.

100 If the great Greek philosophers such as Aristotle, Euclid, Archimedes, Hippocrates, Galen and others formed the basis of dialectic and philosophical study during the renaissance of the eleventh and twelfth centuries, Spain played a major role in the proliferation of the material, as David Knowles points out: 'Although [...] some of the Aristotlean writings reached the West directly from Byzantium, or from Byzantine circles in Sicily, the majority came by way of Spain', via Syria and Persia in a long tradition of translation and commentary. See Knowles, David, *The Evolution of Medieval Thought*, ed. D.E. Luscombe and C.N.L. Brooke, 2nd edn (London: Longman, 1988), 176–7.

101 Weir, Alison, 16.

102 See Parry's introduction to Capellanus, 7.

was the Cordoban Ibn Hazm.[103] This precipitated the advent of wandering poets, the troubadours, who used the Arabic metrical forms.[104] Under this influence, in a multi-lingual and cosmopolitan Spain, troubadours sang songs of the Arabic ideal love – a chaste love in which the hero did not surrender to physical passion but strove instead in tournaments – with a structure resembling *zadjal* [an Arabic poetry form][105] and to the accompaniment of the *'ud'*, or lute, the 'instrument par excellence de la musique

103   Ibn Hazm, or Abu Muhammad 'Ali ibn Ahmad ibn Sa'id ibn Hazm (eleventh century) was a Muslim philosopher, historian and theologian whose writings inspired courtly love and who is mentioned in almost every text on Muslim Spain and early medieval courtly poetry. See Parry's introduction to Capellanus, 8; Vernet, 332–5; and Dozy, 574–80, for examples from his poetic works.

104   See Parry's introduction to Capellanus, 8. The case for the transmission of Oriental concepts via the troubadours is strengthened when considering the word's etymology. Jacques Lafitte-Houssat writes that the word *troubadour* came from the Occitan verb *trouber*, and spread to the north of France where it was *trouvère*. He also makes a distinction between troubadours and *jongleurs*, who were socially and intellectually inferior to the troubadours. Lafitte-Houssat, Jacques, *Troubadours et cours d'amour*, 1st edn, vol. 422, Que sais-je? (Paris: Presses Universitaires de France, 1950), 74–5. The word *troubadour* was then accepted usage in France, denoting the travelling poet.

105   *Zadjal* was a form of popular poetry in the eleventh and twelfth centuries in Andalusia and evolved into the poetry of the Arabic Jews and of the Berbers. It appears in the first texts of Languedoc and has a structure of four lines to a verse, the first three on one rhyme and the last line a recurring rhyme. This virtuous pursuit was to become the pursuit of knights; Elisséeff also writes that 'l'idéal occidental était alors célibataire, sacerdotal, et hiérarchisé, ce qui aboutit aux ordres de chevalerie et, par réaction, à la poésie courtoise empruntée à la littérature arabe (*adab*),' [The ideal Westerner was, then, unmarried, religious and treated hierarchically, something which thrives in the orders of chivalry and, consequently, in courtly poetry borrowed from Arabic literature] showing the relation between chivalry and courtly poetry (Elisséeff, 'Les échanges culturels', 41). Anwar Chejne also writes of *zadjal*, 'the similarity between this Andalusian poetry and that of Europe is so striking as to form and content, that it cannot be relegated to coincidence.' See Chejne, Anwar, 'The Role of al-Andalus in the Movement of Ideas Between Islam and the West' in Khalil I. Semaan, ed., *Islam and the Medieval West: Aspects of Intercultural Relations* (Albany: State University of New York Press, 1980) 110–33, 121.

arabe'.[106] In his article on the transmission of ideas from al-Andalus to Europe, Chejne asserts that 'given the historical setting and circumstances, it is very unlikely that such a popular genre did not penetrate into the popular folklore of Spain and through it into neighboring European countries' and he explores the evidence of oral transmission of Arabic-influenced legends, courtly love, chivalry and epic, as well as proverbs, anecdotes, humour, wisdom and novels,[107] which would have travelled with the troubadours.[108] If Rychner's studies are taken into account, then the music and composition methods of the *chansons de geste* composers as he presents them points to a distinctly southern influence.[109]

In Provence, the permissive conditions among its nobility, the heretical religious movements, the influence of Ovidian literature and the wandering scholars given to composing erotic verse and drinking-songs combined to bring about an environment that was conducive to the travelling composing troubadours from Spain. Thus the courtly love of Baghdad, a 'refined concept of love as an ennobling passion, in whose service a man might exhaust a lifetime's aspirations and, if need be, find death without dishonour,'[110] found its way into southern France and was taken up by Aquitainian Duke William IX, among others, who is credited with being the first courtly poet.[111] That the refined concept of courtly love and love-service was profoundly influenced by Arabo-Islamic ideas is even more

---

106 Elisséeff, 'Les échanges culturels', 41.
107 Elisséeff, 'Les échanges culturels', 41.
108 In the introduction to his edition of the Occitan poem, *Flamenca*, Jean-Charles Huchet writes that 'c'est encore le roman des origines de la lyrique occitane que la critique a tour à tour cherchées dans d'hypothétiques productions populaires perdues, dans des emprunts à la lyrique arabe d'Espagne.' Huchet, Jean-Charles, ed., *Flamenca: Roman occitan du XIIIe siècle* (Paris: Union Générale d'Editions, 1988), 18. [it is again the romance of the origins of Occitan lyric that critics searched for in the hypothetical, lost popular productions lent from the Arabic lyric of Spain.]
109 See Rychner.
110 Owen, 23.
111 William IX Duke of Aquitaine (1071–1127), descendant of William of Orange, Count of Toulouse and grandfather of Eleanor of Aquitaine, is mentioned in almost every history of courtly poetry and troubadours as the first of the genre, including

convincing when one considers some earlier poems such as *Floire and Blancheflor*, which portrays the Saracens in honour equal to the Christians. Love, it is now accepted, 'is a feature of both the classical and the Breton material, but the first vernacular European work to ground its whole plot and motivation solely in love, *Floire et Blancheflor*, probably came from a different cultural source, Arabic Spain: the same culture that may have inspired some elements in the Provençal tradition of love-poetry.'[112]

The form of the *lais* came into its own during this time. Distinguishing 'romance literature' from 'romantic poems', Alison Weir writes that this poetry, the *lais*, 'sang of love. It was the poets of the south, the troubadours, who popularized the concept of courtly love, revolutionary in its day' and they in turn were inspired by Arab writers.[113] She also mentions how the *lais* were transmitted: composed in *langue d'oc* and sung to the accompaniment of various kinds of musical instruments, challenging the image of women, 'according them superiority over men, and [laying] down codes of courtesy, chivalry and gentlemanly conduct.'[114] It can be seen, then, that the promulgation of the ideals of chivalry and courtly code came from the southern regions of France, from Spain and from the Islamic Mediterranean.

With the poetry, music and metre came language, too. Many words from that period in Arabic and Provençal are chivalric terms, indicating that they were borrowed into the French from the Arabic.[115] Concepts of philosophy, spirituality and courtly love that were present in Umayyad Spain and southern France had a refining effect upon Occidental culture as well as on knighthood. As a result, the European knights became more gallant and courtly in action and speech not only towards ladies, but also towards every woman and towards humans generally, and the rough man-

---

the following: Elisséeff, 'Les échanges culturels', 41; Owen, 24ff; Parry's introduction to Capellanus, 12ff; Weir, 9–14; and Fahrner, 133ff.

112   Cooper, 28.

113   Weir, 8.

114   Weir, 9.

115   See Ghali, 16.

ners of armed combat were modified and transformed into a softer, kinder, more gracious manner.[116]

From knight to *chevalier*

One of the phenomena that made a lasting mark upon European chivalry as an institution was the influence of the Church and its role in furthering the ideal of the Christian knight, the *Miles Christi*. Chivalry had become inseparable from spirituality, which was the Islamic Mediterranean's evocative contribution to the ideal of European knighthood. The Church took up the role of institutionalizing what was fast becoming its own order for armed men and their philosophy, supplanting the ethereal spirituality of chivalry with the precepts of a more organized religion. Its influence transformed the loyalty of royal vassalage into religious loyalty and a free form of chivalry was developed: more appearance-oriented, slightly sceptical, kind, gallant, unthreatening to clergy and, through love, a taste for adventure, generous sympathy for the unfortunate, and exaltation of a warrior's honour and motives, the heart of an ideal was constituted.[117]

The concept of a chivalric ideology is one that has been addressed at length in twentieth-century scholarship, seeking to dissect chivalry and what it meant in medieval Europe. DuQuesnay Adams mentions a travelling exhibition of arms and armour from the Metropolitan Museum which was visiting the Witte Museum in San Antonio, citing comments by Frances Leonard on the image of the *chevalier*, 'a fully armoured horse and rider,'[118] as embodying 'what man ought to be: bigger than ordinary life, invulnerable, invincible, clearly dedicated to a higher mission.'[119] It is by way of this image that martial chivalry came to symbolize the code of chivalry;

---

116   Ghali., 23, and Owen, 38.
117   See Ghali, 13.
118   See Adams, 43–4.
119   Leonard, Frances, 'The Art of Chivalry: Portrait of an Elite Culture', *The Texas Humanist* 5/3 (1983), 4–6, 4. (Since 1987 this periodical has been known as the *Texas Journal of Ideas, History and Culture*.)

the code justifies the warrior.[120] Jean Flori examined the development of the *chevalier* in terms of its ideology, exploring the image and ethos of the knight and finding that the ideology was the result of a slow evolution influenced by the Church and romance literature, mingling the rites of the institution, old lay traditions and the assignment to knights of a function by the Church.[121]

The role of the Church was more a functional one, assuming the power of the feudal lord in the age of decline of a French royal authority that never fully assumed its moral obligations to defend the country and protect the poor in the early Middle Ages.[122] This of course raises the issue of the paradoxical nature of chivalry as the Church used it. In the name of an ideal peace, the Church, a pacifist institution, raised unarmed masses against warriors led by ecclesiastics[123] and such an inconsistency in the basis of an ideology led to the introspective and philosophical aspects of twelfth- and thirteenth-century romance literature. This ideological paradox is often overlooked, however, when considering the tremendous impact that the image of the *chevalier* and his ethos had upon medieval society and still has today. This complex development of the *chevalier* came about 'to the degree that chivalric ideals can be considered to have become more and more codified into what one can call an ideology by the end of the twelfth century.'[124] The inner development of the knight was represented and influenced by spiritual as well as practical matters.

---

120 See Adams, 44; and Leonard, 4–6.

121 Flori, Jean, *L'Idéologie du glaive: préhistoire de la chevalerie* (Geneva: Droz, 1983), 1–4.

122 Jean Flori discusses this decline of royal authority and the mobilization of knights as *chevaliers* in terms of the Aquitanian Peace of God. See Flori, *L'Idéologie du glaive*, 144–57.

123 Flori, *L'Idéologie du glaive*, 144. While Flori recognizes an irony in the influence and results of the Church's use of the knight, he stresses that the Peace of God did not create a chivalric ethic itself, but contributed greatly to create a common mentality among those who would call themselves *chevalier* (157).

124 Switten, 434. While Switten concentrates on the occurrences of the term *chevalier* in French and Occitan vernacular literature, she makes an etymological observation distinguishing *miles* from *chevalier*: 'Because *miles* is the more important term, it has

With the refinement of spirituality, generosity and the religious conse-
cration of knighthood and its accoutrements, the investiture of the knight
and his sworn fealty to lord and Church, along with the influence of courtly
poetry, the martial knight developed into the twelfth-century *chevalier*. His
duty was to his lord and to protect the weak, the Church and pilgrims; his
honour was served by the chaste veneration of ladies and by his inner nobility on the field. Of the several common elements Christianity has with Islam
as well as with Judaism, the Decalogue (the Ten Commandments of God)
is essential in prescribing rules of behaviour. It is not surprising that the
rules of behaviour for a knight took the form of the Decalogue, and were
written down thus by Gautier in the nineteenth century.[125] These included
loyalty to truth and to the pledged word, generosity and the championship
of the right and good, and the conquering of Saracens. It is also conceivable
that the Church saw in the knightly orders a means of controlling its own
army, as it did in the Crusades into the Holy Land – a means of control
not immune to political devices and designs of the powerful.

The influence of the Church went to the heart of the chivalric code
and merged with the consolidated social entity that the knightly class had
become, necessitating their demand for a visible indication of their service
in chivalry, the dubbing ceremony.[126] A knighthood consecrated by the

---

been more widely studied. Yet the development *caballarius / chevalier* emphasizes
what has been called a popular or lay usage. *Chevalier* has as its central etymological meaning a man on horseback, a figure that played a key role in twelfth-century
vernacular literature' (403). Likewise, Bumke addresses the etymology of *Knecht* and
Ritter in German literature and history, and their changing meanings from soldier
to service to nobility. See Bumke, *Ritterbegriff.*

125   Gautier, Léon, *Chivalry*, trans. D.C. Dunning, ed. Jacques Levron (London: Phoenix
House, 1965), 9–27.

126   Bumke describes how the term 'nobility' became attached to 'knight' and that the
service that knighthood entailed became the prized title of the elite in medieval
Europe. He also notes how important the dubbing ceremony became to the aristocratic elite, as a social event and expression of wealth. See Bumke, *Ritterbegriff,*
101–8. However, the opinions of scholars such as Georges Duby, Jean Flori and
Maurice Keen have cast some doubt about the actual existence of a 'knightly class'
as such in the Middle Ages and have shifted the discussion of this aspect of chivalry

Church was attractive: one's sword was blessed, one became a servant of God and there was a certain security in ecclesiastical patronage and the promise of salvation.[127] The description of dubbing ceremonies by poets became very popular and the Church even took a hand in such literature in that liturgical texts were supplemented as well as illustrated from these poetic sources rather than from historical texts.[128]

Values that became synonymous with chivalry, those of valour, sacrifice for an ideal, protection of the weak, the religion of honour, moral beauty, smiling in the face of death, grace in strength, courtesy and generosity to the defeated enemy, are identified in 1919 by Ghali as French virtues,[129] and they lie at the heart of unifying sentiments such as nationality, empire and kinship. The innovations to chivalric virtues from the Arabic world, according to Ghali, distinguish the epoch of European chivalry and include the reverence of ladies, horse, armaments, lineage, family, honour and poetry.[130] Though Ghali writes that the effects of these chivalric virtues are the influence of the chivalry of Andalusia,[131] it can also be said that the effects of the Church's role in investiture and dubbing furthered these ideals and played a part in popularizing chivalry in France and transcending royal power.

<hr />

to codes and orders instead of a social class. See: Duby; Flori, *L'essor de la chevalerie*. Furthermore, Maurice Keen poses the opinion that a knightly class cannot be easily defined or identified with any period of European history and also disputes the notion that chivalry or the investiture ceremony were sacramental. See Keen, 143–218. It is interesting to note that, despite pointing out the various ecclesiastical facets of the ceremony of investiture, Keen disputes the notion which many scholars have held that the dubbing ceremony was ever a sacrament in the Christian Church. (Keen, 64–82) However, Flori does not concentrate so much on the sacramental importance but on the symbolic importance of ritual items, such as the sword, the symbol of power that the Church would place in ceremony into the hands of kings at the time of coronation. See Flori, *L'Idéologie du glaive*, 3.

127 Bumke, *Ritterbegriff*, 101–9.
128 Bumke, *Ritterbegriff*, 88–9.
129 Ghali, 2–3.
130 Ghali, 39.
131 Ghali, 26.

If France did not invent chivalry then it is certainly credited with promulgating the sophisticated ideal throughout the Latin world and farther into Europe. With the impetus of Church political motives and the poetic ideals of courtly love and reward in honour, chivalry became a formidable institution. While the chivalry of the Sufis and the Andalusian Arabs was one of inner spirituality and poetic appreciation for the quest, the Christian knight saw his task from a different angle. It was France that assumed the charge of defending Christian interests in the lands of Islam in the first Crusades, and France that assumed the role of reaffirming the brotherhood of all people under the Christian religion, by which humanity would better itself.[132] This drive to propagate Christianity throughout the world via chivalry was an indication that European chivalry had come of age.

The journey of courtly literature

If the Church played a key role in the maturity of European chivalry, so too did the ideal of courtly love and veneration of ladies that was brought into Europe from and via the Arab world. The poetry of the troubadours found a well-disposed audience in France among the ruling ranks of *chevaliers* and their ladies, recording deeds, family lineage and the virtues of chivalry, which would later diverge into its characteristic genre, the romance.[133] Though the influence of Arabo-Islamic poetry on Andalusian

132   Ghali, 2.
133   Dennis Green investigates ways in which romance arose out of historical writing, concluding that the romance genre, employing the *matière de Bretagne*, became associated with fiction and fantasy, untruth for entertainment, more so than other genres. The relation between history and fiction in the twelfth century, however, was both similar and complementary. See Green, D.H., *The Beginnings of Medieval Romance: Fact and Fiction, 1150–1220*, ed. Alastair Minnis, Cambridge Studies in Medieval Literature (Cambridge: Cambridge University Press, 2002). It is also of use to reiterate that the term 'romance' referred to a piece of literature composed in the vernacular tongue, as distinguished from Latin, i.e., French, Occitan and Middle High German. Helen Cooper points this out, giving the Old French *romanz* as an

and Provençal poetry is evident, we know that there has been no clear determination about the way in which the trend of chivalry originated in Europe: whether it was the literature that perpetuated these ideas in medieval culture or whether a social class ripe for aggrandizing its status was reflected in its contemporary literature, scholars have not formed a consensus. Chivalry and courtly literature became tightly linked, together comprising, reflecting and depicting rules of etiquette that were recognized by their contemporary audience.

The ideals of Cluny and the *Treuga Dei*, the Peace of God issued by Pope Urban II, influenced knightly virtues and perpetuated the concept of knightly honour, and the 'knightly cult of womanhood'.[134] It might be said that, even if the origin of a conventionalized courtly etiquette is uncertain, literature did influence ideals such as the veneration of women; the pursuit of the married noblewoman, especially if she was of high rank, was a glorified adventure fraught with obstacles.[135] That this ideal of courtly code or love-service was connected intimately with chivalry is apparent in the interconnection of their values. '[T]he more religious and ascetic components of the spirit of chivalry were further developed by the knightly orders' and the Order of Teutonic Knights went so far as to foreswear the 'knightly love code' to live a monastic life.[136]

The refinement of chivalry through spirituality was again evident as courtly romances began to be composed. In comparing the development of both the figure and the term *chevalier* in Old French and Provençal texts to works by Chrétien, Margaret Switten finds that 'the *chevalier* is invited to rise above killing and plundering to embrace an essentially spiritual ideal: maintaining Christianity in the face of the Saracens; attaining *pretz* and

---

example of the term and emphasizing that the vernacular was the language of the secular world of entertainment, practical legalities, practical politics and imperial rule, and that it was a language that was the vehicle of oral transmission, meant to be heard, not read. See Cooper, 8, 11–12.

134   See Reinhardt, 97.
135   See Reinhardt, 98; see also Weir, 9.
136   Reinhardt, 98.

valor [courtliness] through love of women or of God.'[137] This love becomes the dominant feature of medieval literature, exemplifying itself in terms like chivalry and service, and in the sense of an ideal. Love had developed into the ennobling and refining expression of knightly devotion, marked by loyalty and duty to the beloved, and a complex set of self-imposed literary rules which invited inconsistency, conflicting directives and contradictory often paradoxical morals.

For the warrior knight, love was 'a frivolous distraction from his feudal duties,' a pleasure that was 'found in a well-groomed social existence; and the gradual refinement of manners brought with it an appreciation of the contribution made by women, an appreciation in fact of women themselves.'[138] The woman was responsible socially for raising men to their greatest heights.[139] With the *De Amore* treatise on love written by Andreas Capellanus for the entertainment of ladies of his patron court of Champagne, the term 'courtly love', which some scholars have interpreted as a mutation of 'love as practised at court',[140] a formula or code was imposed upon the interpretation of the literary practice of love.[141] That Andreas's 'code' was in itself ever the defining feature of medieval literary love or of chivalry is not convincing. Of his treatise's influence, 'it has been assumed by many critics that there was a generalized type of courtly love which was practiced or at least sung by all authors in all genres and that it was some-

---

137 Switten, 434.

138 Owen, 22.

139 See Jackson, W.T.H., *The Challenge of the Medieval Text: Studies in Genre and Interpretation*, ed. Joan M. Ferrante and Robert W. Hanning (New York: Columbia University Press, 1985), 8.

140 Jackson, *The Challenge of the Medieval Text*, 3.

141 Bloch writes that 'il était naturel qu'une classe aussi nettement délimitée par le genre de vie et la suprématie sociale aboutît à se donner un code de conduite, qui lui fût propre. Mais ces normes ne se précisèrent, pour, en même temps, s'affiner, que durant le second âge féodal [à l'environ d'1100], qui fut, de toute façon, celui de la prise de conscience.' Bloch, *Société féodale*, 35. [it was natural that a class so sharply confined by the way of life and by social ascendancy managed to give itself an apropriate code of conduct. But these standards became clearer, for, at the same time, to become refined during the Second Feudal Age [circa 1100] was, in any case, to gain awareness.]

how a part of the chivalric code. Such a belief is in complete defiance of the works of literature as we have them. [...] No one conception of love will cover all the relations between all the sexes in medieval lyric and epic, and it is unprofitable to seek for such a definition, especially if we regard this love as a spiritual or even an intellectual phenomenon.'[142] Love in medieval literature, epic and romance, is spiritual and intellectual in nature, but so multi-faceted that it does not lend itself to a neatly defined code of practice. The importance of Andreas's *De Amore* was that it *was* written down: that it was a social phenomenon to consider the occupations of courtly society in a form of entertainment, reflecting the social graces of a budding European nobility. It was an elaborate game, but 'for a social game, a gallant fiction, it has proved remarkably long-lived.'[143]

Love in medieval literature reflected a respect for women and spirituality, and was marked by feudal, chivalric and religious undertones, combining diverse elements into a custom of duty. This was the embodiment of the *amor cortois* (courtly love), 'the conception of knightly service as the corollary of love, without which knighthood itself [was] unthinkable.'[144] These elements were not always in harmony with one another and this was the feature of medieval literature. Tension, dilemmas and consequences of the contradictory nature of a chivalric code and service to love, whilst apparent in French romances, were to become the distinguishing feature of medieval German literature, and one of the driving themes in *Willehalm*.

Eleanor and Chrétien

To follow the *chansons de geste* from Aquitaine to Thüringen is to travel the route of some of the continent's most significant courts and their monarchs. Two of the prominent personalities of the twelfth century, Eleanor

---

142   Jackson, *The Challenge of the Medieval Text*, 3–4. Jackson goes on to clarify that love-making in medieval society is frequently misinterpreted because of being mistakenly connected with a preconceived code of courtly love, which he seeks to find outside the parameters of Andreas's treatise.

143   Owen, 176.

144   Richey, 117.

of Aquitaine and Chrétien of Troyes, can scarcely be mentioned without citing their influence in terms of the promulgation of the concept of love poetry in the Middle Ages. The marriage of Eleanor of Aquitaine to Louis VII of France, from which two daughters were born (one being Marie of Champagne), ensured a blossoming interest in courtly genres. A review of the connection between the courts of Poitiers and Champagne and those of German princes, and the exchange of ideas that took place between them, provides some insight into what influences Wolfram may have encountered before setting out upon his task of reworking the *chanson-de-geste* material into *Willehalm*.

Many accounts of Eleanor are of a lively, intelligent, witty, sophisticated and beautiful woman who wielded power easily and who enjoyed her opulent duchy of Aquitaine in its capital of Poitiers.[145] Among many accomplishments in her long life, she was a keen patron of poetry and is said to have influenced and even commissioned works by poets, from England to the southern regions of Aquitaine, having cultivated an interest in the *matière de Bretagne*. The granddaughter of William IX, she had a taste for love poetry and her courts boasted poets and composers such as Bernard de Ventadour, Rigaud de Barbezieux and Bertran de Born.

Eleanor's daughter, Marie of Champagne, was patroness to Chrétien de Troyes, the poet who popularized the Arthurian material in the vernacular, composed poems in couplets, incorporated ideals of courtly love into the *matière de Bretagne* and included several references to his patroness in his works, most notably, *Le Chevalier de la Charrette* (*The Knight of the Cart*).[146] Both ladies had been fascinated by the Arthurian material (Wace dedicated his work to Eleanor) and it was the subject matter for which Chrétien would become famous. The vehicle was the chivalric romance in which spiritual and cultural memes, elements of behaviour passed on by emulation, met.

145   See Weir, 17ff.
146   See Parry's introduction to Capellanus, 13–15.

Chrétien's patroness, Marie, was an avid admirer of romance and it was at her courts that Andreas Capellanus's treatise was penned for the entertainment of her court and probably for the purpose of Andreas's own ingratiation. These *cours d'amour* [courts of love] that took place in Eleanor's courts in Angers and Poitiers were only fictitious, and both Boyd and Weir write that there is no evidence of a meeting between mother and daughter at these places,[147] as Eleanor's marital circumstances, her divorce of Louis and marriage to English King Henry II, precluded their having lived under the same roof since Marie's childhood. However, even with this lack of information, scholars have been too intrigued by the influences apparent in the works to let the matter rest. June Hall Martin McCash explores cause, effect and the facts that are known about their lives to conclude that it is possible and not entirely disproved that Eleanor and Marie could have met.[148] Similarly, John Bednar, working with the possibility of a mother-daughter meeting, cites evidence to support the possible meeting of Eleanor and Chrétien: 'if Marie left Champagne to visit her mother in Poitiers in 1174, we can be sure that Chrétien was accompanying her entourage.'[149] Whether or not Marie of Champagne or Chrétien ever spent time with Eleanor of Aquitaine to enjoy their passion for poetry together, it is apparent that these ladies exerted considerable influence over the courtly poetry emanating from France, and its propagation and popularity throughout Europe. Certainly Chrétien, whether he visited

---

147 'Recent studies indicate that mother and daughter probably never met or even corresponded.' (Boyd, 137) Also see Weir, 181.

148 McCash's study is well-researched and convincing, and she concludes that 'despite the lack of indisputable documentation, the probability of a friendly relationship between Marie of Champagne and her mother seems strong in view of the apparent connections between Marie and Eleanor's sons and daughters-in-law, interaction between writers associated with their courts, and circumstances that place them in close proximity on several occasions.' McCash, June Hall Martin, 'Marie de Champagne and Eleanor of Aquitaine: A Relationship Reexamined', *Speculum* LIV/4 (1979), 698–711.

149 Bednar, John, *La Spiritualité et le symbolisme dans les oeuvres de Chrétien de Troyes* (Paris: Libraire A.-G. Nizet, 1974), 45–6.

Poitiers or not, would have been exposed to Aquitainian poetry (as was
the court that patronized him and in which the material was preserved
and spread).[150]

To the German courts

The *fin'amors* that permeated twelfth-century French literature was adapted
in Germany as *hohe Minne* [courtly love] and travelled from Poitiers along
the Danube and Rhine until its sentiments were expressed in Friedrich von
Hausen's work: the lady was God's wonder and venerating her was a divine
duty.[151] The means of travel of French poetry and chivalric and courtly ideals
would have been traffic between courts on either side of the Rhine, not only
by troubadours or *jongleurs*, who were not documented as having made the
trip into Germany as often as they were documented having traversed the
borders of Angevin France, but also by kings, princes and other members of
the nobility.[152] Of note is the legend of Hermann I of Thuringia, who would

---

150   Fahrner writes that after Eleanor, 'Man nimmt die Stärke des Willens wahr und
      die unbedingte Entschlossenheit, mit denen er die Taten ausführt, die ihm seine
      Gesinnung und sein innerer Auftrag gebieten. Man fühlt dabei auch die Größe dieser
      Gesinnung, die über alles Unbedeutende hinwegsieht und hinweggeht, die zugleich
      eine großzügige Milde und Güte ausstrahlt und den ihr Zugehörigen den hohen
      Lebensmut schenken kann' [One perceives the strength of the will and the absolute
      determination with which he implements the deeds that proffer his inclination and
      his inner directive. One also feels the size of this inclination which overlooks every-
      thing that is insignificant and which, at the same time, radiates a generous temperance
      and goodness, and which can give his acquaintances great optimism] (162). This is a
      testament to the medieval mentality that would characterise the era of chivalry and
      romance.
151   See Fahrner, 263.
152   French scholars write of the indebtedness of German vernacular literature to the
      influences from the Romance countries and specifically the interaction between
      members of the nobility. Gesa Bonath writes: 'l'éclosion d'une littérature profane en
      Allemagne doit beaucoup aux contacts entre l'aristocratie allemande et celle de ses
      voisins romans, qui s'établissent surtout à la suite du mariage de Frédéric Barberousse
      avec Béatrice de Bourgogne.' Bonath, Gesa, 'Reflets des croisades dans la littérature
      allemande' in Karl-Heinz Bender and Hermann Kleber, eds, *Les Épopées de la croisade*

later become Wolfram's patron, growing up in Paris. It is substantiated that his father, Ludwig II, wrote a letter to Louis VII of France asking permission to send two of his sons to the French court; in it, he also stated that one of them, Hermann himself, was well-versed in literature.[153] Bumke writes that the first German courtly poetry was indeed taken from French models due to the commerce between French and German courts: 'Den größten Einfluß hatten aber zweifellos die weltlichen Fürsten, die damals bereits auf dem Weg zur Landesherrschaft waren und die ihre Höfe der modernen französischen Adelskultur öffneten.'[154] [The lay-nobility had without doubt the greatest influence; during that era, they were building their kingdoms and opened their courts to the modern French courtly culture.] Through the literature came the culture of French chivalry, too: 'for generations the German nobility had sent its offspring to French schools and courts to be educated [because] France had become the home of Chivalry itself and was educating other countries towards that goal.'[155]

There was a difference between the way the idea of courtly love was received and interpreted in Germany and how it was portrayed in France, due to such factors as geographical location, history, cultural background and language. The treatment of courtly love by German authors distinguished itself in that it was portrayed as more spiritual and more service-oriented, and possessed a poignant duality of love and suffering, of temporal

---

(Stuttgart: Franz Steiner Verlag Wiesbaden, 1987) 105–18, 105. [The emergence of a profane literature in Germany owes much to the contacts between the German aristocracy and that of its Romantic neighbors, that established themselves especially following the marriage of Frederick Barbarossa to Béatrice de Bourgogne.]

153   In his research into the court of Thuringia, Bumke presents evidence that when Margarete van Kleve was married to Ludwig III, Ludwig's brother Heinrich brought with him the unfinished *Eneit* by Veldecke circa 1180, and his other brothers, Hermann and Friedrich, commissioned its finishing, shows an active exchange of literature and ideas between French and German resources. See Bumke, Joachim, *Mäzene im Mittelalter: die Gönner und Auftraggeber der höfischen Literatur in Deutschland 1150–1300* (Munich: C.H. Beck, 1979), 159.

154   Bumke, *Mäzene im Mittelalter*, 10.

155   Curschmann, Michael, 'The French, the Audience, and the Narrator in Wolfram's "Willehalm"', *Neophilologus* 59/4 (1975), 548–62, 558.

and divine duty. *Minne* combines the aristocratic idea of love with service: a nobleman gives up his inheritance to serve a lady, a service that is for him a privilege.[156] In addition to the honour of serving came the reward. Love 'bestows dignity and honor on a man, it gives respect to a woman. Without it both knight and lady are incomplete members of society.'[157]

While Chrétien's works can be seen as a commentary on courtly love, and as depicting the irony of love and service as interdependent values, conveying messages about morals and creating 'an illusory sense of unison by sheer magic of style,'[158] German poets expressed the relationship between love and service rather differently. Hartmann von Aue, one of the first to bring out the idea of knightly ethos in romance, related adventure to love, the service of which would bring everything together in harmony, reconciling secular and spiritual ideals, love being a manifestation of God.[159] Gottfried von Strassburg's love was more intellectual, focusing on the individual and asking whether love and society are compatible.[160] Walther von der Vogelweide's poetry tends towards stressing 'the breach between the higher aspirations of the age and their fulfilment.'[161] Wolfram, like Chrétien, makes a critique of love and service, but his emphasis is on the rift between man and God, and how to redeem this relationship. Differences in chronological eras, geopolitical environments and generic models resulted in the depiction of the traditional knightly subject matter with a differing focus.

Love and service are as important in *Willehalm* as they are in *Parzival*, but not merely the love of service to ladies, *Minnedienst*; rather, the love

156 'Der adlige Herr begibt sich seiner Herrenrechte und tritt in den Dienst einer Dame; er dient um Minnelohn, und es ist eine Auszeichnung für ihn, Diener zu heißen.' (Bumke, *Ritterbegriff*, 99). W.T.H. Jackson also writes that German authors regarded the French literary love as characterised by love-service [The noble lord gives up his rights as ruler and enlists in the service of a lady; he serves for Love and it is an accolade for him to be called a servant] (*The Challenge of the Medieval Text*, 33).

157 Jackson, *The Challenge of the Medieval Text*, 30.

158 Richey, 53.

159 Richey, 43–6, 115; Jackson, *Chivalry in Twelfth-Century Germany*, 16–17.

160 See: Jackson, *The Challenge of the Medieval Text*, 24–30; Richey, 46–7.

161 Richey, 115.

between husband and wife, the love between kin and clan, and the love
between man and God, and all of these are bound together by honour of
service, which to Wolfram is represented by spirituality consisting of an
inner journey. This is consistent with observations on the German interpretation and portrayal of *Minnedienst*; the love in German poetry is spiritually portrayed and linked, a struggle within oneself, the human heart as
the battlefield.[162] German poetry saw women as the embodiment of *Minne*;
it was the lady who served as the knight's guide, providing the journey to
knighthood, and for this, the knight was indebted to her.[163] This service was
the noblest element of human life. Fahrner sees the duality of the German
Minnedienst, love and suffering, as always bound together; *Minne* and the
nobility of the struggle are interdependent.[164]

The Poet of Thuringia

The court at Thuringia under Hermann I was famous for the reception of French literary material in Germany and for drawing poets from
all over Germany.[165] Wolfram was inspired, as were his contemporary
compatriots, poets and patrons alike, by the ideas of love service and
chivalry emanating from France's literature and his *Parzival*, perhaps
his greatest work, shows introspect in both concepts, their implications
and the problems they posed. *Parzival* was largely taken from Chrétien's
Le conte du Graal, but when Wolfram composed *Willehalm*, the source
was from a different type of material, the *matière de France*. In a survey
of German Crusade literature, Gesa Bonath writes that 'pendant une
période assez longue Wolfram est le seul à soulever la thématique dans le
genre épique' [during a quite long period of time, Wolfram was the only

---

162 Fahrner, 264.
163 Fahrner, 264–6.
164 Fahrner, 271–5.
165 Bumke, Joachim, *Höfische Kultur: Literatur und Gesellschaft im hohen Mittelalter*
     (Munich: Deutscher Taschenbuch Verlag, 2002), 122.

one to revive the themes of the epic genre].[166] The question must then be addressed: where did Wolfram or Hermann acquire the inspiration for this material?

Joachim Bumke explored the question of whether Wolfram's ideas were his own or his patron's, but no adequate answer could be found as evidence for the source for his choice of material and subject matter.[167] There is, however, sufficient evidence of commerce between the courts of France and Thuringia, as we have seen, and thus in all probability between other German and French courts as well, indicating an exchange of literature as well as of ideas. It would be no surprise then if Wolfram himself had heard *chansons de geste* performed or heard about some second-hand, specifically *Aliscans* or *Prise d'Orange*. In any case, Wolfram gives his patron credit for making him familiar with the material: 'lantgrâf von Dürngen Herman, tet mir diz maer von im bekant. er ist en franzoys genant, kuns Gwillâms de Orangis' [Hermann, Landgrave of Thuringia, acquainted me with this story; in French he is known as Guillaume d'Orange] (*Wh.* 3, 8–11).

If German authors generally depicted a code of chivalry in a philosophical, inner sense, this is especially so in *Willehalm*. In reworking French material, 'each [German] author chose works which suited his purpose and modified the treatment of love which he found there.'[168] In Wolfram's two major works, based on material from differing genres, he imposes his own views and conducts his own explorations of what courtliness is and of what problems are exposed.

With the Grail court in *Parzival*, Wolfram offers a positive alternative to the Arthurian court, which is not separate in Chrétien's work. With Wolfram there is a distinct difference between the spiritual and the secular, criticizing love-service explicitly; all knights obsessed with it prove defective or complete failures.[169] Though both Christian and Saracen in Wolfram's works are depicted as serving love, Wolfram makes a distinction between

---

166 Bonath, 112.
167 See Bumke, *Mäzene im Mittelalter*.
168 Jackson, *The Challenge of the Medieval Text*, 17.
169 Jackson, *The Challenge of the Medieval Text*, 21.

the manner in which they serve and how that service is directed. This holds true especially in the characters in *Willehalm*: 'Love is of vital importance to Willehalm; minne as a quasi-religious cult is not.'[170] In *Willehalm*, as in *Parzival*, Wolfram again examines chivalry, but makes use of its code in a different setting, focusing on honour and the ideal of conversion, and love is an integral part of the balance between secular and spiritual, between chivalric code and Christian duty. The chivalry of *Willehalm* seems to suggest how proper service is rewarded.

Chivalry as it existed in Europe and as it was depicted in medieval literature, with its code of service and spiritual reflection, can be followed from its development as a military institution in Europe and as a spiritual code and unifying force in Persia and the Arab world. The cosmopolitan activity that reached distant geographic regions of Europe and the Islamic Mediterranean resulted in a fusion of the chivalry that was developing, culminating in the emergence of a chivalric code in Europe that encompassed both spiritual and temporal ideals, governing behaviour and directing service, venerating ladies and protecting the weak. This is the chivalry apparent in the *chansons de geste* and upon which Wolfram expanded in his retelling of *Aliscans* in his *Willehalm*. It is in this work that Wolfram explores moral weaknesses; amongst these was the influence of the Church that exploited the ideals of service and motivation, the effect of which was service in the interest of protection and power. Wolfram offers his answer to these weaknesses as a more individually and spiritually guided chivalric service.

---

170   Rushing, James A., 'Arofel's Death and the Question of Willehalm's Guilt', *Journal of English and Germanic Philology*, October (1995), 469–82, 476.

Ethics of Chivalry Put to the Test: The Crusades

Though *Willehalm* includes elements that can be identified in terms of
the Crusade epic, the question arises as to how much this text and its
sources were influenced by Crusade ideology and what they portray in
terms of Crusades and chivalry. Furthermore, what Crusade ideology
denotes in early thirteenth-century German lyric when compared to the
chansons de geste is in need of clarification. We have seen how knighthood
and spirituality became interconnected in a more socially defined chivalry and how the influence of the Church supplied it with the additional
purpose of defence, integrating knighthood with piety. The latter seems
to have occurred most profoundly about the time of the First Crusade,
its starting point an address by Pope Urban II at Clermont in 1095.[171] The
literature contemporary with *Willehalm* and also that of its sources spans
a timeframe from before the Crusades to just after the Third Crusade (led
by Richard the Lionheart, Philip II of France and Frederick I, Barbarossa,
Holy Roman Emperor).[172]

As the majority of the *chansons de geste* of the *Cycle de Guillaume* were
probably composed before the call of the First Crusade, one can scarcely
speak of them as pure Crusade literature. They do, however, have elements
that can be seen as consistent with Crusade ideology, this possibly due to
their having been recorded in writing during the time of the first Crusades
or just before. Jean Flori sees the Crusade elements in the *chansons de geste*
as a revival of the old martial and feudal ideology, included to satisfy the

---

171   See: Keen, 44–5; Flori, 'L'idée de croisade', 476; and Reinhardt, 106–7.
172   The first *chansons de geste* of the *Guillaume* cycle have been placed as early as the
      late eleventh century, though later findings have designated *Couronnement* as the
      earliest to have been written down, dating from 1131, and *Aliscans* around 1185. See
      Ferrante, 15–16. Wolfram's *Willehalm* is generally believed to have been composed
      before 1215; see Richey, 36–7; Bertau, Karl, 'Versuch Über Wolfram' in Karl Bertau,
      ed., *Wolfram von Eschenbach: neun Versuche über Subjektivität und Ursprünglichkeit
      in der Geschichte* (Munich: C.H. Beck, 1983) 145–65, 146–8; Bumke, *Mäzene im
      Mittelalter*, 168.

audience of the Crusading era: 'ces épopées furent conçues pour l'essentiel avant la première croisade et leur rédaction (ou leur remaniement) n'a pas profondément altéré l'idéologie qu'elles véhiculent, et qui demeure celle de la "guerre juste", antérieure à l'appel de Clermont' [these epics were essentially before the first Crusade and their publication (or their rewriting) did not profoundly alter the ideology that they conveyed and that held the idea of the 'just war' before the call of Clermont].[173]

It remains to be considered how this Crusade ideology was received and depicted east of the Rhine and how Wolfram in particular characterized a Crusading knighthood in *Willehalm*. In order to do this, we must look at the relationship between the ecclesiastical and secular aspects of knighthood and chivalry: what influence the Church had upon chivalry via the Crusades; how the Church call for Crusades brought about the questioning of a duality in doctrine; and how this is represented in our texts.

Chivalry and the Church

Chivalry had strong spiritual roots that were independent of the Christian Church; these included the warrior legends of the Germanic cultures and the almost monastic chivalric orders of the Arabo-Islamic cultures. Keen

---

173   Flori, Jean, 'La Croix, la crosse et l'épée, La Conversion des infidèles dans la Chanson de Roland et les chroniques de croisade' in François Suard, ed., *Plaist vos oïr bone cançon vallant? mélanges offerts à François Suard: études recueillies par Dominique Boutet, Marie-Madeleine Castellani, Françoise Ferrand et Aimé Petit* (Lille 3: Villeneuve d'Ascq, 1999), 261–72, 262. See also Bloch, *La Société féodale*, 157: 'Une des caractéristiques essentielles des chansons fut d'ailleurs de ne vouloir retracer que des événements anciens. A peu près seules, les croisades semblèrent immédiatement dignes de l'épopée. C'est qu'elles avaient tout pour secouer les imaginations; sans doute aussi qu'elles transposaient dans le présent une forme d'héroïsme chrétien, familière, dès le XIᵉ siècle, aux poèmes.' [One of the essential characteristics of the *chansons de geste* was, moreover, the desire to revisit only old events. Of these only the Crusades seemed immediately deserving of epic. This is because they had everything to inspire the imagination; doubtless just as they transposed the familiar, Christian figure of heroism of the eleventh century into the present, in the poems.]

notes that two of the main goals of chivalrous life were 'fame in this world, and salvation in the next,'[174] and it was the piety of the eleventh century that began to entwine the two. Likewise, it was the 'interweaving of Christian with heroic and secular motifs [that became] characteristic of the treatment of the crusade in chivalrous narrative and poetry.'[175] The secular can be prudently separated from the ecclesiastic influences on chivalry: early chivalry's moral directives from the more recent Church prescripts sought to impose upon chivalry a purpose: that of the Crusade.[176] This can be seen in the literature that spans the timeframe of the blossoming of chivalry. The Gautier and Ramón Lull prescripts for chivalry attest to the impact of Crusading ideals on chivalry as an institution with a code of practice set out by the Church as it appeared after the First Crusade.[177]

During the early Feudal Age, around the tenth century, German heroic songs were not written down; rather, their material had been preserved by oral transmission in the vernacular, the *lingua theodisca* [German language]. This premise is attested by the existence of several manuscripts: the alliterative *Hildebrandslied*, copied by monks (c. 800) onto the leaves of a theological manuscript;[178] the German heroic story of redemption in characteristic alliterative verse, *Heliand* (c. 850); and even a Latin version of *Waltharius* (c. 930). All of these point to a previous oral transmission and all combine Germanic heroic tradition with Christian values.[179] The

---

174 Keen, 54.
175 Keen, 55.
176 The power struggle between the German Emperor Henry IV and Pope Gregory VII and the ensuing Cluniac reform, which put an end to the imperial power of lay investiture and monasteries and granting it solely to Rome, likely forged a rift between secular and ecclesiastic influence over knighthood, as well as contributing to the power struggle between Church and State. See Reinhardt, 74–5.
177 See: Cooper, 42ff; Keen, 16; and Bloch, *La Société féodale*, 57.
178 Reinhardt, 57.
179 Reinhardt, 56–7. Reinhardt writes that Walther, of *Waltharius*, 'appears as the first German representative of Christian knighthood, the undaunted yet humble protector of noble womanhood' (85). Marc Bloch also surveys early Germanic epic material that was influenced by the French *chansons de geste*. See Bloch, *La Société féodale*, 157–61.

presence of Church influences are more pronounced, however, in the French poems composed during that time, when the German poems were still only being sung.

Whilst France was relatively young as a linguistic and literary entity, the material of her *gestes* did not predate Christian influence in Europe as did the material of the German epic *Lieder*.[180] It was when the French vernacular *chansons de geste* began to proliferate, retold and translated for German audiences, that the appreciation for vernacular poetry in Germany began to flourish[181] – hence the influence of Christian French literature upon the long-established German taste for the heroic epic.[182] However Christian the material of early German vernacular heroic poems and however loyal to the Church of Rome the French epics, these displayed little of what could be called Crusading ideology due to their relating material of traditional knighthood and legend in contemporaneous conditions. It was a result of the Crusades that the value of military skills and prowess were idealized in French literature and, as Koss writes, a 'pervasive presence of the Saracens as primary adversary directly reflects the Crusader ethic [...] the chivalric values expounded in the *chansons* can be seen as

---

180   Bloch writes of the contrast in the German and French literature of the tenth and eleventh centuries, that 'la France, dont la civilisation avait été profondément remaniée dans le creuset du haut moyen âge, dont la langue, en tant qu'entité linguistique vraiment différenciée, était relativement jeune, si elle se tournait vers sa tradition la plus reculée, découvrait les Carolingiens' [France, whose civilization had been profoundly reshaped in the melting pot of the Early Middle Ages, had a language that was, as an essentially differentiated linguistic entity, relatively young, and turned to its late tradition, to discover the Carolingians] (Bloch, *La Société féodale*, 160–1).

181   Bloch, *La Société féodale*, 159–60.

182   Bloch recognizes the more distant past related in German material than in the French: 'l'Allemagne[...].disposait, pour en nourrir ses contes, d'une substance infiniment plus ancienne, parce que, longtemps caché, le courant des récits et peut-être des chants ne s'était jamais interrompu' [Germany, in order to to cultivate its stories, utilized subject matter that was infinitely older, because the stream of narratives and perhaps songs so long hidden had never been interrupted] (Bloch, *La Société féodale*, 161).

an idealization of the military ideals supposedly subscribed to by these soldiers of Christ.'[183]

Crusade ideology

The material of the German *Lieder* and of the *chansons de geste* relates to defiant barons, to pagan forces encroaching upon Imperial land and to the strength and right of feudal principles and loyalty. Flori sums up the Crusading ideology relating those principal themes of Pope Urban II's call at Clermont by using an alliterative device, the letter 'P': penitential pilgrimage, papal address or decree, pardoning of sins, promise of paradise and special privileges.[184] None of these themes plays a strong role, if any at all, in the *Cycle de Guillaume* or in *Willehalm*. However, these themes in Crusading ideology can be seen as being closely related to those memes outlined by Cooper in her investigation of the romance genre, a genre that succeeded the *chansons de geste* in the wake of the *matière de Bretagne*.[185]

Willehalm and its French counterpart were chivalric literature comprising a range of elements of popular medieval literary genres that had little to do with crusading ideology other than that they were composed during the time of the Crusades for an aristocratic audience occupied with these contemporary issues. Keen makes the observation that 'crusading and chivalry were not precisely the same thing. Chivalry [...] was related to a whole range of martial and aristocratic activities which had no necessary

---

183 Koss, Ronald G., *Family, Kinship and Lineage in the Cycle de Guillaume d'Orange*, vol. 5, Studies in Mediaeval Literature (Lewiston: The Edwin Mellen Press, 1990), 198.

184 See Flori, 'L'idée de croisade'.

185 Themes and memes, or elements of cultural behaviour passed on by imitation, that Cooper finds consistent with literature that can be called romance, which resemble closely those themes given by Flori (see above) as elements of Crusade ideology, are those such as pilgrimage, seeking redemption and forgiveness, and the quest. See Cooper: 'One extreme form of penance requires the sinner to act the part of the mute fool at court and to eat only what he can seize from the dogs.' (87) This type of behaviour is adopted by the William character in both *Aliscans* and *Willehalm*, though perhaps he is not quite as severe when he goes to the court at Montlaon.

connection with Crusading.'[186] The ideology, however, can be seen to have appealed in that there were certain elements of chivalry, even in its pagan roots, that merged easily with the themes of the Clermont address and this facilitates the identification of those pieces of literature with the Crusading idea. Flori writes that the inspiration for the *chansons de geste*, while not that of the Crusades, was 'l'ancienne idéologie de la guerre sacralisée telle que la concevaient les chevaliers, avant, pendant, et peut-être encore peu après la première croisade' [the old ideology of a sacred war, such as was conceived by the knights before, during, and perhaps again shortly after the first Crusade].[187] Further, the disposition towards religious wars existed before the call to Crusade and this was taken up and furthered by the activity of the Crusades themselves.

The ideology perpetuated by the kinetic energy of the Crusading centuries had an effect on chivalry in that, because knights were called for the first time by the Church (in defence of Rome from the Saracen threat), knighthood was given the guise of a Christian vocation.[188] Knighthood and chivalry before this call to Crusade was no less Christian and no less a vocation for Christian men. Keen identifies the *chansons de geste* as 'the earliest sources that can fully and properly be called "chivalrous"' and he draws attention to the religious element independent of the Crusades that was present in the chivalry and in the character of the knights of the *chansons de geste*: 'they are "Christian soldiers" because they are both Christians and knights, and not because of any special commission that the

---

186 Keen, 44.
187 Flori, 'L'idée de croisade', 495. Flori also writes that the crusade ideology 'ne [semble] pas avoir modifié profondément la trame initiale et l'idéologie principale de ces chansons de geste qui conservent une forte coloration carolingienne,' [does not [seem] to have profoundly modified the initial quality, and the principal ideology of these epics which preserve a strong Carolingian flavour] thereby drawing a connection between pre- and post-Clermont ideologies in the *chansons de geste* ('L'idée de croisade,' 494). In a subsequent article, Flori expands upon this idea, finding that the *chansons de geste* were not about crusading, but were an expression of war ideology and religiously motivated feudalism ('La croix, la crosse et l'épée').
188 See Keen, 46.

authority of the Church has given them.'[189] With the Crusades, however, knighthood and the ideals of chivalry were given a religious basis, more concrete than spiritual, with God as the knight's liege-lord and honour defined by religion.[190] It was later that Crusading ideology became part of aristocratic knightly pursuits in France and her literature, and even later in Germany that true Crusading ideology played any definitive role in the chivalry and literature of the court. When treated by German authors such as Wolfram, those pre-Clermont themes of Christian knighthood take on a deeper, self-reflective angle, presenting contradictions in terms of world and religious view without denying the firm faith in the Christian Church that characterized the medieval world order.

Christianity and morality

Wolfram allows his characters in *Willehalm* to question Christianization as a moral duty in war and to ask whether morality and courtly ethics can transcend Church doctrine. Besides these questions posed by the characters, the audience is given an opportunity to reflect on the contradiction and duality posed by the Christian imperative in the portrayal of the Saracen adversaries. Such questions are not addressed in the preceding *chansons de geste* which, while Christian, were more concerned with questions of feudal loyalty and courage than the romance-inspired self-reflection of the late twelfth century. Wolfram's scanty knowledge of Saracen culture and

189   Keen, 51. Keen also makes a survey of Germanic literature predating the *chansons de geste* in the search for origins of knightly piety, looking at works such as *Ruodlieb*, *Beowulf*, *Waldhere* and the Saxon *Genesis*. See Keen, 52ff.

190   Friedrich-Wilhelm Wentzlaff-Eggebert explores the dogmatic foundations of a holy war and how Christian and feudal traditions were used in literature to perpetuate the Crusade idea. Wentzlaff-Eggebert, Friedrich-Wilhelm, 'Kreuzzugsidee und Mittelalterliches Weltbild', *Deutsches Vierteljahrschrift für Literaturwissenschaft und Geistesgeschichte* 30 (1956), 71–88, 76–8. Kurt Reinhardt also writes that 'there was also to be found that splendid conception of the loyalty of the Christian knight to his divine Liege Lord who had called him to arms through his representative, the pope' (108).

theological debate shows that his message was of his own concept of chivalry; he does not enter into ecclesiastical criticism in *Willehalm*, but makes a pragmatic case for a positive view of chivalry that is spiritually guided.

Image of the Saracen

The way in which the Saracens are portrayed in the *chansons de geste* and in *Willehalm* is not necessarily consistent nor do these images of Saracens in literature correspond to those for which Crusade ideology became known. However, as the Crusade ideal was more complex than that, so too was the image of the Saracen adversary and consequently the protagonists' interaction with him.

Mary Campbell thoughtfully surveys a number of early European texts on the Orient and of particular interest are pilgrimage books such as Egeria's ethereal *Peregrinatio ad terram sanctam* (c. 375) and the *De locis sanctis* of Bishop Arculf, a Merovingian Gaul (c. 675).[191] Unsurprisingly, the idea of religious war plays no part in the depiction of the peoples of the Orient described in these works, which concentrate more on spiritual experience and Biblical historical sites than on the imperative to convert heathens or to defend sacred ground. The vocation of knighthood and its merging with spiritual and moral ethics likely contributed to the later view of the Saracen just as much as did the threat of conquest, exercised to a greater or lesser degree on the European continent by the expanding Arabo-Islamic caliphates. More so than in Rome and Sicily, this pressure was exerted strongly on the Iberian peninsula, the stronghold of the Umayyad Caliphate, and the southern coast of what is now France.

The image of the Saracen in the *chansons de geste* is one that predates the Crusades; it is modelled on small clashes in Spain rather than on contemporary Crusade experiences.[192] Serper argues, however, that the image

191 See Campbell, *The Witness*.
192 Serper, Arié, 'Sarrasins et chansons de geste' in *Essor et fortune de la chanson de geste dans l'Europe et l'Orient latin: actes du IXe congrès international de la Société Rencesvals pour l'étude des épopées romanes, Padoue-Venise, 29 août–4 septembre 1982* (Modena: Mucchi, 1983) 179–83, 181.

conceived was nonetheless for a Crusading audience and that the exoticism of the Saracens depicted in *chansons de geste* like *Roland* was offered as a stimulus to the popularity of the Crusade.[193] The Saracens depicted in the *chansons de geste*, then, are a result of a Christian religious standpoint imposed upon the heathen adversaries and not upon personal experience from pilgrimage or diplomatic mission.[194] Saracens cease to become merely occupants of a distant Holy Land or a power in the conquest of the European continent; rather, they become a military and religious adversary, formidable conquerors of land previously contained within the Roman Empire. They are religious enemies, distinguished by florid descriptions of lavish courts and of material luxury as well as of the exotic and fantastical features of the Saracen army (*Wh.* 32, 8–37).

Saracens are described ruthlessly in *Roland* as criminals, thieves, traitors and fools, and the image of Marsile, with his mutilated right arm as a punishment for thievery and his treacherous, evil motivations stands out.[195] Ferrante remarks that in the *chansons de geste*, 'Saracens are generally presented as monstrous creatures, often physically deformed, brutal' and terrifying in martial prowess; 'most of them are fit only to be defeated

---

193   Serper, 179. This corresponds to Jean Dufournet's assertion that the *Chanson de Roland* is 'un poème de la croisade, tout pénétré des rêves et des préjugés des seigneurs et des guerriers qui allèrent lutter en Espagne autour de Saragosse, destiné à renforcer, chez un public bouleversé par la menace sarrasine, l'enthousiasme pour la guerre sainte, prônant un choc total entre deux mondes antagonistes, au moment où la société guerrière[...] prenait conscience d'elle-même et se définissait dans la culte de ses héros passés' [a crusade poem, entirely penetrated by the imaginings and the prejudices of the lords and warriors who went to fight in Spain around Saragossa, intended to strengthen the enthusiasm for Holy War in a public troubled by the Saracen threat, acclaiming a clash between two conflicting worlds at a time when the warrior society [...] became aware of itself and defined itself in the veneration of its bygone heroes]. Dufournet, Jean, ed., *La Chanson de Roland* (Paris: Flammarion, 1993), 20.

194   Serper writes that the misrepresentation of the Islamic religion in Roland and the imposed Christian view of the Saracen attest to the extreme religious fervour of the Christians of the crusading era and not from ignorance, resulting in the Saracens being the villains. Serper, 180–1.

195   See Dufournet, *Roland*, 29.

and destroyed; a very few are converted to Christianity, [and] those who convert often turn out better Christians than the Franks.'[196] There are certainly some grey areas in the depiction of Saracens in the *chansons de geste*, for many are described as accomplished knights with beautiful equipage (though Jean-Marc Pastré writes that this could be seen as a deliberate device, making the Christian victor seem even more commendable when he defeats the Saracen knight).[197] Blancandrin, for example, is first described in *Roland* as 'des plus saives paiens: De vasselage fut asez chevaler, Prozdom i out pur sun seignur aider' [the wisest of pagans; a knight of much loyalty who helps his liege-lord with wise counsel].[198] However, it is from his mind that the treacherous plot against Charlemagne is conceived. There is also a general misrepresentation of physical appearance as well as of the Muslim religion in *Willehalm*, as in the *chansons de geste*. The Saracen is described as a fantastical beauty, with dark sometimes horned skin and extra appendages; he is also described as a giant and as having one eye, and his religion is portrayed as having multiple deities – Apollo, Kahun, Mahomet and Tervigant. The misrepresentation can be seen as an element to engender enthusiasm for the Crusade, as an element of exoticism applied to the formidable opponent or as poetic licence. It is most probably due to all three as well as to a lack of direct experience.

An example of the contradictory portrayal of the Saracen in *Willehalm* is that of Gyburg's son, Ehmereiz, or Esmeré. In *Aliscans*, Esmeré appears during the battle as a reasonable knight. He asks his stepfather, Guillaume, why he was disinherited and thrown out, and tells him that Guillaume's bloody act of beheading Esmeré's two brothers (after having them beaten on the marble floor and hanged from a tree) has shamed him and that they must be avenged. This outburst is answered commandingly by Guillaume, who calls him a fool and says that if a man does not love Christianity then he has no right to live, 'jel di par verite' [I say in truth]. He adds

196   Ferrante, 25–6.
197   Pastré, Jean-Marc, 'Étranges Sarrasins: le luxe et l'exotisme dans le Willehalm de Wolfram' in *De l'Etranger à l'étrange ou la conjointure de la merveille, En hommage à Marguerite Rossi et Paul Bancourt* (Aix-en-Provence: Sénefiance, 1988), 329–39.
198   *Roland* III, 24–6. All citations from *Roland* are taken from Dufournet.

that whoever kills such a man has destroyed evil and avenged God, who will be grateful; he then attacks the Saracens' honour and chivalry: 'tuit estes chien par droiture apelé, car vos n'avez ne foi ne lëauté.' [You are all rightly called dogs because you have neither faith nor law] (*Alisc.* XXXII, 1242–62).[199] In *Willehalm*, however, this is depicted differently. Ehmereiz, in beautiful shining armour, attacks Gyburg's integrity and vows vengeance, but Willehalm, knowing he is his stepson, does not respond to Ehmereiz's taunts. He does not harm him and respects that he is Gyburg's son. He wounds or kills every knight he encounters, but shows remarkable restraint with Ehmereiz.[200] This underscores the importance of extended kinship regardless of religion, as well as the significance of mercy and generosity in the chivalric code.

Rüdiger Schnell proposes that the explanation for this seeming contradiction in the depiction of Saracens in contemporary German literature was due to three factors: the genre of the text, the era in which it was composed and the personality of the individual poet.[201] He writes that early German poetry exhibited Crusade and chivalric ideals benevolent to Muslims, but that courtly poets wrote from a spiritual-religious viewpoint, demonstrating a literary re-evaluation of the heathen world.[202] Schnell's opinion of the attitude towards the Saracens here is reasonable, especially as he seems to be referring only to the *Rolandslied* and *Willehalm*; but the Saracens in *Parzival*, in particular Feirefiz, deserve mention too.

Feirefiz is Parzival's half-brother, a Saracen who demonstrates his nobility and loyalty to his brother in thought and deed and is finally given the opportunity by the author to feel the extension of divine love in his desire for Repanse. Feirefiz converts to Christianity so that he can marry her and is blessed with the vision of the Grail. He then returns to his pagan India to spread the story of Christian life. This literary treat-

---

199 All excerpts from *Aliscans* are taken from Régnier, *Aliscans*, unless otherwise indicated.
200 *Wh.* 74, 26–75, 30.
201 Schnell, 'Die Christen und die "Anderen"', 186.
202 Schnell, 'Die Christen und die "Anderen"', 186–7.

ment of people from the pagan world can be seen as respectful rather than entirely governed by prejudice.

Other German verse, due to geographical and historical factors, is concerned with heathens from another realm, namely the Huns. Yet the treatment of Attila in *Nibelungenlied* as well as in *Waltharius* is also respectful and he is depicted as no less capable of chivalry, nobility, loyalty and honour. If a poet were to re-evaluate the heathen world, it would be prudent to depict the heathens as human rather than inhuman, as in Augustine's writings; as capable of embracing chivalric values rather than as bandits to be feared on pilgrimage (as in the *Liber Sancti Jacobi*);[203] and as possessing the capacity for the desire to convert to Christianity, rather than as obstinate and treacherous (as in *Chanson de Roland* and even in *Aliscans*). An exception is the Saracen princess or queen, a popular character in the *chansons de geste*, who converts after falling in love with a French knight, and upon whose decisions and actions so much power rests.

War, peace and duality

Underpinning the contradiction in the portrayal of the Saracen adversary was the conflict between Biblical teaching and Crusade ideology, between the monastic aspects of chivalry and the warrior pursuits of the knight. Even in the Bible, there was a perplexing duality between the generally pacifist teachings of Christ and the warring activity of the Old Testament. Keen observes that the Crusades were instrumental in bringing Church authorities to terms with war, warriors and their place in society, and he traces Church attitudes from the early fathers, among whom a pacifistic tradition was strong, to Augustine, who justified the use of force, highlighting

---

203   Friedrich Wolfzettel cites several texts, including the *Liber Sancti Jacobi*, to illustrate the fantastical and dangerous image given of Saracens in earlier literature. See Wolfzettel, Friedrich, 'Die Entdeckung des "Anderen" aus dem Geist der Kreuzzüge' in Peter Schreiner and Odilo Engels, eds, *Die Begegnung des Westens mit dem Osten: Kongressakten des 4. Symposions des Mediävistenverbandes in Köln 1991 aus Anlass des 1000. Todesjahres der Kaiserin Theophanu* (Sigmaringen: Thorbecke Verlag, 1991) 273–95, 276.

the threat to the old imperial lands, churches and clergy from barbarian invasion.[204] Similarly, Wentzlaff-Eggebert, surveying earlier French, Latin and German poetry, suggests that the origin of the Crusade ideology lies in pilgrimages in which weapons were for defence rather than dominion and that the later idea of a Holy War was a contradiction that demanded justification.[205]

This contradiction between philosophies produced and condoned by the Church was a phenomenon that invited closer inspection and poets from the *chansons de geste* to the romance and epic obliged. The justification came in the rationale that the defence of the Holy Land was the defence of the Christian inheritance and religious and feudal values were drawn together in the heroic deeds of literary heroes. In *Willehalm*, as in *Prise* and *Aliscans*, William's rationale for his conquest of the city of Orange and its queen, Orable, is never questioned, for these both lay in Saracen hands; the land itself had been part of the Holy Roman Empire and this action can be seen as defence. The unity of the Crusade ideal and the medieval world view overcame the contradiction. This unity existed only in literature, however, and Wentzlaff-Eggebert writes: 'diese Einheit des christlichen Glaubens und der höfischen Lehre, die durch die Kreuzzugsidee verwirklicht wird, trug dazu bei, für eine Zeitspanne jegliche Form des mittelalterlichen Dualismus zu überwinden, im ständischen wie im soziologischen Bereich' [this unity of the Christian belief with courtly morals, which was realized in Crusade ideology, also carried with it for a time the notion of overcoming each idea of medieval dualism in society as well as sociologically].[206] Unity existed in the form of the Christian, courtly protagonist, the individual, the knight–hero who in *Prise*, *Aliscans* and *Willehalm* must be accompanied by his liege-lady Gyburg to be complete.

---

204 Keen, 45–6.
205 Wentzlaff-Eggebert, 'Kreuzzugsidee', 73.
206 Wentzlaff-Eggebert, 'Kreuzzugsidee', 87–8.

Wolfram's characterization of knighthood

The Crusading motivations behind much *chanson-de-geste* material invites the audience to look for the same ideals in *Willehalm*. The portrayal of the knights, both Christian and Saracen, in *Willehalm* calls the audience to reflect on the ideals identified as Crusading because of the stance of its *chanson-de-geste* source material. The Crusade ideology itself is not as pronounced in *Willehalm*, yet the reactions to it, the reflection of the contradictory directives of the Church, are questioned. The *chansons de geste* played to the Crusade and the Reconquista experiences of the audience, experiences from which the German audience was more removed. The German view was subtly different from that of the *chansons de geste*.

Crusading ideology in Germany

Pure Crusade ideology does not feature heavily in the lyric of twelfth-century Germany. Gesa Bonath writes that this is because there was no significant German presence in the Crusades until after the 'heroic phase', which was about 1097–9; therefore, there was no interest in portraying these endeavours in literature and Germany's epics pass these contemporary events by.[207] It was during these first Crusades, following the call of Clermont, that the Flemish, French and Norman Crusaders met with victories in the numerous small campaigns that ensued and not until the unified forces of Nur al-Din Zangi and his successor Saladin did the Arabo-Islamic military have its first major successes, defeating the Crusaders at Damascus in 1148, the time of the Second Crusade.[208] Neither of these greater and none of the lesser campaigns had any significant German presence.

Of the seven major Crusade campaigns, only three of them were conducted with the support and participation of the German knighthood,

207   Bonath, 103, 106.
208   Reinhardt, 107.

under the leadership of the German emperor.[209] The Second Crusade, about 1096–9, led by the French king, Louis VII, and the Holy Roman Emperor Konrad III, had been a failure. In the years following the Crusade called at Clermont, the enthusiasm for the victory and adventure waned; meanwhile, the threat in the Holy Land became more formidable, taking on greater importance to the Holy Roman Empire with the Third Crusade (1189–92). Led by the legendary Frederick Barbarossa, the shining example of German chivalry,[210] this Crusade ended in a truce with Saladin (conducted by the son of Eleanor of Aquitaine, Richard the Lionheart). The only other Crusade campaign under the leadership and with the support of the German Empire was the fifth, occurring around 1228–9, during which the Emperor Frederick II gained Jerusalem by negotiation.[211]

Much of the literature of the German High Middle Ages was composed before the Fourth Crusade and in the wake of the defeat of the Second Crusade, with no great interest in the portrayal of these events in literature having manifested itself.[212] In fact, the attitude towards the Crusade in Germany can be seen to have been one of bitterness, especially after the events of the Albigensian Crusade (about 1210) and the tales of the 'Children's Crusade' (about 1212).[213] As a result, the old German themes of loyalty, courage in battle and introspection remained strong in German literature, casting a different light on the reception of Crusade ideology.

---

209 Reinhardt, 107.
210 Reinhardt, 107. Such was the charisma attached to the figure and activity of Frederick Barbarossa, who drowned in the river Saleph whilst on Crusade, that a legend was born which, 'relating to the coming of the Third Empire, pictured the emperor asleep in the depths of the Kyffhäuser Mountain in Thuringia, waiting for the day of his return to lead his people to unity and renewed glory.' (Reinhardt, 92)
211 Reinhardt, 108.
212 See Bonath, 103.
213 See: Bonath, 113; Reinhardt, 107. Though it is generally accepted that chroniclers' accounts of the Children's Crusade was the amalgamation of several large-scale movements of groups in an attempt to address Crusading mentality in Europe rather than the fabled pilgrimage of children who met untimely ends in slavery or disease, the movements themselves demonstrate a questioning of the ideology and an interest in addressing it by the larger populace.

Knapp calls this a reorientation of East and West,[214] and this is apparent
in that, instead of speaking in terms of the 'Crusade', German texts refer to
the 'Orient'. It is not the same Orient or 'foreign' that is portrayed in the
French *chansons de geste*, the invasion of Carolingian imperial territory by
the Saracens from the Mediterranean rim; rather, the German notion of
'Orient' is portrayed much less as an immediate threat to land and more
as a distant curiosity, as it appeared in the *Kaiserchronik*, as Feirefiz in
Parzival,[215] in Gahmuret's journeys or as the distant world of Ruodlieb's
journeys. When Wolfram took up the material that had inspired the *chanson de geste Rolandslied* [*Song of Roland*] and fashioned his version of *La
Bataille d'Aliscans* in *Willehalm*, it was almost a century later, in the wake
of the Third Crusade, but with still no more of a German literary sense of
Crusade ideology.

The Christian moral imperative

When viewing Wolfram's works from a political standpoint, probing
Christian morality and directives in *Willehalm* is perhaps possible if we consider the environment of the author. Hermann of Thuringia was a member
of the Hohenstaufen federation, dedicated to the return of Frederick II
to the throne of the Holy Roman Empire; it also showed an inclination
towards criticism of papal decree and some aspects of the Cluniac reform
relating to the power struggle between Church and State.[216] Whether or
not Hermann's political inclinations matched those of Wolfram, or whether
Wolfram's works reflected the views of his patron (as did Walther's), some
evidence can be seen in that Parzival's 'vocation to the kingship of the Holy
Grail reads like a commentary on the political and spiritual implications
of the Hohenstaufen claims to the *Sacrum Imperium*.'[217]

---

214   Knapp, *Die Grosse Schlacht Zwischen Orient und Okzident*, 143.
215   See Bonath, 113.
216   See Reinhardt, 74f, 92f; Bumke, *Höfische Kultur*, 656f; and Bumke, *Mäzene im
         Mittelalter*, 163–5.
217   Reinhardt, 153.

Wolfram's depiction of the chivalric view of the Christian moral imperative to convert or kill seems to be more based upon the late twelfth-century courtly code of ethics and the spiritual chivalry that was part of it than upon a commentary on his contemporary political environment. It is mentioned by heathen and Christian characters alike, within Willehalm's extended family by marriage to Gyburg, that a better solution than war would be to behave with the family solidarity that propriety would demand. Were it not for Tybalt's lust for vengeance and inheritance land, perhaps a peace could be agreed. However, Christian Crusade ideology is also in play, in that any provocation or move towards the acquisition of land by the Saracens must be answered by a consolidated Christian military victory.

Fighting wars in a duty to love-service earned renown, land and honour; fighting wars to serve revenge assured the survival of the honour of an illustrious clan; and fighting to defend Christian lands earned eternal salvation. The war in *Willehalm*, however, is depicted in a more personal and human way by Wolfram, who tells his audience that 'diz engiltet niht wan sterben, und an freuden verderben' [this fighting will settle for nothing less than death and loss of joy] (*Wh*. 10, 25–6).[218] That the means by which peace might otherwise be accomplished is questioned or contemplated by the characters is novel for Crusade literature, but whether conversion features heavily in the ideal solution of peace remains to be seen. Willehalm, like his compatriots, his adversaries and his wife, the Saracen queen of Orange, is bound to a code of chivalry that is part of his temporal success as well as his spiritual salvation and it is by nature self-reflecting and introspective. Thus, it would be impossible for Willehalm to follow through with the events as they have been laid out before him without asking questions about the justification for loss of life and how to preserve divine grace without detriment to worldly honour.

218 Gibbs and Johnson, 22.

Crusade ideology in *Willehalm*

It was during the time of the composition of *Willehalm*, about 1210, that
the literary recognition of uniquely German themes can be seen to coincide
with the events of the Crusades and with contemporary European affairs
outside the borders of the Holy Roman Empire. From the time of the composition of *Ruodlieb*, there is a manifestation of the German mentality in
literature in the distinctive portrayal of 'wisdom, human understanding,
love of nature, and a keen sense of humor.'[219] Less than a century later, the
most famous German poets of the age, Gottfried, Hartmann, Walther and
Wolfram, had mastered the art of depicting these themes in contemporary
popular material.

Wolfram composed *Willehalm* from the French source, though not
without encountering the obstacle of the depiction of 'the foreign'. This
depiction was understandable enough to the French audience of a century earlier, some of whom had probably participated in the Crusade and
lived in close proximity to the Saracen menace on European soil, but it
was more distant to the German courtly audience, whose participation in
and proximity to such events was less immediate.[220] Wolfram could not
quite assimilate the French empire and the Spain of the *chansons de geste*
into his own sense of German geographic nationality and often interprets
'foreign' by using the term 'French' in *Willehalm*, saving the Saracens for
identification in terms of the 'Orient'.[221]

---

219   Reinhardt, 86.
220   The contrast between the distance from the Saracen threat to Thuringia and the prox-
      imity to it of France is attested in the last lines of the *Chanson de Roland* (3394–8),
      which captures the feeling of an ever-present threat of Saracen invasion. Dufournet
      writes that 'le *Roland* reflète les peurs d'un monde obsédé par le péril toujours renais-
      sant des masses sarrasines déferlant en vagues successives' [the [*Chanson de*] *Roland*
      reflects the fears of a world obsessed with the recurring danger of the Saracen masses
      breaking out in successive waves] (*Roland*, 30–1).
221   See Knapp, *Die Grosse Schlacht Zwischen Orient und Okzident*, 145–9.

Wolfram deals with this French 'foreignness' by identifying it with the unknown: the background of the French cyclical material, French place names and French battle cries. Thus Wolfram crafts a systematic play with what is not known to either him or the audience.[222] The national sense of France in *Aliscans* is a problem for Wolfram as well. There are several powers at play in the story: the literary French Carolingian Empire, the Provence of William of Aquitaine and the historic Carolingian Empire – the Holy Roman Empire. It would have been difficult for Wolfram to have identified and differentiated what is French from what is empire in *Willehalm* geographically, given the limited geographic knowledge of the Middle Ages; what is more likely is that Wolfram differentiated these identities using historical context.[223] Kiening sees this historical sense in terms of the *Rolandslied*, in which France is identified as 'empire', whereas in the later *Willehalm*, France is merely a small nation whose court is centred on the district of Montlaon.[224] In this way, Wolfram avoids the identification of France with 'empire', a concept remaining in the glorious Carolingian past and as a background to *Willehalm*. In order to further distance *Willehalm*'s Provence from the France of the weak king Louis the Pious, Wolfram portrays the French knights as effeminate, decadent and, worst of all, cowardly (as when the French reinforcements flee from battle[225] and must be prodded by Rennewart to rejoin the fight).[226] Kiening points out the use of French

---

222 Kiening, Christian, 'Umgang mit dem Fremden, Die Erfahrung des "Französischen" in Wolframs "Willehalm"', *Wolfram-Studien* XI (1989), 65–85, 72–3.

223 Kiening sees Wolfram's identification of France and what is 'French' in geographical terms, comprising the area surrounding Champagne that was the French kingdom at the time of the composition of both *Aliscans* and *Willehalm*. See Kiening, 78. However, Friedrich Maurer argues that the material of twelfth-century German poetry was seen as neither foreign nor Carolingian, but as Hohenstaufen imperial material. Maurer, Friedrich, *Dichtung und Sprache des Mittelalters: Gesammelte Aufsätze*, 2nd edn (Bern: Francke Verlag, 1971), 456. This latter view seems to correspond to Wolfram's *Willehalm*, in which a wider Carolingian empire with a common and distant history is depicted.

224 Kiening, 76.

225 *Wh.* 325.

226 See Kiening, 79–80.

place names in battle cries, which are avoided in *Willehalm* until after the final victory, at which time the French reinforcements are allowed by the author to show their local heritage by calling the names of northern French cities.[227] In these ways, Wolfram is identifying Willehalm as Provençal and as successor to the values of the empire of Charlemagne, while distancing him from the weak French kingdom and vassals of Louis. Such an intended association of Willehalm with Charlemagne would provide an explanation for the discrepancy in the battle cry of 'Orange' in *Aliscans M* and 'Monschoie' in *Willehalm*, relating the story and the character to *Roland* and to the Carolingian past.

The difficulty that Wolfram encounters in styling Frenchness and foreignness in *Willehalm*, and opposing those to the Saracen adversary, illustrates his own remoteness and possibly that of his audience from the Crusade ideology, though there is the presence of Crusade ideology of a sort in *Willehalm*. During the first battle at the beginning of the story, Wolfram describes the French knights' armour as bearing a cross, the symbol of Christ, and states that those who died in battle earned eternal peace:

> sîne helfaer heten niht vermiten,
> beidiu geslagen und gesniten
> ûf ir wâpenlîchiu kleit
> was Kristes tôt, den da versneit
> diu heidensch ungeloubic diet.
> sîn tôt daz kriuze uns sus beschiet:
> ez ist sîn verh und unser segen
> (*Wh.* 31, 23–9)

His men had not neglected to have the symbol of the death of Christ cut out and fixed on their armour and this the heathens slashed to pieces, those faithless people. His death has granted us the Cross. It is His very Life and a blessing to us.[228]

---

227 Kiening cites the cries of the Champagnois, the Flemish and the Lotharingians after the second battle of Alischantz. (78)

228 Gibbs and Johnson, 31.

des lîbes tôt, der sêle vride
erwurben Franzoysaere dâ.

(*Wh.* 32, 6–7)

In that very place the Frenchmen achieved the death of the body but the peace of the soul.[229]

By means of Flori's summation of the elements comprising Crusade ideology (penitential pilgrimage, papal decree, redemption, promise of paradise and special privileges), correlations can be made between these elements and those found in *Willehalm*, for the purpose of determining the role and importance of the ideology in the work. There is nothing of papal decree, the call to defend the Church, or the Holy Land; in relation to papal authority, there is no guarantee of special privileges like those associated and bestowed upon returning Crusading knights. The elements of penitential pilgrimage, redemption and the promise of paradise in the afterlife do, however, feature in *Willehalm*. Paradise secured in the afterlife can be related to the character of Vivianz, who is described in terms of a Christian martyr. Likewise the theme of penitential pilgrimage: just as Cooper describes quest and pilgrimage as prominent themes of romance genres,[230] they are themes present in *Willehalm*, corresponding more to romance themes than to Crusade ideology. Willehalm, like many romance knights, embarks upon a quest to Montlaon to secure reinforcements; this is a rational and practical mission, although underpinned by certain romance themes: the incognito duel with a brother; Willehalm's depriving himself of a bed to sleep on and of any sustenance other than bread and water; his foregoing any show of affection; and his refusal to bath or change his outward appearance from that in which he had fought the first battle. It is also likely that both author and audience were aware of the armed and penitential pilgrimages initiated by Crusades into the Holy Land. Furthermore, the ideology of a Holy War that might be present in *Willehalm* has its precedent in *Roland*, where the expression of a sanctified

---

229 Gibbs and Johnson, 31.
230 See Cooper, 47–50.

war points to Crusade ideology, including martyrdom and redemption. It is, as Flori writes, 'le combat pour la chrétienté qui, en lui-même, accomplit la pénitence rédemptrice' [the fight for Christianity that, itself, accomplishes redeeming penitence].[231]

Perhaps the most apparent elements of *Willehalm* that would dismiss it from being pure Crusade literature are the absence of any clergy in important roles, together with the lack of any journey to the Holy Land to reconquer territory taken by the enemy. In fact, the entire story remains within the borders of the European continent and within the borders of modern-day France, just as in the *Cycle de Guillaume*. Willehalm himself, a Christian knight and future saint whose life seems divinely favoured, administers the last rites to Vivianz with some consecrated bread he has in his pocket and hears his last confession.[232] He seems to take on characteristics of both Charlemagne and Turpin in *Chanson de Roland*,[233] bypassing the need for a representative of the Church to be present in *Willehalm*. Rennewart acts as the armed bishop in battle, routing the fleeing Frenchmen and reminding them of their Christian duty.[234] Gyburg and the Narbonnais princes deliver their speeches to the assembled reinforcements, inspiring them with ideals of Christian mercy, reminding them of their duty as

---

231   Flori, 'La croix, la crosse et l'épée', 267. Flori illustrates that the simple act of fighting the heathen leads to a Crusade ideology in *Roland* by citing verses 1132–8, which finish, 'E l'arcevesque de Deu les beneïst, Par penitence les cumandet a ferir.' [Pray for God's grace, confess your sins with penitence.]

232   *Wh.* 68, 4–22.

233   Bishop Turpin has a special function in the *Chanson de Roland*, which Jean Dufournet sees as intercession in the debate over celibacy that divided the Church. See Dufournet, *Roland*, 20. Turpin also represents a fusion of clergy and chivalry, functioning as the image of the Christian hero and sanctifying the war. See Flori, 'La croix, la crosse et l'épée', 265–6.

234   *Wh.* 324, 8ff; and 'si slüege aldâ diu gotes hant, von der si flühtic waern gewant.' (325, 3–4) [It was the Hand of God from which they had fled, that was punishing them.] Gibbs and Johnson, 164.

Christian knights and appealing to the Crusade fervour of the French knights to encourage them into battle for Orange.[235]

Still, the fact that a battle is being fought between Saracen and Christian forces draws on a Crusade ideology and although 'the Crusades in the East do not figure in the [French] William poems, [...] there is no question that their existence influenced the treatment of the great struggle for Christianity.'[236] The goal of the inner and external conflicts remains focused on conversion and thereby redemption, a theme that features prominently in Wolfram's version of *Aliscans*. With redemption and the restitution of Willehalm's Christian Orange comes the unification of the Christian and Saracen worlds,[237] the certainty of a life after death and peace after internal conflict. When Willehalm questions his actions and their Christian justifications after the second battle of Alischantz,[238] Wachinger sees this as a questioning of Crusade ideology, thereby activating the already strong imperial conscience of the public.[239] It is for this reason that Wachinger is of the opinion that Crusade ideology remains present in *Willehalm*,[240] though the extent to which it exists in the work can be seen as negligible. Rather, it seems far more important to Wolfram to develop the ideals of the inner knight, such as *Minnedienst*, chivalry and spirituality, than it is for him to awaken in the audience a lust for Crusade. Instead, he introduces a questioning of the directive from Rome and explores the moral duty as opposed to the feudal necessity to Christianize Saracens.

---

235   *Wh.* 306ff. Julius Richter also points out how the Church plays no role in *Willehalm*, illustrating how the power lies not with the Church but with the imperial army, how Gyburg functions as a spiritual weapon via her speech and how Vivianz's last rites are given him by his uncle. Richter, Julius, 'Zur Ritterlichen Frömmigkeit der Stauferzeit: Die Kreuzzugsidee in Wolframs Willehalm', *Wolfram Jahrbuch* (1956), 23–33, 29–30.

236   Ferrante, 25.

237   See Ortmann, 86.

238   *Wh.* 449ff.

239   Wachinger, 52.

240   Wachinger.

In the battle in Wolfram's version of *Aliscans*, there is much more of an emphasis on *Minnedienst* and chivalry than on a pro-Crusade ideology.[241] The battle has in fact been interpreted as a conflict between Christian and courtly ethics.[242] With the dimensions of *Minnedienst* and chivalry worked out so deftly by Wolfram in *Willehalm*, an emphasis on the spiritual and internal ideals of redemption, courage, loyalty, honour, spirituality and religious conversion come into play. In this way, Wolfram remains true to the German idiom, combining the heroic with an intimacy and tenderness that was already apparent in earlier poems such as *Hildebrandslied*, *Ruodlieb* and *Ezzolied*.[243] It can be said that this combination of heroism and compassion, together with internal spiritual and ethical conflict, is unique to the character of German knighthood.

The very idea of the Crusade creates contradictions in ideology that manifest themselves literarily in the image of chivalry, Saracen adversaries and Christian ethics. The influence of the Crusades was felt slowly and less directly in Germany's literature, allowing it to combine with age-old and deep-rooted Germanic themes of heroism, honour and loyalty, which were easily transferable to a Saracen adversary. It is the combination of these Germanic themes and the ethical questions and contradictions brought about by the Crusades that is of interest to Wolfram in *Willehalm*. There is no goal in *Willehalm* either to reinforce or to challenge Crusade ideas, but they do provide part of the environment and they are thematically explored. Though the influences from the East and the West were compelling to German literature, Reinhardt makes the keen observation that:

> it is, however, symptomatic of the growing astuteness of German culture that neither the Romanic nor the Oriental influences that acted upon the German mind in the Age of Chivalry, and especially during the two centuries of the Crusades, were able to silence the voice of a genuine Germany that speaks so unmistakably in German art and poetry, in the games of war and the diversions of peace, in bold political action and in the silence of mystical contemplation.[244]

---

241 See: Bumke, *Wolfram von Eschenbach*, 390; and Ortmann, 86.
242 Ortmann, 86.
243 See Reinhardt, 85–6.
244 Reinhardt, 110.

This is the combination that exemplifies Wolfram's Christian knight and his inner quest towards redemption and unity of Christian and Saracen.

The Saracen knight is portrayed as subject to the same code of chivalry as his Christian adversary and especially so in *Willehalm*. Although he might have fantastical features, the Saracen still has the same capacity for inner reflection, for the striving towards an ideal and for service to love. Conversion to Christianity would make his chivalry complete, as it did for Gyburg, Willehalm's liege-lady, wife, adviser, companion and motivator for the service of his entire clan. This is perhaps why Richey saw in this more inward as opposed to secular reflection of chivalry that 'Wolfram, carrying the self-reliance of knighthood into the domain of thought, could set forth as a sure conviction what others expressed but tentatively [...] Nobility – *werdekeit* – is the touchstone of chivalry, and implies [...] a stronger confidence in the kinship of God and man.'[245]

The chivalry of *Willehalm* strives to retain the honour gained in worldly chivalry without compromising the salvation and promise of redemption granted to Christian knighthood and spiritual chivalry, of justice and right in both worlds, of the highest honour for proper service. Wolfram, 'his language dark and heavy, expressing a dynamic vitality of thought, emotion and imagination that would never submit to the clarity and symmetry of the literary conventions of the age,'[246] reveals an attitude towards chivalry distinctive and unique to the geographical-historical environment in which he wrote.

It is generally accepted that in any given narrative tradition there are many sources of information, themes and material, and that these are transferred between stories and texts, appearing even if the authors and their audience have had no direct contact with the locations of the originating

---

245 Richey, 115.
246 Reinhardt, 153.

ideas.[247] Wolfram's own personal abilities and inclinations, and those ideas that influenced him, though we may never know the extent of them, can be seen to have stemmed at least in part from the Persian spiritual chivalry of Sufism; this was disseminated throughout the twelfth century by vehicles such as diplomatic embassies, libraries and centres for learning and translation in both Europe and the Islamic world, and by the proliferation of scientific, philosophical and religious texts as well as poetry and music. The environment that created the self-reflecting and spiritual European chivalry depicted in twelfth century literature was one almost as cosmopolitan and diverse as the Europe of today, conducive to the transfer, incubation and expansion of ideas and institutions such as chivalric orders. Chivalry's deep-running spiritual undercurrent and ideals of love and service rendered it an establishment that was not immune to the machinations of the Church, resulting in Crusades in the service of Rome with the goal of uniting support via Christianization and the promised reward of salvation. These applications and motivations were to expose moral problems that surfaced in the vehicle of popular literature and to which Wolfram offered an answer: a developed and spiritually guided chivalry that involved self-reflection and evaluation of the direction of service, a resistance to moral contradictions and the achievement of balance and unity.

247 'While Wolfram had access to Arab learning, probably through the medium of Latin
    translations, there is no evidence that he ever went to Arab lands. Nevertheless, the
    Orient and Oriental characters play a major role in both [*Parzival* and *Willehalm*],
    and there is a notable conformity of attitude between the two works, which points to
    a greater degree of compassion and understanding than might be expected at a time
    when the crusading ethos was prevalent.' Edwards, Cyril, 'Wolfram von Eschenbach,
    Islam, and the Crusades' in James R. Hodkinson and Jeffrey Morrison, eds, *Encounters
    with Islam in German Literature and Culture* (Columbia, SC: Camden House, 2009),
    36–54, 36.

Rewriting the *Chansons de geste*

In *Willehalm*, Wolfram retells the story of Guillaume d'Orange from the *chanson-de-geste* material of the *Cycle de Guillaume d'Orange*. This is a story of knights and values, of principles and spiritual chivalry set in the context of history and deeds. Wolfram explores the application of chivalry and its problems in a setting more corporeal than that of Arthur's court or the Grail castle. There are concrete and permanent consequences of actions and words. Though the *chansons de geste* drew their subject from material that was in its essence very different from the *matière de Bretagne*, they were replete with themes which Wolfram masterfully expanded upon and exploited, and both *La Prise d'Orange* and *Aliscans* are presented here as the *chansons de geste* whose themes are most present in Wolfram's *Willehalm*.

By what means did Wolfram rewrite a *chanson de geste* and its epic subject matter in his *Willehalm* and what role does chivalry play in it? As for the choice of subject matter, perhaps Wolfram had accomplished what he had set out to do in *Parzival* and wished to test his art by way of a different genre. Perhaps, having become familiar with the stories in the French cycle of *Guillaume d'Orange*, he saw in it material that inspired him. Or perhaps, as he was wont to express about his modifications to Chrétien's *Le conte du Graal*, he wanted his audience to believe that he could tell the story better. What is most likely, however, is that Hermann of Thuringia, having been exposed to the material in France, was captivated enough by it to commission a version of his own. The motivations and inspirations for this choice of material on either Hermann's or Wolfram's part remain a matter for conjecture. However, considering what is known about this text, its sources and the historical and literary environment that brought them into being, we can derive a reasonable impression of Wolfram's reasons for further developing courtly chivalry in *Willehalm* and the role it played in this work.

In forming a picture of Wolfram's courtly code, we will explore how spiritual chivalry is portrayed, taking into account what courtly elements are present in his sources and how Wolfram explores problems within chivalry in *Willehalm*. We will see how nobility, honour, kinship and love are components in this chivalry, playing a role in the depiction of Saracens in *Willehalm*, a prolific element in the chivalry of medieval literature. Beginning with an overview of Wolfram's sources, *La Prise d'Orange* and *Aliscans*, and considering the socio-historical development and geopolitical environment surrounding these texts, we will look at how and why Wolfram used the themes and material from his sources and from his environment in his retelling of *Aliscans*, at how the depiction of courtliness and chivalry changes from the *chansons de geste* to *Willehalm* and at how Wolfram was working from a genre that had already been infiltrated and infused with courtly themes and material.

From *Aliscans* to *Willehalm*

The material from which Wolfram fashioned *Willehalm*, that of the *chansons de geste*, his modifications to the *Aliscans* material and the presence of material and themes from *La Prise d'Orange* contribute to the question of the genre of *Willehalm*, which has been frequently debated. It is not quite clearly legend, nor romance, nor epic literature, but comprises elements of all three.[1] It also shows elements of Crusade literature that characterizes

---

1   Among the scholars who have recognized a difficulty in placing *Willehalm* into one of the medieval literary genres is Annette Gerok-Reiter. She identifies elements in the work corresponding to different genres, such as the structure and verse form, and the awareness of problems through narration and reflection. These latter suggest a courtly romance genre, whilst the *chanson de geste de Guillaume d'Orange* material suggests heroic epic or Crusade genre. Finally, the identification by Wolfram of William as a

the twelfth and thirteenth centuries: material composed by poets and clerics to advance the popularity of the Crusade ideal. The legendary figure of William of Toulouse, whom Wolfram names the patron saint of knights,[2] famed for driving Saracens from French soil in grand Crusade fashion, is retained as the protagonist. Yet the ideals of courtly love, chivalry and service are pervasive and even *Willehalm*'s verse form, its rhyming couplets and its spiritually incisive and self-reflective tone, link *Willehalm* to the romance. A survey of the thematic and material sources reveal that even they, *Aliscans* and *La Prise d'Orange*, were already too compromised to be pure epic in genre.

To assign a specific genre to early medieval French literature or to German versions composed in a different time and environment is impractical.[3] Clear definitions of genre in the literature of this timeframe are vague and a pure generic structure begins to break down as twelfth century literature takes on more elements akin to romance, while retaining popu-

---

saint and a Christian hero is indicative of a legend: 'Wolfram's Erzählung *Willehalm* ist Heldenepos, Legende, höfischer Roman. Mit gleichem Recht könnte man ebenso sagen, sie ist weder das eine noch das andere noch das dritte' [Wolfram's narrative *Willehalm* is an heroic epic, legend, courtly romance. One could say with equal reason that it is neither the first nor the second, nor the third]. She also mentions Kurt Ruh's suggestion of the work being a kind of *opus mixtum*. See Gerok-Reiter, Annette, 'Die Hölle auf Erden: Überlegungen zum Verhältnis von Weltlichem und Geistlichem in Wolframs "Willehalm"' in Burghart Wachinger, Hans-Joachim Ziegeler and Christoph Huber, eds, *Geistliches in weltlicher und Weltliches in geistlicher Literatur des Mittelalters* (Tübingen: Niemeyer, 2000), 171–94, 171.

2 *Wh.* 4, 3–18.

3 Marguerite Rossi writes that differences between the genres of *chanson de geste* and romance were recognized in France, but in *Willehalm* the *chanson de geste* material loses the distinctiveness of genre and is replaced with a courtly romance structure. Rossi, Marguerite, 'Rapport introductif: épopée française et épopée non française', *Essor et fortune de la chanson de geste dans l'Europe et l'Orient latin: actes du IXe congrès international de la Société Rencesvals pour l'étude des épopées romanes, Padoue-Venise, 29 août–4 septembre 1982* (Modena: Mucchi, 1983), 247–65, 257. She presents a convincing case for this and adds the observation of historical perspective when she writes that later, the influence of cycles of *chanson de geste* constituted grouping older poetry together, e.g., the Dietrich and *Nibelungenlied* material. Rossi, 259.

lar themes and material from its chronological predecessors, the *chansons de geste*, classical epic, Occitan love poetry and oral tradition's sagas and lays. Though it is difficult for scholars to depart from the desire to study a work according to its literary genre, placing it in a generic category so that it can be analysed within that framework, by the thirteenth century it is reasonable to view literature not as belonging to a specific genre but as encompassing elements of several genres which are neither precise nor rigid in their parameters and as products of retelling and rewriting.

Epic and Crusade literature are easier to define than romance, as their subject matter provides much of the key material, but when romance themes permeate the literature of twelfth century Europe, genres become more nebulous and the elements that define them less precise for scholars analysing medieval texts.[4] Helen Cooper writes that although there are a number of elements signifying romance,

> any of the features that might be taken as definitive for the genre may be absent in any particular case without damaging that sense of family resemblance, though the dissimilarity increases, ultimately beyond the point of recognition, in proportion as the various elements are missing – or, alternatively, as an atypical element is given prominence […] no single one is essential for definition or recognition taken individually. Equally, related genres will share some features even though other unshared elements signal generic difference.[5]

Dennis Green approaches romance from a slightly different angle in his exploration of how romance rose out of historical writing, using examples of German literature to support his suggestion that, with the emergence of the *matière de Bretagne*, romance became more associated with untruth than other genres, and was a fiction and fantasy woven for entertainment purposes.[6] From yet another angle, genre is questioned

---

4   In her work on what defines romance, Helen Cooper writes that 'the borders between romance and […] other genres are highly permeable.' (10)

5   Cooper, 9.

6   Green, D.H., *The Beginnings of Medieval Romance: Fact and Fiction, 1150–1220*, ed. Alastair Minnnis, Cambridge Studies in Medieval Literature (Cambridge: Cambridge University Press, 2002), 134–43.

by Robert Hanning, who looks at what constitutes the 'chivalric' in epic and romance.[7] It is also notable that W.T.H. Jackson found a common theme in all genres of medieval narrative to be the structural concept of an epic centre, as in a royal court.[8] What becomes apparent is that romance developed gradually by way of its elements being included in more and more literature and in more and more dominant roles, but in the twelfth century it also combined with other material, making it an ambiguous genre. *Aliscans*, *La Prise d'Orange* and *Willehalm* are indicative of this progression.

Whether or not these texts conform to any one medieval genre is less important than the value of the functions of the major themes within those recognizable genres or narrative frameworks. These modifications can be seen as illustrating Wolfram's intention in rewriting a popular story to create a work conveying his own philosophy, as he did with *Parzival*, within a contemporary courtly idiom. The two themes of *Willehalm* that stand out are religion and chivalry, both including love as a key element and both integrated by Wolfram into the application of a courtly code, reward and service to a religious war, which is to be the context of these texts. The embellishment of these themes is Wolfram's most prominent and complex innovation in *Willehalm*.

The understanding of Wolfram's innovations, how themes in his text and his sources were applied and why, is furthered by closer examination of the use made of both romance and epic elements in *Willehalm*. We can then begin to understand Wolfram's intentions and success in rewriting *Aliscans* as a 'courtly epic'. A comparison and contrasting of *Willehalm* with its sources in terms of courtly, epic and romance genres will show

7   See Hanning, Robert W., 'The Criticism of Chivalric Epic and Romance' in Howell Chickering and Thomas H. Seiler, eds, *The Study of Chivalry: Resources and Approaches* (Kalamazoo, MI: Medieval Institute Publications, 1988), 91–113.

8   Jackson presents a detailed analysis to support this theory, covering French, Old English and German texts in his book under the chapter, 'The Epic Center as Structural Determinant in Medieval Narrative Poetry'. See Jackson, *The Challenge of the Medieval Text*.

that Wolfram, working from an already imprecise genre, combines these aspects into a whole with the vehicle of his narration, encompassing a pro-Crusade courtly epic with the underlying objective of continuing to explore spirituality, service and love.

The *chansons de geste* were a means of retransmitting historical events as well as being very much for entertainment; their subject matter and places were in essence existent rather than fantastical and often engaged the themes of pilgrimage or divine acts, conflict and feudal vassalage, setting examples for Crusade ideology.[9] Even the Crusading ideology, however, is not so clearly delineated. The Crusade ideology in the *chansons de geste* is not that preached by the Church after Urban II at Clermont but of an earlier, Carolingian *Reconquista* milieu.[10]

Aliscans, like the rest of its fellow *chansons de geste*, conforms to its heroic epic genre in verse form and in subject matter. It is constructed of running verses or *laisses*[11] of lines in decasyllabic metre with assonance, to which the language lends itself appreciably. Its subject matter is influenced

9   Suard, François, *Chanson de geste et tradition épique en France au moyen âge* (Caen: Paradigme, 1994), 29–52.

10   See Flori, Jean, 'L'idée de croisade dans quelques chansons de geste du cycle de Guillaume d'Orange', *Medioevo Romanzo* 21/2–3 (1997), 496–506. Here Flori examines the presence or absence of Crusade elements in the Guillaume cycle, concluding that none of them plays a distinct role, if any at all, and therefore these *chansons de geste* cannot be clearly classified as Crusade literature of the kind after Clermont.

11   This structure was one of the points discussed by Jean Rychner in support of oral composition of the *chansons de geste*, which he describes as differing according to the audience for whom they were performed in ways such as length, subject matter, repetition of themes and even light, music and scenery. 'Bien que la distribution d'un texte en séances ait dû varier, bien que le récit lui-même ait pu s'allonger ou se raccourcir selon les circonstances, il ne semble pas impossible que la teneur habituelle d'une séance ait exercé quelque influence sur la composition des chansons.' [Although the delivery of a text in sittings had to vary, although the narrative was amenable to lengthening or to shortening of itself under the circumstances, it does not seem impossible that the usual content of a sitting exercized some influence on the composition of songs.] Rychner, Jean, *La chanson de geste: essai sur l'art épique des jongleurs*, ed. Mario Roques, Vol. LIII, Société de publications romanes et françaises (Geneva: Librairie E. Droz, 1955), 48.

by the socio-political environment of the Capetian period during which it was composed. There were problems posed by weak kings and threats posed by enemies, whether traitors to the crown or Saracens trying to conquer French imperial territory, and there is emphasis placed on vassalage and loyalty in the feudal order. The hero is characterized by physical strength, loyalty and courage. Conflict is a prevailing theme, as is tension, and the superiority of family solidarity to feudal obligation is underscored; in the case of *Aliscans*, it is at the court in Montlaon. The plot of *Aliscans* centres on the death of Vivïen in the first battle, on Guillaume's trip to Montlaon and the conflict with the king there, and on the deeds of Rainouart in the second battle. There are contrasting tones, marked by the sanctity of Vivïen's martyrdom on the one side and the comical might of Rainouart on the other.[12]

La Prise d'Orange, comprising the conquest of Orange and its beautiful queen by the young knight, seems to cross the conceptual boundaries of genre more often in its themes. Rather than the epic hero engaged in single combat, the focus is upon the Saracen princess, the object of desire that led Guillaume to the conquest, and the decisive assistance she offers to him and his knights in conquering her city after she falls in love with him. There are undertones of eroticism, service and courtly love of the lady from afar.[13] The portrayal and importance of Gyburg stands amongst one of the strongest cases for Wolfram's having been familiar with *La Prise d'Orange*. In addition, other *chansons de geste* of this cycle, such as *Enfances Guillaume*, reveal the infiltration of fantastical elements.

12   Summaries of the themes of *Aliscans* as well as of *chansons de geste* in general are given good coverage in Bumke, *Wolfram von Eschenbach*, 381, and in Suard, *Chanson de geste et tradition épique*, 51–5.

13   The idea of *l'amour de loin* [love for the distant or unattainable] in poetry being of Provençal origin can be seen in the works of the twelfth-century troubadour, Jaufré Rudel.

Wolfram's innovations

> unsanfte mac genôzen
> Diutscher rede decheine
> dirre diech nu meine,
> ir letze und ir beginnen.
>   (*Wh.* 4, 30 – 5, 3)

> [No story in German tongue can equal this tale I now have in mind in its
> entirety.]

Of the various innovations applied by Wolfram in his retelling of the *chanson de geste*, the most prominent are those representative of courtly genres. First and foremost of Wolfram's alterations to the *Aliscans* material is the metre and verse form. The decasyllabic assonant *laisse* form of the heroic epic is replaced with octosyllabic rhyming couplets, the form of courtly romance texts, in the German fashion of four accents per line, the Middle High German tetrametre. That *Willehalm* is a more courtly version of *Aliscans* is also apparent in its style and descriptions of its knights and characters;[14] *Minnedienst*, or love and the service of ladies, is a pivotal feature. Other innovations include details during the siege of Orange, descriptions and the sequence of events in Montlaon, and the prominence given to the role of the character of Gyburg; these are all without precedent in Wolfram's sources.

The shift from the heroic tone of *Aliscans* to the courtly emphasis on *Minnedienst*, to the Christian duty of the knight and to spirituality, is achieved by Wolfram in changes to characters and subtle plot modifications. *Minne* and a courtly code is more apparent in *Willehalm* through the actions of the ladies, who are softer yet exert the same subtle profound influence and serve to remind the knights of what motivates service. The court settings are described in detail, every luxury narrated to the audience. By way of this, Wolfram changes the setting slightly at Montlaon by making it a *Hoftag*, at which many nobles will be present, an important

---

14   Joachim Bumke gives a condensed survey of the scholarship comparing *Aliscans* with
      Willehalm. See Bumke, *Wolfram von Eschenbach*, 388–90.

venue for the renewal of vows of fealty at the time when Willehalm arrives. Additionally, Heimrich, Willehalm's father, serves a kind of avuncular role at both palaces, Montlaon and Gloriette, a courtly element that must have pleased the audience and served the purpose of advancing narrative plot while adding atmosphere to the story.[15]

The key change is to the character of Gyburg, who is given more attention and more prominence than her *Aliscans* counterpart. In fact it is more than the ideal of *Minnedienst* in *Willehalm* that is of pivotal importance to chivalry; it is the personage of Gyburg herself, whose role builds on the importance it had in *La Prise d'Orange*. In *Willehalm*, she is Willehalm's equal in heroism, wit and love, his partner in life and his equivalent as a main character. She is given entire scenes in which her character is represented as protagonist, in which she laments, directs knights' service, engages in religious dialogue and speaks at the war council. There are also two new love scenes with Willehalm. It is the mention of her capture by Willehalm at the beginning of the narrative,[16] instead of later on as in *Aliscans*, that brings the courtly ethic of love, service and reward into the foreground, depicting the battles at Alischantz as motivated by duty to liege-lady and not only by the desire for revenge for the death of Vivianz, for in *Willehalm* it is Gyburg who is the focus of the Saracen attack.

How familiar Wolfram was with the cycle to which *Aliscans* belongs can only be surmised, though there are strong indications that he had some knowledge of the material found in other *chansons de geste* in the *Cycle de Guillaume*,[17] such as the themes and material from *La Prise d'Orange* and

---

15   See Huby-Marly, Marie-Noël, 'Willehalm de Wolfram von Eschenbach et la chanson des Aliscans', *Études germaniques*, 39 (1984), 388–411, 401. See also Gibbs and Johnson, 256.

16   Gyburg's role as the reason for the war is intimated after the opening prayer of *Willehalm* (*Wh.* 7, 23 – 8, 29) and again after the fatal wounding of Vivianz (*Wh.* 30, 21ff).

17   John Clifton-Everest investigates the themes of the *chansons de geste* in Wolfram's *Parzival*, such as the rescue of a Saracen woman, love and marriage as a motivation for Saracens to convert to Christianity, conversion of the defeated Saracen, and the idea of deeds surpassing religion. He concluded that Wolfram must have had more knowledge of the *chanson-de-geste* material before writing *Willehalm* and perhaps

Le Charroi de Nîmes: for instance, the disinheritance of the hero. The theme of the disinheritance of the protagonist who must then prove himself as a knight has its precedent in Wolfram's *Parzival*, where Herzeloyde does everything she can to strip her son of his heritage before he sets out on his own. Similarly, Willehalm is a disinherited son:

> von Narbôn grâf Heimrîch
> alle sîne süne verstiez,
> daz er in bürg noch huobe liez,
> noch der erde dechein sîn rîcheit.
> [....]
> er bat sîn süne kêren,
> und selbe ir rîcheit mêren,
> in diu lant swâ si möhten:
> ob si ze dienste iht töhten,
> stieze in diu saelde rehtiu zil,
> si erwurben rîches lônes vil.
>
> 'Welt ir urborn den lîp,
> hôhen lôn hânt werdiu wîp:
> ir vindet ouch etswâ den man
> der wol dienstes lônen kan
> mit lêhen und mit anderm guote.
> hin ze wîbn nâch hôhem muote
> sult ir die sinne rihten
> und an ir helfe phlihten.
> der keiser Karl hât vil tugent:
> iur starken lîbe, iur schoene jugent,
> die antwurt in sîn gebot.
> des muoz in wenden hôhiu nôt,
> ern rîche iuch immer mêre:
> sîn hof hât iwer êre.
> dem sult ir diens sîn bereit:
> er erkennet wol iur edelkeit.'
>
>   (*Wh.* 5, 16 – 6, 16)

---

even before *Parzival*, as he seems to have been influenced by them. See Clifton-Everest, 'Wolframs Parzival und die chanson de geste'.

[Count Heimrich of Narbonne disinherited all his sons, leaving them neither castles nor estates, nor any of his worldly goods. [...] He told his own sons to go out and increase their wealth in whatever lands they might. If they were fit for the service of chivalry, and if Fortune provided them with their proper goals, they would reap many rich rewards. 'If you are prepared to exert yourselves, noble ladies will have rich rewards for you. You will also find a lord somewhere who knows how to reward service with fiefs and other chattels. You should turn your thoughts to ladies to attain [chivalrous] spirits,[18] and involve yourselves in their service. The Emperor Charles is a man of excellence. Put your strong bodies and your handsome youthfulness at his disposal. Unless some grave trouble prevents him, he will heap riches upon you, and his court will gain honour through you. He is the man you should be ready to serve. He will recognize your nobility.'][19]

Wolfram shows that he is familiar with something not occurring in *Aliscans*, although it appears in other *chansons de geste*,[20] and he uses this passage at the beginning of the narrative to set the tone of the poem, creating an anticipation that this courtly theme will have significance in this work, and at the same time including the epic element of Charlemagne's noble legacy. The setting is reminiscent of *Parzival*, though the opening suggests that the story will progress very differently. There is the directive to go out and seek goals through chivalry and to seek ladies in whose service riches as well as *hôher muot* [a chivalric spirit] might be acquired, this recalling the developmental progress of the hero of romance. Nowhere

---

18   Note that Gibbs and Johnson have translated *hôhem muote* as 'high spirits' here, which can be seen to convey only part of its meaning. Included in the idea of 'high spirits' is the buoyant air of self-confidence and pride such as are inspired within the knight who seeks the favour of and service to a lady. Wolfram's own words on the inspiration of *hohe minne* are clear: 'eteslîch durh sandern swester, dâ tet rîterlîche tât. minn gît ellenthaften rât' [Some of them were performing knightly deeds for the sisters of others, for noble Love inspires courage.] (*Wh.* 329, 16–18). Gibbs and Johnson, 165. See also *Wh.* 83, 10–11.

19   Wolfram von Eschenbach, *Willehalm*, 19–20.

20   That Willehalm and his brothers are disinherited by Aymeri only occurs in *Les Narbonnais* (ed. H. Suchier (Paris: SATF, 1898), laisses 266ff) and in *Guibert d'Andrenas* (ed. J. Melander (Paris: Edouard Champion, 1922), laisses 144ff), both of which Bumke cites as having been dated somewhat vaguely in the first half of the thirteenth century; see Bumke, *Wolfram von Eschenbach*, 387.

else in *Willehalm* are chivalric duty and courtly parameters spelled out so clearly and it is through this that Wolfram's rendition of the rest of the story draws its tone. How or even whether Wolfram knew about the two *chansons de geste* in which a disinheritance occurs in the Narbonnais family remains one of the mysteries surrounding his penchant for collecting subject matter and incorporating it into his narration. However, he appears to include this element to supply his version of the epic with a courtly emphasis from the beginning and to relate it to his audience in such a way as to present the parameters within which the issues of the narrative will be played out: chivalry and its intertwined courtly code of spirituality, honour, love and service.[21]

> Wie vil si sorgen dolten,
> und wass ouch freude erholten,
> und wie ir manlîchiu kunst
> wîbe minne unde ir herzen gunst
> mit ritterschaft bejageten,
> und dicke alsô betageten
> daz mans in hôhem prîse sach!
> selten senftekeit, grôz ungemach
> wart den helden sît bekant.
> durch prîs si wâren ûz gesant.
> (*Wh.* 7, 1–10)

[How many troubles they endured and what joys they derived, and how their manly skill pursued with chivalry the love of women and the favour of their hearts, and how they often spent their time in ways that earned them high renown! Seldom ease, but great discomfort, was the heroes' later lot. They had been sent forth to achieve fame.][22]

---

21   In his research on the character of Willehalm and Wolfram's courtly tone, Rushing believes that Wolfram's emphasis is on love in *Willehalm* and not *Minnedienst*, which is central in determining the genre of this piece. See Rushing, James A., 'Arofel's Death and the Question of Willehalm's Guilt', *Journal of English and Germanic Philology*, October (1995), 469–82, 476. However, even if Wolfram's courtly code in *Willehalm* does not embrace the *Minnedienst* ideal, there are sufficient elements of romance to prevent ruling out that genre entirely.

22   Gibbs and Johnson, 20.

Heimrich's sons have earned fame for themselves in chivalric duties. Here it can be seen that, in contrast to Parzival, whose eventual reward was to live out his days with his family, these men, accomplished knights, earn themselves difficulties and suffering; this is what is expected of the romance hero. Wolfram is establishing the conflict that will form the centrepiece of his narrative: reconciling chivalry with the consequences of war, the self-reflection of a Christian knight and his duty. As well as this, Heimrich talks about Charlemagne: about his reputation for integrity, his capacity to recognize nobility and that service to him will bring honour to his court.

The mention of Charlemagne seems to allude to some of the personal history of the main character of Willehalm, who has already attained for himself a sizeable fief and recognition through service to the crown; he has also won a Saracen princess, obtained renown as a military leader and seems also to be in a state of grace with God when the story begins:

> er ist en franzoys genant
> kuns Gwillâms de Orangis.
> ein ieslîch rîter sî gewis,
> der sîner helfe in angest gert,
> daz er der niemer wirt entwert,
> ern sage die selben nôt vor gote.
> der unverzagete werde bote
> derkennet rîter kumber gar.
> er wart selbe dicke harnaschvar.
> den stric bekante wol sîn hant,
> die den helm ûfz houbet bant
> gein sîns verhes koste.
> er was ein zil der tjoste:
> bî vînden man in dicke sach.
> der schilt von arde was sîn dach.
> man hoert in Francrîche jehen
> swer sîn geslähte kunde spehen,
> daz stüende übr al ir rîche
> der fürsten kraft gelîche.
> sîne mâge wârn die hoehsten ie.
> âne den keiser Karlen nie
> Sô werder Franzoys wart erborn:
> dâ für was und ist sîn prîs erkorn.
> *(Wh. 3, 10 – 4, 2)*

[He is called en français [in French] Comte Guillaume d'Orange. Let every knight who calls for his aid in time of trouble be assured that he will never be denied it, but that Guillaume will declare that same distress before God. That doughty, noble intercessor knows every sorrow which can befall a knight. He was often stained with armour himself. His hand was well acquainted with the thong which binds the helmet to the head to keep a knight from paying with his life. Many a lance was broken on his shield, and he was often to be seen in the throng of the enemy. He was born to carry a shield. In France one hears it said that whoever knew how to identify his family maintained that it was equal to the power of any princes throughout the realm. His kinsmen were always the noblest. Apart from the Emperor Charles himself no such noble Frenchman was ever born. Thus his fame was and is outstanding.][23]

Willehalm is brave, famous, noble and has the grace of God; he is portrayed as the ideal knight from the outset, something which took Parzival many years of painstaking effort to achieve. However, this story is not about *attaining* perfect knighthood; rather, it seems to be about how to use and to safeguard it, and about the function of that accomplished chivalry which is exemplified in the main characters. *Willehalm* suggests a message about knighthood and chivalry applied to a situation more historical and practical than ideal, inviting only afterwards the assessment of values, together with that type of self-reflection that marked the courtly genre.

As the story progresses, Wolfram makes other allusions to Willehalm's past. A good knight will have performed brave deeds, gaining renown and rewards in land, amongst other riches; he will have performed in the service of ladies and he will acknowledge these things with a certain measure of humility.[24] These deeds have all been performed by Willehalm and Wolfram makes certain his audience is aware of his past feats throughout the narrative, emphasizing his ability and station as a knight as well

---

23   Gibbs and Johnson, 18–19.
24   '[Es] läßt sich das meiste begreifen, was an durchgehenden Bearbeitungstendenzen beim Vergleich der deutschen Dichtungen mit ihren französischen Vorbildern auffällt ... das Bemühen der deutschen Dichter, die verschiedenen Aspekte höfischer Vorbildlichkeit in einem einheitlichen Programm zusammenzufassen, das um den Gedanken kreiste, daß der vollkommene Ritter zugleich Gott und der Welt gefallen mußte.' Bumke, Joachim, *Höfische Kultur: Literatur und Gesellschaft im hohen Mittelalter* (Munich: Deutscher Taschenbuch Verlag, 2002), 135–6.

as providing a courtly touchstone by which the actions and issues in the story are measured.

> ich was sô lange ein koufman,
> unz ich Nimes gewan, die guoten stat,
> mit wagen. dar nâch ich bat
> in gevancnisse ir minne
> sîn wîp die küneginne.
> ir güete mich gewerte
> al des ich an si gerte
> daz tet si, durh den touf noch mêr,
> mit mir danne ir überkêr,
> denn durh mîne werdekeit.
>   (*Wh.* 298, 14–23)

[I played the part of a merchant until I had conquered that fine city of Nîmes with my waggon. After that, while I was in prison, I sought the love of Tibalt's wife, the Queen. Kind as she is, she granted me all that I desired of her but she did this – and then when she crossed the sea with me – more on account of baptism than through any worth of mine.][25]

This passage mentions events that occurred in *Le charroi de Nîmes* [*The Caravan of Nîmes*]. Another passage makes mention of occurrences in *Le couronnement de Louis* [*The Coronation of Louis*], when Willehalm reminds Loys at Montlaon that it was he who secured the crown for him when it was under threat.[26] There are also many passages alluding to events that occurred in *La Prise d'Orange*. These underscore Willehalm's conquest of that city as well as of the Saracen princess, Arabel, who would become Gyburg, legitimizing his conquest and title to Orange.[27] Wolfram mentions that Willehalm learnt to speak heathen tongues when he was in an Arab

---

25   Gibbs and Johnson, 151–2.

26   *Wh.* 159, 6ff. That Guillaume was instrumental in retaining Louis' crown is, however, also mentioned in *Aliscans* in the corresponding scene, LXIX, 3134ff.

27   Sources for the themes in *La Prise d'Orange* were the topic of an article by Philip Bennett, who concentrated greatly on the popular theme of the Muslim princess and her abduction and conversion by the European knight. See Bennett, 'The Storming of the Other World'.

prison: 'do der marcgrâve in prîsûn gevangen lac dâ ze Arâbî, Caldeis und Côatî lernt er dâ ze sprechen' [when the Margrave had been languishing in prison in Arabi, he had learnt to speak the languages Kaldeis and Koati] (*Wh.* 192, 6–9).[28] In *La Prise d'Orange*, Guillaume hears about Orange and the beautiful Orable from a fugitive knight who can speak Saracen tongues and by the time he is set upon his conquest of Orange, he is able to deceive the inhabitants and King Aragon with his mastery of the African dialect.[29] During a conversation with her father in *Willehalm*, Gyburg relates her and Willehalm's story:

> der begund ouch mîner minne gern,
> dô in der künic Synagûn,
> Halzebieres swester sun,
> in eime sturme gevienc
> dâ sîn hant alsölhe tât begienc
> daz er den prîs ze bêder sit
> behielt aldâ und alle zît.
> diu hôhe wirde sîne
> über al die Sarrazîne
> was erschollen unt erhôrt.
> dô was ich küneginne dort
> und pflac vil grôzer rîcheit:
> sus lônde ich sîner arbeit:
> von boin und anderem sîm versmidn
> macht ich in ledec an allen lidn,
> unt fuor in toufpaeriu lant.
>   (*Wh.* 220, 14–29)

[And, indeed, he sought my love when King Sinagun, Halzebier's nephew, captured him in attack, during which he had performed such deeds that his fame was acclaimed by both sides and for all time. His great nobility was rumoured far and wide among all the Saracens. I was Queen there at the time and enjoyed great wealth. I rewarded him for all his troubles by freeing him from the fetters and other irons that bound him hand and foot and by going with him to Christian lands.][30]

---

28   Gibbs and Johnson, 103.
29   *La Prise d'Orange*, VII–XIII, XVI.
30   Gibbs and Johnson, 116.

Gyburg again relates these events more descriptively when she gives Rennewart a suit of armour, recounting the history of how she came to possess the armour in which Willehalm had performed such illustrious deeds.[31]

Other innovations of Wolfram in this work have given scholars difficulties and generated speculation about their origins. Joachim Bumke writes that since no literary texts have been found to serve as precedent for the mention of Willehalm having fought in and taken control of Rome for Pope Leo III in the service of Charlemagne, it must be deduced that it came from a text no longer extant.[32]

> dô ir durch âventiure
> bî Karl dem lampriure
> nâch hôhem prîse runget
> und Rômaere betwunget,
> Ein mâsen dier enpfienget dô
> durh den bâbest Lêô
> > (*Wh.* 91, 27 – 92, 2)

[When, for the sake of adventure, you were striving after high renown in the service of Charles l'Empereur and oppressing the Romans, you received a scar on behalf of Pope Leo.][33]

However, in *Aliscans* Guiborc asks to see the scar Guillaume received in Rome twice: once when he approaches the fortress at Orange, after the defeat of the first battle, and again upon his return to relieve the city:

---

31   *Wh.* 293–4.
32   Bumke writes that for this mention of a trip to Rome 'findet sich keine direkte Parallele im französischen Wilhelm-Zyklus, so daß damit gerechnet werden muß, daß die Angabe aus einer anderen Quelle stammt' [no direct parallel can be found in the French Guillaume Cycle, so that it must be reasoned that the information comes from a different source] (Bumke, *Wolfram von Eschenbach*, 387).
33   Gibbs and Johnson, 58.

Por san Donis, qui est mes avoeç,
Enceis vera la boce sor lo neç,
Qe devant Roma fist Guillelme Isoreç,
C'est une ensegne qe je conois asseç
                    (*Alisc.* 'M', XLVII, 1851–4)

[By Saint Denis who is with me, I would see the bump on the nose that Guillaume received from Ysorez outside Rome, it is a mark I know well.]

And again:

L'aume deslace, la coyfe veit ostant;
Dame Giborg l'esgarde apertement,
Voit soç lo nes la boce aparisant,
Qe li ot fet Isorez a son brant,
Tres devant Rome en la batayle grant.
                    (*Alisc.* 'M', LXXXI, 4085–9)[34]

[He unfastens his helmet, and lifts his coif; Lady Guibourc sees his uncovered head, sees on his nose the bump that is visible that Ysorez gave him with a sword outside Rome in a great battle.]

Wolfram's reference to the incident in Rome differs from the references in *Aliscans* in that he mentions it only once and he includes the name of Pope Leo. Upon Willehalm's return to Orange, he is recognized by his voice, whereas in *Aliscans*, Guiborc tells Guillaume that his voice sounds like any Saracen and thus demands again to see his nose. Gyburg refers to the Romans whom Willehalm had subdued, but in *Aliscans* it is the

---

34   *Alisc.* XLVII, 1851–4; LXXXI, 4085–9. These passages are taken from the Venice MS
      of *Aliscans*: Holtus, Günter, ed., *La versione franco-italiana della 'Bataille d'Aliscans':*
      Codex Marcianus fr, VIII[=252], Kurt Baldinger, series ed., Beihefte zur Zeitschrift
      für romanische Philologie, vol. 205 (Tübingen: Max Niemeyer Verlag, 1985). As
      mentioned above, this version is believed to be the closest to that of Wolfram's source
      and, as it bears affinities to 'S,' and to the 'A' versions, it is of value to note that Rome
      is also mentioned in both of these versions: XLVIII and LXXXV in the 'S' MS and
      XLVII and LXXXI in the 'A' versions. See Régnier, *Aliscans*, vol. 1, 7–10, regarding
      the manuscripts.

Saracen king, Ysorez, who dealt Guillaume the infamous blow to the nose. These alterations seem to be less an enigma than an instance of Wolfram's inventiveness; they illustrate his subtlety in portraying characters as well as demonstrating that he was working from more than one source.

Asking after the scar on Willehalm's / Guillaume's nose is, of course, one way of explaining the scar that gave him his nickname, *au cort nés* [short-nose], and its variations. For if it were solely for the purpose of identifying Willehalm, Gyburg need not have revealed when and how or even where on his body the scar was obtained; it is likely that it is for the benefit of the audience that this information is disclosed in descriptive narrative. It is also part of an intricate discourse between Gyburg and Willehalm, during which they seem to play out a set of literary rules of engagement in order that Willehalm may enter the palace without engendering fear in the city's inhabitants.[35] However, it is not incorrect to reason that the establishment of the Christian knighthood of Willehalm would enhance the courtly quality of Wolfram's version of the story if the pope were mentioned. Willehalm had been wounded protecting the pope, thereby reinforcing the spiritual aspect of Willehalm's knighthood: that he had fought for Christianity before,[36] that he was loyal to both emperor and pope, thus supporting further his future sainthood, and that he is in a state of grace

---

35   This situation, as well as Willehalm's return to Orange in Book V, deserves closer scrutiny and will be explored in greater detail in Chapter 5.

36   We can only assume that Wolfram and his audience were familiar with the events surrounding the papacy of Pope St Leo III and that it was not Saracens but Lombards Willehalm had been fighting when he 'oppressed' the Romans in support of the pontiff. There had been a threat to God's representative on earth and the Emperor Charlemagne, recently declared benefactor of the Church in Rome and protector of the Holy See by the pope, powerfully quelled it. See Mann, Horace K., *The Lives of the Popes in the Early Middle Ages: The Popes During the Carolingian Empire; Leo III to Formosus, 795–891*, 2nd edn, vol. II (London: K. Paul, Trench, Trubner, 1925), 3–6, 21–33. Also see 'Chapter IV: Empires of the West' of Duffy, Eamon, *Saints and Sinners: A History of the Popes* (New Haven, CT: Yale University Press, 1997); and Pertz, George Henry, ed., *Chronicon Moissiacense, Monumenta Germaniae Historica*, Series Scriptores I (Stuttgart: Anton Hiersemann, 1963), 280–313. It is worthy of mention that one of the surviving manuscripts of *Willehalm*, G (Cod. Sang. 857 St

from the beginning of the story. Because Wolfram's audience cannot have been expected to have been familiar with *La Prise d'Orange* as a part of the background of *Willehalm*, this information was included. This image of Willehalm as the ideal knight is thus strengthened, his right as Margrave of Orange established and the stage for his internal conflict as an already accomplished knight is firmly set.

Romance and epic elements

Though Wolfram's era is seen as the pinnacle of Hohenstaufen splendour and the incubator for Arthurian romance, the *matière de Bretagne* that was popularized throughout Europe by Chrétien and Hartmann among others, the *chansons de geste* of the previous century had not been entirely abandoned. Wolfram took on the challenge of resetting the French *chanson de geste*, the *matière de France*, in a courtly milieu and used its epic elements to his advantage. A valid point is made by Michael Batts that 'in the twelfth and thirteenth centuries, literary virtuosity was demonstrated by the skilful reworking and reinterpretation of existing sources.'[37] Wolfram's intention in taking up established material and refashioning it was possibly, as it was to

Gallen) is included in a volume along with *Karl der Große*, among other works such as *Nibelungenlied* and *Parzival*.

37   Batts's article is summed up in these words, in the introduction by Batts, Michael, 'National Perspectives on Originality and Translation: Chrétien de Troyes and Hartmann von Aue' in Martin H. Jones and Roy Wisbey, eds, *Chrétien de Troyes and the German Middle Ages, Papers from an International Symposium* (Cambridge: D.S. Brewer, 1993), 9–18. Additionally, Batts is clear in his opinion that, 'part of the problem lies, of course, in the fact that the philologically legitimate desire to identify the source leads to a detailed comparison of the texts of the supposed source and the derivate [...] however, if it is agreed that the medieval poet consciously and deliberately used existing material and transferred this into his own language, adapting it *wherever necessary* to his own devices, there is no logical reason for assuming that that which is translated without overt change is any less the author's own than that which deviates from the original.' (11–12) This observation is not considered by Marguerite Rossi, who sees medieval German literature like *Willehalm* as a translation whose

Hartmann and other of their contemporaries, an exercise and an indication of his ability rather than a demonstration of any lack of originality. Much as the *jongleurs* enjoyed adding their own innovations to their performances, suggesting that they could tell the story better than the last man, so too did Wolfram and his contemporaries make alterations to existing material, reflecting their own narrative abilities and retelling a popular thread with their own additions. This newer material was regarded as their own and not analogous to the original material, 'original material' being a concept that was by no means clearly defined for a medieval audience.

In his bantering manner, Wolfram did not neglect to tell his audience that he could relate the story of *Parzival* better than Chrétien and he makes reference to Chrétien's 'lesser' ability in *Willehalm*, though Chrétien had had no hand in the *chanson de geste*.[38] Nevertheless, this is perhaps more an indication of his admiration for Chrétien rather than criticism. Wolfram's comments on his own linguistic ineptitude are no less humorous:

> Herbergen ist loschiern genant.
> sô vil hân ich der sprâche erkant.
> ein ungefüeger Tschampâneys
> kunde vil baz franzeys
> dann ich, swiech franzoys spreche.
> seht waz ich an den reche,
> den ich diz maere diuten sol:
> den zaeme ein tiutschiu sprâche wol:

liberal adaptations were the result of the inability of the poet to comprehend the model of epic narrative as it existed in the French originals. See Rossi, 256–7.

38 'Cristjans einen alten tymit im hat ze Munleun an gelegt: da mit er sine tumpheit regt, swer sprichet so nach wane' [Chrétien dressed him in old dimity in Montlaon: whoever speaks of such fantasies reveals his ignorance] (*Wh.* 125, 20–3). Wolfram remarks that the material in which Chrétien described Willehalm as dressed betrayed his ignorance; however, not only did Chrétien not author *Aliscans*, but there also appears to be no description of the actual material Willehalm was wearing (*Aliscans* LXI). Kiening remarks that the reference to Chrétien here is simply a way in which Wolfram shows off his abilities by mentioning a well-known poet and trumping his work (74). We cannot dismiss the possibility of the occurrence of this in the MS with which Wolfram was familiar, now lost.

mîn tiutsch ist etswâ doch sô krump,
er mac mir lîhte sîn ze tump,
den ichs niht gâhs bescheide:
dâ sûme wir uns beide.
                              (*Wh.* 237, 3–14)

[Setting up camp is called *loger* in French. I've learnt that much of the language. A
rude peasant from the Champagne could speak much better French than I, the way
I speak it. Now look how I am treating those to whom I should be telling this tale in
translation! They would be better off if I used German, but sometimes my German
is so involved that a man can easily become quite perplexed, if I do not explain it to
him quickly. Then we are both wasting our time!][39]

Wolfram is commenting on his command of both the French and
German languages and, if the Champagne peasant can be correlated with
Chrétien, he is paying his fellow poet an indirect compliment. Wolfram's
misinterpretation of the French language has its precedent in *Parzival*, yet
one can never be certain whether it is actual or intended. Arthur Hatto
observes a typical misunderstanding or mistranslation in *Parzival* of the
term for a silver carving dish, which Wolfram interprets as 'carving knives'
(in the plural): 'But what matter? To a man of Wolfram's temperament and
imagination such minor irritations to narrative logic produced pearls.'[40]
The two silver knives are there to remove the ice-like 'glass' left on the lance
from Anfortas's wound, illustrating Wolfram's narrative and imaginative
abilities. Wolfram's extensive use of French words throughout his narration
of *Willehalm*, too, attests to the process of retelling stories and his own
ability and confidence in telling the story just as he would have it told.

Gyburc moht ir wâpenroc
nu mit êren von ir legn:
si unde ir juncfrouwen megn
dez harnaschrâm tuon von dem vel.
si sprach 'gelüke ist sinewel.
mir was nu lange trûren bî:

39   Gibbs and Johnson, 123.
40   Wolfram von Eschenbach. *Parzival*, 429.

dâ von bin ich ein teil nu vrî.
Al mîne juncvrouwen ich man,
leget iwer besten kleider an:
ir sult iuch feitieren,
vel und hâr sô zieren,
daz ir minneclîchen sît getân,
ob ein minne gerender man
iu dienst nâch minne biete,
daz er sihs niht gâhs geniete,
und daz im tuo daz scheiden wê
von iu. daz sult ir schaffen ê.
Und vlizet iuch einer hövescheit,
Gebaret als ob iu nie dahein leit
Von vienden geschaehe.'
(*Wh.* 246, 24 – 247, 13)

[Now Giburc could lay aside her surcoat in honour, and she and her ladies could wash the armour rust from their skin. She said: 'The wheel of Fortune is round. I was beset by sorrows for a long time. Now I am partly relieved of them. I urge all of you, my ladies, to put on your best clothes. You should deck yourselves out, do your face and hair so that you look lovely, so that a knight seeking love and offering service in return for love will not quickly have too much and that parting from you will be painful. Do that first of all, and put on your best courtly manners, as if you had not suffered from the enemy.']⁴¹

Willehalm is not the knight of the romance genre who undertakes a journey in order to find a love to serve, as does his character in *Le Charroi de Nîmes* and *La Prise d'Orange*, or even Gahmuret in *Parzival*. But he remains fervently faithful to his wife, Gyburg, his partner and liege-lady, who has, because of his love and the love of God, become Christian. He is a successful military leader not because he is striving to attain knight-hood, but because of the practical side that his more human, less fantastical qualities allow.⁴² Willehalm serves God through his deep sense of chivalry and in doing so is confronted with ethical dilemmas and conflict which

---

41 Gibbs and Johnson, 127–8.
42 Jean-Marc Pastré finds that this human quality of the characters in *Willehalm* is pre-eminent, unlike in the romances. See Pastré, 'Un avatar courtois', 341.

he must resolve. Though there is none of the ethereal aspect of Arthur's court or the Grail castle in *Willehalm*, there is the self-reflection of a courtly class, the close inspection of a religious ideal of chivalry and the spiritual consequences of the duty of Christian knighthood.

The transformation that seems apparent in the character of Guillaume in *La Prise d'Orange* has enjoyed repeated scrutiny. As Claude Régnier points out in the introduction to his edition, none of the extant manuscripts is the original[43] and elements in them seem to suggest that certain changes have been effected, reflecting a more courtly and humorous version of the story than do its companions in the *Geste de Garin de Monglane*.[44] The principal change is to the character of Guillaume. 'Le renouveleur [...] a métamorphosé cet homme de guerre en personnage de chanson courtoise, troublé par le retour du printemps, amoureux d'une princesse lointaine et confessant le pouvoir souverain de l'amour' [The new author transformed this warrior into a character of courtly songs, anxious as the spring returns, in love with a distant princess and confessing the undeniable power of love].[45] Indeed, Guillaume's actions in *La Prise d'Orange* seem uncharacteristic of the epic hero of other *chansons de geste* in the cycle. Although *La Prise d'Orange* offers an incontestably epic tone, it ignores one of the major epic themes of the cycle: loyalty to a sovereign.[46]

43   Régnier lists evidence of structural modifications as well as incomplete assonances, shortening of the *laisses*, omissions, displaced verses and other errors that support the theory of an earlier, no longer extant manuscript of *La Prise d'Orange*. Régnier, *La Prise d'Orange*, 25ff, and 31–4.

44   Régnier cites evidence of the changes to the character of Tiébaut and to the marriage of Guillaume with Orable and suggests that these changes were effected after the *chansons* of *Guillaume* and *Aliscans* had become popular. Régnier, *La Prise d'Orange*, 30.

45   Régnier, *La Prise d'Orange*.

46   Lachet, Claude, *La Prise d'Orange ou la parodie courtoise d'une épopée*, Editions Slatkine, vol. 10, Nouvelle bibliothèque du Moyen Age (Genève: Libr, H. Champion, 1986), 146. Joan Ferrante writes that 'It is the causes that the heroes of the William cycle serve which distinguish them from the rebellious barons of the feudal epics; these are loyalty to the king, despite his unworthiness, and dedication to Christianity.' (4)

These markedly different characteristics of Guillaume's character and the tone of *La Prise d'Orange* contribute to the riddle of Wolfram's sources for *Willehalm* and his knowledge of *chansons de geste*. It also shows that, well before *Willehalm* was composed,[47] the Guillaume character had undergone, at least once, a transformation from the epic hero into the courtly knight. Perhaps Wolfram was familiar with this innovation in *La Prise d'Orange* or perhaps he made his courtly modifications to the French material independently, influenced by his contemporary environment. Whichever the case, the courtly tone and modifications to the Guillaume character are of a different nature in *Willehalm* to those of *La Prise d'Orange*. Whereas in *La Prise d'Orange* there is the parodic humour of knights looking for something to do, the knights in *Willehalm* are driven by a sense of duty to lineage and love-service, and reflect upon the consequences of their actions as knights with a broader view of religion, love and redemption.

There are parallels between elements in *Willehalm* with those of romance as a genre, but the general tone does not strongly suggest romance. Characteristics of the epic, such as a commanding sense of duty to the empire, military conflict, individual mounted combat and the motif of the religious importance of feudal values,[48] remain present in *Willehalm*. Wolfram's underscoring of the significance of courtly ethics and chivalry is achieved without detriment to the epic tone of the poem, but not without an important contrast which renders *Willehalm* uniquely Wolfram's. The reworking of the heroic epic into a courtly epic enabled Wolfram to depict the Saracens as equals in chivalry and knighthood. They suffer the same losses in the name of *Minne*, they fight by the same rules of courage and honour, and they have the same weaknesses in ignoring the importance

---

47   Ferrante dates *La Prise d'Orange* and *Aliscans* as mid- to late twelfth century (10); also see Régnier, *Aliscans*, vol. 1, 40. *Willehalm* is generally believed to have been composed after 1210; see Pérennec, René, *Wolfram von Eschenbach* (Paris: Belin, 2005), 15–16; Richey, 36–7; Bertau, 'Versuch über Wolfram', 146–8; Bumke, *Mäzene im Mittelalter*, 168.

48   See: Suard, *La chanson de geste*, 33–9, and Suard, *Chanson de geste et tradition épique*, 39ff.

of feudal vassalage.[49] Placing the adversaries on a level playing field fore-grounds the religious element of the epic genre and allows for its scrutiny in a self-reflective courtly fashion. The ambiguity of the genre of *Willehalm*, in that it combines romance motifs and elements in the historical setting of the *matière de France*, is indicative of the trend in medieval literature in the twelfth and thirteenth centuries. Just as chivalry is a fusion of ele-ments from different sources, *Willehalm* can be seen as a combination of different genres that were more recognizable in earlier French literature but that have begun to break down with the flourishing of literature in Europe's vernacular tongues.

Wolfram's message

Wolfram applied a more courtly tone to the heroic epic, appealing to the romance audience and at the same time rewriting a story in a unique genre: a form of courtly epic, what has been termed '*deutsche chanson de geste*'.[50] The goal of the characters in *Aliscans* was the destruction of the Saracen threat. Any non-Christian in *Aliscans* does not escape a description akin to that of an inhuman entity.[51] Even in *Chanson de Roland*, Marsile, the Saracen

---

49 Jörn Reichel mentioned the importance of vassalage to the feudal system and how it was shown as problematic for the Saracens as well as for the Christians in his article: Reichel, Jörn, 'Willehalm und die höfische Welt', *Euphorion. Zeitschrift für Literaturgeschichte* 69 (1975), 406.

50 Ortmann, 88.

51 At the beginning of the work, during Vivianz's battle: 'Quant Viviens cele jent venant, De tel façon et de si let semblant' [Then Vivien sees these men coming, with their strange behaviour and ugly appearance] (*Alisc.* IV, 87, 88); and in the battle between Guillaume and Aérofle, Aérofle's entrenched ideas against Christianity justify his death as an infidel (XXXVII, 1502, 1503). In the last battle as well there are descrip-tions of exotic ugliness and crude qualities in the Saracens, making them seem less than human and unworthy of such considerations, e.g., the fight between Renoart and Grishart, who eats people after killing them with a hatchet, is described, as is the struggle with Flohart who fights with a scythe (CLII). Friedrich Wolfzettel surveys several texts, including the *Chanson des Saisnes*, in which foreigners from the East

king of Saragossa, though possessing rich lands and an opulent palace, is by definition a pagan incapable of integrity and this despite his closest advisor, Blancandrin, being described as a loyal knight. Both are guilty of treacherous schemes, disregarding even their families' safety to avoid loss of power.[52] By permeating the story with courtly ethics, Wolfram shifts the goal from the complete annihilation of the Saracens to a Christian victory in Orange, which looks towards a possibility of reconciliation through ties of kinship and chivalry. He praises Christian and Saracen alike throughout the narrative for their chivalry, even immediately after Vivianz is mortally wounded, placing the opposing armies and knights on an equal plane where chivalry is concerned. This shifts the focus of the disparity to that of a disagreement of religion, this being the only difference between the Saracens and the Christian knights.[53] The Christian religion is the only thing remaining that marks the Christians as superior to the Saracens, for they are otherwise equally matched.[54]

> daz was almeistic minnen her,
> die manlîch ûfes lîbes zer
> wârn benant für tjostiure:
> manec heiden vil gehiure
> was dâ ze vorflüge komn.
> (*Wh.* 26, 9–13)

are depicted as fantastical and inhuman. He concludes that it was the Crusades and Crusade literature, like the *chansons de geste*, that changed the image of the foreign and the Saracen to that of antagonist. See Wolfzettel, 273–95. Likewise, Mary Campbell discusses several travel texts written before the *chansons de geste* and Mandeville, that also depicted the foreign as fantastical, as well as the fifth century BC book of Ctesias, Herodotus, and Augustine, and the *Wonders of the East* manuscript that is accompanied by *Beowulf* and *Judith*. See Campbell.

52   Dufournet, *Roland*, III, 24–46.

53   Franziska Wessel-Fleinghaus points out how Wolfram has both sides lamenting the sacrifice to love, marking them as equals in courtly ethics (42) and discusses this aspect further, concluding that the reason Wolfram did this was in order that he could ask religious questions (53ff), in Wessel-Fleinghaus, Franziska, 'Gotes hantgetat, Zur Deutung von Wolframs Willehalm unter dem Aspekt der Gattungsfrage', *Literaturwissenschaftliches Jahrbuch* 33 (1992), 29–100.

54   See Pastré-Marc, 'Un avatar courtois', 339.

[They were predominantly knights in the service of Love, those jousters who had been summoned there and boldly risked their lives. Many a splendid heathen made his way to the head of the army.][55]

The introduction of a more refined courtly code of chivalry in place of stark feudal prescripts also allows Wolfram to further inspect and to question the duty of a Christian knight, bringing together religion, chivalry, service and love. If both sides in the war are ideal knights and abide by an exemplary code of chivalry, then the only justification for their slaughter is that they have not been baptized; this raises issues of salvation and redemption, and how one becomes deserving of them. Willehalm laments the necessity to kill Gyburg's kinsmen and also the sin he will commit by doing so. Even after victory has been secured in the second battle and revenge exacted for the death of Vivianz, Willehalm laments lugubriously. He questions God and the Christian motives for the situation in which he finds himself: he has lost a great many Christian kinsmen to protect his conquest and slain what are described as noble knights in the service of love, whose deaths will be mourned. Later he confides in his nephew Bernart and resigns himself to the situation, seeing it as the enactment of God's will.

> got weiz wol waz er hât getân.
> nu geloube, manlîch wîser man,
> ob du sîst sô gehiure,
> dirre sige mir schumpfentiure
> hât ervohten in dem herzen mîn,
> sît ich guoter vriunt muoz âne sîn,
> an den al mîn vreude lac.
> (*Wh.* 459, 23–9)

[God knows what He has done, but believe me, brave, experienced man that you are, if you are so perceptive, this victory has wrought a defeat in my heart since I have lost good friends, in whom all my happiness lay.][56]

55   Gibbs and Johnson, 28.
56   Gibbs and Johnson, 222.

Emphasis is placed upon religion and spirituality when the individual and inner conflicts of characters like Gyburg and Willehalm are related, allowing the poet and audience to question the function of courtly duty.

Some scholars have interpreted it as a work with anti-courtly or anti-chivalric undertones.[57] Jörn Reichel, however, concludes that *Willehalm* is a work exemplifying the function of chivalry within a more lifelike setting, where political conflicts are played out on a personal and ethical level, and not one in which, as it might seem at first glance, the hollowness of the rigid courtly world is mercilessly exposed.[58] Reichel determines that Wolfram's incorporation of the courtly code of chivalry into *Willehalm* shows that, despite conflicts, the courtly world does not fall apart through its encounter with reality and is not rendered powerless so easily; its disillusioning representation is not simply discarded, but its values are modified and integrated with tangible situations, enabling the continuing validity of the courtly world to be recognized.[59] When viewing *Willehalm* as an evolving text, the latter stance seems to suggest a more accurate state of affairs.

The importance of chivalry and a courtly code in *Willehalm* has also been discussed in more recent scholarship. Marie-Noël Huby-Marly writes that adding a courtly tone to the poem was Wolfram's reason for changing *Aliscans* and that Wolfram's intention was to create a new international code of chivalry within the story which followed the same code of chivalry and had the same values as that of the early Feudal Age: courage, family and honour.[60] Kathryn Starkey undertook a detailed analysis of gestures and staging within the scene at Montlaon, showing

---

57   See: Bumke, Joachim, *Wolframs Willehalm. Studien zur Epenstruktur und zum Heiligkeitsbegriff der ausgehenden Blütezeit* (Heidelberg: Carl Winter, 1959), esp. 111–12. Trends have differed somewhat in the latter part of the twentieth century and the beginning of the twenty-first, and the definitions of what is courtly and what constitutes epic have been recognized as less rigid.

58   Reichel, supporting the later trend, disagrees with Bumke's earlier view of the role of chivalry and courtly ethics in *Willehalm*. See Reichel, 401–2.

59   Reichel, 402.

60   See Huby-Marly, 'Willehalm', 406.

how a courtly code of chivalry was drawn upon in *Willehalm*.[61] It is not difficult to see the role chivalry plays in the scene at Montlaon and how the courtly code proves to be the mediating device in conflict. It also remains that Wolfram had not yet finished conveying his message about chivalry in *Parzival* and questioning established orders. The material of *Aliscans* provided him with further opportunity.[62] The role of chivalry, courtly ethics and Christian knighthood is placed under scrutiny in *Willehalm* and is accentuated by the themes that underpin their applications. Love, *Minnedienst* and spirituality are examined, this time within the context of an epic. The underlying theme of love plays nicely into the courtly and religious motifs of the work, provoking questions as to whether *Minnedienst* and religion are at odds with one another, and how love can be a binding as well as a dividing force.

Wolfram is also conveying a message about feudalism. The scene in Montlaon centres on Willehalm's vow to secure imperial support to save Orange and Gyburg. It culminates in Willehalm threatening to withdraw his fealty, surrounded by assembled nobles, and the serene power of Irmschart and Alyze to remind the knights of their chivalric duty. This

---

61   Starkey.

62   John Clifton-Everest saw an extension of the underlying concept and role of love from one work to the other: 'Die Metaphorik dieser Liebe des Feirefiz scheint mir auch in einem gewissen Sinn eine Vorwegnahme der Thematik des *Willehalm* zu sein, und damit ist eine Brücke zum späteren Werk Wolframs geschlagen. [...] Das Stadium der Bekehrung hat Wolfram mit Parzival hinter sich, hier setzt die Erzählung später ein und führt das Thema fort. Nun steht diese christliche Liebe unter dem Angriff einer reaktionären, heidnischen Welt, besitzt jedoch in den Liebenden die Macht, die versammelten militärischen Kräfte des Christentums zu ihrer Verteidigung zu mobilisieren' [The use of metaphor for this love of Feirefiz also seems to me in a certain sense to be an anticipation of the theme of *Willehalm* and with it is suggested a bridge to Wolfram's later work. [...] Wolfram has accomplished the platform of conversion with *Parzival*; here the story begins later and follows on with the subject. Now this Christian love stands under the attack of a reactionary heathen world; however, the lovers possess the power to mobilize the gathered military forces of Christianity in their defence] (Clifton-Everest, 'Wolframs Parzival und die chanson de geste', 713).

indicates the importance of a courtly code of chivalry in difficult and potentially destructive situations. The feudal ideology in the *chansons de geste* can be said to lend meaning to chivalry and *chevalerie terrestre* [secular chivalry] had a spiritual model which was essential to the religious element in that genre, the *chevalerie celeste* [spiritual chivalry].[63] Wolfram used this element of chivalry and feudalism from the *chansons de geste*, where reconciliation is necessary to re-establish the feudal order,[64] and he challenged the way a courtly code functioned jointly with religion and spirituality.

Whether Wolfram misunderstood the irony in French romances or took the material more seriously, he conveyed a message about chivalry and the courtly code in which he saw value. Through *Minnedienst* and spiritual chivalry come the hope for redemption and through courtly code and feudal order, Christian supremacy is justified and legitimized. Wolfram's goal of Christian victory unifies opposing knights on the battlefield in religion, salvation and redemption, in addition to their already recognized accord in a courtly code of chivalry.[65] However, the defeated Saracens do not convert; instead, they are assisted in their departure, leaving conversion an open question. In a text that resists clear genre classification, Wolfram successfully makes use of metre and subject matter, as well as themes and structural symmetry from differing origins, and bonds them together in his unique and characteristic work. Comprising elements of romance also present in *Aliscans* and *La Prise d'Orange*, with the addition of Wolfram's courtly innovations *Willehalm* is a masterpiece exemplary of medieval German courtly literature, the epic romance.

63 See Suard, *Chanson de geste et tradition épique*, 39.
64 See Huby-Marly, 'Willehalm', 396–7.
65 Christa Ortmann explored the utopian theme of *Minne* and observed that only through this unity under Christianity can the chivalry of Christian leadership be legitimized (86).

Wolfram's Answer to a Problem

Chivalry, as it had become in twelfth-century Germany, connoted a code
of behaviour by which an individual could be identified and to which one
should aspire, with the complex and often contradictory background elements of martial activities which defined the occupation, spiritual reflection
and the added complication of the courtly love poetry and of the code that
are exemplified in literature. It is no surprise, then, that chivalry penetrated
the courtly life of the Middle Ages to the great extent that it did and that
the contradictions and dilemmas that it posed were exposed and examined
in literary material traversing several genres.[66] This chivalry, with its moral,
ethical and spiritual problems, was of great importance to Wolfram. He had
explored its problematic code and implications of self-reflection in *Parzival*,
but in *Willehalm* he uses it as a tool, depicting its significance in human
relations between allies as well as adversaries and as a measure by which
one's integrity and spiritual fortitude are assessed. Chivalry thus serves as
a means in *Willehalm* by which to address something which concerned
Wolfram: the problem of how to overcome the fundamental duality of the
world order with one's spiritual and temporal integrity intact. The striving for the peaceful coexistence of values within and by means of chivalry
was of the greatest importance. Within this framework are the prominent
themes of religion and *Minnedienst*, which are problematic in *Willehalm*
and which can be seen as both binding and divisive.

Chivalry in 'Willehalm'

Richey writes that in German literature 'Hartmann was the first to bring out
the value of the knightly ethos' and that Wolfram, although his narrative

---

66   Alois Wolf points to themes and metaphors such as tragic conflict and religious
      debate as Wolfram's innovations to his French source, indicating that these themes
      are absent in *Aliscans* (Wolf, 379–80).

talents were greater, was indebted to his predecessor for this.[67] Wolfram explored the knightly ethos that Hartmann introduced and demonstrated its significance on spiritual and temporal levels, expounding upon and slightly changing the theme of sin and redemption. The world of Hartmann has been contrasted to that of Wolfram and the goal to live in the world in such a way as to attain grace in both the terrestrial and celestial realms, as recognized by Walther von der Vogelweide, was expressed in terms of sin: for Hartmann, suffering is the consequence of sin and grace saves the hero; for Wolfram, suffering is the cause of sin, dishonour, doubt and the denouncement of God.[68] At the heart of this aspiration in *Willehalm* lies chivalry in its elegant complexity; the problem of the coexistence of values and integrity in both worlds is applied to both human fallibility and spiritual aspiration.

Though the war is the focus of the action in *Willehalm*, emphasis is placed on the interaction between characters and the way in which conflicts are resolved. The battlefield is merely an arena for the description of martial prowess and skill; it is not a determinant of victory or a mode by which suspense is drawn out and the victor decided nor is it a testing ground for the chivalric values of the protagonists. Once the war has begun, a Christian victory is inevitable and the battle is already well underway when the story begins. This gives rise to the question of how Willehalm can follow through with the course of action, that of fulfilling his vow to Gyburg to save Orange, without compromising either the spiritual or temporal worlds. So what we see is a battle that takes place not only on the battlefield but equally in the interaction between individual characters, honour in service, loyalty and solidarity on temporal and spiritual levels.

Honour

Of the values of chivalry, honour was very important in the traditional German consciousness. Wolfram evaluates this ideal in *Willehalm* by

---

67   Richey, 43.
68   Maurer, 39–40.

elaborating on the hero's interactions with the Saracen characters;[69] the
duel between Willehalm and Arofel provides powerful material for this.
Willehalm's honour as a knight is first exposed to the audience in this duel.
Willehalm has suffered the loss of his entire force and of many of his kinsmen, through death or capture; he also bears the grief of Vivianz's recent
and tragic death when he encounters Arofel and several Saracen kings on
his way back to Orange and engages them in battle. One after the other the
Saracens are cut down by Willehalm. Wolfram then describes the Saracen
who will oppose Willehalm next: Arofel.

> ein swert der künec Pantanor
> gap dem künege Salatrê:
> der gabz dem künege Antikotê:
> der gabz Esserê dem emerâl:
> der gabz dô als lieht gemâl
> Arofel dem küenen:
> der kund ouch wênic süenen.
> Sus kom daz swert von man ze man,
> unz ez der Persân gewan,
> Arofel, derz mit ellen truoc
> und ez vil genendeclîchen sluoc,
> wand er mit strîte kunde
> und niemen für sich gunde
> deheinen prîs ze bejagenne.
> ich het iu vil ze sagenne
> von sîner hôhen werdekeit,
> und wie er den ruoft erstreit
> undr al den Sarrazînen,
> daz er sich kunde pînen
> von hôher kost in wîbe gebot
> ouch durch sîner vriwende nôt,
> bärlîch im selben ouch ze wer.
> undr al dem Terramêres her
> was ninder bezzer rîter dâ,
> denne Arofel von Persîâ.

---

69   Friedrich Maurer writes that *Willehalm* is Wolfram's critique of the knightly ideal
     of honour, a concept Wolfram sees as central to human existence (409, 420).

Gyburge milte was geslaht
von im: er hetez dar zuo brâht,
daz ninder kein sô miltiu hant
bî sînen zîten was bekant.

(*Wh.* 77, 24 – 78, 22)

[King Pantanor once gave a sword to Salatre, who gave it to king Antikote, who gave it to Essere, the emeral, who gave – this beautifully decorated sword – to Arofel the bold, who was not given to relenting either. Thus the sword passed from hand to hand until it came to the Persan [sic], Arofel, who bore it bravely and wielded it courageously, for he was skilled in fighting and never let anyone outstrip him in pursuing renown. I could tell you a great deal about his nobility, and about how he gained the reputation among the Saracens of venturing much in the service of ladies and for the sake of any friends in trouble and, of course, in order to defend himself. In the whole of Terramer's army there was no better knight than Arofel of Persia. Giburc's generosity came from the same family as his, and he himself excelled to such an extent that no more generous hand was known anywhere so long as he was alive.][70]

Arofel is described as bold, loyal and generous and as a performer of services to ladies; in short, he possesses all of the qualities of an ideal knight. Wolfram also writes that this nobility is a family trait from his Saracen lineage; he is related to Gyburg, whose nobility is well-known. Wolfram's descriptions of Arofel as a shining example of chivalry centre on his inner ideals and on his sword. That Arofel's sword has an illustrious history indicates that he is a worthy knight just as much as the descriptions of his chivalric qualities. Arofel is, however, bested by Willehalm, who cuts his exposed thigh and he offers an oath of surrender, promising Willehalm riches beyond measure to spare his life.[71]

helt, dun hâst deheinen prîs,
ob du mir nimst mîn halbez lebn:
du hâst mir freuden tôt gegebn.

(*Wh.* 79, 22–4)

---

70   Gibbs and Johnson, 51–2.
71   This duel is investigated in more detail in the section 'Arofel' in Chapter 4.

[Noble hero [...] you will gain no honour if you kill me now that I am half-dead, and you have already slain my joy.][72]

There follows a conversation between the two combatants, during which Arofel tries to reason with Willehalm. Willehalm will hear none of it and angrily blames him for the death of Vivianz; nor will he listen to Arofel's pleas or to his reasons for leaving Persia (this being his ten nephews, who are in his care). That Wolfram includes this explanation as the reason for Arofel's being part of Terramer's attacking forces says much for Arofel's sense of duty and devotion to his kinsmen – Willehalm also has had nephews under his charge and the Christian knightly practice of honouring and caring for kinsmen would have been a trait instantly recognizable as noble by the medieval audience.

Willehalm, nonetheless, quickly kills Arofel; he then strips him of his armour and beheads him. His death is punctuated by Wolfram with the lines: 'da erschein der minne ein flüstic tac. noch solden kristenlîchiu wîp klagen sîn ungetouften lîp' [it was a day of loss for love and Christian ladies should still mourn the death of this heathen man] (*Wh.* 81, 20–2). Willehalm's next action is to remove his own armour and exchange it for Arofel's better and more costly armour (though what becomes of the broken straps that held Arofel's shield and hauberk in place is not explicitly revealed). This is a disguise that Wolfram suggests will work against him when he arrives at the gates of Orange. As his horse, Puzzat (Baucent in *Aliscans*) is badly wounded, Willehalm also trades his horse for Arofel's mount, Volatin.

Again, the emphasis of the Christian polemic of Crusade ideology can be questioned, as in *Aliscans* the tone is quite different between the combatants. Guillaume encounters Aérofle, whose prowess is described in his appearance rather than through inner qualities: he carries a sword a fathom long and rides a charger big enough to carry two fully armed men at full speed for a day without sweating. Guillaume likes the horse and tries to make peace with Aérofle. Aérofle responds by insulting Guillaume and

---

72   Gibbs and Johnson, 52.

his religion, telling him that the only way he will make peace is if Guillaume rejects Christianity and returns Orange and Guiborc to the Saracens. When Guillaume refuses, he is met with further religious insults from Aérofle. Guillaume plucks a lance from the ground and the fight begins. They hurl themselves at each other, wounding each other each time they meet. Finally, Aérofle's leg is exposed and Guillaume cuts it off. It is Guillaume's sword, Joyeuse, that is lauded instead of Aérofle's, and it is compared to Roland's Durendal. When Aérofle asks ransom, Guillaume refuses and beheads him. He then takes Aérofle's armour and horse.

Whereas in *Aliscans*, the mere fact that opponents like Aérofle and Esmeré are heathens justifies, for the audience, their deaths at the hands of a Christian knight, there is introspection and afterthought in *Willehalm*. There is none of the boyish naiveté of Parzival, who kills Ither for his red armour, ignorant of the code of combat; rather, Wolfram is at pains to depict the very real consequences of grief and blind vengeance in battle, and the practical consideration of returning to Orange in worn armour on an injured horse (for such a disguise had served him well in the past – in *Charroi* and *Prise*).[73] This is an action that will return to haunt the protagonist, for not only does Willehalm later lament the killing of the distinguished knight, he must also approach Orange twice in Saracen armour, provoking questions as to his identity.

Upon returning with Loys and the reinforcements to the monastery outside Orléans where he left Arofel's costly shield on his way to Montlaon, Willehalm reflects upon his actions in the combat, recognizing that he has committed a dishonourable act which has, by way of love's justice, cost him possession of the shield.

> mîn hant iedoch den selben sluoc,
> sînen bruoder den getiwerten,
> vor wîben den gehiwerten.
> ich hân der minnen hulde
> verloren durch die schulde:

---

73   Guillaume entered both Nîmes and Orange to conquer them by disguising himself as a Saracen in *Le Charroi de Nîmes* and *La Prise d'Orange*.

ob ich minne wolde gern,
ich mües ir durch den zorn enbern,
wand ich Arofele nam den lîp,
den immer klagent diu werden wîp.
(*Wh.* 204, 22–30)

[My hand has slain that man who wore the crown in Samargone in Persia, in the presence of the noble princes, Terramer's cherished brother, who was favoured by the ladies. For this reason I have lost the favour of Love. If I were to desire Love, I should nevertheless have to do without it because of Love's anger towards me, for I took the life of Arofel whom noble women will bewail forever.][74]

By presenting the Saracen adversary as an honourable knight who respects a code of chivalry, love and duty to kinsmen, and does not attack the religion of his Christian adversary, Wolfram asks the audience to reflect upon the actions taken and whether they are honourable. Is it honourable for Willehalm to kill a noble knight only because he is not a Christian? What will the cost be to Willehalm's honour in doing so? Willehalm feels he has committed a sin against *Minne* and the price is Arofel's shield – the booty Willehalm gained by killing him.

Loyalty and solidarity

ez enwart nie man sô künnehaft,
durch die wir dienen müezen.
(*Wh.* 141, 28–9)

[Never did a man have so many relatives for whose sake we have to fight.][75]

Closely linked to honour in the values of chivalry were the feudal ideals of loyalty in vassalage and loyalty to kin and clan. The most striking example of the importance of these ideals in *Willehalm* is in the court scene at Montlaon, where it can be said that the final battle is won, rather than on

---

74   Gibbs and Johnson, 108.
75   Gibbs and Johnson, 80.

the battlefield itself, and both loyalty in vassalage and family solidarity are central to the eventual victory that is gained by Willehalm.

When Willehalm arrives at Montlaon, he is armed and dirty, looking fierce and wearing the armour of Arofel. He refuses food, drink and bedding, as he has promised Gyburg that he will take no comfort until she has been relieved in Orange. In addition, it is a *Hoftag*, a day on which vassals come to pay court, to renew vows of fealty and to exchange advice with the king. Of the nobles who are in Montlaon, none acknowledges Willehalm, leaving him to himself under a tree outside the palace in disgrace. The queen, who is Willehalm's sister, and her husband, King Loys, see him outside but refuse to let him in, knowing that he has come to ask for help which they do not wish to give.[76]

When looking out from the palace at the man under the tree, Willehalm's sister, assuming that he has come to ask for resources for another conquest, recognizes him and gives orders to lock the gates and to turn Willehalm away should he knock. This act is far worse than the silent disdain of the nobles, for Loys is Willehalm's liege-lord and the queen is his family. The royal couple are weak, disrespecting the value of vassalage and kinship, and the responsibility that accompanies it, in favour of the preservation of their own personal comfort. Willehalm remarks that by refusing to acknowledge him, the king and queen have disgraced their court, a court which he served under the rulership of Charlemagne: 'die

---

76　It is perhaps interesting to note that, while Loys does not speak to the Marquis until he enters the palace in *Willehalm*, in *Aliscans* Louis leans out of the window to show him that his appearance is unfit to pay court: 'Looïs prist un baston de pomier / A la fenestre s'est alez apoier' [Louis holds a branch of apple in his hand at the window] (*Alisc.* LXIV, 2872–3). That he holds a branch of apple is worthy of mention in that apples can connote either fame or a charm for deceit. However, in the 'M' and 'S' MSS, Louis holds *un baston d'allier*, a mustard sprig, indicating indifference. In either case, the symbolic language of gesture and appearance is significant. Though the symbolism of flowers and plants was largely a Victorian occupation, we know that it has been in practice since at least the time of the Persian empire. See *Collier's Cyclopedia of Commercial and Social Information and Treasury of Useful and Entertaining Knowledge*, Nugent Robinson, ed. (New York: P.F. Collier, 1882).

hânt des hoves unprîs getân, daz ich beleip sus wîslôs' [they have disgraced
the court leaving me unattended so] (*Wh.* 131, 12–13).

When Willehalm enters the palace the next day, amongst the assembled nobles, he confronts the king immediately. He reminds Loys that he
is avoiding his duty and dishonouring his station by failing to acknowledge
his vassal and that it was Willehalm who served Loys's father and secured
the crown for him as well as the loyalty of the nobles who doubted Loys's
capability to be sovereign. Then Willehalm delivers his most forceful blow:
he threatens to withdraw the fealty that put Loys in power: 'Ouwê der mis-
sewende, daz ich mîne hende zwischen de iweren ie gebôt!' [Alas, that I ever
had the misfortune of placing my hands between yours!] (*Wh.* 146, 1–3).[77]
After Willehalm's outburst, he is greeted warmly and enthusiastically by his
brothers, who offer their support and embrace him in front of the king.
Loys is naturally shaken and he begins a contrite offer to Willehalm.

Blancheflor earns worse treatment from her angry brother when, after
the king acquiesces to Willehalm's request for support, she interjects with
reservations, disregarding her duty to intercede on Willehalm's behalf: 'mir
ist lieber daz er warte her, dan daz ich sînre genâde ger' [I would rather have
him serve us than seek his favour myself] (*Wh.* 147, 9–10).[78] Willehalm's
anger turns from the king towards his sister; he tears the crown from her
head, insulting her and threatening her life with his sword. In *Aliscans*,
Guillaume viciously insults Blancheflor, calling her such things as 'pute
lisse provee' and 'putein folee' [veritable filthy bitch; stupid whore], even
going so far as to describe her motivations and inclinations during acts of
infidelity and lecherousness, before finally threatening her life.[79] However,
the earlier style of the *chanson de geste* seems to be too harsh for Wolfram
here: in *Willehalm*, Blancheflor is not insulted until after she has fled to
her room, i.e., he does not say these things in her presence. Even then,
Wolfram admits to his audience that 'die namn het ich bekennet, ob ich
die wolte vor iu sagen: nu muoz ich si durh zuht verdagen' [I would have

---

77   Gibbs and Johnson, 81.
78   Gibbs and Johnson, 82.
79   *Alisc.* LXIX.

said those names, if I had wanted to say them in your presence, but I must suppress them out of propriety] (*Wh.* 153, 4–6).[80] He adds:

> er schalt se et mêre denne genuoc
> ob er ie manheit getruoc,
> oder ob er ie gedâhte
> daz er sîn dienst brâhte
> durch herzen gir in wîbe gebot,
> ob er freude oder nôt
> ie enpfienc durh wîbes minne,
> an sînem manlîchem sinne
> was doch die kiusche zuht betrogen.
> (*Wh.* 153, 4–6; 7–15)

[Still, he insulted her more than enough. If he had ever exhibited manliness, or if he ever intended following his heart's desire, to put his service at the disposal of ladies, and if he ever received joy or sorrow for the sake of a lady's love, then chaste propriety was done a disservice in his 'manly' behaviour now.][81]

Here Wolfram's reaction to the earlier French epic style demonstrates a respect for propriety and reflection on actions and their motivations that did not feature as much in *Aliscans*, though the emphasis on loyalty remains central.[82]

Willehalm's anger and actions are only checked by their mother, Irmschart, who throws herself between the margrave and the queen. Loys again reminds the court and perhaps himself that Willehalm is his vassal and that the wrong he has done to Willehalm should be put before the princes, appealing to Willehalm's sense of propriety. Willehalm has put the compliance of the king to his demands in jeopardy with his punishment of Blancheflor for disregarding clan loyalty, indicating the importance of family solidarity over vassalage. His niece, Alyze, later approaches him to

---

80   Gibbs and Johnson, 85.
81   Gibbs and Johnson, 85.
82   Blancheflor's depiction in both texts, the way she is treated so harshly by both Guillaume and the poets and why, is treated in detail in Hathaway, 'Women at Montlaon'.

appeal on behalf of her mother the queen, reminding him of his familial duty as well: 'wer hât dich zorn gelêret, gein der tumben muoter mîn? diu doch dîn swester solte sîn, ob sich diu kan versprechen, wiltu daz danne rechen, dâ von sich krenket unser art' [who has made you angry toward my foolish mother? If she, who is supposed to be your sister, makes a slip of the tongue, and if you want to take revenge for that, then our whole family will suffer] (*Wh.* 157, 12–17).[83] In both texts, it is the display of Narbonnais solidarity that finally persuades Loys to lend support to Willehalm.

Throughout the scenes at Montlaon, clan solidarity and loyalty in vassalage is emphasized. In this, *Aliscans* does not differ. That the importance of kinship was so prevalent in the *chanson-de-geste* material can perhaps be explained, as Koss writes, in the fact that 'the individual relied on a family or lineage, as much as on any personal or individual trait, to supply a sense of social identity.'[84] Koss also sums up the function of kinship and its duties in the stories, pointing out that a kin group in the *chansons de geste* 'often comprised several generations and numerous degrees of consanguinity, as well as relatives by marriage. It was to this group that loyalty was due, and which stood as a source of comfort, assistance, protection, and justice […] or the exaction of vengeance.'[85] Such was the extent of the influence and importance of kinship in these stories that Koss, citing Frappier and Wathelet-Willem, recognizes it is not only possible but also probable that 'the family unit served as the breeding ground for the *chansons* themselves'[86] which came to celebrate the illustrious lineage of Guillaume d'Orange in this cycle. That kinship features so strongly in *Willehalm* would indicate that this kind of solidarity was still understood and recognized more than a century after the *chansons de geste* were composed and also suggests that it was a key influence on the characterization of the individual knight-hero who figured so profoundly in romance.

83   Gibbs and Johnson, 86.
84   Koss, 1.
85   Koss, 1.
86   Koss, 1.

As well as their respect for kinship, the knights and ladies in Wolfram's *Willehalm*, Christian and Saracen, are measured by their honour and loyalty, central values in Wolfram's chivalry. Richey also recognizes this emphasis on honour and loyalty, in which 'lies a firm recognition of help and fellowship – *triuwe* – as forming the chief cornerstone of that noble structure.'[87] It is this that facilitates redemption from the sin and dishonour caused by suffering: Willehalm's grief at Vivianz's death; his reaction to killing Arofel in disregard of honour in combat; and his dishonour before the court at Montlaon. The loyalty of his family and the fulfilment of the duties of his liege-lord, the king, to him offer the promise of redemption and are under scrutiny. It is the honour, solidarity and loyalty of chivalry which determine the moral victory and the martial outcome of the battles in *Willehalm*.

Religion and 'Minnedienst'

nâch senfte hoeret ungemach
(*Wh.* 95, 10)

[Suffering and solace go hand in hand.][88]

Though Saracens in *Willehalm* are depicted with the same values of chivalry and service to love, the same ideals and ethics of knighthood as their Christian counterparts, the Saracen chivalry is lacking for Wolfram because of religion and thus conversion to Christianity would complete an otherwise exemplary chivalry which only serves love. Service for love is important in Wolfram's concept of chivalry, but, as it is seen in *Parzival*, he is also clear that it should not be the only motivation. That Wolfram links service to love closely to the Christian relationship with God poses the problem of how to reconcile the two in the chivalry of *Willehalm*. The importance of Wolfram's *Minne* reveals itself in how the questioning of the Christian moral imperative in dealing with heathens is resolved.

---

87   Richey, 125.
88   Gibbs and Johnson, 59.

Love for God vs *Minnedienst*

The role that *Minne* assumes in *Willehalm* is, like Wolfram's chivalry, one that is applied to a more lifelike and less fantastical setting. It encompasses a fellowship of man and woman that is a source of consolation, comfort and hope. Willehalm returns to his fortress at Orange twice and each time he confides in Gyburg, taking comfort in his relationship with her as liege-lady, friend and lover. In this, *Willehalm* differs from the earlier *Aliscans*. On his return from losing the first battle at Aliscans, Guillaume waits only long enough to have his wounds tended by Guiborc before setting out for Montlaon. Similarly, upon his return with reinforcements, Guillaume and Guiborc enjoy a few embraces at the window of the palace before reviewing the reinforcements.

In contrast to their French counterparts, Willehalm and Gyburg lament together the devastating losses of the first battle *before* Gyburg removes Willehalm's armour, an act that is narrated at length, followed by an intimate interlude. Gyburg then offers up a prayer while Willehalm sleeps. Willehalm asks for her order as liege-lady before departing to secure reinforcements and pledges that he will serve no other lady until his return. Wolfram expands upon the theme of intimacy when Willehalm returns again to Orange, using the removal of armour and description of clothing and skin to set the atmosphere as well as representing a symbolic state of affairs between the margrave and his city and its queen. More time is spent at the window as Willehalm and Gyburg recline together in its recess, watching the arriving troops and discussing the situation. Gyburg provides refreshment for Willehalm's knights from the stores of her beleaguered citadel, presenting herself, her ladies and the palace beautifully and opulently as inspiration for the arriving knights of Willehalm's clan. They then go together to meet Willehalm's father, Heimrich, and the rest of Willehalm's family. When all are cared for, Willehalm and Gyburg enjoy another intimate interlude and Wolfram again speaks of the intertwining of joy and sorrow, as well as of redemption. The next day, when the French troops arrive, a banquet is held and speeches are delivered at the war council before the battle.

The duty of service to liege-ladies and women keeps stable a necessary element of twelfth-century vassalage and social order which, when seen as inspired by service to love, is perhaps more refined and ethically agreeable in comparison to the earlier feudal necessities of power and might for protection. Alyze and Irmschart are the gracious inspirations for adherence to the duty and service to love in the Montlaon scenes. It is Alyze who stays Willehalm's anger at his sister, her mother, by reminding him of his duty towards courtly honour and it is Irmschart who inspires deferential obedience and influence as matriarch of Heimrich's clan. Blancheflor, too, later redeems herself in *Willehalm*, regaining her position as a worthy liege-lady. These women in their embodiment of liege-ladies stay tempers, resolve conflict and motivate and influence actions. However, Wolfram's attitude towards the duty to love as being the knight's only motivation is clear, for without the spiritual bond with God and the Christian veneration of Christ, this service is nothing but a hollow shell:

> von gesteine und von golde
> was rîchiu kost niht vermiten
> in die banier was gesniten.
> Amor der minne zêre
> mit eime tiuren gêre
> durh daz wan er nâh minnen ranc.
> (*Wh.* 24, 2–7)

[Expense was of no account, where costly jewels and gold were concerned. His banner was adorned with a precious spear in honour of Amor, the god of Love, for this knight was fighting in the service of Love.][89]

Wolfram describes the motivation of the knight Noupatris as beautiful to behold, but his naive striving for the love of ladies, coupled with his not being Christian, leaves him lacking. The god Amor serves him poorly; he dies unobserved because his compatriots are themselves striving in the service of love.

---

89   Gibbs and Johnson, 27.

ungesehen und unvernomn
was mangem heiden dâ sîn tôt
der doch sîn verch en wâge bôt
durh prîs und durh der wîbe lôn.
                        (*Wh.* 25, 6–9)

[His death went unseen and unheard by many heathens there, who were themselves
risking their lives for glory and the favour of ladies.][90]

The embodiment of Christian love on earth is the marriage between
husband and wife, and the union between Willehalm and Gyburg is given
great importance, especially since it was love for Willehalm that inspired
Gyburg to convert to Christianity. It is also this love which results in so
much sorrow: 'Arabeln Willalm erwarp, dar umbe unschuldic volc erstarp'
[Willehalm won the love of Arabel, and because of this innocent people
died] (*Wh.* 7, 27–8).[91] Wolfram often couples joy with sorrow, and love
with suffering: 'nach senfte hoeret ungemach' and 'Arabele Gyburc, ein
wîp, zwir genant, minne und dîn lîp, sich nu mit jâmer flihtet' [suffering
and solace go hand in hand [...] Arabel-Giburc, one woman with two
names, love and you have become intertwined with sorrow] (*Wh.* 95, 10;
30, 21–3).[92] It is for this reason that love for God can be seen to be at odds
with the duty to *Minne* in *Willehalm*, suggesting that only faith in God
can lead to salvation, and not *Minne*.[93]

Wolfram, however, does not seem to place one over the other in rank,
or to depict one as at odds with the other; rather, he presents *Minnedienst*
and love for God side by side, just as he does joy and sorrow, love and
suffering, and the spiritual and the secular.[94] In *Willehalm*, love for God
and *Minnedienst* each cause joy and sorrow, and indeed Wolfram suggests
that there can never be one without the other: 'jâ sol diu manlîch arbeit,
werben liep unde leit. die zwêne geselleclîche site, ouch der wâren wîpheit

90   Gibbs and Johnson, 28.
91   Gibbs and Johnson, 21.
92   Gibbs and Johnson, 59, 30.
93   Miklautsch, 'Minne-flust', 233.
94   See Wessel-Fleinghaus, 44.

volgent mite, sît daz man freude ie trûrens jach.' [A man's efforts should be directed towards joy *and* sorrow, and true womanliness also knows this dual companionship, since sorrow has always been associated with joy.][95] (*Wh.* 280, 7–11) It is human love that draws people together, acting as the motivation for Saracen conversion to Christianity, and no amount of humiliation, reasoning or imposed suffering, will persuade a Saracen towards conversion otherwise. When Rennewart is given to Alyze as a playmate, he tells her of the humiliation he suffered at the hands of Loys, who pressured him to convert, with the result that he resisted. Finally, he is denied the company of Alyze. Later, in Willehalm's charge, Rennewart finds in Alyze more than companionship: 'ir zweier liebe urhap, volwuohs: die brâhtens an den tôt, und liten nâch ein ander nôt' [The seed of their love grew to maturity, and they sustained it to the end of their lives, each enduring grief on account of the other] (*Wh.* 284, 14–16).[96] Here Wolfram describes a love that in its nature embraces both joy and sorrow. This can be seen as a secular model of the celestial love exemplified in the Christian story of the crucifixion, in which both the joys and sorrows of love are embraced and the secular and spiritual are united. Gyburg, Willehalm's converted liege-lady, is the one who calls the audience's attention to this union in her conversation with her father, Terramer, during the siege. When Terramer asks Gyburg to reconsider her position and to end the war by converting back to Islam, she refuses, replying:

> dô Jêsuses mennischeit
> der tôt am kriuce müete,
> innen des sîn leben blüete
> ûz der gotlîchen sterke.
> lieber vater, nu merke:
> innen des diu mennischeit erstarp,
> diu gotheit ir daz lebn erwarp.

95   Gibbs and Johnson, 143.
96   Gibbs and Johnson, 145. This is the extent of Wolfram's description of Rennewart's future activity in *Willehalm*, whereas in *Aliscans*, he converts and marries Alyze. In *Willehalm*, however, his future conversion is not indicated, showing that *Minnedienst* could precede conversion and love for God.

Möhten hôher sîn nu dîne gote,
sô wolt ich doch ze sîme gebote
unz an den tôt belîben,
der ie werden wîben
vor ûz ir rehts alsô verjach,
daz man in dienestlîchen sach
under schiltlîchem dache
bî sôlhem ungemache
dâ man den lîp durch wirde zert
unt dem laster von dem prîse wert.
                    (*Wh.* 219, 24 – 220, 10)

[While Jesus, the man, was struggling with death on the Cross, His life was blossoming forth from His divine strength. Father dear, pay heed to what I am saying: while human life was dying, the Godhead was achieving life for humanity. Even if your gods were greater, I should still want to remain in the command of him who always recognized an obligation to noble women especially and was therefore often seen in their service, wearing a shield and performing such feats, in which for the sake of honour, the body is not spared and is preserved from dishonour by fame.][97]

Gyburg parallels the dual nature of love, joy, and suffering: the *Minnedienst* of Willehalm and the Christian knight parallels the trials of Christ at crucifixion and points to the assurance of redemption and salvation for humanity. The chivalry of the heathens lacks this assurance. She tells Terramer that she serves both Willehalm and God, and concludes that she will remain true to her Christian baptism: 'ich diente im und der hoesten hant. Mîns toufes schôn ich gerne' [I have given myself to Willehalm and to God, and I will guard my baptism] (*Wh.* 220, 30 – 221, 1).

When the speeches are concluded after the war council, before the second battle, Wolfram (through Gyburg) talks about the relationship between *Minnedienst* and love for God:

Ich diene der künsteclîchen hant
für der heiden got Tervigant:
ir kraft hât mich von Mahumeten
unders toufes zil gebeten.

des trag ich mîner mâge haz;
und der getouften umbe daz:
durh menneschlîcher minne gît
si waenent daz ich fuogte disen strît.
dêswâr ich liez ouch minne dort,
[...]
ey Willalm, rehter punjûr,
daz dir mîn minne ie wart sô sûr!
waz werder diet ûz erkorn
in dîme dienste hânt verlorn
ir lîp genendeclîche!
der arme und der rîche,
nu geloubt daz iwerr mâge flust
mir sendet jâmer in die brust:
für wâr mîn vreude ist mit in tôt.

(Wh. 310, 1–9, 21–9)

[I serve the Hand of God the Artist in place of the heathen God Tervigant. Its power has led me away from Mahmete and towards baptism. Because of that I am enduring the hatred of my kinsmen, and of the Christians, too, for this reason: they believe I brought about this conflict out of desire for human love. It is true that I left love behind me there [...] Alas, Willehalm, true fighter, that my love should ever have become so bitter for you! How many supreme men have lost their lives gallantly in your service! Rich and poor alike, all of you must believe that the loss of your kinsmen sears my breast. Indeed, my joy lies slain with them.][98]

Gyburg speaks to the Frenchmen as she spoke to her father, reminding them of the grace of God and of the difference between Christian love and *Minnedienst* without that spiritual power. *Minnedienst* serves as a courtly means of addressing and measuring spiritual and religious belief. After the victory of the second battle, Willehalm laments the losses incurred by the entire campaign, relating the love between man and woman to spirituality, addressing Christ:

---

98   Gibbs and Johnson, 157.

sît entwarf dîn selbes hant
daz der vriunt vriundinne vant
an dem arme sîn durch minne.
reht manlîche sinne
dienent ûf wîplîchen lôn.
manegen sperkraches dôn
hân ich gehôrt umb ein wîp,
diu nu leider mînen lîp
mac dirre flust ergetzen niht:
mîn herze iedoch ir minne giht.
wan dîn helfe unde ir trôst,
ich waere immer unrelôst
vor jâmers gebende:
                    (*Wh.* 456, 9–21)

[It was Your Hand that ordained that man should have woman in his arms for love.
Men of proper manly spirit serve for women's reward. I have heard many a spear break
in the service of a woman, who now unfortunately cannot recompense me for this
loss, but my heart still declares my love for her. Were it not for Your help and her
consolation, I would be ever unrelieved of the bonds of misery.][99]

Ortmann notes that the Christian dogmatic premises of the old historical poems being interpreted by knightly standards marked a new quality in the hero, whose chivalry worked as an integrative power.[100] Though
Miklautsch is in disagreement with Ortmann that *Minne* holds the promise
of absolution, being a utopian quality and symbolizing God on earth,[101]
Wolfram's message is that, just as suffering and joy go together, so too does
Christian *Minnedienst* and love for God. Even in *Parzival*, we can see the
notions of a balance between and the interdependency of joy and grief.[102]
The focus in *Willehalm* is on comfort, support and redemption from the
necessary suffering, misery and guilt of the courtly knight-hero.[103] While
service to ladies and love and its reward are not the deciding motif in the

99   Gibbs and Johnson, 220.
100   See Ortmann, 114.
101   See Miklautsch, 'Minne-flust,' 234; and Ortmann, 114–16.
102   See: Lofmark, *Rennewart*, 230.
103   See Ortmann, 115.

chivalry of *Willehalm*, they are an integral and indispensable part of the character and spirituality of the courtly knight-hero.

The quest for a peaceful coexistence

The obstacle to the peaceful coexistence of temporal and spiritual values in *Willehalm* is the war that must be fought. The Saracen attack and siege of Orange must be answered in order to preserve Willehalm's claim to Orange, the legitimacy of his power and the justification of a Christian southern march. Willehalm, already an accomplished and experienced knight at the beginning of the story, recognizes that this obstacle is insurmountable without a high physical and spiritual price being exacted; he also realizes that his developed inner chivalry must serve him well (and he serve it in return) and that his service must be directed impeccably if he is to succeed. The very title by which Wolfram's text is known, *Willehalm*, suggests that it is more about the character himself, his inner conflicts and values, than is its source, *La Bataille d'Aliscans*. As with *Minnedienst* and the Christian love for God, Wolfram depicts the fallibility and imperfection of the knight – a human being – by presenting those elements that would seem to be at odds as coexisting side by side, integral parts of each other. In *Willehalm*, chivalry is shown from a contemplative angle: 'not the grace and glory alone, but the shadow-side also,'[104] as Willehalm questions his motive for going to war both before and after he has attained victory.

Burghart Wachinger uses *Willehalm* as an example to support his view that, whereas the French epic maintained a black-and-white stance in the depiction of heathens and Christians, the German only depicted grey areas.[105] However, Wolfram's views suggest more of a partnership between the opposing elements: in his world, although the heathens are not Christians, they can still be appraised according to their code of chivalry and *Minnedienst*, in which the dual components of joy and sorrow, pain

---

104 Richey, 125.
105 Wachinger, 57.

and solace, and spiritual and temporal consequences always accompany
each other. It is Gyburg, in her speech to the French reinforcements, who
expresses the fundamental basis of the dual nature of divine creation:

> sîn erbarmede rîchiu minne
> elliu wunder gar besliuzet,
> des triwe niht verdriuzet,
> sine trage die helfeclîche hant
> diu bêde wazzer unde lant
> vil künsteclîch alrêrst entwarf,
> und des al diu crêatiure bedarf
> die der himel umbesweifet hât.
> diu selbe 'han&tcirc; die plânêten lât
> ir poynder vollen gâhen
> bêdiu verre und nâhen.
> swie si nimmer ûf gehaldent,
> si warment unde kaldent:
> etswenne'z îs si schaffent:
> dar nâch si boume saffent,
> sô diu erde ir gevidere rêrt
> unde si der meie lêrt
> ir mûze alsus volrecken,
> nâch den rîfen bluomen stecken.
>
> (*Wh.* 309, 12–30)

[His love which is so full of mercy embraces all miracles and in His loving loyalty
He will not cease to hold out the helping Hand which first brought into being both
land and water: all creatures contained beneath the heavens have need of this. That
same Hand allows the planets to run their full courses both near and far. Never
ceasing in their activity, they bestow warmth and cold alike, sometimes creating ice,
then bringing sap to the trees so that the earth may seem to be shedding its plumage
and the month of May instructs the earth to accomplish its moulting process and
to bring forth flowers in succession to the frost.][106]

Gyburg, her love for Willehalm and her conversion to Christianity
symbolize the divine gift of redemption after suffering and sorrow. This hope
for the future is personified in the liege-lady here, comforting Willehalm

---

106 Gibbs and Johnson, 156–7.

after he has brought back the French reinforcements to relieve Orange and rescue her. Although the battle remains to be fought and losses remain to be suffered, and although the losses already suffered cannot be altered, Willehalm and Gyburg take solace in their love and companionship upon his return, with support from the Holy Roman crown:

> an sînem arm ein swankel rîs
> Uz der süezen minne'rblüete.
> Gyburc mit kiuscher güete
> sô nâhe an sîne brust sich want,
> daz im nu gelten wart bekant:
> allez daz er ie verlôs,
> dâ für er si ze gelte kôs.
> ir minne im sölhe helfe tuot,
> daz des marcgrâven trûric muot
> wart mit vreuden undersnitn.
> diu sorge im was sô verre entritn,
> si möhte erreichen niht ein sper.
> Gyburc was sîner freuden wer.
>
> (*Wh.* 279, 30 – 280, 13)

[In his arms now a slender shoot was blossoming forth from sweet love. In her pure tenderness Giburc snuggled so close against his chest that he was recompensed: he claimed her as his compensation for everything that he had ever lost. Her love afforded him such aid that the Margrave's sadness was streaked with joy. Sorrow had ridden away from him so far that no spear could have reached it. Giburc was the guarantor of his joy.][107]

Through Gyburg's love for him, which led to her conversion to Christianity, Willehalm receives confirmation of the promise of redemption after suffering and of his duty to service. He is bound by Christian chivalry, service to his liege-lady and duty to fallen kinsmen to return the assault on Orange and drive the Saracens from French soil and it is this act that will result in the deaths of Christian and Saracen knights, his family and Gyburg's.

---

107 Gibbs and Johnson, 143.

Willehalm recognizes from the beginning that once the war has begun and once Orange has been threatened by the Saracens, he must follow through with the inevitable course of action: to secure reinforcements by leaving Orange and Gyburg in danger and to return to defeat the Saracen forces. Alternatives to this course of action are only passing thoughts, such as that which Willehalm twice asks Gyburg to consider before leaving for Montlaon:

> Nu sag ûf dîne wîpheit
> ist dir mîn dar rîten leit
> od liep mîn hie belîben?
> swar mich dîn rât wil trîben
> dar wil ich kêrn unz an den tôt.
> dîn minne ie dienst mir gebôt
> sît mich enpfienc dîn güete
>   (*Wh.* 95, 29 – 96, 5)

> [Now tell me on your honour as a woman: will it grieve you if I ride off, or please you if I stay behind? Whichever way your counsel sends me, that is the direction which I shall take, even unto death. Your love has commanded my service ever since, in your goodness, you received me.][108]

Willehalm asks for Gyburg's directive before they discuss the situation, and again after they have taken consolation in each other: 'frowe, nu solt du sagen mir, belîbens ode rîtens rât: dîn gebot ietwederz hât' [my lady, you must advise me now whether to remain here or to ride away. Your command is all I need, in either case] (*Wh.* 103, 6–8).[109] He seeks the verbal endorsement of his wife as his liege-lady whose family will endure defeat and suffering should he abide by his Christian duty. She has chosen salvation through Christianity, keeps her vow to remain loyal to her new religion, and can expect the support and salvation promised to one of the Christian fold in the guise of Willehalm's kinsmen and feudal lord, the king. This dilemma puts them both in peril: in either case they will suffer

---

108   Gibbs and Johnson, 59–60.
109   Gibbs and Johnson, 63.

losses and also the guilt of being the cause of those deaths. In the end, Christian fortitude and the necessity to legitimize and hold a Christian Orange decide the course of action.

The motivation for the decision to go through with the battle is mentioned by Wolfram at the beginning of the story, when he reflects upon what might have spurred the Pfalzgraf Bertram to fight when he would much rather have fled:

> Bertram dô strîts ernande.
> seht ob in des mande
> Munschoy diu krîe:
> oder twancs in âmîe?
> oder müet in Viviânses nôt?
> oder ob sîn manheit gebôt
> daz er dâ prîs hât bejaget.
> hât mirz diu âventiure gesaget,
> sô sag ich iu durh wen er leit
> daz er mit Gorhande streit
> und Viviânsen lôste dan.
>
> (*Wh.* 42, 1–11)

[Berthram summoned his courage for battle. Did the cry 'Monjoie!' urge him to do that? Or did a lady's love compel him? Or did Vivianz' predicament move him? Or did his manly nature order him to seek renown there? If my source has told me, then I shall tell you on whose account he endured fighting with Gorhant and rescued Vivianz.][110]

The answer does not come in simple terms, for Bertram is taken prisoner, along with seven others, by Halzebier and they are held captive on a Saracen ship until Rennewart frees them in the second battle. Upon their release by Rennewart, they secure mounts and engage in the battle alongside the Christians, going on to achieve victory. Would Willehalm embark upon this course of action for the salvation of Orange, for the love of Gyburg, to avenge the death of his nephew Vivianz or to gain fame in battle? He was already renowned for his martial abilities, which had gained him land,

110   Gibbs and Johnson, 35.

riches and the love of ladies. He is sorely grieved for Vivianz, but this seems to be more of a motivator for the extended clan than for Willehalm personally, after he has slain Arofel in anger. Orange represents the 'prize', the inheritance that he will leave his clan, and Gyburg is closely tied to it, for she, who is also his prize, was the motive for the conquest. She also enabled Willehalm's taking of Orange, and legitimized it by her conversion and marriage to him. For Wolfram it is not this conquest alone which binds Gyburg to Willehalm; it is also the winning over of her heart in love and service, and her conversion to Christianity. This is the prize that motivated Willehalm more than any other: not *Minnedienst* alone but *Minnedienst* combined with a love for God that was strong enough to win Gyburg over to conversion and grant restitution and salvation. It is after the long separation and suffering that both Willehalm and Gyburg endure during his trip to Montlaon that this connection and balance between *Minnedienst* and love for God becomes clearer. Likewise, it is after the imprisonment on the Saracen ship that Bertram finds his mettle and strength in battle. Whether this parallel was intended by Wolfram must remain speculation, though the questioning of motive appears more clearly than in the French source, as Wolfram seems to have remarked.

Once the decision is made, however, it remains only for the events to be played out: for Willehalm to leave Gyburg defending Orange and ask his family and liege-lord for support troops; for him to bring back an army capable of annihilating the Saracens besieging Orange; and for him to defeat them, suffering the loss of illustrious knights belonging to both Willehalm's and Gyburg's families.

This dilemma is underscored by Wolfram in Willehalm's questioning of motives; this brings it to the foreground and allows the alternatives and consequences of action to take precedence. Christian knightly duty has consequences. Spiritually, Willehalm risks his salvation by slaying kin; temporally, he risks his power and happiness by putting his wife and heirs at risk. The consequences will emerge after the victory, which is why there is no jubilation and victory party after the second battle. Instead, there is prayer, lament, the quiet fortitude and resolve of serving chivalric honour by seeing the defeated Saracens safely to their ships instead of keeping them for gain in ransom and caring for the Saracen dead with honour. Willehalm's dilemma is that he risks his spiritual or his temporal honour and salvation; it is the preservation of and service to both that is desirable. A partnership of the temporal and spiritual seems to be the answer.

Attaining this balance between temporal and spiritual service and honour and maintaining that balance proves problematic, but Wolfram sees the striving towards that goal as worthy. Though Wolfram recognized that this coexistence would never be realized, the quest was nonetheless important. In this, *Willehalm* shows itself to be a product of the romance era. Typical of the romance genre, Cooper writes, 'is a concern with ideals, especially secular ideals, and with human perfectibility within a social context [...] even if perfection is not achieved, [...] the ideals themselves are not therefore treated with cynicism.'[111] It is not so much the struggle between people of different religions that is the problem but what is done about it by means of the ideals of spiritual and temporal chivalry. Willehalm serves both his temporal and spiritual honour in his behaviour towards the defeated Saracens, but there is no reconciliation and, as Gibbs and Johnson write, 'the problem remains, much as one may admire the words and the action of Willehalm, and acknowledge the enlightened nature of Wolfram himself.'[112] True, religious war and the security of Orange remain insoluble problems, but the focus must be seen to be upon the application of the ideals of spiritual and temporal chivalry.

A product of the French-influenced German courts of the early thirteenth century, Wolfram's *Willehalm* can be seen as the pinnacle of expression for a knighthood and chivalry conceived and refined by introspection, self-reflection and a deep sense of duty to love in its many manifestations. *Willehalm* expresses the inner striving for a balance of temporal rewards and honours with that of the ideals of spiritual chivalry that featured strongly in Wolfram's notion of divine love. Because of an old tradition of oral transmission of deeply rooted legend material in Germany, there was time for the image of the Saracen adversary to filter through to German poets

---

111   Cooper, 10.
112   Gibbs and Johnson, 273.

and audiences from sources predating the *chansons de geste* and Crusades, and for that image to mingle with the older Germanic material. This was an opportunity to see Saracen knights in a different way to the pagans described in the literature of the regions which were more immediately threatened by them and which had no oral traditions predating European Christianization.

In rewriting the *chanson-de-geste* material, Wolfram combines elements of the French Carolingian and Crusade epic with older Germanic themes of honour and predestined dilemmas, and with that of the *matière de Bretagne* that had become popular in the medieval world. This combination of diverse elements and themes, coupled with the self-reflection and spiritual undertones of a refined chivalry, furthered a philosophical questioning of ethics and justification for actions, and literature was the vehicle. Like the epic genre, people of the medieval world and their ideas were more mobile than previous scholarship has suggested. For Wolfram, the crowning achievement of Christian knighthood is finding harmony between duty to God and to the world, through divine love, the love of women and family and clan, thereby achieving redemption and salvation. Set amongst historical events, the imperfection of the human character and irreconcilable cultural and religious differences demand consideration and *Willehalm* suggests that all humans, despite these contradictions, can strive for a balance between the spiritual and the profane through a chivalry that combines spirituality, love and service without compromising one ideal for the other.

The examination of the themes and their development and background surrounding the depiction of the Saracens in *La Prise d'Orange*, *Aliscans* and *Willehalm* builds a framework around which specific Saracen characters and their roles in these texts can be explored. The element of political and practical motivation manifests itself in the importance of a feudal order, its power to legitimize conquest and its dependence upon loyalty in vassalage, symbolized in the conquest of heathen territory by and dependent upon baptism and vows of fealty. The other driving and legitimizing element in conquest and confrontation between Christian and Saracen in these texts is chivalry, as it developed in the twelfth century into a social institution as well as a spiritual ideal, encompassing service and love as the touchstones by which all knights, Christian and Saracen, are appraised in *Willehalm*.

In the following chapters we will become acquainted in more detail with the Saracen characters in the texts. The prominence of chivalry will reveal itself in these figures, as it had developed across continents, time and genres. The driving themes of the story and of chivalry are exemplified in the Saracen characters, culminating in the complex and eminent character of Gyburg/Guiborc, the converted Saracen queen of Orange, upon whose chivalry and direction of chivalric service rests the fate of Willehalm's own chivalry, his legitimacy as Margrave of Orange and the power and prominence of the Narbonnais clan.

CHAPTER 4

The Saracen as Protagonist

Deus, quel baron, s'oüst chrestïentét![1]

[God, what a baron! Were he only Christian!]

The role that the Saracen plays in *Willehalm* is one of prominence not just because he is a formidable enemy to the French empire. It is possible to speak of various Saracen figures as protagonists within *Willehalm*, where the roles they play intermingle with themes developed by Wolfram, those themes from the *chansons de geste* that develop key actions and plot substance. The treatment these Saracens receive by Wolfram differs in some measure from their depiction by the *jongleurs* in *Aliscans*. Commenting on Wolfram's innovations to Saracen characters in *Willehalm*, Lofmark writes:

> The characters who played minor parts in *Aliscans* or were little more than names gain most in stature by being integrated into the structure of the armies; many of them, particularly the Saracens, are at the same time integrated into the noble families by being related to the chief characters and are provided with fiefs or kingdoms [...] All this gives them quite a specific function and makes them important for their contribution to the whole action rather than as individuals.[2]

It is by such integration that Wolfram transforms these prominent Saracens into key figures who are seen by the audience as contributing to the broader plot as the story develops. They are given greater individual

---

1   *Chanson de Roland* 3164, about Baligan. Matthew Bennett points out that this is a 'stock phrase descriptive of noble Saracen knights' in the *chansons de geste*. Bennett, 105–6.
2   Lofmark, *Rennewart*, 86–7.

attention by Wolfram than by the *jongleurs* of *Aliscans* and are accorded more human and personal qualities, which allows insight into their thoughts and feelings and depicts them as characters with which the audience can identify. These Saracens also further the inner development of other main characters in *Willehalm* and in some cases they exemplify chivalric traits that Wolfram chooses to emphasize, contributing towards a message important to him.

The hitherto-received view that the Saracens of the *chansons de geste* are fundamentally two-dimensional and that those depicted in Wolfram's works are given more significance as characters has established a limitation on the wider understanding of earlier medieval narrative, if not on the understanding of the relationship between themes in *Willehalm* and its *chanson-de-geste* sources. Though Wolfram's Saracens are more developed and have more individual significance than their *Aliscans* counterparts, there are marked exceptions, illustrating that characters and attitudes in *Aliscans* served as clear precedents to Wolfram's depictions of the Saracens and their functions. Themes such as loyalty, solidarity and clan, important to Wolfram, were already strongly in play in the *chansons de geste* and he expands upon them in *Willehalm*, making use of the Saracen characters to exemplify these themes as well as newer themes such as love, chivalry and spirituality.

When these prominent Saracens are seen alongside their *Aliscans* counterparts, it becomes clear that Wolfram's depiction of them is not entirely new and that the Saracens of *Willehalm* had already undergone a literary transformation due to political and geographical changes, the shifting perspective of audiences and the influence of popular generic themes.[3] Because many of the *chansons de geste* are not studied in conjunction with the romance material contemporary with them, a gap has formed between the conception of the Saracens in each, affecting the perception

3   Ferrante describes how the depiction of Saracens and Arab life in *Prise d'Orange* 'indicates a closer acquaintance with that life than is found in other poems', illustrating how factors of time and political climate affect portrayals in literature. (27). See also Chapter 2, section: 'Genre'.

of the way they are depicted in *Willehalm* as compared to its sources. In effect, the Saracens in *Willehalm* differ from those in *Aliscans* only moderately: enough for Wolfram to engage his distinctive imaginative talent in the creation of his characters and his ingenuity of plot-weaving, but not enough to assert without reservation that their depiction is remarkably unprecedented.

As with the female characters, Wolfram's innovations to the prominent Saracens can be subtle, but the effects are far-reaching within *Willehalm*. Influenced by his German audience and its political and popular environment, Wolfram's Saracens convey a similar message about kinship, solidarity, chivalry and loyalty to that in the *chanson de geste*, but in a way more involved than in *Aliscans*. We will focus on several key Saracen characters whose depiction has gained from Wolfram's innovations: four prominent Saracen kings, those Saracens who are related to Willehalm by his marriage to Gyburg and Gyburg herself as protagonist. In inspecting these characters and their counterparts in Wolfram's source, we will see that their depiction in *Willehalm* is not so far from that of *Aliscans* in most cases and that Wolfram's innovations should be seen as valuable in themselves as well as valuable in relation to the message he is conveying in *Willehalm* and not hindered by the notion that Wolfram's image of the Saracen character differs so greatly from other medieval literature as to be very extraordinary.

Four Saracen Kings

The number of Saracen kings are numerous in *Willehalm* and almost every combatant met by a Christian knight is a king of some distant and exotic land. Willehalm himself faces fifteen of these kings during the first battle and we see a further twenty-three who died during it, lying on biers. In addition, Vivianz and his company encounter several kings and there are, of course, those kings who survive the second battle. On the whole, Wolfram, makes most of them of little consequence, as does *Aliscans*, with the notable exception of four significant figures.

In the characters of Arofel, Noupatris, Halzebier and Matribleiz, Wolfram takes some rather unidimensional Saracen figures who play little or no role at all in *Aliscans*, builds upon their reputations and develops their characters, fashioning four distinctive and remarkable figures. These kings become individual personalities with important roles and a specific purpose. Wolfram's reasons for the innovations to these four Saracen kings can be seen more clearly when compared to their *Aliscans* counterparts. By exploring the developments Wolfram makes to these characters, their purpose and role in *Willehalm* is clarified, as is Wolfram's message. Whereas in *Parzival* it was the Christian knight who conveyed a message of chivalry and conduct by his trials, in *Willehalm* it is the heathen knight and specifically these four kings from whom the Christian protagonists learn and through whom they are able to hone their chivalry.

Arofel

Most beautifully described of all the Saracen knights in *Willehalm* is Arofel, the king of Persia and Terramer's brother, who has brought his large and illustrious army across the sea to support the campaign. Wolfram's interpretation of the *Aliscans* counterpart, Aérofle, and his importance to the story is distinguishable in that it differs markedly from his source, *Aliscans*. Wolfram gives much more attention to Arofel's personal history, kin and deeds, to his appearance, his thoughts, principles and chivalry, and to his reasons for finding himself on the battlefield with Terramer's army. Though Arofel is killed in the first battle by Willehalm, the manner of his death is given a very different perspective from that of his counterpart in *Aliscans*, Aérofle, and Wolfram uses this as a recurring motif throughout the rest of the story, allowing Arofel's death to influence Saracen and Christian characters as well as the audience.

Presentation

From his first appearance, Arofel is presented as a capable and formidable knight, the commander of a great force who comes to the rescue of his countrymen when they have been overcome by Vivianz and Bertram: his arrival heralds the beginning of defeat for the Christians in the first battle. He is first mentioned by Wolfram as Terramer's loyal brother, the leader of a great force renowned for its knighthood:

> Terramêr was ir vatr:
> Arofeln sînen bruoder batr,
> und den starken Halzebier.
> die zwêne manec urssier
> in sîne helfe brâhten:
> wol si des gedâhten.
> Terramêrs rîcheit
> was kreftic wît unde breit
>   (*Wh.* 9, 21–8)

[Terramer, her [Gyburg's] father, summoned his brother Arofel and the mighty Halzebier, and these two men brought many warships to his aid. They were sincere in their intention. The power of Terramer was immense and extended far and wide.][4]

In just a passing mention of his name, Arofel's character has taken on the attributes for which he will be renowned in *Willehalm*: might and loyalty to kin. When he is next mentioned, Wolfram subtly and deftly builds upon this image.

> allererst ich nennens grife zuo
> Arofel der Persân,
> dem was in manegen landen lân
> prîs ze muoten und zer tjost.
> er het ouch dâ die hoehsten kost
> von soldiern und von mâgen:
> an sîme ringe lâgen
> zehen künege, sînes bruoder kint.
> der heiden rîterschaft ein wint
> was, wan die er fuorte.
>   (*Wh.* 29, 12–21)

---

4   Wolfram von Eschenbach. *Willehalm*, 21.

[Now here is a name. Arofel of Persia had been accorded fame in many lands, for multiple and single combat. Moreover, he was best provided of all those present with soldiers and kinsmen. In his camp were ten kings, his brother's children. Indeed, the heathen army was a mere nothing without those whom he was leading.][5]

Wolfram makes a point of naming Arofel in this passage, the message being that although the Saracen numbers are great and the kings numerous, one name in particular deserves mention. He then tells us that Arofel has built an illustrious reputation around his combat abilities and also that he has a loyal following of kinsmen in his army who are the strength of the Saracen forces. This tells us a great deal about Arofel's leadership and reputation. That his battalion is renowned for its knighthood is apparent in Wolfram's summary of the Saracen forces who broke through the Christian defences: 'diu Josweizes heres kraft und Arofels rîterschaft und Halzebiers koberen' [The great army of Josweiz, Arofel's knights and Halzebier's re-assembled forces] (*Wh.* 33, 27–9).

Arofel's kinsmen, his nephews who fight in his army, are important to Wolfram for they account for Arofel's reputation as knight as well as commander and Wolfram makes mention of them several times before the duel. In doing so, Wolfram ensures that Arofel, his nephews and their father, Terramer, establish a reputation with the audience of loyalty to kin as well as of knighthood and that they fulfil their duties and obligations.

> mit maneger rotte swancte
> Terramêrs bruoder her,
> Arofel, durh strîtes ger.
> dô kôs man ûfme gevilde
> manec zimier wilde,
> der diu rîterschaft erdâhte,
> die Arofel brâhte.
> Daz was des schult, er mohtez hân.
> Terramêr het verlân
> der jungen hôh gemuoten diet,
> ich mein daz er in underschiet
> sunderrîcheit sunderlant

sînen zehen sünen was benant,
dâ ieslîcher krône
vor sînen fürsten schône
truoc mit krefte und mit art.
ieslîcher ûf der hervart
selbander rîcher künege reit.
seht ob ir her iht waere breit,
die in ir dienste wârn geriten.
ouch dienden si mit zühte siten
ir vetern und leisten sîn gebot.
er lag ouch in ir dienete tôt,
Arofel von Persyâ,
in des dienste sie dâ
wâren unde ouch er durch sie.
der milte enpfiel sölh helfe nie.

(Wh. 29, 24 – 30, 20)

[Arofel, the brother of Terramer, moved forward with many bands of men, pressed on by the desire for battle. On the plain of Alischantz could be seen many strange helmet decorations, devised by the knights whom Arofel had brought with him. That was his obligation and he was able to fulfil it. Terramer had made bequests to the high-spirited young men. I mean that he had designated certain portions to them; particular lands were assigned to his ten sons, where each reigned in splendour over his princes, according to his power and innate skill. Each one was riding into battle in company with other wealthy kings. Just see how vast the army was of those who had ridden in their service, and they themselves were serving their uncle with appropriate good manners and fulfilling his commands. Arofel of Persia, in whose service they were and who in turn served them, lay slain in that service. A generous man never lacked such aid.][6]

The last four lines complete the image of Arofel's character: he is a formidable fighter and commander and, most importantly, loyal and honour-bound; they foreshadow his death in the service of his brother and his nephews for whom he is responsible.

Wolfram does not leave it at that, however: he then goes on to tell the audience the names of Arofel's nephews and recounts how they bravely join

6   Gibbs and Johnson, 30.

the fight.[7] It is only then, when Wolfram relates the death of Arofel's sister's son at the hand of Vivianz, alongside seven other kinsmen in Halzebier's battalion, that Wolfram draws sympathy from the audience.[8] Wolfram mentions these seven kings by name, telling us that Lybilun was Arofel's nephew. To further assert the importance of kin relationships in the story, Wolfram refers to Arofel as Gyburg's uncle a few lines before he describes Willehalm's disposition as he goes into battle against Arofel and Tenebruns: 'er wolde et ze Oransche hin, dâ Gyburc diu künegin sîn herze nâhen bî ir truoc' [he was wanting to ride on towards Orange, where the Queen held his heart in her safekeeping] (*Wh.* 77, 9–11).[9] The connection is made between the woman Willehalm loves and serves and her uncle whom he now faces.

When Arofel and Willehalm meet in single combat, the description puts a face to the character who has been mentioned in several passages describing might, knighthood and loyalty to kin. At first Willehalm faces Tenebruns and Arofel together, but while Tenebruns is slain, Arofel is not easily bested and thus warrants a more detailed description. In the middle of a charge, when their shields are splintered and fragments are flying, Wolfram embarks upon a story of the sword of King Pantanor.[10]

This more formal introduction of Arofel, after having heard him mentioned in passing descriptions of the Saracen forces during battle, expresses, in Wolfram's distinctive style, the image of a knight in whom he wants his audience to see chivalry exemplified. Here is the knight about whom we have heard; this is the commander whose ten nephew kings, famous in their own rights, follow him loyally with their great and formidable armies; this is the knight whose reputation as a great fighter and leader is known far and wide. Here he stands, presented in grand fashion by the narrator. He is not just any Saracen king accompanying Terramer's forces; he is one whose chivalry is attested to by the possession of an illustrious

---

7   *Wh.* 32, 8–18.
8   *Wh.* 46, 13–23.
9   Gibbs and Johnson, 51.
10   See Chapter 3, section 'Honour'.

sword. Wolfram spares Arofel no expense in his depiction: he is courageous, skilled at fighting, noble, chivalrous and generous. He is also well loved by ladies, and Wolfram says that his accoutrements are beautiful beyond description.[11] It is his boldness and zeal in battle, however, the very trait that has won him knightly fame, that will be the cause of his defeat:

> daz ors mit hurte in nâher truoc,
> daz die riemen vorme knie
> brâsten dort unde hie:
> ame lendenier si entstricket wart
> von der hurteclîchen vart,
> Diu iserhose sanc uf den sporn.
>   (*Wh.* 78, 24 – 79, 1)

[His horse carried him forward with such force that the straps above his knee snapped in several places and came loose from his belt; in the sudden charge his chain-mail leg-covering slipped down to his spurs.]

By contrast, the Aérofle in *Aliscans* plays a minor role, relegated to the part of an indistinctive Saracen king who has brought his great army to join forces with Tiebaut and Desramé. He first appears in the poem when the heathen army, no match for Vivien, Bertrand and five kinsmen, is in retreat. Aérofle's 10,000-strong force arrives to turn the tide of the first battle in favour of the heathens: 'Icele eschiele fu bien desbaretee, Quant Aarofle lor sort d'une valee/ O tot .X.M. d'une gent deffaee; La gent fuiant est o lui retournee' [This squadron was in great disarray when Aérofle suddenly appears from a valley with ten thousand pagans. Then the cowards turn around and join him] (*Alisc.* X, 262–5). He is described in single combat as brutal, violent and ferocious. When he encounters the seven French counts, Vivien, Bertrand and their cousins, he attacks Guichart with a hatchet, cutting through his *bouclier* and horse with a single blow, driving it more than two feet into the ground. Looking at the empty saddle of the collapsed horse, he cuts a fearsome figure and the audience is permitted a description of his physique: 'Grant et fort, s'ot la

---

11   *Wh.* 76, 13–29.

brace quarree, N'ot si fort home jusqu'a la mer Betee' [Arofel was big and strong with powerful arms and his strength was unmatched all the way to the Arctic Ocean] (*Alisc.* X, 288–9). Guichart, beaten by Arofel whose stupefying violence receives one more line of description, then attempts to recover his sword and call out to Bertrand. His cousins rush to his aid, but all are taken prisoner except Vivien, who has suffered a mortal wound.[12] The brutal Saracen is not seen again until the duel with Guillaume, but his image is already a very different one from that which Wolfram has built up of the corresponding character in *Willehalm*.

In *Aliscans* the audience sees a fierce pagan enemy whom the seven beloved nephews of Guillaume must face and by whom, in the end, they are overcome; his forces are so powerful that the Christians are driven to defeat. In *Willehalm*, however, the audience has seen the development of an image of a knight who has honour and nobility and who fights in loyal service to his family and nephews who are in his charge. Where Aérofle fights with brutality, Arofel fights with courage; he is presented not as a fierce enemy, but as a worthy adversary.

Duel

In *Aliscans*, the combat between Guillaume and Aérofle is significant to the broader plot only in that Guillaume kills one of the Saracen commanders whose forces have brought disaster to the Christians, enabling the fall of the southern march to Terramer's Saracen army. It is also a kind of plot device, enabling Guillaume to adopt the armour and horse of a Saracen in order to make his way back through the Saracen army to Orange and out again towards Montlaon. This also serves as a recurring disguise motif in which Guillaume is not recognized by family and peers but is, ironically, by the Saracens. The only characteristics of Aérofle that are of any significance are his reputation for strength and brutality in battle, both standard

12   *Alisc.* XI.

for a pagan enemy in the *chansons de geste*.[13] Although this combat with Guillaume is the focus of the action, the exchange of seven *laisses* as words and blows being described in detail, the horse, Folatile, seems to be the motivating feature of the scene and is the prize that causes the manner of both combatants to change completely.

The emphasis at this point in *Aliscans* is on Guillaume, his unequalled ability in combat and his firm reliance on God's grace to protect him. However, in the depiction of Aérofle and Guillaume's reactions to him, certain features are distinguishable in his character. After defeating fifteen kings and setting two (Corsuble and Esmeré) to flight, Guillaume chooses not to pursue them, instead making his way towards Orange. He is ambushed by the fierce duo, Danebron and Aérofle: 'Quant devant lui li saillent d'un aguet, .II. roi i ot, qui sont de mal estrait; Ce est Arofles et Danebron qui brait; Onques el mont n'ot rois ou tant mal et' [When suddenly before him in ambush appeared two kings of a foul race: Aérofle and Danebron who did not cease shouting; there were no more wicked kings in all the world] (*Alisc.* XXXIII, 1299–1302). Believing that if he can best fifteen kings without much trouble, two should pose no great danger, Guillaume resigns himself to the inevitability of the fight ahead.[14]

The words and actions of the two Saracens are marked by insults and viciousness, to which Guillaume responds that two against one is shameful and that they must, therefore, have no honour. He then attempts to reason with them to let him go on his way.[15] Danebron will have none of it, saying that nothing can compensate for his losses at Guillaume's hands and that he will not eat until Guillaume's head hangs from a tree, to which Guillaume replies that he must be completely mad.[16] The two then engage in combat with one another and Guillaume is almost run through by Danebron's lance. (He is saved by divine protection.) These passages

---

13 Though Aérofle is fierce and cruel in *Aliscans*, his counterpart in *Willehalm* has certain similarities with the Baligan of the *Chanson de Roland*, in that their prowess and chivalry are admirable, but their flaw is that they are not Christian.

14 *Alisc.* XXXIII.

15 *Alisc.* XXXIV 1316–39.

16 *Alisc.* XXXIV 1340–8.

show Guillaume to be the most clear-minded of the combatants, striving for a non-violent resolution – possibly because he knows that in his state the odds are stacked against him. He tries to provoke shame in his opponents for their behaviour, hoping that this will persuade them to let him go on his way. It is the Saracens, however, who obstinately insist on avenging their losses upon Guillaume. When Danebron is finally killed, Aérofle is angrier still.[17] Guillaume can only reply that he has never seen anything like Aérofle's anger; Guillaume has broken the blade of his sword, his horse is losing blood and he feels failure looming.[18] As a Christian knight, there is nothing for him but to invoke divine assistance, which, of course, he will be given; without it, he fights a losing battle.

In the next *laisse*, XXXVI, the audience is given a description of Aérofle's appearance as Guillaume surveys the enemy he is about to face. He is larger than anyone Guillaume has ever seen, his armour is beautiful, expensive and set with brilliant gemstones, his lance is tipped with the poison from a dangerous serpent and he is full of wicked thoughts. This opulence is indicative of the might of Aérofle, of his success as a warrior and of his fierceness in battle. It is the horse Folatile, however, that catches the eye of Guillaume: Aérofle is mounted on a huge charger, beautiful beyond description, capable of carrying two fully armed knights at a gallop for a day without breaking a sweat. The practicality of battle and necessity takes precedence over anything else and Guillaume's discouragement gives way to motivation. Guillaume wants the horse and asks God for assistance in acquiring it; he then tries to bargain with Aérofle, saying: 'Sarrazins, frere, dit par ta loiauté, Que t'ai meffet dont m'as cuilli en hé?' [Saracen, *brother*, tell me honestly: what bad thing have I done to you for you to hate me so?] (*Alisc.* XXXVI, 1469–70).[19]

No bargain will be struck, so a long, hard fight ensues during which shields are broken and both men are bloodied. Guillaume is spared from

17   *Alisc.* XXXIV 1349–75.
18   *Alisc.* XXXV, 1396–1406.
19   Guillaume addresses Aérofle in a personal manner instead of as an anonymous enemy troop.

mortal blows by God's protection, cursing his sword, Joyeuse, when it fails him, and the story of his having received it from Charlemagne for reassurance is recounted.[20] He is impressed with Aérofle's sword, though, and says he has never seen its equal, save Roland's famed blade Durendal, but the Saracen's anger remains unabated. In this mention of the swords, the audience is reminded of *Chanson de Roland* and invited to draw a parallel between Charlemagne and Guillaume: the emperor's sword, Joyeuse, is now wielded by Guillaume. If Aérofle has a sword that can be compared to Durendal, which could not be broken even by stone, then he is most fearsome indeed. He has the best horse, the best equipment, is rich and fierce ... All of this makes it all the more estimable that Guillaume, in his defeated state, can face him and all the more impressive when Guillaume wins (something that could not be hoped for without divine assistance). Guillaume finally tears away a piece of Aérofle's hauberk and shatters it to pieces, severing his *cuisse* [protective thigh covering] with the blow.[21]

The next *laisse* begins again with a description reinforcing the fierceness of the Saracen assailant: Aérofle is big, hideous and of such an impressive stature that he is a head taller than Guillaume. When Guillaume invokes Christ's protection and calls on Joyeuse, Aérofle's thigh is cut through by the count who then blesses his Joyeuse. His manner then changes completely when he addresses Aérofle. He calls him a devil, insults him, his religion and his gods, and tells him that he can go to hell, for victory is now his.[22]

---

20   *Alisc.* XXXVIII, 1577ff.
21   *Alisc.* XXXVIII, 1593–1600. Though a cuisse is a piece of armour covering the upper leg, here it is possible that *cuisse*, or *coisse*, means 'thigh', as Aérofle's leg is, indeed, cut through by Guillaume, line 1612; in *Aliscans* 'M', XXXVIII 1439. Wolfram will refer to both armour and thigh when Willehalm meets Arofel in battle. It is interesting to note that Wolfram's version also adds to Arolfel's thigh the adjective *blanke* (*Wh.* 79, 2), which Kartschoke translates to 'nackt', bare or naked, and Gibbs and Johnson translate to 'white', consistent with the French, *blanc*. Wolfram von Eschenbach. *Willehalm*, 51; and Gibbs and Johnson, 52. This addition indicates the influence and application of romance-style symbolism attached to the human body and its coverings. Refer to the discussion in Chapter 5, section: 'Dress and Appearance.'
22   *Alisc.* XXXIX, 1611–33.

Aérofle's horse continues to be the focus of the action. Guillaume mounts Folatile immediately; trying him out, he finds him beyond compare and is very pleased. Aérofle, however, whose manner is now more reserved, pleads for mercy, attempting to strike a bargain to keep his horse: 'Guillelmes, entendez; Parlez a moi, gentix quens henorez' [Guillaume, listen! Answer me, noble and honourable count] (*Alisc.* XL, 1644–5). They continue to argue, Aérofle pleading and Guillaume insulting him until Aérofle passes out from his wound. Guillaume takes his sword and beheads him then and there; taking the horse and the armour, his language matches that of the Saracen in his taunting and insults. This is the last the audience hears of Aérofle in *Aliscans*. Guillaume's actions were motivated by his desire for the horse and the desperate bid for self-preservation in adverse circumstances. Willehalm's motivations will be subtly different.

When Willehalm meets Arofel and Tenebruns in *Willehalm*, he is a hero blinded by grief for his dead nephew, Vivianz. The audience already has an image of Arofel as an honourable and noble knight, albeit a heathen, and he and Tenebruns are granted only a few words of description as they approach Willehalm. They are meaningful phrases, however, as the beauty of their armour is credited to the favours of ladies, which must have been won deservedly.[23] Here, the opulence of armour and equipment is more indicative of misplaced service than it is of power. Wolfram does not waste words on describing the combat itself, and uses less detail in his summary:

> Schoyûse wart der scheiden blôz
> und manlîch gezucket,
> und bêde sporn gedrucket
> Puzzât durch die sîten.
> manlîch was ir strîten.
> der künec Tenebruns lac tôt.
> (*Wh.* 77, 14–20)

---

23   *Willehalm* 76, 16–30.

[Schoiuse was unsheathed and bravely wielded, and both spurs were dug into Puzzat's flanks. They fought courageously, and King Tenebruns was slain.][24]

It is then that Wolfram elaborates upon the story of Arofel's sword. This story serves to ennoble Arofel rather than Willehalm and leaves Willehalm and his enraged grief in the background. There is very little that Wolfram can add to Arofel's image now and it suffices to say, 'Arofel der riche streit genendecliche: er bejagt e werdekeit genuoc' [The mighty Arofel was fighting boldly now, and indeed he had already attained renown in full measure] (*Wh.* 78, 23–5).[25] It is not Willehalm's sword-stroke that severs the strap holding up one of Arofel's *chausses*, his chainmail leg-covering, but the force of his own charge that snaps it; his leg exposed, the chain mail slides down to his spur. Thus far, there is no mention of any blows from Willehalm.[26] It is his own zeal in battle, his own enthusiasm during the charge, marking his bravery and courage, that exposes his leg to Willehalm's sword and not, as in *Aliscans*, an error in his swordsmanship. This is a significant yet subtle innovation on Wolfram's part, elevating the character of Arofel from the enraged pagan enemy to a respectable and more level-headed warrior, all the while endowing him with the fatal flaw of having too much fervour for the charge and perhaps lacking in measure.[27] Arofel then suffers the mortal blow from the margrave, who cuts deeply into his bare thigh, rendering him defenceless.[28]

A conversation ensues between Willehalm and Arofel, who has so far in the story said nothing. He who brought his army to answer the call of his brother, he who fought beside his nephews as they fell, he whose nobility and honour were presented before the audience earlier in the

24 Gibbs and Johnson, 51.
25 Gibbs and Johnson, 52.
26 It is worthy of mention that Arofel does not seem to be wearing cuisses in *Willehalm*, as is Aérofle in *Aliscans*, but chausses. Whether this is a mistranslation by Wolfram or an intentional innovation to the detail must remain conjecture.
27 Here we can see a parallel with the consequences for the sin of *démesure* [excess] in knights of the romance genre, with which Wolfam would have been familiar from *Parzival*.
28 *Wh.* 79, 1–7.

battle, 'der e genendeclichen streit' [he who fought courageously], offers
Willehalm his oath of surrender and the payment of a ransom (*Wh.* 79,
9–21). Willehalm asks after Arofel's background and family and he is told
that Arofel is the powerful ruler of Persia; here, Wolfram adds a sombre
warning to Arofel's words: 'Arable unde Tybalt, laegt ir für mich beide
erslagen, iwern tôt man minre solde klagen' [Arabel and Tibalt, if you both
lay dead, here in my place, people should not mourn your death so much
as mine] (*Wh.* 80, 12–14).[29]

These warriors have exchanged no words prior to this and this is the
first time that the audience hears Willehalm talk to his adversary. Arofel's
composure can then easily be credited to his quiet resolve and the margrave's anger and refusal of parley is seen as the result of grief, having just
left the body of Vivianz and having ridden in haste towards his endangered
city, Orange. Wolfram states simply to the audience: 'der künec niwan der
wârheit jach. der marcrâve mit zorne sprach' [the King was speaking the
truth, but Willehalm replied in a rage] (*Wh.* 80, 15–16).[30] He does not
depict Arofel as evil or wicked by word or action, nor does he make excuses
for Willehalm. Willehalm refuses any ransom and riches with vehemence
and Arofel tells him that he has come to fight with his nephews who are
there in his care. Volatin is mentioned only once, as an offer to Willehalm
for ransom; this is refused. Instead of replying, Willehalm kills Arofel on
the spot, takes his armour and cuts off his head.[31] Wolfram's own feelings
about this are revealed in his words:

> und dez houbet sîn vür unbetrogen
> balde ab im geswenket
> und der wîbe dienst gekrenket.
> ir freuden urbor an im lac:
> da erschein der minne ein flüstic tac.
> noch solden kristenlîchiu wîp
> klagen sîn ungetouften lîp.
>   (*Wh.* 81, 16–22)

29   *Wh.* 53.
30   *Wh.* 53.
31   *Wh.* 81.

[He struck off Arofel's head and so deprived the ladies of a servant who had been a fertile ground for their joy. Thus had dawned a day of loss for Love, and even today Christian ladies should still be mourning this heathen man.][32]

With the death of Arofel, Willehalm has taken upon himself a heavy burden which he will carry to the end of the fragment. He has committed a sin against love, *Minne*, and this is tied closely to his spiritual relationship with God, becoming one of the defining elements for his inner conflict and development as a character. That Wolfram used a heathen, this Saracen king, to put across this message is innovative in itself. It means that Gyburg is not the only heathen who has value for the audience and in the story, and Arofel's significance is heightened by the integrity of his character.

The fact that Arofel is a heathen and never converts is also significant. His death at the hands of Willehalm can be seen as a waste of a noble knight's service and knightly code on the battlefield is questioned: who is entitled to it and who is governed by it. Arofel has proved himself both on the battlefield and in the service of love and Willehalm sends his soul to eternal doom with a heated act of revenge. With Arofel's death comes the question of whether it is right to dispose of heathen lives, for in this story all are related, even if distantly, to the same clan. This will have a great impact as the narrative progresses; Wolfram does not let the audience forget Arofel of Persia.

Legend

Like the heroes of the Germanic past, Arofel's illustrious name lives on long after he has been killed. He is mentioned frequently throughout the rest of the story, in references to his horse, his armour and his sword, which Willehalm has taken and uses until the second battle, symbolizing his own coming to terms with the deaths of both Arofel and Vivianz.[33] The references to Arofel's accoutrements arise not only as memories but are present wherever the hero, Willehalm, goes, for it is he who wears the armour, car-

---

32   Gibbs and Johnson, 53.
33   *Wh.* 85, 25f; 89, 14; 91, 5; 105, 23; 125, 25f; 137, 2ff; and 232, 7ff.

ries the shield and rides the horse, all symbols of Arofel's knightly status as well as of his metonymic presence. Willehalm's killing of Arofel is never questioned by other characters but is reflected on by Willehalm himself, who must justify and answer for this behaviour.

After the proceedings at Loys's court, Willehalm undergoes a change, and begins to regret his actions on the battlefield with Arofel. Returning from Montlaon with reinforcements, Willehalm stops at the monastery where he left Arofel's shield, only to find that everything has been burnt down and lost. Willehalm laments the killing of Arofel; he realizes that he slew Arofel in anger and that this is a sin against *Minne*, costing him the beautiful shield. Moreover, Willehalm realizes that the death of Arofel will be a great blow to Terramer,[34] and proceeds to remember the other kinsmen he has killed in battle. These will be mourned by the heathen king and Willehalm reflects on his motives for each duel, marking a significant milestone in his inner transformation and readiness for the second battle. This self-reflection and lamentation is spurred by the memory of Arofel's nobility and his loss of life at Willehalm's hands.[35]

Arofel is also mourned by his Saracen kinsmen, namely Gyburg and Terramer. In a conversation with Heimrich of Narbonne, Gyburg laments the deaths of many heathen kings, all of them her family. She lists the names of the fallen,[36] including Arofel, and mentions the courage and honour with which they fought. This serves to remind the audience of two things: that Gyburg is in mourning for fallen kinsmen who are also the enemy and that these heathens are mourned for the same values – love, honour, bravery in battle – present in Christian knights. Whereas in *Aliscans* the death of a heathen king signalled a victory for the Christian side and for the knight who slew him, in *Willehalm* the death of a heathen knight is reflected upon long after the battle, their absence felt by Christian and Saracen alike. Arofel is a figure who remains present in the memories of

34   *Wh.* 203–4.
35   Bumke sees a contrast in the image of Arofel in life and then in death; in life he could serve *Minne*, but in dying, shame is brought down upon this service. Bumke, *Wolfram von Eschenbach*, 285.
36   *Wh.* 254–7.

the other characters throughout the story because of his chivalry, his courage in battle, his service to love and his loyalty, and because the manner of his death seems somehow unbecoming of a knight of such description. This is something Wolfram seems to wish to address by referring to Arofel repeatedly throughout the story, long after his death.

One of the ways in which a warrior's illustrious name could live on after he had died was for his deeds to be sung by those who remembered him. So it is for Arofel and his mighty forces. Arofel's army is mentioned in *Willehalm* with references to its power, its reputation and its fame under his command. Willehalm mentions Arofel's great force and his overpowering of the Christians, telling the court at Montlaon that they were outnumbered by the heathens, and naming Arofel's forces as being a decisive factor in defeating the Christians.[37] The Saracens mourn the king and Terramer vows revenge for the death of his brother, along with his other kinsmen, revenge featuring as a key motivator for the second battle on both sides of the conflict: 'Thesereiz und Nöupatrîs, die zwêne künege manegen prîs heten, und der bruoder mîn, Arofel: des muoz ich sîn âne vreude, ine gereche sie.' (*Wh*. 337, 25–9) [Tesereiz and Noupatris, two kings who had won renown, as my brother Arofel: I must live in sorrow if I do not avenge them.] Arofel's absence is felt keenly by his division and Terramer speaks to his ten sons who were in Arofel's command, preparing them for the second battle:

> ir sult ouch bî iu leiten
> iwers vetern her schône,
> die von Samargône,
> und die fürsten gar ûz Persîâ.
> Arofel hât si dicke aldâ
> vil rîterlîche gelêret
> daz ir prîs wart gemêret.
> an des ringe ir lâget hie,
> nu denket hiute daz er ie
> iwer ieslîchen ze sun erkôs,
> unz er den lîp durh iuch verlôs.

---

37   *Wh*. 151, 6–10.

ach wer sol nu minne pflegn,
sît sô hôher prîs ist tôt gelegn?
waz wunders tet der Persân!
kunnen diu wîp iht triwe hân,
sît wir alle sîn von wîben komn,
ir jâmer wirt nâch im vernomn.
                    (*Wh.* 345, 15–30)

[You shall also have in your command the splendid army of your uncle, those from
Samargone and the princes all the way from Persia. Arofel had often instructed them
closely there in matters of chivalry so that their renown increased. Just remember
today that he in whose camp you were staying always treated each of you as his own
son until he lost his life for your sake. Alas, who shall now cherish courtly love since
such high renown lies slain? What amazing feats did the Persan [sic] perform! If
women have a sense of loyalty at all, they will be heard mourning for him: we are,
after all, all born of women.][38]

To inspire them to victory, Terramer reminds his ten sons of their
uncle and of the image that carries on after him in his battalion. They are
reminded of Arofel's ability to command, as he had instructed his army and
looked after its reputation. They are also reminded that he was a loyal kinsman who died for them, whose death must now be avenged. Lastly, they are
reminded of the service to love that Arofel represented and that his death
is a loss to that service, which incites fervour for avenging him. Wolfram
shows Arofel to be a well-respected knight who is not forgotten, like his
counterpart in *Aliscans*, but whose image is remembered by the audience
as well as by the characters. This is because his death still has a role to play
in *Willehalm*. It has already caused Willehalm to reflect upon his actions
and the wider conflict and now the memory of Arofel's deeds inspires the
Saracen horde. It remains conjecture that this is another feature pointing
towards a reconciliation in the conclusion of the fragment, for both sides
have been profoundly affected by Arofel's death.

When his nephews are seen in the heat of battle against the Christians,
their fervour for their uncle remains strong:

38   Gibbs and Johnson, 172.

Arofel der Persân
was in ûf Alitschanz erslagn.
die sîne begunden in dâ klagn
mit den ecken und mit dem dône.
ir krîe Samargône
in manegem poynder wart geschrît:
Arofels wart in dem strît
von den sînen manlîch gedâht,
der si selbe dicke hête brâht
an die vînde werdeclîche.
ûz Arofels rîche
vil fürsten dâ mit kreften sint:
sîn selbes darbten doch diu kint,
wand er ir ander vater was.
weder starp noch genas
getriwer künec nie dehein,
den tages lieht ie überschein.
(*Wh.* 374, 14–30)

[Their kinsman Arofel the Persan [sic] had been slain at Alischantz and his men were mourning him there with the edges of their swords and with their shouts. Their cry of 'Samargone!' accompanied many an onslaught. Arofel was recalled by his men in acts of courage in that battle, he who had himself many times led them nobly to confront the enemy. Many princes from the kingdom of Arofel were there in full force, but Terramer's sons still missed Arofel himself, for he had been a second father to them. Never did the sun shine on any more faithful king, alive or dead.][39]

With Wolfram's final remarks on Arofel, his image vanishes along with the Saracen hope of victory in the second battle. The Saracens fight

39 Gibbs and Johnson, 185. *Mit den ecken* is translated here by Gibbs and Johnson as 'the edges of the swords,' which, whilst perhaps ambiguous in this context, refers to the sharp blade edge as it does in other passages describing Willehalm's sword, *Schoiuse* or *Joyeuuse* (*Wh.* 90, 26; 295, 2–5; 442, 12–13). However, in a more general context it refers simply to the blade or sword (*Wh.* 397, 25–6; 407, 28; 410, 23–4; 430, 24–5; 450, 26–7) or to the cutting action that was done with it (*Wh.* 430, 28–9). In this passage, *ecken* can be taken to mean the swords which were beaten against things such as shields to augment the *dône*, or shouts, and to increase the noise in mourning Arofel, an Arabic custom that would have been encountered during Crusades.

bravely, but the Christians overcome them in the end, although the price is felt keenly, Wolfram having described the admirable nobility and chivalry of Saracen knights (this epitomized by Arofel, a leader mourned by his kinsmen, who cannot avenge his death).

Even though *Willehalm* only survives as a fragment, there is enough evidence to suggest that Wolfram might have intended Arofel's death to mean more than any other victory in single combat for a Christian protagonist; it is perhaps symbolic of the direction and overall plan of the story, acting as a parallel to Willehalm's inner conflict and redemption. Wolfram is certain, however, that great meaning is attached to Arofel's death; Wolfram introduces him slowly, allowing his appeal to grow on the audience, then, after his death, he mentions him again and again. There is also the manner of his death at the hands of Willehalm, which is markedly different from that of his counterpart in *Aliscans*.

Wolfram makes no reference to religion when describing Arofel and his illustrious qualities or when recounting the combat against Willehalm. He never faults him for anything, except perhaps indirectly, in describing his motivation to gain renown in the service of love; the spiritual counterpart, service to God, is only conspicuous by its absence, if at all. Still, this Saracen ranks highly in Wolfram's world and Christian ladies should still mourn his death. If Arofel is not Christian, no eternal rewards await him in the afterlife, but that the memory of his renown and reputation are kept alive long after his death is reminiscent of the pagan Germanic warrior's hope that the stories of his deeds would be sung for generations. The Christian victory, however, is proof of who is right. Nonetheless, Wolfram's portrayal of certain heathen adversaries, especially Arofel, can do nothing but expose grey areas in a largely black-and-white Crusade ideology and raise questions about justifying the manner by which heathens are killed, and whether they really are enemies in this story, or respectable adversaries, knights and kinsmen without proper direction.

Noupatris

A heathen king who is described as the '*Minneritter* par excellence',[40] Noupatris stands out as a symbol of the exoticism and ostentation of the Saracen adversary in *Willehalm* and as the embodiment of the knight who blindly serves love alone, meeting a lonely end. He is a young and beautiful warrior, loved by his kinsmen and, like Arofel, mourned long after his death. He has a key role in *Willehalm* as the enemy who deals Vivianz the mortal blow. He has no counterpart in *Aliscans*.

That Wolfram should have invented this character himself when working, as he was, from a well-known source, might seem unlikely, though not entirely implausible. However, it is much more probable that he misunderstood the French, as he was wont to do in many passages in both *Willehalm* and *Parzival*, and compensated with his characteristic flair for invention and imagination: Chandler's catalogue of names cites the word 'l'aupatris, an oriental title of distinction,' as having been the phrase that Wolfram misinterpreted as the name of Noupatris.[41] Though Vivianz is wounded in *Aliscans* III, the reference to an emir does not occur until IX, 229 in Régnier's edition:

> Mes Vivïen tieng je au plus hardi,
> C'ainz por paiens une foiz ne foï,
> Devant les autres a veü l'ampatri,
> Qui le jor l'ot navré et maubailli

---

40 Wiesmann-Wiedemann, Friederike, *Le Roman du Willehalm de Wolfram d'Eschenbach et l'épopée d'Aliscans: Étude de la transformation de l'épopée en roman*, Göppinger Arbeiten zur Germanistik, ed., F.H.a.C.S, Ulrich Müller, vol. 190 (Göppingen: Alfred Kümmerle, 1976), 95.

41 Chandler, Frank W., *A Catalogue of Names of Persons in the German Court Epics*, ed. Martin H. Jones, vol. VIII, King's College London Medieval Studies (Exeter: Short Run Press, 1992), 213. Chandler also mentions Singer's 1918 assertion that Wolfram must have worked from a manuscript of *Aliscans* using the indefinite article instead, 'un aupatris,' 213. See Singer, S., *Wolframs 'Willehalm'* (Bern: A. Francke, 1918), 13, cited in Chandler (xxix). On these occurrences alone, a case could be made to support the oral transmission of Wolfram's source.

Tel li dona de son espié forbi
Parmi le cors que l'ame s'en parti.
Dïent li conte: Dex, quel vassal a ci!
                    (*Alisc.* IX, 227–9)[42]

[But I consider Vivien the most resilient; he hasn't once fled before the heathens. He marked the emir ahead of the others; he who had, that very day, wounded Vivianz grievously with his sharp spear. It was the most serious wound he had ever received. Recognizing him perfectly, Vivianz severed his soul from his body with a blow of his spear. 'God,' said his companions, 'What a knight!']

This passage connects the nameless emir to Vivien's fatal wound, resulting in his entrails spilling from his body in *laisse* IV. To this emir, Wolfram assigns the name Noupatris, and with it a character befitting the heathen who meets his death in the mortal joust with Vivianz, the young and beloved hero and kinsman.[43] Noupatris is youthful and attractive and strives for nothing but the reward of serving love:

die fuort ein man den nie verdrôz
strîts noch rîterlîcher tât.
sîn werdekeit noch volge hât,
daz er warp um rîterlîchen prîs:
der hiez Nöupatrîs:
er het ouch jugent und liehten schîn.
ze Oraste Gentesîn
truoc er krône: ez was sîn lant.
dar verjagt und dar gesant
het in der wîbe minne:
sîn herze und des sinne

---

42   The corresponding lines in the 'M' manuscript mentions the 'emir' as well: 'Devant les autres a oncis l'ampatri' [Ahead of the others was the *emir*] (*Alisc.* 'M,' IX 227). All citations from the the 'M' MS are taken from Holtus, Günter, ed., *La versione franco-italiana della 'Bataille d'Aliscans': Codex Marcianus fr, VIII [=252]*, Kurt Baldinger, series ed., Beihefte zur Zeitschrift für romanische Philologie, vol. 205 (Tübingen: Max Niemeyer Verlag, 1985).

43   Régnier notes that lines 230–45 of *laisse* IX are missing from four MSS. See Régnier, *Aliscans*, note on 52, vol. I, and 315, vol. 2. These lines are, however, present in either the 'M' or the 'S' ms.

ranc nâch wîbe lône.
von rubîn ein krône
ûf sînem liehten helme was:
lûter als ein spiegelglas
was der helm unverdecket glanz.
gegen dem kom Viviânz
(*Wh.* 22, 14–30)

[Leading them was a man who never tired of fighting, nor of knightly deeds. People are still in agreement about his excellence: he strove for knightly fame. Noupatris was his name and he had youth and radiant good looks. In his land, Oraste Gentesin, he wore the crown. The love of women had driven him forth and sent him yonder in the world. His heart and all its sensibilities strove after the reward of women. On his bright helmet was a ruby crown and the helmet itself shone without blemish, shiny as a looking-glass. Riding towards him came Vivianz.][44]

There is certainly in Wolfram's descriptions an element of the formulaic presentation of the enemy as formidable, and beauty and riches were the sign of strength and favour, so that the victory would sound even more impressive to the audience. More than that element of the awe-inspiring adversary in the descriptions and presentation of the heathens in *Willehalm*, however, is the humanity with which they are attributed, the remarkable and admirable qualities that they possess and the continued references to them after they have been killed in battle and are mourned by their kinsmen.

Decisive duel

Noupatris, a necessary figure for Wolfram to fashion, it would seem, because of the cyclical nature of his source material, is a short-lived character whose purpose in *Willehalm* extends beyond providing an adversary for a Frenchman. The audiences of *Aliscans* would have already known the history of Vivien through hearing other *chansons de geste* in the *Geste de Garin de Monglane*, namely the later *Chevalerie Vivien* and *Enfances Vivien*, which came about because of the popularity of the character. Wolfram's

---

44   Gibbs and Johnson, 27.

German audience would not have been as familiar with the character and
this is why Vivianz receives a fairly detailed description when he is introduced in the combat with Noupatris. Vivianz is the beloved nephew of
Willehalm and his death will spur Willehalm's clan to revenge:

> und der clâre Viviâns:
> ich waere immer mêr ein gans
> an wizzenlîchen triuwen,
> ob mich der niht solde riuwen.
> ouwê daz sîniu jungen jâr
> âne mundes granhâr
> mit tôde nâmen ende!
> von hôher freude ellende
> wart dar under sîn geslehte:
> daz tâten si mit rehte.
>   (*Wh.* 13, 21–30)

[There, too, was the radiant Vivianz, and to the end of my days I should be a stupid
ass with regard to my understanding of loyalty if I were not to mourn for him.
Alas, that his tender years should have ended in death before he had time to grow
a beard! Because of this his whole family became strangers to joy, and with good
reason.][45]

Because this death is pivotal to the plot, Wolfram must have considered the character who dealt the fatal blow carefully. He matched the two
opponents, both young and brave, Vivianz and Noupatris:

> si wurben bêde umb den tôt.
> ich bin noch einer, swâ manz sagt,
> der ir tôt mit triwen klagt;
> disen durh prîs und durh den touf;
> und jenen durh den staeten kouf:
> sîn jugent vil prîses gerte
>   (*Wh.* 23, 14–19)

---

45   Gibbs and Johnson, 23.

[Both men were duelling to the death. I am one of those who still mourn their deaths sincerely, whenever this tale is told, the one because of his renown and because he was a Christian, and the other because of his constant striving.][46]

Wolfram depicts this knight as noteworthy – just as he must be, to cause the death of a beloved kinsman and hero. He is not without flaw, however, and his youthfulness is used to imply that he serves love above all things and is brazen, extravagant and bold. Going into the duel, he, like Vivianz, is the first to spur his horse on to the head of the charge, meeting Vivianz as if jousting in a tournament:

Sin manheit in werte
maneger rîterlîchen ger.
sîn schaft was roerîn ime sper,
und daz ysen scharpf unde breit.
mit volleclîchem poynder reit
der heiden vor den sînen.
undr al den Sarrazînen
was niender banier alsô guot,
als die der künec hôh gemuot
in sîner hende fuorte.
Als er tjostieren wolde.
von gesteine und von golde
was rîchiu kost niht vermiten,
in die banier was gesniten
Amor der minne zêre,
mit eime tiuren gêre,
durh daz wan er nâh minnen ranc.
daz ors von rabbîne spranc
gein dem jungen Franzoys,
der ouch manlîch und kurtoys
was und dar zuo hôh gemuot,
als noch der prîses gerende tuot.
                    (*Wh.* 23, 20 – 24, 12)

46   Gibbs and Johnson, 27.

[His [boldness] craved for fame, [and] afforded him many a knightly goal. The shaft of his lance was made of bamboo with an iron tip which was broad and sharp. The heathen came riding at full tilt, at the head of his men. Among Saracens there was no banner so fine as that which the high-spirited king carried in his hand. He touched the horse with his spurs, as though he were going into a joust. Expense was of no account, where costly jewels and gold were concerned. His banner was adorned with a precious spear in honour of Amor, the god of Love, for this knight was fighting in the service of Love. The horse leapt from its charge towards the young Frenchman who was likewise brave and chivalrous and high-spirited, as to this day is any man who hungers after fame.][47]

Noupatris is called *der heide*, the heathen, by Wolfram, and is portrayed as having his courage and honour misplaced: love, instead of an ideal or embodiment of the divine promise to humans in spirituality, is Noupatris's deity and love's reward and renown are his motivations for fighting. Noupatris is young and proud, perhaps even arrogant and over-confident; he is also beautiful to behold, having spared no expense on his appearance. He looks the part, from his tipped spear and his ornate banner to his leaping charger. Wolfram's opinions about this are underscored by the depiction of Noupatris's comrade-in-arms, Tesereiz, an equally young and bold knight who is described as the Garland of Love. Tesereiz is the knight who recognizes Puzzat, Willehalm's horse, who is following his master who is mounted on Volatin. In his desire to learn the identity of the Frenchman, Tesereiz confronts Willehalm, who has just left Vivianz's corpse and slain Arofel. Tesereiz reveals his own naivety and fervour in love's service, for which Wolfram is lenient with him:

> er sprach 'ob du getoufet sîs,
> so enpfâch ein tjost durch den prîs.
> ob duz der marcrâve bist,
> half dir dô dîn hêrre Krist
> daz diu Arâboysinne
> Arabel durch dîne minne
> rîchiu lant und werde krône
> dîner minne gap ze lône

(trüeg sölh êre ein Sarrazîn
als wont an dem prîse dîn,
des waern al unser gote gemeit),
ich wil durch dîne werdekeit
dich vor al den heiden nern,
benamen durch dîne minne wern.
mir enhât hie niemen vollen strît:
mîn her wol ebenhiuze gît
von Grikulâne unz an den Roten.
ich wil dich unsern werden goten
wol ze hulden bringen:
dâ mac dîn dienst wol ringen
nâch wîbe lôn und umb ir gruoz.
ob ich mit dir strîten muoz,
ich weiz wol, dêst der minne leit.
sô unsanfte ich nie gestreit
mit deheiner slahte man,
wand ich dir keines schaden gan.'
                    (*Wh.* 86, 5–30)

['If you are a Christian,' he said, 'then joust with me for the sake of fame. If you really are the Margrave, if your Lord Christ once gave you his aid, so that out of love for you Arabel, the Araboise, gave up rich lands and a noble crown, to gain your love, then, for the sake of your nobility, I shall protect you from the heathens, indeed defend you for the sake of your love. For, if a Saracen had been so honoured as you, with your reputation, then all our gods would have rejoiced. No one can match me here in fighting power; my army rivals all others from Girkulane to the River Rhône. I intend to convert you to the worship of our illustrious gods; then you will be able to serve the ladies with your fighting and so win for yourself their greeting and their reward. If I am obliged to fight with you, then I know very well that this will be damaging to Love. I was never so reluctant to fight with any man before, for I have no desire to harm you.']⁴⁸

Tesereiz shows all the bravado and naive enthusiasm reminiscent of Herzeloyde's darling young Parzival.⁴⁹ He addresses the margrave as if he had

48   Gibbs and Johnson, 55–6.
49   See the comparison of Tesereiz to young Parzival encountering the knights for the first time in Wolf, 379.

no clear idea of battle or enemies and he clearly misjudges Willehalm's ability to kill him effortlessly; the margrave is the better and more experienced fighter. Tesereiz is also bold enough to suggest that Willehalm convert to Islam, almost as if he were one of the knights in *Parzival*, inviting the margrave to join in the chivalrous pursuits at Arthur's court. It is his naive confidence that, in worshipping his gods, he serves ladies as he should and is thereby entitled to win fame and love's reward. The spirituality of the Christian knight is absent from his boldness. That Wolfram sees Tesereiz's and Noupatris's youthful ignorance as endearing and their desire to serve love as worthy is evident in his own words upon the young Saracens' encountering the experienced and harried Willehalm, who makes quick work of them:

> hie wurden d'ors mit sporn genomn.
> dâ was manheit gein ellen komn,
> und diu milte gein der güete,
> kiusche und hôhgemüete,
> mit triwen zuht ze bêder sît:
> der ahte schanze was der strît.
> daz niunde was diu minne:
> diu verlôs an ir gewinne.
>   (*Wh.* 87, 15–22)

[Then the horses were spurred, and Manliness came face to face with Courage, and Generosity with Goodness, and on each side were Purity and High Spirits, Loyalty and Good Breeding. The combat was a game of chance played by these eight. Love was the ninth player, but their gain proved to be her loss.][50]

Love is not served when the knights on both sides endeavour to kill each other in her service and Wolfram draws attention to this tragic conflict when the young knights, Vivianz and Noupatris, face each other in a fatal clash. The duel is quick and furious: the opponents lunge at each other, smashing through shields and breaking their lances, each inside the body of the other, each sealing the other's fate: 'ietweders kraft alsô versniten, daz

---

50   Gibbs and Johnson, 56.

es der tôt sîn bürge wart' [the strength of each man was so weakened that
death became his surety] (*Wh.* 24, 24–5).[51] Vivianz, the hero, wounded
though he is, strikes Noupatris through his helmet, killing him then and
there. He then removes the spear from his torso and replaces his own escaping entrails before tying himself together with the banner of Amor so that
he can go on fighting before dying a saint's death in the arms of his uncle,
Willehalm. For Noupatris, the poor misguided heathen, however, death
is a cold and shameful event:

> Da ergienc ein schädelîch geschiht
> und ein jaemerlîchiu angesiht
> von den sînen die daz sâhen.
> si wolten helfe gâhen:
> ir helfe was ze spâte komn.
> ungesehen und unvernomn
> was mangem heiden dâ sîn tôt,
> der doch sîn verch en wâge bôt
> durh prîs und durh der wîbe lôn.
> (*Wh.* 25, 1–9)

[That was when the heathen gave up the ghost, and there occurred for those of his
men who witnessed this a pitiful experience and a wretched sight. They wanted to
rush to his aid, but their help came too late. His death went unseen and unheard
by many heathens there, who were themselves risking their lives for glory and the
favour of ladies.][52]

The only difference between the characters of Noupatris and Vivianz is
their religion. Noupatris's religion is childlike, he appears to be in the service
of love alone, almost reminiscent of an innocent young Parzival who was
so inspired by birdsong, whereas Vivianz's service is directed by God and
its reward is the service to love and renown. In this, Wolfram juxtaposes
the knights on the battlefield as well as the opposing sides in the war by
contrasting their religion but setting their chivalry and spirituality on a
level field. What differentiates the heathen from the Christian is a naive

51 Gibbs and Johnson, 28.
52 Gibbs and Johnson, 28.

ignorance about God and conversion is the only act that will redeem him. Noupatris dies without the redemptive promise granted by conversion to Christianity, but he is nevertheless remembered.

Legend of a *Minneritter*

Like Arofel, Noupatris is mentioned again and again throughout the story, long after his death in the first battle, though for slightly different reasons. Noupatris, the narcissistic heathen king, will always be the man who dealt Vivianz the mortal wound. He represents folly in chivalry and serves to remind the audience of the flawed characteristics of heathen chivalry. Misguided though the motive might be, the spear remains sharp enough to kill even the most beloved Christian.

Noupatris is mentioned along with his fallen compatriots in several passages,[53] but he stands out most in those passages describing his renown for service to love and his vast riches.[54] His reputation continues on in his army after his death and Gyburg describes how her honour was defended during the siege of Orange by the knights who served love:

> Nöupatrîses rîterschaft
> was hie mit grôzer heres kraft:
> die der minne gerende ûz brâhte,
> sêr daz den versmâhte,
> der sich gein mir armen vrouwen
> in sturme lieze beschouwen.
> sît diss landes hêrr was überstritn
> und der nâch helfe was geritn,
> si jâhen, gein werden wîben
> solten werde man belîben
> dazs se immer diens werten
> und ir lônes wider gerten.
> hie was vil hers hêrrenlôs,
> von den ich starken haz erkôs:

---

53   *Wh.* 28, 4–9; 106, 20–5; 337, 21–6.
54   *Wh.* 55, 1–6; 255, 15–17.

wan Nöupatrîses diet
und Thesereizes her sich schiet
ûz den andern, als ich hân gesagt.
ich waen, si wârn doch unverzagt.
(*Wh.* 267, 3–20)

[Noupatris' knights were here with the strength of a great army. Those whom that Seeker after Love had brought disdained whoever showed himself in an attack on a poor woman like me. Since the lord of this land had been defeated and had ridden off for help, they maintained that noble men should act towards women in such a way as to be ever at their service and to seek reward in return. Many an army was here without its leader, and from them I suffered severely. Only Noupatris' people and Tesereiz' army kept apart from the others, as I explained. But I am sure they were not lacking in courage.][55]

Here the audience sees the practical advantage to Gyburg that was afforded by the same extravagance that caused Noupatris' death. The duty to the service of love for which he and his knights were renowned brought them recognition by Gyburg, who defended the Christian fortress at Orange. As is characteristic in Wolfram's telling of this story, there are consequences for every action and ideal, and the balance between the spiritual aspects and the practical aspects of these ideals is one goal: to live in this world without compromising spiritual ideals, to live by spiritual standards in such a way as not to compromise earthly standing. In Gyburg's gratitude to Noupatris's knights for the benefits of their idealization of the service to love, Wolfram treats the memory of this bold and ostentatious knight less harshly than might be expected for the man responsible for the death of Vivianz, whom Gyburg had doted on. Although Noupatris's misguided service to love became his own undoing, his memory and inspiration, surviving in the knights of his army, ensures his renown after death. Thus the question of how a knight should let his service be directed by a lady is addressed in *Willehalm* in a more practical manner than in *Parzival*, albeit with a less concrete answer: with measure.

---

55   Gibbs and Johnson, 136.

His knights having received a favourable report from Gyburg, Noupatris's memory is granted due pardon from Wolfram for the role he played in Vivianz's death. When he is mentioned thereafter, it is with a distant respect for the traits that, before, were wielded with such frivolity. Noupatris's boldness becomes courage, his worship of love becomes service. Terramer addresses his forces and assigns the battalions without leaders; command of Noupatris's battalion goes to Halzebier, who is to form the spearhead:

> ich schaffe ouch zuo dem vanen dîn
> die von Oraste Gentesîn,
> die der süeze Nöupatrîs
> brâhte. die hânt manegen prîs
> erstriten mit roerînen spern:
> si beginnt ouch hiute tjoste gern.
> ir hêrren herze truoc ein wîp:
> durh die verlôs er hie den lîp
>   (*Wh.* 341, 15–22)

[I assign also to your banner the men from Oraste Gentesin whom dear Noupatris led. They earned much renown with their lances of bamboo. They will be eager to joust today too. A woman held the heart of their lord, and for her sake he lost his life here.][56]

Here again, we see the narrative function of a naive folly: a knight who lived and died for love and renown in love's service is survived by his band of men whose devotion to the same ideal will serve a practical use in battle, for they fight with passion and boldness at the head of the armies. Terramer reminds his troops that Noupatris was in the service of a lady, and that is how he is remembered. Noupatris's character is not one that is developed for the audience before his decisive action in the story; rather, it is after he has been killed that his character begins to take shape. His memory serves to remind the audience not just of the folly of serving love only but also of the balance that service to love is capable of bringing to chivalry.

---

56   Gibbs and Johnson, 170–1.

Halzebier

Perhaps the most imposing Saracen is Terramer's brother, King Halzebier of Falfunde, who, along with Arofel, has come to Terramer's aid with warships and a massive army. He is described as strong, mighty and powerful, *küen*, *kraft* and *stark*, and he is responsible for the deaths of many Narbonnais kinsmen. Unlike Arofel, he does not die in the first battle, but remains a harsh and threatening Saracen commander until he meets his fate in the second battle of Alischantz.

First battle of Alischantz

In *Aliscans*, Haucebier is introduced when he comes riding at the head of 20,000 heathens under his command to reinforce the gaps forged by Vivien and Bertrand.[57] Strong and imposing, the arrival of Haucebier strikes fear in the hearts of the French heroes. The *jongleurs* indulge their audiences immediately with a grotesque physical description of Haucebier. This image is of one of the fiercest of the Saracens in *Aliscans*, symbolic of the formidable strength of the Saracen forces and the impossibility of a Christian victory. When Bertrand and six of Vivien's cousins are captured by the Saracens under Aérofle, Haucebier faces the young count Vivien who, though mortally wounded, is still fighting, cutting through the heathen ranks with his charges:

> Es Haucebier d'outre Carfanaon.
> En tote Espaigne n'ot paien si felon,
> Niés fu Tiebaut et oncle Sinagon,
> Cil ot Guillelme meint jor en sa prison.
> En tote Espaigne partot en parloit on,
> Plus ot de force que .XIIII. Esclavon.
> Plest vos oïr un pou de sa façon?
> Demie lance ot de lonc au penon,
> Et une toise par les flans environ;
> Et les epaules lees a grant foison.

57   *Alisc.* VI, VII.

Les braz ot gros, les poinz quarrez enson;
Demi pié ot entre les els del front,
La teste ot grosse et de cheveus foison
Et les elz roges ausi comme charbon.
Une charree portoit il bien de plon;
Forz Renouart ainz ne fu si fort hom
Qui puis l'ocist, si com dist la chançon.
                    (*Alisc.* XIII, 355–71)

[And here is Haucebier from beyond Carfanaon, the wickedest of all the pagans in Spain, nephew of Tiebaut, uncle of Sinagon, who held Guillaume long in prison. All of Spain speaks of him, for he has more strength than fourteen Slavs. Would you like to hear how he looks? He stands half a lance tall at the banner [of the lance at his side], his haunches are of great circumference, he has massive square shoulders, great arms and powerful fists. The distance between his eyes is half a foot, his head is huge, with thick hair, and his eyes are red like burning coals. He carries a leaden club. Except for Rainouart, never was there so strong a man. Rainouart later killed him, as we learn in the story.]

Haucebier is the strongest heathen, save Rainouart, and is presented as a fearsome enemy who deals Vivien the final blow, putting an end to the count's charge and turning the tide for the heathen forces.[58] Haucebier, an inhuman heathen enemy, also represents the strength of the Saracen army, strong, confident and tenacious as he immediately turns to the task of finding Guillaume, intending to take him to Tiébaut.

Again, Wolfram's sensitivities can be discerned here in the difference between the depiction of this Saracen king in *Willehalm* and that of his source. The character of Halzebier is softened, the 'dog-and-whore' imagery is dispensed with, yet he remains the backbone of Terramer's forces. True to form, Wolfram does not try to astound us with a physical description of Halzebier until after he has been introduced in various passages throughout the first battle; in these, his motives are alluded to and his reputation and kin revealed.

58   *Alisc.* XIII, 372–82.

His name is first heard when Wolfram talks about Terramer's brothers, Halzebier and Arofel, who brought warships to join Terramer's forces;[59] then, the audience is introduced to this powerful Saracen gradually, through battle scenes. His army is formidable and his arrival heralds disaster for the Christians. Just as his arrival in *Aliscans* signals defeat in the heart of Bertrand, his arrival on the scene in *Willehalm* is terrifying, yet Wolfram achieves this more by way of a description of Halzebier's reputation than through grotesque physical appearance and crude behaviour. Wolfram's image of Halzebier derives more from the narrator's distanced perspective and less from the perspective of the Christian combatants.

> nu was mit al den sînen
> ze orse komen, swiez drumbe ergê,
> der starke küene Halzebier.
> manegen stolzen soldier
> Unt manegen edelen amazzûr
> er fuorte: die nam untûr,
> sît si fürsten hiezen,
> sô wolden si geniezen
> ir kraft unde ir edelkeit,
> daz in der prîs waere bereit
> vor ander heres fluot.
> manec fürste hôh gemuot
> kom dâ mit scharn zuo geriten,
> die durch Halzebieren striten.
> in sîn helfe was benant
> drîzec tûsent werlîch erkant,
> sarjande und rîterschaft.
> Halzebier kom mit kraft.
> (*Wh.* 17, 26 – 18, 14)

[And now, however things might turn out, powerful, bold Halzebier, King of Falfunde, had arrived on horseback with all his men. He was riding at the head of many proud soldiers and many a noble amazur.[60] Since they bore the name of

---

59   *Wh.* 9.
60   *Amazur*, akin to 'emir', is one of several exotic-sounding terms employed by Wolfram as Saracen titles of command, though he had no knowledge of these titles himself.

prince, it seemed to them a matter of little consequence that renown should come
to them in advance of the mass of the army. Many a high-spirited prince came riding
up with his men to fight in the service of Halzebier. Thirty thousand doughty foot-
soldiers and knights on horseback were numbered among those who supported him.
Halzebier came in force.][61]

Halzebier's warriors are numerous, his reputation powerful, and he,
as well as those under his command, radiates a boldness and confidence
that, while not altogether worthy, proves effective and decisive in the first
battle. The audience hears more of him in the first battle as gaps are broken
in his lines, two-thirds of his 30,000 men fall and he makes a retreat.[62]
Kin and clan remain significant when Wolfram writes that Terramer is
shaken when he hears of Halzebier's defeat and of Noupatris's death;[63] it
is related that the Saracen king, Synagun, who fights with honour in the
battle, is Halzebier's nephew.[64] We also learn that Pinel, who met his death
at the hands of Willehalm,[65] is another of Halzebier's nephews, whose
death Halzebier grieves when Vivianz and the eight barons are breaking
through his lines.[66]

In this way, Wolfram changes the character of Halzebier markedly
from that of his source, *Aliscans*, before he even supplies us with a first
full description. While Haucebier is huge, fierce and vicious, and his massive army the formidable backbone of Terramer's forces, Halzebier is the
other of Terramer's powerful and loyal brothers who has fulfilled his kinship obligation by bringing his own warships and great numbers of foot
soldiers and knights to Terramer's aid. Accompanying the Saracen army are
his nephews, Pinel and Synagun, both respected kings, young and brave,
who fight for honour and for the favour of ladies and love. Wolfram obliges
the audience with the anticipated description of Halzebier just before the
decisive and much-anticipated meeting with Vivianz:

61   Gibbs and Johnson, 25.
62   *Wh*. 22, 1–5; 27, 18–21.
63   *Wh*, 28, 3–9.
64   *Wh*. 27, 12–16.
65   *Wh*. 21, 1–9.
66   *Wh*. 45.

Halzibier der clâre
mit reidbrûnem hâre
und spanne breit zwischen brân,
swaz sterke heten sehs man,
die truoc von Falfundê der künec.
der was al sîner lide frümec
und manlîches herzen,
zer zeswen und zer lerzen
gereht, ze bêden handen.
sîn hôher prîs vor schanden
was mit werdekeit behuot:
in wîbe dienste het er muot.

                    (*Wh.* 46, 1–12)

[Halzebier was handsome, with curling brown hair and a span's breadth between his eyebrows. He had the strength of six men, this king of Falfunde. He was powerful of limb and bold of heart, equally adept at fighting with his right hand and with his left. His lofty reputation was protected from disgrace by his nobility. He was courageous in the service of women.][67]

Halzebier cuts a handsome figure despite his being a heathen and an enemy on the battlefield. Wolfram's narrative felicity allows the perspective of the audience to shift from that of the Christians fighting against monstrous and fierce heathens, whose goal is domination of the French imperial territory, to the more removed position of narrator and audience watching a battle between Charlemagne's descendants and their worthy opponents. The fact that the opponents are heathens is barely mentioned after the prologue, nor is it given significance through reiteration.

Halzebier surveys the scene in a second, as does his *Aliscans* counterpart, and he acts as any warrior and commander would, albeit with the feelings and motivation of grief included, even magnified, by Wolfram:

nu wart gerochen Pînel
von Halzibier dem künge snel,
do er an Vivîans ersach
daz er die schar mit hurte brach,

---

67 Gibbs and Johnson, 36–7.

und daz er sluoc Libilûn,
Arofels swester sun,
Eskelabôn und Galafrê,
Rubîûn und Tampastê,
Gloriôn und Morhant.
die siben künege sâ zehant
lâgn vor Viviânze tôt.
Halzebier die grôzen nôt
mit einem swertes swanke galt,
daz Vivîans wart gevalt
hinderz ors ûf d'erde.
unversunnen lac der werde,
der ê was heidenscheft ein schûr:
des jach dâ manec amazûr.
                                    (*Wh.* 46, 13–30)

[Now Pinel was avenged boldly after King Halzebier had seen Vivianz scattering the heathen troops by his charge and killing Libilun, Arofel's sister's son, as well as Eskelabon and Galafre, Rubiun and Tampaste, Glorion and Morant. These seven kings quickly lay dead, slain by the hand of Vivianz. Halzebier repaid these great losses with one stroke of his sword. Vivianz was felled from his horse to the ground. That gallant man lay there unconscious, he who previously had been a veritable hailstorm to the heathens, as many an amazur could attest.][68]

Halzebier, driven by both a desire to avenge his kinsmen and his duty as a knight in combat, puts an end to Vivianz's surge of desperate fighting after his mortal wound by Noupatris, quashing any hope of French victory.[69] He then takes eight barons captive, including Bertram, all of Vivanz's companions who had thrust into the gaps of the Saracen line. His thoughts on this are disclosed by Wolfram: he means to keep these as prisoners to exchange for Queen Arabel.[70] This purposeful disposition in the character of Halzebier is entirely Wolfram's innovation, and one which facilitates his plans for the future of this figure; in *Aliscans*, Haucebier is not named

68   Gibbs and Johnson, 37.
69   Wolfram described each of the kings killed by Vivianz earlier; see *Wh.* 26, 25 –7, 15.
70   *Wh.* 47, 1–13.

as being responsible for the taking of prisoners, nor does any reasoning for his actions come into play.

Siege of Orange

When the first battle has been fought, Orange is besieged by the Saracens and Halzebier's considerable forces are among the most notable to hold the siege. In *Aliscans*, Haucebier's great army is included by name in the list of those besieging Orange when Guillaume surveys the siege from inside the fortress and again when he reminds Guiburc of the might that surrounds Orange before he takes his leave to secure reinforcements.[71] That Haucebier is a force that must be reckoned with again and that he remains answerable for the final blow to Vivïen is demonstrated in the passages when his death at the hands of Rainouart is foreshadowed by the *jongleur*: 'Forz Renouart ainz ne fu si fort hom Qui puis l'ocist, si com dist la chançon' [Only Rainouart is stronger than [Aérofle], and could kill him in an instant, according to the song] (*Alisc.* XIII, 369–71) and later when Aélis appears at the banquet at Montlaon:

> C'est Aaliz, ou il n'a qu'enseignier,
> Que Renoart reçust puis a moillier;
> Mes Looÿs ne le vost otraier,
> Li quens Guillelmes la li fist esposer.
> Cil Renoart ocist puis Haucebier
> En Aleschans el grant estor plenier,
> .VII.M. des autres de le gent aversier.
> (*Alisc.* LXXI, 3384–90)

[Here is Aélis, who attracts nothing but praise, whom Rainouart received later as a bride. Louis did not wish to authorize this, but Count Guillaume commanded the marriage. This Rainouart killed Haucebier later on in the great battle of Aliscans, as well as seven thousand other combatants of the opposing army.]

71   *Alisc.* XLIX, LI.

Haucebier is mentioned here to lend credit to Rainouart's strength
and ability, because he is the mightiest of heathens, massive, powerful and
formidable, and the man who can best him must be impressive. It also serves
as a reminder to the audience that this heathen, responsible for a blow to
the beloved character Vivien, will get his come-uppance. Haucebier is not
only formidable and fearsome in *Aliscans*; because of his role in Vivien's
death, he is loathsome as well.

It is Wolfram, the narrator himself, and not Willehalm, who surveys
the siege as it is established at Orange after the first battle in *Willehalm*.
Wolfram lays out the siege plan for his audience, describing who was camped
at each gate and under whose command different battalions were, describing the mettle and chivalry of each heathen prince, king and commander
that is mentioned and, above all, to whom they are related.[72] The image of
a rambling storyteller enjoying narration as much as his audience enjoyed
listening comes easily with Wolfram's descriptions. It is here only that
Halzebier's army is mentioned, it seems, simply because he is part of the
landscape, and one would hardly expect him not to be: 'wie diu fünfte sî
behuot? der pflac der künec Halzebier. noch mêr ist ir benennet mier' [and
how was the fifth gate guarded? Protecting it was King Halzebier, but my
source names still more].

Military deployment alone does not suffice for Wolfram's description
and account of heathen activity during the siege of Orange and it is not
the only reason Halzebier's name is mentioned. The theme of nephews
together with uncles in battle remains significant as Halzebier's nephew,
King Synagun, is mentioned several times by Wolfram.[73] The importance
kinship seems to have for Haucebier in the *chanson de geste*, however, is
negligible. Before the second battle, he is mentioned in a list of heathens
who are described as descendants of Judas, indicating their treacherous

---

72 *Wh*, 97–8.
73 The story of his capture of Willehalm in a previous battle is related in *Wh*. 220; 293;
    294, and he can be found in *Enfances Vivien* as well as in *Aliscans*. It is Synagun's
    armour and sword that Gyburg gives to Rennewart when she bestows accoutrements
    upon her brother, and it is then that we learn that Synagun is also *her* nephew; see
    Wh. 295–6.

nature and the *jongleurs'* favour towards the other side in the battle.[74] It is also mentioned in passing that Desramé is Haucebier's uncle and, later, that his nephew is Corsuble, one of the fifteen kings Guillaume faced before duelling with Aérofle.[75] Neither of these family ties seems to have any significance in the development of the character of Haucebier.

Defeat

When the second battle of Alischantz is being staged, Halzebier and his immense army are chosen to lead the Saracen charge. Terramer organizes the attack and Halzebier finds it a great honour to spearhead the assault.[76] Wolfram makes certain to mention, as the battle begins and Halzebier's forces attack the slowly advancing Frenchmen, that Halzebier still grieves for Pinel, whose army now rides under the command of Halzebier, giving the audience an insight into the mind and emotions of the adversary that is not present in his source.[77] Despite his grief, Halzebier goes on to fight bravely and capably as the battle rages.[78] It would seem that Wolfram wanted his audience to sympathize with Halzebier to some degree, rather than to indulge in cheers as he meets his death at the hands of Rainouart (as is the fate of Haucebier in *Aliscans*).

The *jongleurs* of *Aliscans*, however, present a different picture of this Saracen king. Haucebier's grotesque physique is described once more as the battle commences and yet again when he faces Rainouart, reinforcing the audience's image of the formidable and terrifying enemy whom the Franks must defeat with their courage and knightly skill. He is described with a series of superlatives, radiating power, force, violence and vehemence; he is just the sort of adversary that only the bravest man would face.[79]

74 *Alisc.* LXXXV 4379ff.
75 *Alisc.* XC, 4679. Haucebier is also the uncle of Sinagon and the brother-in-law of Aérofle; see *Alisc.* X.
76 *Wh.* 341–2.
77 *Wh.* 362, 8.
78 *Wh.* 362–3.
79 *Alisc.* C 5280–2; CLVII 6875–93.

When the battle is lost, Halzebier and his intrepid army fight their way back towards their ships.[80] Later, Wolfram allows the king to meet his end at the hands of the French prisoners he had taken on board. Freed by Rennewart, who is looking for mounts, the prisoners recognize Halzebier as the man who felled Vivianz and they attack him. The fight rages until Halzebier, weary after having fought hard and valiantly all day on foot and on horseback, is thrown to the ground and killed.[81] In *Aliscans*, Haucebier meets a fitting end at the hands of Rainouart, who is angry because a blow to Haucebier has damaged his beloved *tinel*, or club;[82] it is a combat long-anticipated in the *chanson de geste* and is carried through four *laisses*, complete with pre-combat taunting and florid descriptions of brutality and violence.[83] Wolfram softens the final combat for Halzebier from that of his source, giving him an epitaph befitting the character he developed:

> ime sweize muose erkalten
> sîn werder lîp, ê der erstarp,
> der ie nâch sölhem prîse warp
> des andern künegen was ze vil.
> er stiez sô kostebaeriu zil
> mit manheit und mit milte,
> daz er durch nôt bevilte
> ander künege sîne genôze.
> sus starp der schanden blôze
> ân alle missewende.
> man giht daz sîne hende
> wol getorsten strîten unde geben,
> zuht mit triwen, al sîn leben
> al dise werdeclîchen site
> unz an den tôt im wonten mite.

---

80 *Wh.* 414, 7–16.
81 *Wh.* 218–19.
82 Renneweart / Rainouart, the Saracen comical giant, and hero of *La Bataille Loquifer*, favours an enormous tree trunk or club over a sword as a weapon, which appears in *Aliscans* as *tinel* (*Alisc.* XLV 1927–1929), and in *Willehalm* as *stange* (*Wh.* 196, 20). See the section 'Renneweart', in this chapter.
83 *Alisc.* CLVII–CLX.

ûz sehs hern der er pflac
manec fürste umb in gestreut lac,
die smorgens zuo zim wârn geschart.
gerne het in Terramêr bewart.

           (*Wh.* 419, 12–30)

[His noble body covered with sweat grew cold before he died, he who always strove
for a renown that was too much for other kings. He set such a magnificent example
with boldness and generosity that other kings, his peers, simply could not equal it.
Thus that faultless man died, free of ignominy. People say that his hands were equally
adroit in fighting and in giving. Courtesy with loyalty, all these noble qualities he
possessed all his life until death. Many a prince from the six armies that he had led
and that had been assigned to him that morning lay dead around him. Terramer
would have liked to save him.][84]

The praise given Halzebier at his death is that of a worthy opponent
in battle, one who is familiar with chivalry and commands respect from his
army. The Saracen king, described in *Aliscans* with superlatives of height,
ferocity and size, is described by Wolfram with superlatives geared more
towards the ideals of chivalry and the unspoken code of combat. That
Wolfram credits him with bravery is not diminished by his necessary retreat;
Halzebier retains his honour into death.

This demise is a great blow to Terramer, because Halzebier represents
the military might of the Saracens, which, by the end of the second battle,
has been conclusively broken. From the figure of an enormous and fearsome
heathen enemy, Wolfram has fashioned a character with a subtle depth
and evocative significance. His life as it comes to the audience by way of
accounts of his reputation, his role in the Saracen assault on Orange and
his demeanour in battle corresponds not only with the tone of the narration but also with the development of the plot. Wolfram is consistent
in his portrayal of the Saracen knights as kinsmen and as practitioners of
chivalry, and is slow to devalue them because of their religion alone, despite
his medieval Christian milieu. Halzebier is portrayed by him, then, as a
capable commander and worthy knight who meets an honourable death

---

84   Gibbs and Johnson, 206.

and not as a soulless heathen enemy. Halzebier himself develops little, but the role he plays can be seen as symbolic of the fate of the entire Saracen assault as it runs its disastrous course from the initial attack to the siege and to the final battle and defeat at the hands of the Christians.

Matribleiz

Wolfram's pleasure in fashioning characters of individual substance is apparent in the Saracen king, Matribleiz. Matribleiz has no more precedence in Wolfram's source, *Aliscans*, than being mentioned in a list of names, inconsequentially and incidentally.[85] In *Willehalm*, however, this character takes on more significance as the story progresses and in the end Matribleiz plays one of the most important roles of all the Saracens.

Minding the gate

Matribleiz, Saracen king of Skandinavia, Gruonlant and Gaheviez, first appears in *Willehalm* guarding the fifth gate of Orange during the siege.[86] He is mentioned in a list of kings who were guarding this gate with Halzebier and no more is said of him until Willehalm has returned from Montlaon with support and reinforcements.

Gyburg tells Heimrich of the happenings in Orange during the siege and it is then that the audience learns more of Matribleiz's role. She recounts to Willehalm's father the bargain her son Ehmereiz sought to make with her: if she would surrender and renounce her faith in Christianity, he would see that she was compensated ten times over for the land and its resources. Ehmereiz assures her of his promise by telling her that Matribleiz shall be the one to oversee the transaction:

---

85   Matribleiz's *Aliscans* counterpart is mentioned as one of the Saracen kings, Mautrblez, encamped before the gate of Orange, laying siege to the city (*Alisc.* XLIX 2175). A character of a similar name, Maltriblez, is mentioned when Rainouart lists his brothers when confronting Valegrape (*Alisc.* CXLII 6569).

86   *Wh.* 98, 12–15.

der staete Matribeleiz,
der künec von Scandinâvîâ,
der bêde hie unt anderswâ
sîne triwe hât behalten,
der solt der prüefer walten
mit vride und mit geleite,
und des geltes wern bereite.

(*Wh.* 257, 4–10)

[Steadfast Matribleiz, the King of Skandinavia, who everyone knows is to be trusted and who both here and elsewhere has preserved his loyalty, was to protect the assessors, ensure safe conduct for them and pay out the money in cash.][87]

In this passage, Wolfram supplies a personal reputation to the Saracen King Matribleiz and it is one which will have a specific and important function as the second battle plays itself out. The audience, anticipating the French victory now that reinforcements have arrived and are amassing at Orange for the final defeat of the attackers, looks back through the eyes of Gyburg over the time spent in the defence of the city during the siege. That Matribleiz is mentioned by name to Gyburg in the parley with Ehmereiz speaks a great deal of this reputation, for Ehmereiz, wanting to assure his mother that his promise is credible, knows that Matribleiz's name will assuage any doubts she might have. Further to Matribleiz's credit is the report to Heimrich that people everywhere know of his integrity.

Through relatively small narrative innovations to the Saracen king, Wolfram has fashioned a trustworthy knight, exemplifying chivalric virtues respected universally; he has given him a kingdom with a name, Skandinavia,[88] and has described a little of his soldiering ability (by way of his not being prominent and having played no part at all in the first battle). It is in the second battle, however, that Matribleiz's character will begin to excel.

87 Gibbs and Johnson, 132.
88 Wolfram uses the place name, Skandinavia, possibly because of its exotic sound; it is not necessarily to be understood here, either geographically or politically, as comprising the nordic countries on the Baltic and North Seas.

Representative of the defeated

Matribleiz's rise from the ranks begins when Terramer addresses his ten sons before the second battle, assigning commanders and battalions. Matribleiz is to be in the sixth wave under Aropatin of Ganfassashe. We learn that Matribleiz has brought every knight from his three kingdoms, Skandinavia, Gruonlant and Gaheviez.[89] In battle, his battalion is met by old Heimrich himself and the fighting is tough, but Matribliez exhibits *staete* [reliability].[90] The sixth wave is broken by Heimrich's ruthless knights and Matribleiz is not seen again until he is taken prisoner by the victorious Willehalm.

When Matribleiz is captured with the defeated heathen nobles, Heimrich is left guarding them and Matribleiz's honest reputation convinces Willehalm to leave him unshackled. Willehalm realizes that he is Gyburg's relation and addresses him:

> mit zuht des marcrâven munt
> sprach 'mir ist ein dinc wol kunt
> an iu, künec Matribleiz,
> daz ich die wâren sippe weiz
> zwischen iu und dem wîbe mîn:
> durch si sult ir hie gêret sîn
> von allen den diechs mag erbiten.
> ir habt mit werdeclîchen siten
> Iwer zît gelebt sô schône,
> daz nie houbt under krône
> ob küneges herzen wart erkant,
> den beiden vor ûz waere benant
> sô manec hôhlîcher prîs.
> ich mag iuch lobn in allen wîs,
> zer manheit und zer triuwe,
> und zer milte ân riuwe,
> und zer staete diu niht wenken kan.

89 *Wh.* 348, 2–26.
90 *Wh.* 383, 10–14.

ich künd iu, wol gelobter man,
mînen willen, des ich bite:
ich getrûwe iu wol, ir sît dermite.'
                    (*Wh.* 461, 23 – 462, 12)

[The Margrave spoke with propriety, saying: 'There is one thing I know very well about you, King Matribleiz, and that is that you are truly related to my wife. Because of that you shall be honoured here by all of whom I request it. You have lived your life nobly and so properly that there has never been known a crowned head over a king's heart to which higher renown in such fullness could be attributed. I can praise you in every respect for your courage and loyalty, for your unstinting generosity and for your constancy that knows no change. I shall tell you my intent and what I shall ask of you, highly honoured man, and trust in you to carry it out.'][91]

Willehalm pays Matribleiz the compliment of respecting his relationship with Gyburg, recognizing also that he exemplifies chivalric virtues and that he is trustworthy. This is why Matribleiz, not known to the audience for his individual deeds in battle, is now in the position of carrying out Willehalm's most innovative and important command for the text, to act on behalf of his fallen kinsmen and to care for those dead that he can find, relying upon the embalming materials that Willehalm has put at his disposal.

Arofel and Halzebier, Gyburg's uncles and the important Saracen commanders, are dead. The specific roles given them by Wolfram having played themselves out, now Matribleiz can step in as the recipient of Willehalm's knightly and Christian compassion. Wolfram has set up his character carefully, and the audience respects him as a trustworthy knight; there is no ignominious blood on his hands from the first battle and no dishonourable actions from the second. He behaves with dignity in defeat when he is taken prisoner and makes a fitting figure to whom Willehalm can entrust his act of reconciliation with himself and with God: the showing of compassion to his defeated enemy.

It is almost as if Wolfram extends the gift of redemption through the words of Matribleiz to the conquering margrave:

---

91   Gibbs and Johnson, 223.

Matribleiz zehant sich bôt
ze tal gein sînen fuozen nider.
der wart schier ûf gehaben sider.
dô danct er dem markîs,
und sprach alsô, daz al sîn prîs
mit der tât waere beslozzen,
und sîn triwe mit lobe begozzen,
des sîn saelde immer blüete
und sîn unverswigeniu güete.
(*Wh.* 463, 2–10)

[Matribleiz immediately cast himself at Willehalm's feet, but he was quickly lifted up again. He thanked the Marquis, saying that this deed had set the seal upon all his renown and had showered his loyalty with praise so that his fortune would ever blossom and his much-proclaimed virtue too.][92]

Matribleiz then talks with regret about how he fought and was taken captive, calling his own race 'heathen' and blaming the folly of his gods. Releasing Matribleiz from his word of honour, his parole, Willehalm entrusts him with the task of finding, embalming and returning all of the fallen heathen kings to their ships and with carrying a personal message to Terramer of compassion and generosity: that the fallen kings are being sent back to him out of respect[93] and that Willehalm desires to earn his favour and grace.[94] With this prominent task ahead of him, Matribleiz is granted Willehalm's blessing:

ich bevilh iuch, künec Matribleiz,
dem der der sterne zal weiz
Unt der uns gap des mânen schîn.
dem müezet ir bevolhen sîn,
daz er iuch bring ze Gaheviez.
iwer herze tugende nie verliez
(*Wh.* 466, 29 – 467, 4)

---

92   Gibbs and Johnson, 223.
93   It is worthy of note that in the parodic *Chanson de Rainouart*, Guillaume negotiates to have a pagan statue returned to the Saracens after battle.
94   *Wh.* 463–6.

[I commend you, King Matribleiz, to Him who knows the number of the stars and who gave us the light of the moon. May you be in his care, and may he bring you to Gaheveiz, for your heart has never abandoned virtue.][95]

After a few more lines we reach the end of the fragment. Wolfram's story is unfinished, but his message is manifest. Though the Saracens are defeated and though there is open recognition of differing religious views and their perceived consequences, there is, at the end of the final battle, no discussion of conversion to Islam or to Christianity between Willehalm and Matribleiz, and they each listen to the other's reference to his own gods without derisive or judgmental comment. Matribleiz is even extended Willehalm's Christian blessing as he embarks upon his task. Though *Willehalm* does not present the heathens as equals to their Christian enemies in being worthy of God's grace, Wolfram recognizes that it is neither he nor the characters in the story who will be their judge and Matribleiz receives on their behalf the Christian charity and compassion of the reconciled Willehalm, who has God's favour and grace.

Deliberately, though sometimes due to misinterpretations or misunderstandings of the source material, Wolfram has effected profound changes to the characters of Arofel, Noupatris, Halzebier and Matribleiz from that of his source. He has made certain details more prominent, such as their being distant kinsmen of Gyburg, Willehalm's beloved wife, and their status as kings due to illustrious lineage or reputation.[96] An innovation common to all four is their courtliness and service to love and ladies; this is mentioned repeatedly by Wolfram, possibly as a result of his chronological and geo-political milieu. It would appear that he also wanted the audience to see these characters as complete in their chivalric values, save for the one component that they are understood to be missing in the foundation of

---

95 Gibbs and Johnson, 225.

96 The fact that Saracens were often depicted as possessing a natural right to noble privilege as knights and heroes in the *chansons de geste* was not new to Wolfram (see Daniel. *Heroes and Saracens*, 35), though he certainly makes a point of narrating the illustrious lineage and nobility of these heathen kings.

Christian courtly chivalry: the love for God, who directs and influences that service to ladies and all humans. What is certain is that Wolfram had specific intentions for these four heathen kings whose transformation from the pagan enemies of *Aliscans* to the worthy knight-adversaries in *Willehalm* enables them to be seen as protagonists of a sort.

Though none of these kings features as prominently in *Aliscans*, in the heroic romance of *Willehalm* the episodic nature of the songs of the *jongleurs* gives way to the more uninterrupted plot development of the epic romance structure. This more continuous narrative facilitates Wolfram's desire to develop a specific character in each heathen king in order to build his story and to convey a message. Each represents an aspect of chivalry that is praiseworthy and admired, and each serves a specific function in the story. Arofel, whose chivalry is attested to in his renown, exemplifies loyalty to his kinsmen; it is his death that serves to measure Willehalm's own inner conflict and call into question the motivation for killing. Noupatris, beloved kinsmen of the Saracens, who embodies youth and fervour in the service of love and ladies, makes a fitting opponent for Vivianz to whom he deals a mortal blow, falling himself in the combat and being mourned deeply by his kinsmen. Halzebier, the mighty and powerful knight-commander whose forces represent the backbone of the Saracen assault, carries out his duty until he is killed in combat in the second battle, his role paralleling the ill-fated course of the Saracens against the Christians. Matribleiz, renowned for integrity and honesty, remains trustworthy to the end, when he is assigned the specific task of carrying out Willehalm's compassionate wishes and receives on behalf of all the heathens the Christian *largesse* that symbolizes the tone of redemption after the conflict.

Wolfram recognized that if there was any quality at all mitigating in the character of a villain, then the audience could not reject him as entirely evil. In the case of Aérofle and Haucebier, the *chanson-de-geste* portrayal left no hint of a redeemable quality; they were described as monstrous, unfeeling, and vicious, fit only to be killed. When Wolfram transformed these characters into individuals with chivalric qualities and human emotions, he made it possible for the audience to see them as humanly fallible, as unfortunate heathens endowed with a child-like ignorance of God, though not without the curiosity to look beyond their own religion, unable to see that their faith is flawed, yet worthy of respect as human beings. They remain, however, unable to realize the rewards of chivalry unless they are converted to Christianity. Their folly underscores the message Wolfram seems intent on conveying about loyalty and kinship, and how they are joined in chivalry and spirituality.

Gyburg's Kinsmen

How Wolfram portrayed the principal Saracens in *Willehalm* was not always so innovative as to be entirely original, for the *chansons de geste* often told of Saracen enemies with exceptional virtues, clan nobility and family connections to the Christian protagonists.[97] There were certain notable cases in which the heathen enemy recognized the error of his ways and converted to Christianity, such as Baudins, Rainouart's cousin who converts after being defeated, or the famous Fierabras.[98] These characters have certain qualities that endear them in some way to the audience. Even Rainouart himself, with his *tinel* and his child-like temper, converts to Christianity to marry Louis' daughter, Aélis, and goes on to be the favoured protagonist in many *chansons de geste*, fighting on the side of the Christians. Wolfram recognized the importance of kinship in the portrayal of the heathen protagonists with a purpose beyond that of *Aliscans*. This purpose was to recount the deeds of the Narbonnais heroes and those serving the Christian cause. Wolfram was interested in exploring a message about humanity, loyalty and love in *Willehalm* and Willehalm's Saracen in-laws play a central role.

---

97 In his volume on Rennewart, Lofmark examines the treatment of the Saracen in *Willehalm* and *Aliscans*, and observes that in composing his version, 'Wolfram generally avoids contradicting his source and follows it more closely than he has been given credit for in recent years.' *Rennewart*, 236.

98 Norman Daniel, writing on Fierabras, notes that 'public villains are no doubt charming when you get to know them.' Daniel, *Heroes and Saracens*, 41.

Wolfram's pleasure in narration is apparent in his largest work, *Parzival*, and the dimension and richness of character with which he endowed his protagonists alone demonstrates a propensity to surpass the thematic scope that marked the era of the heroic *chansons de geste* even before he began his version of the *Aliscans* material. His purpose in *Willehalm* is similar to that in *Parzival*, in which conversion of the heathen made a worthy theme. Saracens and the prospect of their conversion to Christianity, of joining in kinship or brotherhood through service to God, constituted an idea that Wolfram seeks to explore more closely. It was Feirefiz, Parzival's brother, who, loyally accompanying his brother to the Grail, converted to Christianity for the love of Repanse, and participating in the spreading of Christianity throughout the world via the kinship of Grail maidens. Having given his audience this precedent, Wolfram's themes in *Willehalm* would fall short of expectations were they not to converge on the same ideas of brotherhood between adversaries and kinship through conversion.

Wolfram draws on the circumstance of war being fought between adversaries who are family relations to give emphasis to the tragic aspect of death in battle, combining virtues of love, chivalry and spirituality in the Saracen protagonists in order that the audience can view the war from a wider perspective. Though the four Saracen kings discussed above are distantly related to Gyburg and thereby must be of virtuous character, her immediate kinsmen, Terramer, Ehmereiz and Rennewart, are represented with even more significance, as they embody the hope that 'family connections may also bridge the two societies.'[99] Terramer, Ehmereiz and Rennewart, portrayed as no less ignorant in their religious beliefs than the four Saracen kings whose roles were purposefully changed by Wolfram, symbolize the hope of redemption through conversion and, thereby, the unifying power of kinship, the forgiveness of wayward deeds and the beginning of peace and understanding for all humanity as God's creation.

99   Daniel, *Heroes and Saracens*, 37.

Terramer

> ir muget wol mîme sweher jehen
> mîner mâge tôt, des landes brant:
> sölhe heimstiur gît mir sîn hant.
> ez ist manec mîn übergenôz geriten
> ûf mînen schaden: daz waere vermiten,
> soldez Tybalt hân geworben.
>
> (Wh. 261, 6–11)

[You can blame my father-in-law for the deaths of my kinsmen and the devastation of the land. Such is the dowry he gives to me. Many men, more powerful than I, have attacked me. This would have been avoided, if Tibalt had been acting on his own.][100]

In the character of Terramer, one finds conflict and tension, a man torn between his duty to command an army against Willehalm out of loyalty to his clan, and his chivalric duty as a knight and father. Terramer, who is both Gyburg's father and Willehalm's enemy, is trapped between loyalties and subject to obligation. By Terramer's joining and adding his support to Tybalt's attack on Orange, the relatively simple issue of revenge and the desire to reconquer from Willehalm what has been stolen becomes a large-scale war between Christianity and the Arab world. Terramer is at once a hardened adversary and a tender parent, an obstinate leader and a curious intellectual. It is in Terramer's character that Wolfram allows the embodiment of the tragic conflict between kin and between knights to manifest itself.

Tragic villain

Wolfram introduces Terramer from the beginning as a powerful man, rich with loyal vassals:

---

100 Gibbs and Johnson, 134.

Terramêrs rîcheit
was kreftic wît unde breit,
und daz ander künge ir krône
durh manneschaft ze lône
Von sîner hende enpfiengen
und dienst gein im begiengen.
        (*Wh.* 9, 27 – 10, 2)

[The power of Terramer was immense and extended far and wide, and other kings
received their crowns in fief and fealty from him and performed their services to
him.][101]

He is also presented, however, as a man who is caught between two families and Wolfram suggests that Terramer is a victim of these circumstances,[102]
bound to play out a battle which will only end in disaster for him. Although
Terramer knows that things might have been different, it is too late now.

Terramêr wart des enein,
ûf Alitschanz er kêrte,
dâ strît sîn her gelêrte
des er nimmer mêr wart vrô.
wie tet der wîse man alsô?
si wârn im sippe al gelîche,
Willalm des lobes rîche
und Tybalt Arabeln man,
durh den er herzesêre gewan
vor jâmer nâch dem bruoder sîn
und mangen werden Sarrazîn
dem tôde ergap ze zinse.
ein herze daz von flinse
ime donre gewahsen waere,
daz müeten disiu maere.
        (*Wh.* 12, 4–18)

---

101 Gibbs and Johnson, 21.
102 Wolfram describes how Terramer summoned Arofel and Halzebier with their armies,
     'durh den künic Tybalt' [on behalf of King Tibalt], who was deeply grieved at the
     loss of Gyburg as well as of his lands (*Wh.* 10, 15).

[Terramer had resolved to move towards Alischantz, where the fighting taught his army such a lesson that he was never happy again. How could such a wise and experienced man behave like that? They were both equally related to him, the renowned Willehalm and Tibalt, Arabel's husband, because of whom he endured heartache through grief for his brother and surrendered many a noble Saracen in tribute to death. A heart turned to flint by a clap of thunder would be moved by this tale.][103]

Terramer is torn between two sons-in-law, both worthy of his loyalty, and Wolfram calls attention to the tragedy of this. Wolfram foreshadows the defeat Terramer's forces will suffer and makes it clear that this will affect him personally. He does not use the word 'heathen' to identify Terramer's character; instead, he merely mentions that Terramer served his favourite gods,[104] thereby drawing the audience's attention to the individual and his reactions to his situation, rather than to a common but fearsome Saracen enemy. The audience is asked the rhetorical question of how a man of Terramer's years could embark upon such an endeavour as a consequence of Tybalt's grief and lust for revenge.[105] That Wolfram finds this course of action ill-befitting such a man is evident. Wolfram derides Terramer's behaviour as foolish, though not without supplying an insight into the man who carries out these actions:

> Terramêr unfuoget,
> daz in des niht genuoget,
> des sîne tohter dûhte vil.
> bescheidenlîch ich sprechen wil,
> swen mîn kint ze friwende erkür,
> ungerne ich den ze friwent verlür.
> Willalm ehkurneis
> was sô wert ein Franzeis,
> des noch bedörfte wol ein wîp,
> ob si alsô kürlîchen lîp
> durch minne braehte in ir gebot:
> sîn sweher hazzet in ân nôt.
>
> (*Wh.* 11, 19–30)

103 Gibbs and Johnson, 22–3.
104 *Wh.* 9, 8–9.
105 *Wh.* 11, 6–15.

[(Terramer was foolish to disdain the man whom his daughter prized so highly. Let me tell you one thing: I would not want to lose as a friend the one whom my daughter had chosen as her beloved.) Willehalm au court nez was such a noble Frenchman that, if today a lady were to acquire an equally distinguished knight to serve her for love, it would have to be Willehalm and no other. His father-in-law had no reason to hate him.][106]

The contrast with which Terramer's complex character is depicted in *Willehalm* is marked by his extremes of temper and the discrepancy between Wolfram's description of his physical grandeur and his emotional disposition.[107] Indeed, Wolfram describes him as a first-rate warrior and highly respected commander who has no need to utter commands himself; instead, he is followed without hesitation, his reputation preceding him.[108] When Terramer is told by his scouts that Halzebier is retreating and Noupatris has been slain, he says nothing; it is his scouts who do the talking. Wolfram maintains this sense of distance in Terramer by describing the effect of allowing the news to circulate that he is to join in the battle personally:

> 'wir soltens umbestecken
> mit dem zehenden unserr phîle:
> si mugen deheine wîle
> vor dem her getûren.'
> eskelîrn und amazûren
> unden künegen die dâ houbetman
> wârn, den wart dô kunt getân,
> man begunde jungn und alten sagen
> daz selbe wâpen wolde tragen
> Terramêr der zornic gemuot.
> dô regete sich diu heres fluot.
> (*Wh.* 28, 12–22)

106 Gibbs and Johnson, 22.
107 Gibbs and Johnson, 257–8.
108 When all detachments have formed around Orange after the second battle, Fabors, Terramer's son, gives the orders: 'Fâbors Terramêres suon gap ieslîchem künege stat als in sîn vater ligen bat' [Terramer's son Fabors assigned each king his siege position, as required by Terramer himself] (*Wh.* 97, 12–14). Gibbs and Johnson, 60.

['We should surround them with one tenth of our archers,' they said. 'They cannot hold out long against our army.' The word was passed to eskelirs[109] and amazurs, and to those kings who were commanding the forces there, and to all men, young and old alike, that the enraged Terramer himself was proposing to enter into battle. At that, the lines of the heathen army began to move like flood water.][110]

Terramer has brought countless warships and other vessels across the sea; he has summoned the forces of Arofel and Halzebier, commanded the deployment of troops, lost beloved kinsmen and been involved in combat, yet he speaks very little in the story and only then as a leader. The impression Wolfram probably wishes to give his audience is that of an aloof and respected commander, experienced and wise in his leadership, both loyal and commanding loyalty from his vast dominions. The things he does say are always in the midst of action, in the heat of the moment and contradict the image the audience is forming of the man himself. In one passage, he must rally a counter-assault out of a broken line and passionately recounts how the war came about, inciting motivation in his troops to re-form against the Christian defence:

> mir und den goten ist benomn
> der ich ê jach ze kinde,
> von taverne ingesinde:
> von salsen suppierren
> sich Tybalt muose vierren
> von sînem wîbe und alle ir kint,
> die hie durh rehte râche sint.
> daz uns die luoderaere
> alsô smaehiu maere
> getorsten ie gesenden!
> held, ir sult ernenden:
> êrt die got und dar nâch mich,
> daz Tybalt und des gerich
> noh hiut ein sölh phant hie nem,
> daz Arabeln des gezem,

---

109 Like *amazur*, this is another term invented by Wolfram for a Saracen military commander. See also note 517.
110 Gibbs and Johnson, 29.

ob es geruochet Tervigant,
daz si diu kristenlîchen bant
und den touf unêre.
ê si von Jêsus kêre,
ich sols ûf einer hürde ê sehen,
diu fiuric sî: daz muoz geschehen.
                    (*Wh*. 44, 10–30)

['She whom I used to call my child has been stolen from me and from our gods,
and by a tavern mob at that! Those soup-swillers have forced Tibalt to part from
his wife, and all their children, too, who are here for just revenge, were parted from
their mother. Just imagine those milksops daring to send us such disgraceful news!
Men, take heart! Honour the gods and then me, so that Tibalt in his revenge will
exact here this very day such a toll that – Tervigant willing – Arabel will have to bring
shame upon her Christian ties and upon her baptism. She says that before she would
turn away from Jesus I should see her burning at the stake. So be it!']¹¹¹

There is passion, but no real hatred in his words: they are those of a
commander mustering his warriors who are in disarray. This he does capably, for they regroup and fight against Vivianz and his comrades, taking
eight barons prisoner. The image Wolfram gives of Terramer's position in
the predicament is one of the unfortunate father whose daughter has been
led astray by the enemy, causing Tybalt shame; it is an act that demands
revenge. Even Terramer's declaration that he will see Arabel burn if he must,
to exact revenge, is less of a vow of intent than it is a challenge to his troops
to re-engage in the battle and to secure a victory. By limiting the compass of
Terramer's words to that of a respected and capable leader, the expectation
is allowed to build in *Willehalm* about what his speech away from combat
and battle will further reveal about this intriguing Saracen.

Similarly, Terramer's *Aliscans* counterpart, Desramé, says very little
before the second battle, but the intention of the *jongleurs* differs from
Wolfram's carefully orchestrated accrual of personality. Desramé is seen
at some distance during the first part of *Aliscans*, but the audience is left
with the impression that this is because, being the supreme commander
of the pagan forces, his entry proper into the battle will signify that it has

---

111   Gibbs and Johnson, 36.

come to a climax. Part of the climactic build-up of action in the *chanson de geste* is foreshadowed in that, when Desramé is mentioned earlier, it is his paternal relation to Rainouart that is emphasized, which must end in the ultimate meeting between father and son upon the battlefield. In fact, it is Rainouart, not Desramé, who is the primary focus for the audience of *Aliscans*.

When Terramer finally speaks after the battle in *Willehalm*, it is to reflect upon his situation. The tragic disposition of his character is underpinned by his comments about the losses he has suffered. We see the image of a great man who has taken a grave course of action due to his loyalty and his misplaced belief in his gods, whose heart grieves at his misfortune when the losses are taken into account after the first battle:

> diu flust dô Terramêren treip
> in sô herzebaere klage,
> dês waere erstorben lîhte ein zage.
> dô sprach er trûreclîche
> 'swer giht daz ich sî rîche,
> der hât mich unreht erkant,
> swie al der heidenschefte lant
> mit dienste stên ze mîme gebote.
> ich mac der kristenheite gote
> alêrst nu grôzes wunders jehen:
> selh wunder ist an mir geschehen,
> daz ein hant vol rîter mich
> hât nâch entworht durch den gerich,
> [...]
> für wâr nu ist mîn hervart
> kreftiger und wîter brâht.
> ich wil und hân mir des erdâht,
> daz ich manege unkunde nôt
> Arabeln gebe und smaehen tôt,
> des Jêsus gunêret sî:
> der wille ist mîme herzen bî.'
>
> (*Wh.* 107, 10 – 108, 22)

[The loss drove Terramer to such heart-felt lament that it would have killed a lesser man. He spoke in sorrow: 'Whoever says that I am mighty, does not know me properly, even though all the lands of heathendom stand ready to serve at my command. I can only now ascribe a great miracle to the god of Christendom, for it is a miracle indeed which has befallen me, that a handful of knights almost destroyed me on account of my vengeance. [...] To be sure, my army is more powerful and more broadly based. It is my firm intent to give Arabel unheard-of torment and a shameful death to disgrace Jesus. I cherish that desire in my heart.']¹¹²

Terramer's image as a man with torn loyalties is established. He reasons out both the advantages and disadvantages of his position in his speech, attempting to justify his actions and to come to terms with the losses that he has suffered. This lament and the compassion in Terramer's character, however, is not understood by the Christian protagonists until the end of the fragment where Wolfram's text breaks off; Terramer's heartache is kept to himself, despite his questioning of motive and reason. He is ignorant of the Christian mysteries, but not so ignorant as to underestimate the power of their influence on the French army. This, along with the reference to his uncle, Baligan, the Saracen adversary of Charlemagne in the *Rolandslied*, softens his image somewhat, while also elevating his importance and stature above that of Désramé.¹¹³ He is bound to ride out his decision to invade the southern march. In the end, he vows to sacrifice his daughter as vengeance against Christianity; he has reasoned that Christianity must be to blame for his downfall, but there is no satisfaction derived from this conclusion nor does it seem that comfort is reflected in Terramer's bearing. Although vengeance is a central motive and theme in *Willehalm*, as it was in *Aliscans*, Wolfram seems to be conveying the idea, the truth, that revenge grants neither comfort, redemption nor peace; though driven by loyalty and duty, it reveals a deep spiritual crack in the unspoken code of chivalry.

---

112   Gibbs and Johnson, 65–6.
113   Lofmark considers the rank given Terramer by Wolfram who refers to other tales
       that the audience would have known: besides being *admirat* and steward of Baldac,
       he is 'a father *Kanabêûs*' and cousin to Baligan from *Rolandslied*, and becomes heir
       of Pompeius from *Parzival*, 'which places him in historical perspective among the
       Saracen emperors.' Lofmark, *Rennewart*, 89.

Waging an imposed war

The image of Terramer, as fashioned by Wolfram, is less of a terrifying warrior than that of one more resolute, martially capable to a high degree, formidable and imposing without being petrifying. The *jongleurs* of *Aliscans*, however, supply little of Desramé's individual character for the audience to wonder at until the first physical descriptions of Desramé, before the second battle, when the awaited confrontation between Desramé and Rainouart is imminent. It is then that his awe-inspiring albeit grotesque physical appearance is first described, in the scene where he first learns of his poor military position:

> Desramez l'ot, mout s'en es aïrez,
> De mautalant est tainz et enbrasez,
> Les elz rooile, s'a les sorcilz levez,
> Estraint les danz, s'a les grenons crollés.
> Ne vos sai dire com est grant sa fiertez;
> Cil ne l'esgarde qui ne soit effreez.
> (*Alisc.* XCVIII, 5207–12)

> [Desramé listened to [the scout] and became angry. First he paled, then he turned red with rage; his eyes rolled, his eyebrows raised, he ground his teeth and contorted his moustaches. I cannot describe to you how great was his fierceness. One could not look at him without being frightened.]

Descriptions of his appearance in the next *laisse* include that of his armaments.[114] The detail of the size and costliness of these armaments and the strength of their bearer is elaborated on, with short histories of each (their lineage reflecting on his reputation). It is also noted that his armour has not once been hit. By the time he meets Rainouart, a portrait has developed. He charges forward with four *rois mescreüz* [pagan kings],[115] appears *toz irascuz* [utterly furious][116] and enters the fight:

---

114 *Alisc.* XCIX 5223–40.
115 *Alisc.* CXV 6093.
116 *Alisc.* CXV 6106.

Desramez fu fort et grant et corssuz,
Lonc ot le col, noirs ert et toz chenus;
En tote Espaigne n'ot paien si membruz.
                    (*Alisc.* CXV, 6112–15)

[Desramé is brawny, big, corpulent; he has a long neck and is black with white hair.
He is the mightiest heathen in all Spain.]

This is Desramé as he goes into battle in *Aliscans*, although we do not
see him as an individual before the second battle, as we do Terramer in
Willehalm. Terramer's character is established for the audience before the
second battle commences, without the need for any physical description.
With the help of Terramer's developing personality, his thoughts, his feelings and his reflections, Wolfram allows the war to become the focus, the
thematic centre of *Willehalm*, and not the background as in *Aliscans*.[117]
It is through Terramer's ruminations and tragically torn loyalties that the
audience is shown that this war between people of different religions, yet
of the same extended family, can be questioned, that its outcome can be
scrutinized and that the means by which victory is attained and actions
are motivated can be inspected on a spiritual level. The war encompasses
every individual and every action and is, in Bumke's words, 'eine furchtbare
Erfahrung, die die ganze Ordnung des menschlichen Zusammenlebens zu
erschüttern droht' [a terrible experience that threatens to shake the entire
community social order].[118] The war threatens more than mere territory and
inheritance, as in *Aliscans*: for Wolfram, it threatens the code of chivalric
behaviour which encompasses spiritual chivalry, family loyalty and service
to love, and enables people to live together in harmony, peace and spiritual
accord. When Terramer considers his actions, their motivations and consequences, he questions the reasons for the war and the behaviour of knights,
establishing the idea that there are chivalric alternatives to such a war.

Though Terramer is the villain, he is not portrayed as evil and his
defeat brings no great celebration. He is respected for having followed his

117   See Bumke, *Wolfram von Eschenbach*, 320.
118   See Bumke, *Wolfram von Eschenbach*, 320.

course of action out of loyalty and honour, and is not without his own sentiments of detached respect for Willehalm or for the Christian religion. It is a devastating loss for him, and he is forced to depart in defeat after being heavily wounded in combat against Willehalm:

> wan der admirât wart sêre wunt
> geleit ûf sînen tragamunt
> der niemer schunphentiur enphienc.
>
> (*Wh.* 443, 13–15)

[The Admirat, who had never been defeated, was laid sorely wounded on his warship.][119]

This is the last we see of Terramer in *Willehalm*, yet the effects of his chivalric actions will be evident in one more important scene. When speaking to King Matribleiz after the battle, Willehalm tells of a tent he found with kings slain in the first battle, whom Terramer had provided with biers and golden and jewelled name-plates; it is only then that Willehalm perceives Terramer's compassion, generosity and grief.[120] When both battles have taken place, as well as a siege and a rumination on the situation, this scene is perhaps the most important of all for Terramer's character development, as well as for the tone of the story, for it allows the audience to see the emergent inner nobility of Terramer through Willehalm's eyes. Willehalm's realization of Terramer's integrity even in defeat prompts him to send an embassy to the admirat[121] via Matribleiz:

> swaz ir künege vindet dâ,
> die bringet Terramêre,
> der die grôzen überkêre
> tet âne mîne schulde,
> des genâde und des hulde

---

119   Gibbs and Johnson, 215.
120   'Such honouring of the slain goes beyond the duty of the ruler and betrays, again, the personal response of a man whom Wolfram refrains from actually criticizing but sees rather as a victim of circumstances.' Gibbs and Johnson, 215, 258.
121   *Admirat* is another of Wolfram's invented titles. See also notes 517 and 566.

ich gerne gediende, torst ichs biten,
swie er gebüte, wan mit den siten
daz ich den hoehsten got verküre
und daz ich mînen touf verlüre
und wider gaeb mîn clârez wîp.
für wâr ich liez ê manegen lîp
verhouwen als ist hie gesehen.
hêr künec, ir muget im dort wol jehen,
ich ensendes im durch forhte niht,
swaz man hie tôter künege siht:
ich êre dermit et sînen art,
des mir ze kürzwîle wart
an mînem arme ein süezez teil,
dâ von ich trûric unde geil
sît dicke wart, sô kom der tac
daz Tybalt gein mir strîtes pflac.
                    (*Wh.* 466, 4 –24)

[Whatever kings you find there bring them to Terramer, who launched his huge invasion through no fault of mine and whose grace and favour I would like to earn, if I
dared seek it, in whatever way he might command, except for asking me to renounce
Almighty God and to lose my Christian baptism and to give back my lovely wife.
Indeed, I would sooner send many men to their deaths, as you have seen here. Your
Highness, you may tell him when you get there that I am not sending the dead kings
that are here out of fear. I am simply showing respect for his family, a sweet member
of which it has been my pleasure to hold in my arms and who has often made me sad
and happy since the day Tibalt attacked me.][122]

This scene might suggest that Terramer's losses in the assault on
Orange were not entirely ineffectual, for his chivalry is being recognized
and remembered, and the hope is born that reconciliation is still possible.
This realization stands in sharp contrast to the departure of Desramé in
Aliscans, who escapes, wounded, to his ships:

N'en i a nul ne soient effondrez
Fors un tot seul qui en est eschapez;
En cel entra li forz rois Desramez,

122   Gibbs and Johnson, 224–5.

Li rois i entre entre lui et Huré;
Traient lor ancre, s'ont lor voile levé;
En mer s'enpaignent; or sont a sauveté.
Li vis deable lor dona tel oré
Desi a Cordres ne se sont aresté.
(*Alisc.* CLXII, 7001–8)

[All have fallen except one who escaped. It is the powerful king Desramé who takes refuge with the company of Huré. Hoisting their anchor, raising their sail, they put to sea; they are saved. The living devil gives them a favourable wind that does not cease until they reach Cordres.]

Father and kinsman

'Min tohter vrumt mir herzeser, Arable.'
(*Wh.* 351, 1–2)

[My daughter Arabel is causing me heartfelt pain.][123]

Wolfram's characterization of Terramer places an emphasis on kinship; Terramer is depicted as a man with conflicted loyalties, in terms of his family.[124] He answers the call of his son-in-law, Tybalt, to take revenge upon Willehalm for taking his lands and his wife; nonetheless, he remains tied to his daughter, Gyburg, because of his relationship to her. This also means that he must at some point accept the fact that Willehalm is his son-in-law and acknowledge Rennewart as his son. True to his word, he follows through with his duty to support Tybalt's campaign and the audience has the impression that, although he feels anger and shame towards his daughter for her actions (as well as the fact that her behaviour has led to war), he accedes to Tybalt's request because of devotion and duty to his clan and not out of fury towards his daughter. In Terramer's character, the contrast between a father of Gyburg and a kinsman of Tybalt and

---

123 Gibbs and Johnson, 174.
124 Bumke remarks how Wolfram develops almost every theme in the context of kinship (see Bumke, *Wolfram von Eschenbach*, 321) and Terramer is one of the pivotal figures in this tendency.

his brothers is evident during the siege of Orange, where he acts as both commander of the invasion and mediator with his daughter, the queen of Termis (the castle at Orange).

> Terramêr der warp alsô,
> hiute vlêhen, morgen drô,
> gein sîner lieben tohter.
> mit deheinen dingen mohter
> si des überlisten,
> sine wolte Oransche fristen
> > (*Wh.* 222, 1–6)

[Terramer behaved like this towards his dear daughter: beseeching her one day and threatening her the next. But by no means could he induce her to cease defending Orange.][125]

In every way, Terramer fulfils his duty as commander of the forces for Tybalt: he is not only capable and respected as a military leader, he is also enthusiastic and imperturbable. He lent his own capabilities to the forces of his son-in-law, remaining true to his word regardless of the ever-growing certainty of defeat. When the first battle subsides and Willehalm returns to his fortress, Terramer can be seen riding his horse around the city gates, pressing his advantage and securing the perimeter for his forces:

> Terramêr dô selbe niht vermeit,
> ze vâre umb Oransch er reit,
> sîner tohter schaden er spehte.
> > (*Wh.* 97, 3–5)

[Terramer himself did not neglect to ride around Orange, eager for battle and contemplating his daughter's downfall.][126]

His energy was directed towards the defeat of Orange, but when he saw that no attack could break through the city, he ordered a siege.[127] His

---

125 Gibbs and Johnson, 117.
126 Gibbs and Johnson, 60.
127 *Wh.* 111.

military skill is further demonstrated in his relationships with his advisors. Though on numerous occasions he allows his orders to his forces to be relayed, such as during the first battle through his scouts and before the second through his sons communicating the battalion assignments, he does not let anyone speak for him, least of all his advisors.[128] In a meeting during which he is advised to withdraw from the siege, he insists upon one last strike, a strategy of reinforcing his initiative and ensuring that no counter-attack would pursue the army as they fell back to the water.

> die wîsen, sheres râtgebn,
> rieten Terramêre
> eine wîl die dankêre,
> sît waere verwüestet al daz lant
> unt ninder werlîchiu hant
> dâ waer wan in der einen stat.
> daz her in al gemeine bat,
> er solte kêren gein der habe:
> sô si genaemen spîse drabe
> unt si der luft erwaete,
> ob er sis danne baete,
> si herbergeten der wider für,
> und taetenz mit gemeiner kür.
> Daz erloubte in der von Tenabrî
> und jah, er wolt dâ wesen bî
> daz ê ein sturm geschaehe,
> sô man die naht ersaehe.
> (*Wh.* 222, 20 – 223, 6)

[Terramer's experienced military advisers recommended a temporary withdrawal, since the whole land was devastated and there was not a single hand capable of fighting, save in the one city. The entire army asked him to head for the harbour, saying that as soon as they had fetched supplies from the ships and enjoyed the fresh air they would encamp before Orange again, if he asked them to, and they would do it

---

128 The idea of a commander making decisions that are contrary to the wishes of his *consilium* becomes a minor theme here, especially as Terramer's decision leads ultimately to the defeat of the Saracens.

with one accord. Terramer of Tenabri granted their request but said that he wanted an assault to take place first, as soon as night fell.][129]

Terramer, apparently against his better judgement, must follow the wishes of his army, which will ultimately lead to his demise when he is caught unprepared by the French reinforcements. His reconsidering is shown as a deviation from the views of his peers precisely because Wolfram wants to reveal an inner nobility in his character: though he does not make the best decisions, he is not one of the masses and remains torn in his loyalties. Terramer maintains his firm command and military wisdom, however, by attacking Orange and burning it to devastation,[130] an act that can be seen as desperate, for he can no longer hold it under siege and he knows that if French reinforcements arrive, he is ultimately lost. Burning Orange is his only hope of retaining the initiative and it corresponds to his wishes that, if he cannot win Arabel back, he will see her die.

When among his advisers and his army, Terramer acts as a motivator to action: he knows exactly what words to use when their position looks grim. Upon hearing the news of the approaching French reinforcements from his scout, he musters his men with stories: of the Holy Roman crown and his rightful inheritance; of Tybalt's shame that must be avenged; of the might of the heathen gods; and of his plans to take Paris and Aachen to gain the imperial seat.[131] His speech is florid and his words strong, but given his disposition, his experience and his penchant for contemplation, one cannot help but wonder how seriously he takes his speeches himself (even if he has little doubt as to their effect on his warriors). Although he is certain that his assault on Orange will now end in defeat, he never betrays this to his forces nor does he balk at his duty as Tybalt's kinsman.

Terramer's military experience and prowess contrasts with the deliberations he has with Gyburg during the siege of Orange. It becomes clear that he does not like the idea of threatening his own daughter, but that he will do what he must. When, after repeated attempts to bring her to

129   Gibbs and Johnson, 117.
130   *Wh.* 223, 7–21.
131   *Wh.* 337, 30 – 341, 3.

submission, Gyburg refuses yet again, Terramer bemoans his situation
and the consequences of Gyburg's decision to marry Willehalm. Gyburg
admonishes him:

> ir verlieset michel arbeit,
> Du vater und ander mîne mâge,
> daz ir lîp unt êre en wâge
> lât durh Tybaldes rât,
> der deheine vorderunge hât
> von rehte ûf mich ze sprechen.
> waz wiltu, vater, rechen
> an dîn selbes kinde?
> bî tumpheit ich dich vinde.
>
> (*Wh.* 216, 30 – 217, 8)

[You are wasting much effort, you, father and my other kinsmen, risking life and
honour to help Tibalt, who has no just claims to lay on me. Why are you taking
revenge on your own child? I think you are acting foolishly.][132]

Terramer does not like to be told this by his daughter, possibly because
it prompts him to question his own actions:

> 'ach ich vreuden arm man,
> daz ich sölh kint ie gewan,'
> sprach Terramêr der rîche,
> 'daz alsô herzenlîche
> an sîner saelde kan verzagn
> unt sich den goten wil entsagn!
> ey süeziu Gyburc, tuo sô niht.
> swaz dir ie geschach od noch geschiht
> von mir, daz ist mîn selbes nôt.
> jâ gieng ich für dich an den tôt.
> daz ruoch erkennen Mahumete,
> daz ich durh Tybaldes bete
> ungerne ûf dînen schaden fuor,
> unz michs bî unserr ê beswuor
> der bâruc unt de êwarten sîn:

die gâben mirz für sünde mîn,
daz ich dich taete lîbelôs.
mîn triwe ich doch sô nie verkôs,
ich hete dich zeime kinde.
ob ich dich bî saelden vinde,
sô êre dîn geslehte
unt tuo den goten rehte.'
(*Wh.* 217, 9–30)

['Alas, unhappy man that I am,' said the mighty Terramer, 'that I ever had such a child, who can despair so totally of her own salvation and deliberately renounce the gods! Oh, sweet Arabel, don't behave like this! Whatever has happened or will yet happen to you because of me, is my very own misery. Indeed, I would lay down my life for you. May Mahmete deign to recognize that I did not want to take up arms against you at Tibalt's request, until the Baruc and his priests entreated me by our religion to do so. They told me to kill you as penance for my sins. Yet I never did betray my loyalty to that extent. I always thought of you as my child. If I find you in a state of blessedness, then honour your family and give the gods their due!']¹³³

Terramer fluctuates between expressing love and loyalty to his child and loyalty and obedience to his religion, each in opposition to the other.

When he speaks to Gyburg about Christianity, it is almost as a puzzled child. His contempt for the religion is something akin to awe rather than hatred.¹³⁴ He tries to reason out the paradox of the Trinity and Christ, and when he is unable to arrive at a satisfactory explanation, he simply entreats Gyburg to give up her new religion.¹³⁵ Refusing him again, Gyburg, who is resilient and determined, tries very sensibly to talk terms.

Tybald ich Todjerne
lâz, dâ du mich krôntes.
dannoch du, vater, schôntes
dîner triwe, dô daz selbe lant
ze heimstiwer mir gap dîn hant.
wilt du Tybalde volgen,

---

133   Gibbs and Johnson, 115.
134   See Gibbs and Johnson, 258.
135   *Wh.* 219, 2–22.

du muost mir sîn erbolgen.
nâch sîm erbeteile
er füert dîn êre veile.
er giht ouch ûf Sybilje:
daz liez im Marsilje
sîn oeheim, den Ruolant ersluoc.
hie dishalp mers er sagt genuoc
daz er für erbeschaft sül hân:
sît dîn veter Baligân
den lîp verlôs von Karle,
halp Provenz unt Arle,
er giht daz sül er erben.
wiltu durh lüge verderben
dîn triuwe an dîn selbes fruht,
ouwê waz touc dîn altiu zuht?
du verwurkest an mir al dîn heil.
mahtu Todjern, mîn erbeteil,
Tybalde und Ehmereize gebn,
und lâz mich mit armuot lebn.
(*Wh.* 221, 2–26)

[To Tibalt I leave Todjerne, where you crowned me Queen. At that time, father, you still preserved your loyalty when you yourself gave me that land as a dowry. If you are going to side with Tibalt, then you will have to be angry with me. He is selling out your honour for his inherited territorial rights. He lays claim indeed to Sibilje, saying that Marsilje, his uncle, whom Roland slew, left him that. Here on this side of the sea, there is much land that he claims as his inheritance. He says that he should inherit Arles and half of Provence, since your uncle, Baligan, was slain by Charles. If you are going to let your loyalty to your own offspring die for the sake of such lies, then, alas, of what value is your former courtesy? You will forfeit all your hopes for salvation by your behaviour towards me. Go ahead and give Todjerne, my property by right, to Tibalt and Ehmereiz, and let me live in poverty.][136]

Terramer's answer to this is not narrated – and indeed, what could he say? Gyburg not only attacks his chivalry; she also attacks his motives and his salvation. To a wise and experienced man, these words from his daughter, no matter how sensible or true, are impertinent; thus, the battle

136 Gibbs and Johnson, 116.

continues both around the city and within the man. What magnanimity Terramer has in his character remains distanced from the battle itself and is not discovered until after the second battle has finished, when Willehalm finds the tent with the fallen kings. Whether or not Terramer will redeem himself remains conjecture, as the fragment breaks off after Willehalm sends the embassy to his father-in-law.

Terramer's wider fate, like that of Rennewart, remains outside the scope of the fragment, but the qualities with which Wolfram has endowed him indicate a future appearance. It would be difficult to support the notion that an author such as Wolfram would not have had intentions for the return of this character, even were Terramer not compared to Baligan, who returned after Roncesvalles to fight against Charlemagne. Terramer's conflict, like that of the entire story, looks towards resolution, redemption, and peace.

Ehmereiz

Once again, a figure who carries little weight in *Aliscans* is given a greater role by Wolfram, who continues to develop his Saracens thoughtfully, giving depth and meaning to their presence in his story. Although he is presented as more of an individual than some of the other Saracens in the *chansons de geste*, Esmeré is transformed subtly into the young prince Ehmereiz, worthy because he is a blood-relative of Gyburg and because he behaves chivalrously.

Young warrior

Not only is Esmeré's role in *Aliscans* of less consequence than that of Ehmereiz in *Willehalm* but the portrayals of Guillaume's stepson are in sharp contrast, too. Esmeré d'Odïerne appears only three times in *Aliscans*, but in each appearance he is further developed. Guillaume first sees Esmeré from afar, accompanied by two other kings, Corsuble and Ahenré, and ten thousand troops as they disembark from their ship; they are elaborately turned out with jewelled armour and beautiful weapons.[137]

When Guillaume next sees Esmeré, the encounter is less than civil and words are exchanged between stepfather and stepson. Esmeré is in the company of six other kings when they find Guillaume alone on the battlefield and surround him. Guillaume recognizes him as Guiborc's beloved son and realizes that this makes him his stepson. Esmeré addresses him:

> Sire paratre, dist li rois Esmeré,
> Por quoi m'as tu a tort deherité,
> Et fors d'Orenge par traïson gité,
> Et pris ma mere trestot estre mon gré,
> Et mes .II. freres a grant tort decolé?
> Tant les batis, voiant tot ton barné,
> Desor un marbre el pavement listé,
> Que de leur sanc corurent grant li gué;
> Puis les pendis a un arbre ramé.
> Sire Guillelmes, ne l'ai pas oblïé.
> Par Mahomet, mout en oi grant vilté.
> Fel soie je, se ja n'est comparé!
> De cele teste me sera amendé.
> *(Alisc.* XXXII, 1242–54)

[‘Step-father,’ says King Esmeré, ‘why have you unjustly disinherited me, treacherously thrown me out of Orange, stolen away my mother despite me and unjustly beheaded my two brothers? You beat them so severely before your barons on the decorated marble floor that their blood ran in streams, then you hanged them from the branches of a tree. Sir Guillaume, I have not forgotten that. By Mohammad, I am shamed greatly. Wretched am I if I do not avenge them. Your head will be my compensation.’]

Here, the audience is presented with Esmeré's viewpoint: he has been thrown out of Orange and thus shamed; he has been disinherited of land; and his brothers have been beaten and hanged. He has plenty to complain about, and refers to events that the *jongleurs'* audience would have known

---

137 *Alisc.* XVII.

from the *Prise d'Orange*. His duty is to avenge his brothers and, realizing this, Guillaume tells him:

> Respont Guillelmes: Vos dites cruauté!
> Puis que li hom n'aime crestïenté
> Et qu'il het Deu et despit charité,
> N'a droit en vie, jel di par verité;
> Et qui l'ocist, si destruit un maufé;
> Deu a vengié, si l'en set mout bon gré.
> Tuit estes chien par droiture apelé,
> Car vos n'avez ne foi ne lëauté.
> (*Alisc.* XXXII, 1255–62)

[Guillaume responds, 'You speak cruel words! If a man does not love Christianity, hates God and despises charity, he has no right to live, I speak the truth. And he who kills him has destroyed a demon; God is avenged and is approving. You are all rightly called dogs because you have neither faith nor loyalty.']

As if by rote, and also because of his past experience in *Prise d'Orange*, about which Wolfram and his audience might know little, Guillaume addresses Esmeré. Guillaume tells the audience and perhaps reminds himself why Esmeré is fit to be killed and why he must combat him. He refutes Esmeré's claims to the right to avenge his brothers by attacking his chivalry and his religion. Guillaume reinforces his own position by declaring that he has God's approval.[138] A fight then ensues, but Esmeré and Corsuble escape Guillaume who, not being in a favourable position to pursue, does not give chase. When Esmeré is next seen, he is encamped

---

138   Joan Ferrante writes that Guillaume's actions can be seen as consonant with the context of the *chansons de geste*, that his killing of heathens rather than holding them for ransom is meant to be seen as Guillaume putting 'the service of God before his own personal gain' (26). It is, however, telling of Guillaume's character and of the climate of the *chansons de geste* that he has already killed Esmeré's brothers, who might also be Guiborc's sons, and is ready to kill Esmeré as well, believing himself justified in doing so. Lynn Tarte Ramey concludes that the inclusion of these killings in some versions of *Aliscans*, *Le Moniage Guillaume* and *Foucon de Candie* were rare, however, because they were unpopular to audiences who admired the image of Guiborc. See Ramey, 'Role Models?', 137–8.

outside a gate of Orange with the Saracen forces who are laying siege to it.[139] What becomes of him is not recounted in *Aliscans*; he does not emerge during the second battle, the confrontation with him already having been concluded.

Such a simplistic portrayal of Gyburg's son would never do for Wolfram, who places great importance on the theme of kinship, and he embellishes the figure of Ehmereiz accordingly, endowing him with further dimensions. Futhermore, for the sake of his audience's limited knowledge of the *Cycle de Guillaume*, if not for the character development of Ehmereiz, his kinsmen and the central themes in *Willehalm*, the reference to his past experience with his stepfather is entirely omitted. Ehmereiz plays a much greater role in representing the connection between the two camps via kinship than does his *Aliscans* counterpart; he is also endowed with an innocence that is in stark contrast to Terramer's hardened experience among the kinsmen who fight on the side of the Saracens.

Wolfram first mentions Ehmereiz in passing, as he joins the forces of his father, Tybalt, and Terramer to repel the French onslaught led by Vivianz and his peers.[140] After this, Wolfram indulges his audience with descriptions of the young knight; he refrains from giving him an entirely corrupt character and even confirms his standing by having Willehalm spare him despite the situation. When Willehalm encounters the fifteen kings on his own, Ehmereiz is among them:

> Ehmereiz von Todjerne
> in bekant und sah in gerne,
> der werden Gyburge suon.
> er wolde de ersten tjost dâ tuon.
> des enweiz ich niht, ob daz geschach;
> wan ieslîcher balde brach
> swaz in sîner hant kom her.
> (*Wh.* 72, 19–25)

---

139 *Alisc.* XLIX.
140 *Wh.* 28, 25.

[Ehmereiz of Todjerne, the son of noble Giburc, recognized him: he was glad to see him and wanted to be the first to joust with him. I do not know whether that took place, for each of them soon afterwards broke the weapon which he had in his hand.][141]

Ehmereiz does not seem to want to make friends with his stepfather and Willehalm has raised a sword against him. Although Wolfram says that he does not know the details of the conflict between parent and child, it is not clear whether Willehalm actually recognizes Ehmereiz. The vagueness is soon clarified. Wolfram begins by mentioning Ehmereiz as renowned in a list of the kings in combat with Willehalm, alongside the lord of the race of the Baruc, who, he reminds the audience, had Gahmuret buried according to his Christian custom in *Parzival*.[142] Then, as if recognizing his stepson, Willehalm kills all of the kings who face him, but deliberately spares Ehmereiz:

> daz bluot in durch die ringe vlôz
> allen, wan Gyburge suon:
> dem enwolt er dâ niht tuon.
> daz enliez er durch in selben niht:
> Gyburg diz maere des frides giht,
> in der geleite er dannen reit:
> der marcrâf niht mit im enstreit.
>   (*Wh.* 74, 26 – 75, 2)

[The blood of all these kings flowed through their chain-mail, except for the son of Giburc: Willehalm did not wish to harm him, and yet he did not spare him on his own account. My story attributes his protection to Giburc: it was in her safe conduct that Ehmereiz rode away, for the Margrave did not fight with him.][143]

Wolfram makes it clear that, no matter his source, his own story holds courtly love and kinship in high regard. It is for the sake of Gyburg that Willehalm spares Ehmereiz and this is part of the function of his character.

---

141 Gibbs and Johnson, 49.
142 *Wh*, 73, 17–24.
143 Gibbs and Johnson, 50.

Ehmereiz represents the family connection between the two sides and that his life is spared by Willehalm, who could easily have killed him on the spot, is indicative of the power of Gyburg's influence and the effect of service to love. When Ehmereiz confronts Willehalm, telling him that he must seek revenge upon him for the shame his mother's actions have caused him and his kinsmen, the emphasis is on Gyburg's decision to marry Willehalm; there is no mention of the fate of other family members at the hands of Willehalm.[144] This keeps the cohesion and nuclear nature of the story intact, whilst further establishing the thematic centre of love and kinship.

Parts of Ehmereiz's address give the impression of a passionate youth, unaware of how harmless his words and his ability to substantiate them really are:

> dô Ehmereiz Gyburge barn
> sô rîterlîche kom gevarn,
> und al sîn wâpenlîchez kleit
> nie dehein armuot erleit
> (wan ez was tiwer unde lieht),
> der marcrâve tet im nieht,
> gein sîner rede er ouch niht sprach:
> swes er von Gyburge jach,
> daz wart im einen gar vertragen:
> die andern wunt unde erslagen
> (*Wh.* 75, 21–30)

[When Ehmereiz, the child of Giburc, came riding up so chivalrously and his whole suit of armour showed no sign of poverty whatsoever, for it was expensive and brightly gleaming, the Margrave did not harm him; nor did he reply to what he had said. Whatever he said about Giburc, the Margrave put up with from him, but from him alone: the others were wounded or slain.][145]

Willehalm takes little notice of the young knight and his taunts. This is a theme that does not come into play in the corresponding scene in *Aliscans*; there, Guillaume is the hero defending his land and Christendom.

---

144 *Wh.* 75, 4–20.
145 Gibbs and Johnson, 51.

In *Willehalm*, however, the margrave is in the service of his wife, of love and of his kinsmen, and Ehmereiz must therefore be spared.

Noble prince

Despite his arrogant taunts, Ehmereiz possesses a chivalry that allows him to respect kinship and love's service, and this is revealed at intervals during the siege, when he is guarding the fourth gate with Gyburg's brothers.[146] He is seen to disagree with his father's treatment of his mother: 'der künec Tybalt hin zer wide Arabelen dicke dreute: Ehmereiz in drumbe steute' [Tibalt repeatedly threatened Arabel with hanging, but Ehmereiz upbraided him for that] (*Wh*. 221, 28–30).[147] Ehmereiz is also listed foremost among those kings besieging Orange who refrained from avenging their losses upon Gyburg out of respect for women and their role in the service of love:

> si sprach 'die werden alle mir
> erzeigeten zorn, swaz i'r dâ weiz,
> niwan mîn sun Ehmereiz.
> der hete doch rîter hie genuoc:
> von sîme rinc man nie getruoc
> gein mir bogen schilt noch swert
> dar zuo dûhte er sich ze wert,
> swaz volkes im ist undertân.'
>   (*Wh*. 266, 10–17)

[She [Gyburg] replied: 'All the noblemen were hostile to me, as far as I know, except my son Ehmereiz. He had many knights here, but no one from his camp raised a bow, shield or sword against me. He didn't want to stoop so low as to cause me fear from the people who were under his command.'][148]

As Ehmereiz is a young king, Queen Gyburg's son, heir to Tybalt's possessions and Terramer's bloodline, the legacy of a family divided in religion and loyalties, Wolfram allows him to receive advice on his chivalry. He is not

---

146 *Wh*. 98.
147 Gibbs and Johnson, 117.
148 Gibbs and Johnson, 136.

as experienced as his grandfather, Terramer, though he strives for renown on the battlefield; he also preserves a kind of respect for his mother, despite her actions having shamed his family. During the siege, he offers Gyburg compensation for the land and its resources, whilst Terramer and Tybalt desire Gyburg's death.[149] Gyburg admonishes his actions, refusing to be moved from Orange while at the same time giving him advice on his conduct.

> dô sprach ich 'sun, wie stêt dir daz?
> dir zaeme ein ander rede baz.
> wilt du mich veile machen
> und dînen prîs verswachen,
> daz man mich gelte sam ein rint?
> du bist von hôher art mîn kint:
> daz schadet dînem prîse.
> bistu sölher manheit wîse
> alsô der marcgrâve ie was,
> der alz gebirge Kaukasas
> dir gaeb (daz waere ein rîcher solt:
> wand ez ist allz vil rôtez golt),
> du naemestz ungern für ein wîp
> diu alsô kürlîchen lîp
> hete als ich noch hiute hân.
> dîn bieten hât missetân.
> zem marcrâven hân ich muot:
> niemen mac geleisten sölch guot
> daz mich von im gescheide.'
>
> (*Wh.* 257, 11–29)

[Then I said: 'Son, what are you thinking of? Some other kind of speech would be more fitting. Do you want to put me up for sale and thereby demean yourself when I am paid for just like a cow? You are my son of lofty lineage, but what you propose will damage your reputation. If you are as wise and manly as the Margrave ever was and if someone would give you all the mountain Kaukasas – that would be a rich reward, for it is all solid red gold – you would not want to accept it for a woman who was just as beautiful as I still am today. Your offer is ill-made. I have committed myself to the Margrave, and no one can offer me such wealth as to separate me from him.']ced[150]

---

149 *Wh.* 256–7.
150 Gibbs and Johnson, 132.

Ehmereiz is young and can be influenced, unlike Terramer, who remains set in his ways, and Gyburg offers him advice on how he should direct his efforts. Gyburg does not demoralize her son nor does she give in to his offer. Instead, she reasons with him, cautioning him against actions that might bring him dishonour and also appealing to his sense of honour and clan loyalty by advising him of his folly in offering her riches in exchange for deserting her new husband and clan. As the Saracen forces prepare for the second battle, Terramer offers his advice to Tybalt and Ehmereiz, too:

> Ehmereiz, dîn hôher muot,
> swederthalp der edelt hin,
> daz wirt an prîse dîn gewin,
> nâch dînem vater oder nâch mir.
> dîns vater ellen râte ich dir:
> sô biste in allen landen
> bewart vor houbetschanden.
>   (*Wh.* 342, 24–30)

[Ehmereiz, your high courage, whether you get it from your father or from me, will gain renown for you. Be brave like your father. Then you will be preserved from disgrace in all lands.][151]

Terramer reminds both Tybalt and Ehmereiz that their courage will preserve their renown and good name despite the shame they have suffered (or might yet suffer, for Terramer already sees that the battle is lost). They are the warriors whose honour rests upon the outcome of the battle and it is also for the revenge of their dishonour that the battle has been waged. If Ehmereiz's honour cannot be restored with victory, Terramer reminds him that his courageous actions will still be recognized everywhere. Ehmereiz then fights with great bravery, as do his knights, in the second battalion with his father, Tybalt, but his motive is still guided by courtly service:

> Manec unverzaget kristen hant
> dâ wurben umbe sölhiu pfant
> die Berhtram möhte machen quît

---

151   Gibbs and Johnson, 171.

dâ warp ouch Ehmereizes strît
nâch phande umb die diu in gebar.
(*Wh.* 368, 1–5)

[Many dauntless Christians were fighting for the kind of ransom which could be
exchanged for Berthram, while Ehmereiz was fighting to gain ransom for the woman
who had borne him.][152]

As is his integrity in his courtly duty to serve love and ladies, Ehmereiz's
courage is exceptional on the battlefield, for he appears to have taken both
Terramer's advice as well as Gyburg's. He fights at the front of the charge
with his battalion, once barely escaping capture,[153] and perseveres against
greater odds, almost being overcome by Rennewart's company.[154] Even in
retreat, he never forgets his courage:

[...]
und Ehmereiz Tybaldes sun,
daz si wol kobern kunden.
swâ si bekumbert funden
bêde ir mâge unde ir man,
alsô hulfen si den dan,
dês ir rîterschaft hât êre
(*Wh.* 435, 20–5)

[[...] and Ehmereiz, Tibalt's son, showed that they could rally their forces even in
retreat. Wherever they found their kinsmen or vassals being pressed, they helped
them then in a way that did honour to their chivalry.][155]

Ehmereiz is last seen fighting in front of the ships as his countrymen
reach the water in retreat, securing the way for Terramer, who has fled on
Brahane.[156]

---

152 Gibbs and Johnson, 182.
153 *Wh.* 367–8.
154 *Wh.* 388–9.
155 Gibbs and Johnson, 212.
156 *Wh.* 438, 22–30.

Ehmereiz takes on more importance in *Willehalm* than Esmeré in *Aliscans*. Kinship and service are the dominant themes in the portrayal of Ehmereiz. His character not only reflects his familial ties, which lie on either side of the conflict, but also the heritage which he represents. He is the only heir of Gyburg and Tybalt, Willehalm's only semblance of an offspring after the death of Vivianz, and the decisions he makes after the battle of Alischantz will be the measure by which the Christian moral victory can be gauged. He has already displayed courage and courtly integrity befitting his station and his moral fibre would indicate that he still has some role to play in the future relations between the Christians and the Saracens. But what Wolfram had planned for him after the battle remains undetermined in the fragment of *Willehalm*.

Rennewart

Little has been written to surpass the eloquent volume on Rennewart by Lofmark, published in 1972,[157] although some more recent critics have addressed Rennewart's role to support opinions about the ending of *Willehalm*.[158] It can certainly be established that Rennewart is one of the most prominent figures in Wolfram's *Willehalm* and his role and Wolfram's intentions for this Saracen have always been a topic for discussion. He starts out as a captured prisoner, a kitchen-hand, unbaptized and ridiculed, and during the second battle he excels as the noble leader he has been born to become, instrumental in the Christian victory.[159]

---

157   Lofmark, *Rennewart*.
158   See: Knapp, Fritz Peter, *Rennewart: Studien zu Gehalt und Gestalt des 'Willehalm'
         Wolframs von Eschenbach* (Wien: Verlag Notring, 1970), esp. 344; Knapp,
         'Heilsgewißheit Oder Resignation?'
159   Rennewart bears striking resemblance to some romance figures, such as Gareth of
         Mallory's *Le Morte d'Arthur*, who has large hands and works in the kitchens. The
         scene in which Gareth is about to joust with Lancelot, who pulls out, is reminiscent of
         the scene in which Guillaume and Rainouart appear about to joust when Guillaume
         tells him he is only coming to help him carry his *tinel* (*Alisc*. LXXVIII). Because

Rennewart proves to be one of the figures most capable of representing Wolfram's ideas and message regarding heathens and their conversion to Christianity and this is accomplished by Rennewart's individual
development. Reminiscent of Ajax in his size, strength and value on the
battlefield, Rainouart does not develop in *Aliscans*; he remains violent,
impetuous and naive. However, the popularity of this character is attested
in the rituals he undertakes to become a part of the Christian community
– baptism, marriage, knighthood – as well as in his inner conflict about
his identity and recognition.[160] In contrast, Rennewart learns to control
his temper, is motivated by love for Alyze and appears as a respectable
knight.[161] Rennewart's character development betrays a literary genre quite
different from the *chansons de geste* and it is through this that Rennewart
fulfils a purpose.[162]

Because the story is a fragment, Rennewart's destiny does not come
to fruition within the narrative. What we do know, however, within the
fragment, is that Rennewart's pivotal role, his contradictory elements and
personal realization, will centre on his anticipated investiture, baptism
and marriage to Loys's daughter Alyze, making a reconciliation possible.
For Wolfram, this is only achievable with God's grace; spirituality must be
linked with chivalry and sanctified by God. Wolfram's Saracens fit within
that plan: their chivalry confirms his ideal and fulfils his 'longing for a more
immediate presence of the guidance and spirit of God in the institutions
of this world.'[163] Rennewart, the young Saracen prince, beloved kinsman of
Gyburg and brother-in-law to Willehalm, seems the character best suited
to traverse this cleft between the spiritual and temporal in *Willehalm*.

---

this is a later work, it might indicate the popularity of the Rainouart character type.
Wolfram's *Willehalm*, however, does not include this incident.

160   See Besnardeau, 329, 339.

161   See Huby-Marly, 'Willehalm', 403.

162   Parts of this section are included within the article: Hathaway, 'Chivalry and
       Spirituality'.

163   Lofmark, *Rennewart*, 185.

The formation of a hero: Chivalry and investiture

> 'Dex, dist Bertran, trop me voiz deleant;
> N'avrai cheval por quoi vois attendant;
> car a ces cops n'avra ja nus garant.'
>   (*Alisc.* CVIII, 5702–4)

['God,' says Bertrand, 'you're taking too long; I'll never get the horse I am waiting for, there is no protection against your blows.'][164]

In *Aliscans*, Rainouart emerges as a comical, God-fearing Saracen, destined to marry Aélis, to be baptized and to be the hero of *Aliscans* as well as of *La Bataille Loquifer* and the *Moniage Rainoart*. The audience is reminded of Rainouart's destiny in the *chansons de geste*; his deeds are foreshadowed repeatedly in *Aliscans*, long before his first appearance,[165] in passages punctuated by such phrases as 'Se Dex garist Renoart l'aduré / Et son tinel, qu'il a grant et quarré, Par lui seront paien desheritez' [May God protect the valiant Rainouart and his enormous *tinel*; the heathens shall be expelled at his hands] (*Alisc.* XLV, 1927–9). His beloved *tinel*, fashioned from a tree large enough to shade one hundred knights, becomes his hallmark;[166] it is comical in both its size and in the fact that Rainouart is strong enough to wield it easily (which he does, rather than brandish the sword of a knight as

---

164 Ferrante, 242–3. Ferrante's translation is from the Oxford/Halle edition of the 'S' manuscript, which, whilst contrasting with the 'A' and 'M' MSS in many aspects, is consistent in this passage; her translation brings out the humour of the *chanson de geste*. In this scene, Bertrand, taken prisoner in the first battle and now having been freed by Rainouart, is longing for a horse to ride into the fighting and aid the Frenchmen, but he must wait whilst Rainouart learns, very slowly, how to kill a knight without also killing the mount with a single blow of his new sword. Time and again Rainouart tries in vain to kill the knight but not his horse while Bertrand looks on impatiently, giving him advice on how to strike blows. Finally a horse is spared the blow that kills its master and Bertrand is satisfied.

165 *Alisc.* X, XIII, XIV, XLI, XLV, XLIX and LXXI. Before Rainouart even appears, it is foretold that he, the kitchen boy in Montlaon, will be the one to kill Haucebier, release the Christian prisoners from the Saracens and marry Aélis.

166 *Alisc.* LXIV–LXXV.

his preferred weapon). He is ignorant in the ways of gentility and etiquette, as can be seen by his behaviour at the monastery on the way to Orange, and his conduct throughout the second battle and during his baptism shows that there has been no great alteration. Rainouart remains a strong hero, rough around the edges, a source of buffoonery as well as impressive heroics; nevertheless, he is always firm in his persuasion towards Christian values, a born leader and a formidable warrior. Because of this courage, strength and energy, the values of his new society are exalted, new converts can be rallied and Christianity can be regenerated.[167]

Perhaps it was that Rainouart proved one of the most capable and fervent Christians, despite his Saracen background and humble slavery in the kitchens, that inspired Wolfram to fashion his Rennewart. Willehalm recognizes and supports this diamond-in-the-rough and sees Rennewart reach his potential in terms of the grand plan for Wolfram's idea of a complete Christian victory. This is a victory that would encompass more than a military success; it would also achieve peace and concord between kinsmen and knights and between people of different religions, cultures and political motives. To accomplish this, Wolfram required a character who was at once tied to both sides and free from the cycle of vengeance;[168] a character whose humility could be realized spiritually and whose noble background predestined him for chivalry and leadership. Rennewart would have to develop from a kitchen hand into a knight in the eyes of the audience. An investiture for Rennewart would mean the attainment of armour, a knight's weapon, a prized warhorse and most of all, chivalry; it would mean the realization of inner nobility and the service of *mâze* [moderation] to control his temper and it would likely include a vow of fealty. This investiture would signal his position in the story.

When Rennewart is first seen in *Willehalm*, there has been no foreshadowing of his appearance or role. Willehalm first sees this kitchen hand at the banquet in Montlaon and is impressed by his size and strength, but it

---

167   See Besnardeau, 339.
168   See Lofmark, *Rennewart*, 241.

is Wolfram who seems fascinated by the possibilities for him. In his description of Rennewart's grimy appearance, he immediately draws parallels with
gold in a muddy puddle and an eaglet being cast out of his nest to learn
to fly.[169] Rennewart's silence before Willehalm implies his disdain, as if,
though a slave, he cannot hide the aversion he feels at being given to one
of Loys's barons.[170] In fact, the mystery of Rennewart's lineage becomes a
recurring motif for Wolfram: Rennewart is asked about his family twice,
once by Willehalm in Montlaon and again by the persistent Gyburg at
Orange.[171] However, he is not forthcoming about his background.[172] When
Rennewart is received by Willehalm from Loys, he is stirred by a desire for
revenge, but his true nobility is also apparent:

> eteswenne ich in den werken bin,
> daz mir diu schame nimt den sin:
> wand ich leb in lekerîe.
> sol iemmer wert âmîe
> mînen lîp umbevâhen,
> daz mac ir wol versmâhen:
> wan ich bin wirden niht gewent,
> unt hân mich doch dar nâch gesent.
> (*Wh.* 193, 23–30)

169 *Wh.* 187, 30 – 189, 27; 195, 4–6. Wolfram also compares Rennewart's grimy skin to
      a rosebud that is opening to reveal the beautiful petals inside the rough leaves (*Wh.*
      270, 12ff). Lofmark discusses Rennewart's deceptive appearance and concealed
      nobility, comparing him to young Parzival, as does Wolfram himself (*Wh.* 271; 147,
      234).
170 Though Rennewart can understand French well, he feigns deafness when Willehalm
      addresses him, ignoring him until Willehalm speaks to him in his native tongue,
      chaldeis (*Wh.* 192). It is worthy of mention that the name of this fictitious language
      bears resemblance to the sacred tongue of *Chaldean* in *La Queste del Saint Graal*;
      it dates from around 1220, just after the composition of *Willehalm*. See Williams,
      Andrea M.L., *The Adventures of the Holy Grail: a study of La Queste del Saint Graal*
      (Oxford: Peter Lang, 2001), 11.
171 *Wh.* 193–4; 290–1.
172 Similarly, Rainouart in *Aliscans* does not completely reveal his identity to Guiborc
      until after the second battle and before his baptism, a point at which *Willehalm* has
      not yet arrived when the narrative breaks off. See *Alisc.* CLXXXf.

[Sometimes I do things which make me faint with embarrassment, for I am living the life of a pig. If ever a noble love takes me into her arms she may disdain me for this, for I am not accustomed to honour, even though I have yearned for it so.][173]

Only the audience knows about Rennewart's lineage and the story of his capture, although they are only let in on it when it best suits the character and plot development.[174] In this way, the audience is privy to Rennewart's concealed nobility before the main characters and this puts them in a position to best witness the transformation taking place. Though on arrival in Orange Rennewart is in the service of Willehalm, he seeks refuge in the kitchen and Wolfram tells the audience the sad story of his enslavement, indulging in foreshadowing phrases such as 'diu saelde künste-clichen tuot' [such is the intricacy of fate] (*Wh.* 283, 2).[175] When his temper is tried in the kitchen in Orange, Rennewart cannot control himself: he kills the chef and laments bitterly afterwards that if Willehalm only knew his lineage, things would be different: 'bekant er mich, daz waer sîn klage' [if he knew who I am, he would be regretful about this] (*Wh.* 287, 10). His reflection and introspection at this point are pivotal in his development as a knight, the knight he is meant to become; he realizes that his lineage and nobility demand something better for him (both in terms of his treat-ment by others and most of all of his own behaviour) and he declares, 'ich bin doch Terramers barn' [after all, I am the child of Terramer] (*Wh.* 288, 30).[176] A significant step in Rennewart's progress towards investiture will be the recognition of his lineage by society and the other characters in the

173   Gibbs and Johnson, 103. Kartschoke translates line 25 more liberally, though with a similar tone: 'denn ich lebe fern jeder ritterlichen Bewährung' [because I live cut-off from any knightly trial] (Wolfram von Eschenbach, *Willehalm*, 125). More accurate might be *roguish*, though the preceding translations seem to have expressed the connotation.

174   When Rennewart is in the kitchen at Glorjet in Orange, he is taunted by the chef, and his background is related to the audience by Wolfram, with the poignant story of how he was sold into slavery (*Wh.* 283–4).

175   Gibbs and Johnson, 144.

176   Gibbs and Johnson, 147.

story; the fulfilment of his right to leadership[177] also acts as a mirror of his steps towards maturity, although neither objective is complete when the fragment ends.

The scenes following the violence in the kitchens of Glorjet (the palace of Orange) are of central importance for Rennewart's role in the story. Willehalm implores Gyburg to talk to Rennewart, who is upset after the incident with the chef.[178] In their conversation, Gyburg asks after his family, but Rennewart's replies reflect only his belief that he has been made to suffer for a reason and he gives Gyburg no information about his background. Wishing to establish Rennewart's loyalty to Willehalm, Gyburg bestows upon him the armour and sword of King Synagun, won as a prize; it is costly, beautiful and very strong.[179] Though he is reluctant to take the sword at first and even casts it aside, Rennewart accepts the assistance of Gyburg's maids in putting on the armour, after which the sword is fastened around his waist.[180] He maintains, however, that he will still use his *tinel* in the coming battle. During the council of war, held after mass, Wolfram

177   See Lofmark, *Rennewart*, 198–204, 240. Alain Labbé investigates the character of Rainouart from the perspective of contrasts rather than development in *Aliscans* and sees in his depiction an intricate reflection of life's trials because of lineage and, perhaps, destiny. He writes that Rainouart can be seen as 'l'irrémédiable contradiction entre les attributions de l'opulence vivrière, où l'a plongé un destin paradoxal, et celles de la caste guerrière auxquelles le promettait sa naissance et ou le ramène, burlesque en ses effets et grave en son propos' [the irremediable contradiction between the attribution of agricultural opulence, where he was plunged into a paradoxical destiny, and the warriors' life assured him by his birth and to where he returns, comic in his actions and earnest in his words]. Labbé, Alain, 'De la cuisine à la salle: la topographie palatine d'*Aliscans* et l'évolution du personnage de Renouart' in Jean Dufournet, ed., *Mourir aux Aliscans: Aliscans et la légende de Guillaume d'Orange* (Paris: Honoré Champion, 1993), 207–25, esp. 222–3, 210.

178   This is a markedly different reaction to the news of the chef's death than that of Guillaume in Wolfram's source, who is much amused. As Lofmark remarks, 'Killing cooks is good fun by the standards of *Aiscans*' (*Rennewart*, 121).

179   *Wh.* 295–6.

180   *Wh.* 296, 10–11. That his sword is not used until later in both *Aliscans* and in *Willehalm*, until after he can no longer use his *tinel* because it has been broken, seems to suggest a similarity to those swords in romance that could only be used by certain people, at

indulges the audience in another anticipatory passage, explaining why he does not mention by name the French princes who attend the council: it will be they who flee in battle and it will be Rennewart who manfully turns them back at Petit Punt, emphasizing that 'der die starken stangen dans, den habt ir tumber danne ein rint: er was doch des rîchsten mannes kint, der bî den zîten krône truoc' [you think that he who was bearing the enormous club was dumber than an ox, and yet he was the son of the most powerful man reigning at that time] (*Wh.* 302, 14–17).[181] The incident at Petit Punt acts as the starting point for Rennewart's decisive actions in the battle and his gaining of victory for the Christians.

By the time of the council and commencement of the second battle, Rennewart has realized that his strength must be tempered to the demands of his station, that he is in service to Willehalm who is loyal to God and to Gyburg, and that he has acquired a suit of armour and a sword.[182] One of the significant attributes of knighthood that, although implied by Wolfram, remains to be entirely accomplished in Rennewart's development, is that of horsemanship. Lofmark mentions the importance of Rennewart's association with horses, the quintessential indicator of knighthood, pointing out that 'towards the end of the battle there is a clear indication that he is going to have a horse of his own.'[183] It is the mention of the horse, Lignmaredî, who is won as a prize from Poydwiz *after* Rennewart has put on a suit of armour, has learnt battle leadership, and has learnt how to use a sword (all indications of his coming of age as a man and as a knight) that leads Lofmark to the supposition that Wolfram intended to invest Rennewart as a knight.[184]

---

certain times, or under certain circumstances, thus imparting a sense of destiny and greatness. See Williams, 101–28.

181   Gibbs and Johnson, 153.

182   Lofmark notes the difference of Rennewart's weapons as being symbolic of his rank and stature: he progresses from an unarmed kitchen boy to a club-wielding foot-soldier to a leader using his club as his spear. (*Rennewart*, 163)

183   Lofmark, *Rennewart*, 157.

184   Lofmark, *Rennewart*, 157–8; also *Wh.* 420. The indications of Rennewart's investiture by the mention of this horse seem clear as Li Margaris was given to Rainouart

While Rainouart's *tinel* is a source of humour in *Aliscans* (he forgets it because of drunkenness the night before the reinforcements leave Montlaon and continually holds up the army to fetch it), Wolfram uses Rennewart's *tinel* and his forgetfulness to signal developmental steps in his character. If he is to become a knight, Rennewart must learn some responsibility in the eyes of the audience before carrying a sword. The first time he forgets his *tinel*, it is due to oversleeping and Willehalm reminds him about it. On his way to fetch it, he is able to serve Willehalm by gathering the soldiers that were left behind when the army left Montlaon. When the army moves out for the second battle, Rennewart forgets his *tinel* because he is captivated by the armaments of the warriors; he is again reminded by Willehalm of its absence and feels great shame.[185] The third time Rennewart forgets his *tinel* – again because of his interest in the advancing army – he is embarrassed and goes back for it without telling anyone. The first instance of forgetfulness arises because of Rennewart's newly awakened inclination towards the pursuits of his station: he is excited to be serving Willehalm and to be accompanying an army, and he is curious about armaments and

upon investiture in *Aliscans*, CLXXXIV–CLXXXV. Incidentally, the lines in *laisse* CLXXXIV mentioning the horse by name, Li Margaris, are among many lines missing in the 'A' (Paris and Milan), as well as in the 'M' manuscripts (*laisse* CXLVI), but are present in the 'S' manuscript (*laisse* CLXXXVIII), now at Oxford. See: Wienbeck, Hartnacke and Rasch, *Aliscans*. Régnier attributes the many missing lines after *laisse* CLXI to carelessness rather than gross differentiation in material, and points out that the 'M' and 'S' manuscripts can be seen as closer in form to the earliest editions, however incomplete. See Régnier, *Aliscans*, vol. 1, 9, 10. That the name of this horse appears in only one extant manuscript and that Wolfram has used it seems to point to yet another piece of evidence indicating a no-longer-extant version of *Aliscans* that served as a source for *Willehalm*.

185   The shame suffered by Rennewart is the topic of Yeandle's article describing one of the three major characteristics with which Wolfram imbued Rennewart: *zuht, kiusche* and *schame* [lineage, self-control and shame], pointing to the use of this element in *Parzival* to signal an innate nobility. See Yeandle, David N., 'Rennewart's "Shame": An Aspect of the Characterization of Wolfram's Ambivalent Hero' in Martin H. Jones and Timothy McFarland, eds, *Wolfram's 'Willehalm': Fifteen Essays* (Rochester, NY: Camden House, 2002), 167–90. It is also possible that this shame is one of the reasons that Rennewart feels compelled to refuse baptism in *Willehalm*.

organization. The second time he forgets it, he is aware enough of his integrity and station to be ashamed. The third time, he is angry with himself and self-reflective. He wonders whether it is God's way of testing his courage and worries that he will be seen as a coward if anyone spots that he is missing. As he talks to himself, Wolfram expresses Rennewart's desire to achieve his proper and destined role and how his own mistakes hinder his progress towards it:

> er sprach 'nu hât mir tumpheit
> alrêrst gefüeget herzenleit:
> diu scheidet selten sich von mir.
> der dem grimmen vederspil die gir
> verhabt, daz hân ich doch gesehen,
> man muoz im dâ nâch plûkeit jehen.
> wan ich hân mîn selbes gir verhabt.'
> (*Wh.* 317, 3–9)

[He said: 'Now my stupidity has really struck again! It never seems to leave me alone. If one keeps frustrating the desire of a wild falcon – and I've seen that myself – he later becomes shy and timid. I alone have frustrated my own desires.'][186]

Rennewart reflects upon the consequences of his forgetfulness and wonders whether he has hindered his own progress towards service in Willehalm's army. However, Wolfram compensates the young warrior with two new developments. When Rennewart finds his *tinel*, it has been burnt in the fires of the breaking camp and has been made stronger by the heat.[187] On his way back, Rennewart then encounters the retreating Frenchmen at Petit Punt; his resolve is now up to the task of checking their loyalty,

---

186 Gibbs and Johnson, 160.
187 There have been propositions of the symbolism in the burning of Rennewart's club. Lofmark's comment that 'the strengthening of his club in the fire is comparable to Rennewart's own experience, becoming more deadly and resolute in his purpose through the disgrace he has suffered' (Lofmark, *Rennewart*, 162). There is also the possibility, however vague, of a religious symbolism here as well, indicating Rennewart's turning towards the Christian God and accepting his role.

thereby performing an important and decisive function for both his character's development and for the Christian army going into battle.

It is during the course of this second battle that Rennewart comes into
his own, realizing his innate nobility and his significant role in God's plan
of victory. The height of this realization in the *Willehalm* fragment comes
when Rennewart recognizes the sword's superiority over his crude *tinel* as
a weapon and, although he has carried the sword at his side all the while,
'it is in the crisis of the battle that Rennewart reaches the maturity which
makes his sword appropriate.'[188] After his *tinel* is shattered by the crushing
blow Rennewart delivers to Purrel in his dragon armour, he fights with his
fists until he is reminded by Kibelin to draw his sword. This is paralleled
in *Aliscans* almost exactly,[189] yet the meaning that has been attached to the
scene in Wolfram's careful narration proves more climactic in nature.

> Dist Renoart: 'Ceste arme entre souëf[z].
> Bien ait la dame qui la me ceint au lez!
> Se ge cuidasse que costel fussent tel,
> [A Monloon n'en eüst nus remés;]
> Tos les eüsse avec moi aportez.[190]
> [...]
> Dist Renoart: 'Mout me merveil, par Dé:
> Si petite arme qui a tel poësté!
> [Ja nus frans hom qi teint a bonté
> N'en deuroit estre senz .V. a son costé;
> Se l'une faut, que l'altre ait recovré.]
> Par moi seront paien desbareté.'
>   (*Alisc.* CLXI, 6979–82; CLXII, 6983–93)[191]

188 Lofmark, *Rennewart*, 163.
189 In *Aliscans*, Rainouart's *tinel* is shattered on Haucebier, and he beats the heads of
     the pagans with his fist which, in due course, bumps into the sword hanging at his
     waist. It is then that he decides to use it. (*Alisc.* CLVIII–CLXI)
190 These lines correspond to *laisse* CXX, 6169–72 in the 'M' MS. The line in this cita-
     tion, absent in the 'A' and 'M' editions, is in brackets and corresponds to *laisse* CLXV
     in the 'S' MS.
191 Lines in brackets from 'M' MS: *laisse* CXXII, 6258–60. It is noteworthy that these
     lines, corresponding to *laisse* CLXVI in the 'S' MS, mention having four swords by

[Rainouart says, 'This weapon is easy to wield. Blessed be the lady who fixed it to my side! If I had known that blades were like this, I would not have left one at Montlaon; I would have brought them all with me. [...] God, how marvellous that such a small weapon can have such might! No good man should be without five at his side. If one fails, the others can be used. I will put the pagans to flight!']

Rainouart's boyish excitement at the discovery of the facility with which the blade can be used is tempered in *Willehalm* to a more introspective yet still practical reaction:

> er warf ez umbe in der hant,
> er lobt im valze und ekken sîn,
> er sprach 'diu starke stange mîn
> Was mir ein teil ze swaere:
> du bist lîht und doch strîtpaere.
> (*Wh.* 430, 28 – 431, 2)

[Rennewart tossed the sword about in his hand, praising its groove and its edges, saying: 'My strong club was a little too heavy, but you are light and battle-worthy all the same.']¹⁹²

Rainouart learns to use his sword and shield and then to mount a horse, and his investiture takes place after the battle. Ferrante writes that 'all this is meant more to reconcile the presentation of the character with the Rainouart who is the hero of other epics, than it is essential to his nature in *Aliscans*.'¹⁹³ This is why the realization of nobility and the development of the character of Rainouart never seem to come about in *Aliscans*. In *Willehalm*, however, Rennewart can be seen to reflect upon each new development and Wolfram uses each one as a milestone towards Rennewart's coming of age, fulfilling his purpose in the grand plan of Christian victory and the attainment of peace.

---

one's side, rather than five, indicating how certain details were subject to the individual style of a *jongleur*.
192 Gibbs and Johnson, 210.
193 Ferrante, 58.

The development of Rennewart's character is signified by his learning how to direct his noble qualities properly, how to check his temper and his strength (which must be moderated by chivalry) and in being recognized by society. Lofmark points out the medieval concept of character development with regard to Rennewart when he writes that no evolution of the person is expected, no essential change necessary, but that inherent character qualities must be realized by conquering impediments; the development comes in the 'revelation of true nature,' in 'putting the natural qualities into their proper order,' in being what God meant one to be.[194] Rennewart's task is to realize God's purpose for him.

In becoming a true knight, Rennewart's battles are not fought for personal glory, as are Rainouart's; rather, they are 'distinctly represented as service to the Christian cause' which 'subordinates him to a cause greater than himself and raises him by giving him a place and purpose in world history and a direct relationship with God (as the tool that executes the divine will) to which Rainouart of *Aliscans* could not aspire.'[195] Becoming God's tool is what gives Rennewart's character its value in *Willehalm* and it is through his realization of his innate nobility, his becoming a knight and Wolfram's allusions to his investiture that he is able to fulfil that charge.

Conversion and baptism

> waz ob ich, hêrre, im sîn lebn
> baz berihte, op ich mac?
>   (*Wh.* 191, 22–4)

[My lord, ... what if I were to guide him better, if I can?][196]

Becoming a knight and realizing his inner nobility and duty to chivalry is only one aspect of Rennewart's development in *Willehalm*. An integral part of the chivalry that Rennewart attains and of the victory that Wolfram

---

194   Lofmark, *Rennewart*, 144–5.
195   Lofmark, *Rennewart*, 95–6.
196   Gibbs and Johnson, 102.

would depict in *Willehalm* is the guidance and protection by the hand of God that comes with embracing both the Christian religion and chivalry's spirituality. The conversion and baptism of Rainouart are not as important to the story of *Aliscans* as they are for Wolfram, for they represent a development of character and plot of greater scope in *Willehalm*. The emphasis on and depiction of Rennewart's conversion to Christianity and the correlation between baptism on the one hand and investiture, spirituality and chivalry on the other hand yields a central theme in *Willehalm*: turning towards Christianity, chivalry and spirituality through recognition of God's plan for humanity, for all His children. Though the ultimate fulfilment of such a worthy goal remains incomplete in the fragment, Rennewart is the character whose conversion to Christianity and baptism will carry the theme through to a definitive reconciliation and peace.

In *Aliscans*, Rainouart is never depicted as anything other than Christian in his inclinations; he swears he is a Christian and he is not bereft of certain medieval Christian values such as charity.[197] It is Louis who refuses to let him be baptized and Guillaume who permits it and his later marriage to Aélis (his actual conversion to Christianity not being necessary).[198] It is a different perspective on religion with which Wolfram characterizes the Christianity in *Willehalm* more than a century after his source. Lofmark writes that Wolfram contemplates religious and chivalric values side by side and in doing so attributes certain values to the Saracens, which is why he cannot portray Rennewart with the same naive Christianity with which he is represented in *Aliscans*.[199] Rennewart must come to the realization of the path towards God and the decision to convert to Christianity; he must *change* into a Christian knight from a humble kitchen slave in the

---

197   In an incident in the peasant's bean field, Rainouart's compassion shows itself when he berates the Saracens for stealing and destroying the harvest that is the livelihood of the farmer and his family (*Alisc.* CLXXI–CLXXIII).

198   Lofmark sees this depiction of Rainouart as an indication of the kind of explicit form that comprised religion in the *chansons de geste*. See Lofmark, *Rennewart*, 129. See also, Ferrante, 29. Rainouart's actual baptism is unclear, but is tied closely to the scene in which his defeated cousin Bauduc is baptized.

199   Lofmark, *Rennewart*, 132–5.

eyes of his society and of the audience. In converting to Christianity, his status as slave dissolves and he becomes a free man.[200]

Like his attainment of knighthood, the completion of the spiritual complement of chivalry must slowly be achieved by Rennewart, culminating in his baptism, his formal acceptance of the Christian faith and the guidance of God. The development towards this realization by Rennewart is part of Wolfram's bringing 'non-Christians within the scope of God's plan of salvation,'[201] and a broadening of the theme of salvation from that of *Aliscans*. Rennewart's story as it is known by Loys is related to Willehalm at Montlaon, just before Willehalm takes him into his service:

> Ich weiz wol daz er edel ist:
> mîn sin ervant ab nie den list,
> einvaltic noch spaehe,
> von wirde noch von smaehe,
> der in übergienge
> daz er den touf enphienge.
> ich hân unfuoge an im getân:
> got weiz wol daz ich willen hân,
> op er enphienge kristenheit,
> mir waere al sîn kumber leit.
> in brâhten koufliute über sê:
> die heten in gekoufet ê
> in der Persen lande.
> nie dehein ouge erkande
> flaeteger antlüz noch lîp:
> geêret waer daz selbe wîp
> diu in zer werlde brâhte,
> op der touf im niht versmâhte.
>
> (*Wh.* 191, 1–18)

---

200 It was common practice not to allow Saracen slaves to convert in the twelfth century, because it was believed that conversion to Christianity bestowed freedom, hence Louis' decision not to allow Rainouart's baptism. Later, in 1237–8, it was established by Pope Gregory IX that baptism did not release a slave from servile status. See Kedar, 321–2, 326–7.

201 Lofmark, *Rennewart*, 133.

[I know for a fact that he is of noble birth, but I've never found the knack, simple or complicated, by raising or demeaning him, to persuade him to accept baptism. I have treated him harshly, but, God knows, if he would agree to become a Christian, I should not be slow to regret any trouble which befell him. Merchants brought him across the sea after buying him in Persia. No one saw a face or a body more handsome. The woman who brought him into the world would be honoured if only he did not reject baptism.][202]

Whilst in *Aliscans* Rainouart is refused baptism despite his Christian inclinations, in *Willehalm* Rennewart himself refuses baptism, remaining bitter and resentful until he is taken into the service of Willehalm. The conscious decision to be baptized is never reached in the fragment, though the introspective realizations leading up to it parallel and complement the impending investiture of this young Saracen knight. He first begins to recognize that a change must occur as his frustration reaches its peak. This occurs when Willehalm speaks with him in his native tongue, Kaldeis, after having secured him from Loys who has become annoyed at his behaviour.

> der mac mich wol ergetzen
> swar an ich hie vertwâlet bin,
> hât er gotlîchen sin.
> doch hân ich im sô vil geklagt,
> daz ich sîner helfe bin verzagt,
> und hân michs nu gehabt an Krist,
> dem du undertaenic bist.
>   (*Wh.* 193, 6–12)

[[Mahmete] will compensate me in full for what I have lost here, if he is truly divine. Yet I have so often made my lamentation to him that I have despaired of his ever helping me, and now I have turned to Christ, to whom you are also subject.][203]

It becomes clear that force will not accomplish his conversion, but that Wolfram means for this to be a development beginning from within,

---

202 Gibbs and Johnson, 102.
203 Gibbs and Johnson, 103.

influenced by the realization of Rennewart's true nobility, chivalry, and by the presence of God. The acceptance of God's grace and guidance will enable Rennewart to overcome the obstacles that hinder the attainment of baptism, investiture and marriage, victory for Christians and peace between clans and kinsmen, and this in turn enables him to embrace chivalry fully. The development of Rennewart's religious maturity is an integral part of the victory that Wolfram seems inclined to depict after the second battle and this completeness would have been signalled by Rennewart's baptism. 'The religious development, which began with Rennewart's willingness to trust in the Christian God and led to God's acceptance of that trust and his employment of Rennewart for a divine purpose, is incomplete without Rennewart's acceptance of Christian baptism.'[204]

Scholars are of many opinions about the importance of Rennewart in *Willehalm*. Lofmark sees the Rennewart subplot to have been subordinated by Wolfram, via religion, to a cause greater than himself.[205] Wiesmann-Wiedemann observes that he does not play a role in the key revelations of the story:

> Rennewart, qui s'est tourné vers le Christ mais qui n'est pas encore baptisé, est aveugle comme les païens, mais il fait de bonnes actions comme les chrétiens. Ainsi, il ne participe pas à la révélation de l'idéologie. Il n'est présent ni quand, près de l'abbaye, Willehalm raconte les événements de la première bataille ni quand Gyburg donne son commandement de charité.[206]

> [Rennewart, who turns towards Christ but who is still not baptised, is as blind as the pagans, but he performs good deeds like the Christians. Thus, he doesn't witness the revelation of [Christian] ideology. He is not present at the abbey when Willehalm recounts the events of the first battle nor when Gyburg gives her command of mercy.]

Though there is no question that Willehalm is the hero of Wolfram's story, it is Rennewart whose development towards baptism, investiture

---

204 Lofmark, *Rennewart*, 217–18.
205 Lofmark, *Rennewart*, 96.
206 Wiesmann-Wiedemann, 227.

and marriage enables much of the outcome for the other protagonists; his absence at the moments during which Wolfram's message is conveyed is balanced by his decisive actions elsewhere. Rennewart's background and development and his influence upon other characters suggest that his fortuitous marriage to the daughter of the French king will herald reconciliation and peace.

Reconciliation and marriage

The third of the essential aspects of Rennewart's maturity in *Willehalm* is the manifestation of courtly ideals in his behaviour and appearance, in his consequent acceptance into Christian society, in his marriage to the princess and in the resulting reconciliatory effect this has. Reconciliation, closely related to chivalry and spirituality for Wolfram, is the most incomplete feature in Rennewart's development when the poem discontinues. Rennewart's budding relationship with Princess Alyze, an embodiment of the courtly liege-lady, gradually reveals a maturity in his character and points towards a marriage that will have the power of reconciliation between the Saracens and the Christians. This progress towards a reconciliation between kinsmen and enemies can be seen before the end of the fragment in the ways in which Rennewart's character development, as well as Wolfram's innovations to this character, serves to ennoble other protagonists and their roles in the story. When the fragment ends, however, much of this is yet to be realized and Rennewart's role, though reasonably well determined by Wolfram, remains incomplete.

That Alyze, who has already proven her ability to reconcile conflict in the scene at Montlaon,[207] is attracted to Rennewart is a sign of his nobility and potential to fulfil his role as a Christian knight and her courtly attention is the catalyst that brings him towards the fulfilment of this role.

---

207 When King Loys's wife refuses imperial support for Willehalm's beleaguered Orange, Willehalm's temper flares: he threatens the queen's life and threatens Loys with the withdrawal of his fealty. The situation is smoothed over by Alyze, who shows a commanding presence and keen awareness of a courtly code (*Wh.* 145–58).

Wolfram draws upon the symbolism of Rennewart's beard, sometimes humorously, to show his coming of age, referring first to its absence when Willehalm first sees him in Montlaon: '[D]er marchgrave nach Rennewart sande: der was noch ane bart' [Willehalm sent for Rennewart, who was as yet without a beard] (*Wh.* 191, 29–30).[208] But later, when he is part of Willehalm's retinue and is preparing to relieve Orange, it is Alyze's love that has made it grow:

> gedanc nach prise erliez in niht,
> sit er von Munleun uf die vart
> schiet, im wuohs sin junger bart.
> Er enhete der jare doch niht so vil,
> diu reichent gein des bartes zil:
> Alyzen kus het in gequelt.
> (*Wh.* 270, 28 – 271, 3)

[Desire for fame drove him on since he had left Munleun to go into battle. His beard was only then beginning to grow, for he was not yet old enough to have a full beard. The kiss from Alyze had caused it to sprout.]

Rennewart recognizes the reason for his beard's new growth and grieves bitterly when it is singed in the kitchen scuffle at Orange:

> mine grane, die mir sint an gezunt,
> gesaet ir minne uf minen munt,
> diu mir stiure uf dise vart
> mit kusse gap. den selben bart
> hat uz mime kinne
> noch mer gezogen ir minne,
> danne miner kurzen zite jar,
> oder dan der smaehlîche vâr
> des mich ir vater wente.
> (*Wh.* 287, 11–19)

208   Gibbs and Johnson, 102.

[This beard of mine which has been burnt was sown upon my mouth by the love of her who gave me her kiss to guide me on this journey. Her love has done more to pull these hairs out of my chin than the few years I have lived, or that shameful treatment to which her father subjected me.][209]

In this scene, Rennewart is in Orange and he is just beginning to realize his true nobility and to seek his destiny. In his lack of a beard prior to this, he suggested the same youthfulness we see in Vivianz, who also had smooth cheeks. The virility that the beard's first appearance symbolizes is threatened when it is singed, in addition to being an affront to his developing character. In retrospect, Rennewart and the audience can see that this nobility was present before, in Montlaon, and that Alyze in her role as courtly lady recognized it in him. He laments:

ich getrûwe ir wol, si sente
um mich, ze swelher zît si sach
daz der künc sîn zuht an mir zebrach,
und ich spehte die gelegenheit
der rîterlîchen arbeit
in turneyn unde in strîten,
dar ich lief ze mangen zîten,
wie man ein ors mit künste rite,
gein wîben gebâren ouch die site.
                    (*Wh.* 287, 20–8)

[I know for sure that she grieved on my behalf whenever she could see how the king was acting against his natural courtesy in his behaviour towards me and when I myself investigated the whys and wherefores of chivalry in tournaments and battles which I would often run to in order to observe the art of horse-riding, or how one should behave towards ladies.][210]

Here we can see how, even as a kitchen hand in Loys's palace, Rennewart was curious about the pursuits of knights: he is interested in tournaments, horses and service to ladies. This inquisitiveness is Wolfram's way of showing the audience that Rennewart's inner nobility will soon surface and that he

209 Gibbs and Johnson, 146.
210 Gibbs and Johnson, 146.

is worthy of the role which Wolfram has set out for him. Though chivalry and conversion to Christianity were instrumental in Rennewart's development and role, it is love and its service that will give them their significance and direction, and lead the knight towards God's purpose for him. Even as the Saracens prove formidable knights, capable in the service of love, this service must be influenced by the Christian God if it is to mature.

The defining moment in Rennewart's courtly influence for the audience and the one that spurs him on in the direction of chivalry and Christianity, is the scene in Orleans when he takes his leave of the princess. She is found sitting alone in the grass under a tree and the young Rennewart stands before her. Wolfram comments: 'wan daz mirz d'âventiure sagt, des maeres waer ich gar verzagt, als ez im Alyze erbôt' [if my source had not told me, I should be completely at a loss to say how Alize received him] (*Wh.* 213, 13–15).[211] As Wolfram's intentions for Rennewart's character are communicated in several places in the text, it would seem that it is not the kiss itself to which Wolfram refers in these lines, but the words of regret that Alyze has for his past treatment:

> si klagete sîne manege nôt
> die er in Francrîche het erliten.
> dar nâch begunde si in biten
> daz er ir vater schult verkür,
> swaz der ie prîss gein im verlür.
> 'do solt mit mîme kusse varn.
> dîn edelkeit mac dich bewarn
> und an die stat noch bringen
> dâ dich sorge niht darf twingen.'
> diu magt stuont ûf: der kus geschach:
> Rennwart ir neic unde sprach
> 'der hoehste got behüete
> iwer werdeclîchen güete.'
> den anderen vrowen wart ouch genigen,
> gein in sîn urloup niht verswigen.
>   (*Wh.* 213, 16–30)

---

211   Gibbs and Johnson, 112.

[She lamented the many difficulties which he had endured in France and then she went on to beg him to forgive her father's guilt, no matter how much the King had lost in renown through his treatment of him. 'You shall take my kiss away with you. May your nobility protect you and bring you to where no sorrow will oppress you.' The maiden stood up: the kiss was given. Rennewart bowed to her and said: 'May the highest God protect your noble kindness.' He bowed to the other ladies too and did not neglect to take his leave of them.][212]

Alyze's appeal for forgiveness and her bestowal of a kiss symbolizes her own recognition and the acceptance by courtly society of Rennewart's nobility and capability in the task before him: to assist Willehalm in securing the Christian victory. Rennewart accepts her offer; indeed, after Aélis's embrace in *Aliscans*, Rainouart 'tot li pardona' [Rainouart forgave everything] (*Alisc.* LXXIX, 4085) and takes his bow before departing with the army. Alyze has charged Rennewart with the role of assisting Willehalm to repel the Saracens from the southern march, and he has accepted her favour; after this, he is referred to as Alyzen soldier.[213]

In *Aliscans*, Aélis's love for Rainouart blossoms when she watches him wash the dung from his *tinel*, an act symbolizing the cleansing of Rainouart's pure character. In *Willehalm*, Wolfram allows the relationship to build gradually. In childhood, Rennewart was given to Alyze as a playmate and later Alyze convinces her father to give him to Willehalm who now has no nephews in his charge. Her kiss upon his departure and her guilt at his prior treatment in France show a culmination of courtly acceptance of Rennewart's role in the story as well as her command to him to help her uncle. It is now Rennewart's duty to succeed for Willehalm; he is in the service of a lady for love. By convincing her father to give him to Willehalm, Alyze has made it possible for him to go with the army to relieve Orange and she has enlisted Rennewart's service. Even Willehalm recognizes that Rennewart belongs to the princess, if even as a slave, and he asks her permission before speaking to Rennewart after he has acquired him from Loys.[214] If

---

212 Gibbs and Johnson, 112.
213 *Wh.* 418, 14. See also Lofmark, *Rennewart*, 226.
214 'bien sei venuz' er zuo im sprach mit der jungen künigin urloup' ['Welcome' said [Willehalm] to [Rennewart] with the permission of the princess] (*Wh.* 192, 14–15).

the kiss and bow were to be accepted as his vow of service to Alyze, it would contribute greatly towards the implication of a marriage between the two characters and a possible reconciliation of differences between Terramer and the Frenchmen. As it is, however, Rennewart has yet to become a knight and, though he shows inclinations towards his true and noble nature, in Orleans he has not yet embraced those things which will signal his coming of age and formal acceptance in society: investiture and baptism.

When the army arrives to relieve Orange, Wolfram's description of Rennewart's appearance leaves little doubt about his intentions for this character. Without saying a word, Rennewart walks down the great hall of Glorjet to the head of the forces assembled there to eat, and all of the warriors regard him: 'în gienc des rîchsten mannes suon, des houbet krône bî der zît truoc: daz was gar âne strît' [it was the son of the most powerful ruler of the time who had come in and there was no disputing this] (*Wh.* 269, 28–30).[215] Wolfram then describes how the perspiration running down his dirty skin exposes a shining interior, and also strength: 'der starke, niht der swache, truoc ougen als ein trache vorm houbte, grôz, lûter, lieht' [the powerful man – no weakling, this – had eyes in his head like a dragon, huge, clear and shining] (*Wh.* 270, 25–7).[216] Still not having spoken, the impression given by Rennewart in the palace at Orange is considerable, going beyond his rough exterior:

> man kôs der muoter êre
> an im, diu sölhe vruht gebar.
> al sîn antlütze gar
> ze wunsche stuont und al die lide.
> sîn clârheit warp der wîbe vride:
> ir necheiniu haz gein im truoc.
> ich sag iu lobs von im genuoc,
> genaehet er baz dem prîse
> und bin ich dannoch sô wîse.
>   (*Wh.* 271, 6–14)

215   Gibbs and Johnson, 138.
216   Gibbs and Johnson, 139.

[You could detect in him the nobility of the mother who had borne such a child. His whole face and all his limbs were perfection itself, and his handsome appearance earned him the approval of women, so that not one of them was ill-disposed to him. I shall have plenty to say to you in praise of him if he gets closer to renown, and if I am still clever enough for that.][217]

Already then, before the battle and before he has been introduced to the court at Orange, there is a detectable difference in his demeanour and reception from that in Montlaon. He is formidable because his inner nobility is, if not recognized, certainly intimated. His strength is seen not so much as brutish but as an indication of his capability. His physical beauty is noticed, rather than his clumsiness. Most telling of all is his attractiveness to ladies, a sign that Rennewart has come of age in the recognition of his station and the direction of his service. Now that he has recognized himself as noble, he can become a knight and he must see that his chivalry serves well and properly, that it is directed by *Minnedienst* and by God, not merely by his own desire for revenge. This will not be an easy lesson for Rennewart and he will be taunted by the chef as well as by knights and warriors in the coming battle. But Wolfram has given the audience a clear indication of his ability to be accepted in courtly society.

Wolfram compares Rennewart here to the young Parzival, indicating the same reasons for his initial lack of knowledge of courtly behaviour:

> eins dinges mir geloubet:
> er was des unberoubet,
> sîn blic durh rost gap sölhiu mâl
> als dô den jungen Parzivâl
> vant mit sîner varwe glanz
> der grâve Karnahkarnanz
> an venje in dem walde.
> jeht Rennewart al balde
> als guoter schoene, als guoter kraft,

---

217 Gibbs and Johnson, 139. Though Rennewart's mother is not identified, it is clear that Wolfram distinguishes between those characteristics that are the result of the influence of women and those that come from Terramer, the warrior: nobility would be perceived as a maternal inheritance, whereas honour is a paternal one.

und der tumpheit geselleschaft.
ir neweder was nâch arde erzogn:
des was ir edelkeit betrogn.
                    (*Wh.* 271, 15–26)

[One thing you can believe, for no one could take this away from him: through
the grime he shone forth like the young Parzival when Count Karnahkarnaz came
upon him on his knees in the forest, so radiant in his beauty. Right now you are to
attribute a similar beauty to Rennewart, as well as the same inexperience. Neither of
them had been brought up in accordance with his lineage and so they were robbed
of their nobility.][218]

Wolfram refers to a story with which the audience is already familiar
to establish Rennewart's claim to nobility; it also indicates that he has an
important role to play in *Willehalm*, if he can only gain the proper experience and wisdom. The comic element is not lost in Wolfram's innovation
to the source material, however, as Heimrich finally remarks to Gyburg:
'wer ist sô starc, sô manlîch dâ her în für uns gegangen mit einer sô grôzen
stangen?' [Who is this coming in before us, looking so strong and so vigor-
ous and with such a huge club?] (*Wh.* 271, 28–30).[219] Although all of the
knights assembled are looking on with marked curiosity, Heimrich cuts
straight to the point and mentions the great club this warrior is carrying.
Not only is it unusual as a weapon and in its size; it is also intimidating.
Gyburg's answer reaffirms Wolfram's intentions for Rennewart, intimating
his nobility and the role he will play in the rest of the story: 'hêrre, ez ist
ein sarjant, dem sîner kurzen jâre lebn ze rehte, ich waene, ist niht gegebn.
mich dunct, man sold in halden baz' [my lord, it is a sarjant who, in the
course of his short life, has not, I think, received his due. I believe that
he should be treated better] (*Wh.* 272, 2–5).[220] Gyburg continues, telling
Heimrich about Rennewart's bravery, modesty, gentility and loyalty, con-
fiding that she feels a special affinity to him because, as the audience knows
already, though Gyburg does not, he is her brother. This is a fact that rein-

218   Gibbs and Johnson, 139.
219   Gibbs and Johnson, 139.
220   Gibbs and Johnson, 139.

forces Rennewart's claim to nobility and its implications, because Gyburg has already been described by Wolfram as the most admirable queen and Terramer, Rennewart's father, as the most powerful ruler. His development is not yet complete, however, as his appearance as a foot-soldier armed as a knight is contradictory; he has not yet matured enough to assume his role.[221] Rennewart comes to stand before Willehalm, offering his services to him as well as to Gyburg and Heimrich with all of the courtliness demanded of his station.

It remains for Rennewart to embrace the legacy of his lineage and to rise to meet the challenges of his role. He is the son of a powerful king, so he has been born to lead, and he is a knight in the service of Alyze, the princess of the Christian Empire, charged with the defense of Orange with the Christian army. Since leaving Orleans, he has been in a position to do this because of Alyze's kiss; he has matured as a nobleman and is consequently accepted into Christian courtly society. Although no marriage takes place between Rennewart and Alyze in *Willehalm*, it is an event that would signal a reconciliation between the defeated Saracens, namely Terramer, and the Christians, Willehalm and Gyburg, paving the way for a possible conversion of Terramer and the acceptance by both sides of the marriage between Willehalm and Gyburg and of their seat at Orange. It would not be a convincing argument to propose that by reconciliation Wolfram intended all of the Saracens to convert to Christianity. That both sides would reach some understanding through gaining respect for each other's nobility, facilitated by spirituality, thereby offering the hope of future conversion, seems more likely.[222]

---

221 Wiesmann-Wiedemann remarked on Rennewart's contradictory appearance in Orange (203).

222 Wolfram's ending in *Parzival* implies a future Christian world as well, by telling how the Grail knights would become kings of the pagan kingdoms. Knapp is of the same opinion as he asserts that Wolfram intended no great conversion of the heathens, rather reconciliation and hope that would be accomplished through the character of Rennewart. See: Knapp, Fritz Peter. 'Heilsgewißheit oder Resignation?', 612. Lofmark also recognizes Alyze's role in this implied reconciliation by marrying Rennewart,

Another feature of Rennewart's ability to bring about reconciliation in *Willehalm* is the ennobling effect he has on other main characters; this is one of Wolfram's innovations to his source material. King Loys is portrayed as a more compassionate man than Louis in *Aliscans*, because in place of Louis's refusing Rainouart's baptism in *Aliscans*, in *Willehalm* Loys expresses regret that Rennewart has declined it.[223] Instead of feeling fear for this young Saracen, Gyburg and Heimrich treat him with kindness and respect, allowing more civility in their characters than their *Aliscans* counterparts had.[224] Even Willehalm's behaviour is more consistent from the first battle through to the end of the second because of the innovations Wolfram made to the character of Rennewart. Willehalm treats Rennewart with respect and affection and is not indifferent when Rennewart goes missing after the second battle. This lends a compassion and gentility to Willehalm's personality.[225] Terramer is spared the humiliation of fighting with his son and being wounded by him, as Wolfram has Willehalm wound him instead, allowing the battle to take precedence over combat between father and son.[226]

A significant innovation allowing the ennobling of another character by the presence and role of Rennewart is the interaction with Poydjus, the

---

writing that 'if reconciliation is at all possible, they are best able to bring it about' (Lofmark, *Rennewart*, 241).

223 Lofmark, *Rennewart*, 122.

224 Lofmark, *Rennewart*, 122.

225 See Lofmark, *Rennewart*, 236–8. It can be posited that the reason for Guillaume's hostility towards Rainouart because of his absence after the second battle is due to Guillaume's mistrust of Louis's Frenchmen sent to support Guillaume; he knows that Rainouart comes from the court at Montlaon and is not Narbonnais. See Chapter 5, section: 'The Public Arena.'

226 See *Wh.* 43, 3–15, and Lofmark, *Rennewart*, 95, 231. Lofmark comments on the parallel made between this clash and that in the *Hildebrandslied*, that the audience would recognize (though it must be noted that Wolfram's audience would have been familiar with the Middle High German *jüngere Hildebrandslied* [Younger Lay of Hildebrand], that retained the father-son confrontation) (*Rennewart*, 225). More current for Wolfram's timeframe is the comparison of this confrontation with that of Arthur and Mordred.

maternal nephew of Rennewart and Gyburg whose banner carries the heraldic device of Feirefiz;[227] it is from him that Rennewart wins Lignmaredî, his first mount. The last that is seen of Poydjus is when he flees from battle against Rennewart, but his role seems far from concluded. Lofmark gives a detailed account of the reasons why more should be expected from the Poydjus exchange, comparing it with his counterpart in *Aliscans*, Baudins, and citing five major motives for the continuation of his role by Wolfram: first, Poydjus is given a more prominent position in *Willehalm*; second, there is marked similarity between the action of Baudins to that at the end of *Parzival*; third, the career of Poydjus is not one that can plausibly end in flight (he must avenge his maternal uncle, Tedalun, as is consistent with the importance of the *swestersun* [maternal nephew] relationship in the stories); fourth, because Poydjus and his battalion are still fighting after Terramer has sailed with the ships, leaving him stranded in Provence with his uncle, Rennewart.[228] The fifth and most compelling argument for this character's future in *Willehalm* is the role of his counterpart in *Aliscans*. There is a reconciliation and ensuing friendship between Rainouart and Baudins after their battle during which Rainouart defeats Baudins and Baudins must convert to Christianity and be baptized.[229] These are events that have parallels in *Parzival*.[230] However, it must also be taken into account that the continuation of the material as it was presented in Wolfram's source would also serve the purpose of raising Poydjus to the degree which Wolfram has led his audience to expect of him: he would be exonerated from any act

227 See *Wh.* 376, 19–30; 379, 24; and Lofmark, *Rennewart*, 233–4.
228 See Lofmark, *Rennewart*, 232–6.
229 There are several spellings for this name in the various MSS of *Aliscans*: Bauduc, Baudin and Baudus, who seem to have been separate characters at times and were possibly conglomerated or confused when the *chansons de geste* were sung or written down. In the 'A' manuscripts, the character is Bauduc and he is the cousin of Rainouart, nephew of Désramé. However, Lofmark remarks that, as Wolfram has made a distinction between Poydwiz and Poydjus, these characters correspond more closely to those in the 'M' manuscript, whose characters, Baudus and Baudins, are similar: Baudus dies in battle, as does Poydwiz. Lofmark, *Rennewart*, 233.
230 'Wolfram is more likely to have noted and responded to such similarities at the end of his two great poems than to have got rid of them.' Lofmark, *Rennewart*, 234.

of cowardice in fleeing battle if he were to return and thus be worthy of becoming Rennewart's opponent and companion.[231] These innovations to the character of Rennewart allow other characters in *Willehalm* to display more compassion and grace than do their counterparts in *Aliscans* in their dealings with Rainouart / Rennewart, making the implication of a reconciliation between Saracen and Christian more plausible and consistent with what the thirteenth-century German audience might have come to expect from Wolfram.

In courtly epic, 'man derives his importance from social integration'[232] and this seems to tally with Wolfram's plan for his story regarding Rennewart, as with all of his characters. It is in Rennewart's development that he moves from the marginal realms of human society as an outcast, slave and heathen, towards the centre of chivalric importance, recognized by both family and courtly society as the noble warrior he is and instrumental in the Christian victory. That Rennewart's role is pivotal in *Willehalm* but remains incomplete, that the goals that are alluded to remain unrealized, is one of the most plausible reasons put forward by those who assert that *Willehalm* is not a finished work.[233] One of the most convincing arguments is the incomplete social integration which is expected to take place and which has already begun when Rennewart arrives at Orange. When compared with *Aliscans*, *Willehalm* can be seen to both diverge from and conform to its source in different ways and at different places in the text, but it seems to have been Wolfram's intention to follow some passages of *Aliscans* more surely than others in *Willehalm*. Among those is the reconciliation between Gyburg and Rennewart when he reveals his lineage to her, enabling him to be recognized as her brother, the son of Terramer, and as Willehalm's brother-in-law, knight, peer and kinsman in the eyes of society. In *Aliscans*, Rainouart does not reveal his lineage to Guiborc until *laisse* CLXXXIV, after his baptism, neither of which occur in the *Willehalm* fragment. As with the Baudins episode, this is a conclusion that has been too well set

---

231   See Lofmark, *Rennewart*, 236.
232   Lofmark, *Rennewart*, 128.
233   Lofmark, *Rennewart*, 215–43.

up by Wolfram to assume that it will not happen in *Willehalm*. Even as a buffoon in *Aliscans*, Rainouart serves the distinct purpose of answering the challenges facing Christianity resulting from the weak leadership of Louis and the discouragement of Christianity's champions, Guillaume and the Narbonnais princes.[234] The Rennewart character has been developed in *Willehalm* to serve the same function: to aid Willehalm in achieving victory for the Christians and to bring about stronger leadership of the Frenchmen. There is also the discussion between Willehalm and Bernart of Brabant of plans to secure Rennewart's release from capture by the Saracens.[235] Therefore, evidence in the texts of *Aliscans* and Wolfram's narration of *Willehalm* only reinforce what Lofmark deduced years ago: that Rennewart's role in *Willehalm* is incomplete and that it would logically continue with a formal acceptance of his knighthood, kinship and role in Christian courtly society.

It is already clear that Rennewart is the character best suited to serve the function of aiding Willehalm in the Christian military victory. Wolfram's innovations are key to the formation of the Rennewart who will accomplish this task. Wolfram's Christian victory will be no simple military victory. Rather, it must be a complete victory of Christian chivalry over misguided Saracen knighthood; a victory of strong leadership over weak kings, such as Louis, and unruly vassals, such as Tybalt; it also must be a victory of kinship and solidarity over discord and hostility, sanctioned by divine grace. The investigation of Rennewart's maturity with regard to reconciliation and marriage, conversion and baptism, and chivalry and investiture shows not only how Wolfram used Rennewart to this purpose but also how Rennewart's development parallels the unfolding of Wolfram's message of reconciliation within the plot.

---

234 See De Combarieu du Grès, Micheline, 'Aliscans ou la victoire des "nouveaux" chrétiens (étude sur Guibourc et Rainouart)' in Jean Dufournet, ed., *Mourir aux Aliscans: Aliscans et la légende de Guillaume d'Orange* (Paris: Honoré Champion, 1993), 55–77.

235 *Wh.* 458–9.

The goal of reconciliation in *Willehalm* is not a simple one; nonetheless, it is a clear one and the role of the Saracens who are also the extended family of Willehalm, the protagonist upon whose shoulders the fate of the empire as well as the concord between kinsmen on opposing sides rests, is one of prime importance. Kinship, as in *Parzival*, and clan loyalty continue to be key features in *Willehalm* as the extension of family lines traverses the breach between opposing religions and kingdoms. This emphasis seems to suggest that Wolfram sees the obstacle to a reconciliation more in terms of disloyal vassals rather than in terms of religious difference. Wolfram makes use of Willehalm's Saracen kinsmen to convey his message that chivalry with God's sanction and love with divine direction is the path to solidarity and concord, and gives the hope of reconciliation not only between warring sides, but also between kinsmen, vassals and their liege-lord, and between the knight and God.[236] This message of hope includes the idea of a conversion of heathens to Christianity, which is depicted as a part of the spiritual aspect of Christian chivalry. Although the Saracens do not convert within the confines of the fragment that is *Willehalm*, the message pointing towards such a conversion is clear before the text breaks off: through conversion, it is recognized that there will be a brotherhood between all men and Gyburg's Saracen kinsmen exemplify this message in their depiction.

By giving greater prominence to certain Saracen characters in *Willehalm*, Wolfram emphasizes the themes of loyalty, kinship and solidarity, as well as engaging concepts of love, chivalry and spirituality. Wolfram develops these Saracens to a greater extent than his source; he imbues them with human qualities, depicting their thoughts, motivations, fallibility and capacity for love. However, when comparing these characters to their *Aliscans* counterparts, we can see that the Saracens of the *chanson de geste* had a substance and a specific purpose for the *jongleur* that was different

236   That these ideals are closely dependent in Willehalm is supported by Alois Wolf's statement: 'Wolfram never tires of demonstrating that human love and religion ought not to be separated from one another and that human love, minne, presents a first-rate salutary spiritual force.' (Wolf, 378)

from the purpose for which Wolfram recrafted them. Therefore, Wolfram's innovations cannot be said to 'work against the grain of his source material' as Martin Jones writes, nor was his 'even-handed treatment'[237] of the two sides in the conflict an original innovation, any more than war was wholly glorified in the *chansons de geste*. The difference between the depiction of the Saracens in *Aliscans* and in *Willehalm* is due to Wolfram's own intentions regarding the story he wants to tell and the message he wishes to convey, and has little bearing on his understanding of the themes in the *chansons de geste* or on his criticism of the ideals that are portrayed in them. He did, however, know the story well enough to draw certain themes from it to work with them, supplement them and expand upon them, as did all good medieval composers,[238] with the result that many of the Saracens who appear in *Willehalm* are more prominent and individually developed, taking their place as protagonists.

The reasons behind Wolfram's differing depictions of these prominent Saracen characters vary from the more obvious, such as time, geo-political environment, popular interests and epic structure, to more personal interests in his message about chivalry and spirituality. As was discussed in Chapter 2, chivalry is very important to Wolfram and his is a chivalry which must be guided by spirituality to have true value. His Saracens exemplify this chivalry in part or convey messages to the Christian protagonists and to the audience about how it should be retained and employed. The other contributing factor to Wolfram's depiction of the Saracens is his perspective

---

237 Jones, Martin H. 'Giburc at Orange: The Siege as Military Event and Literary Theme' in Martin H. Jones and Timothy McFarland, eds, *Wolfram's 'Willehalm': Fifteen Essays* (Rochester, NY: Camden House, 2002), 97–120. Helen Cooper employs the same phrase when referring to a different work, *Floire et Blancheflour*, dating from the mid-twelfth century, which she writes gives 'even-handed treatment' to both Saracens and Christians. Cooper, 28. This appears then to be a literary attitude that was neither new nor unique.

238 Similarly, this not-unprecedented phenomenon can be seen not only in the works of the *jongleurs*, but in the romances, a genre of which Wolfram had already become master in his *Parzival*, just as 'the author of *La Queste* succeeded in transforming and enriching the elements he borrowed from the works of his predecessors.' Williams, 190.

of what is 'French' and what is 'foreign', and what values German traditions hold in high regard and how. We can see in the representation and behaviour of his Saracens that Wolfram did not view Christianity and Empire as one and the same, as was depicted in the *chansons de geste*, and that the 'we' becomes, rather than the Frankish-ruled Holy Roman Empire, the Narbonnais clan of Willehalm. The French and their idea of empire is depicted as unreliable and given to disloyalty, a reputation detestable to Wolfram's chivalry. The 'they' then becomes not only the Saracen aggressors but also the French imperialists, who emerge as obstacles to Willehalm's fulfilment of his saintly life in Orange and its territory. Religion itself is only a feature in that it is a motivator for the French Empire to support his claim to the land. Thereby, the Crusade ideals of an empire under threat from Saracen invasion remain outside the scope of *Willehalm*; it was not the focus of this work to either reinforce or to challenge these ideals and they remain in the background of the main story as a device rather than the central theme.

Similarly, conversion to Christianity in *Willehalm* is presented only in terms of spirituality and union with God, not as a motivation for war or killing heathens. Religion is recognized as a source of irreconcilable difference and conflict, but it is not the focus of the story. We have seen how the portrayal of some prominent Saracens in *Aliscans* shows that there was a distinction between good Saracens who had value as human beings and those who were seen as evil and threatening, suggesting that religion in itself was not the main focus of the stories of the *jongleurs*. In *Willehalm*, those Saracens, even those who do not convert, are still instrumental in the plot, in God's will and in the Christian victory.

The Saracen Queen

As a woman and as the only Saracen in *Willehalm* who has converted to Christianity (this having occurred in *La Prise d'Orange*), Gyburg occupies a unique position within the text. She is the one figure, too, who links the Saracens to the Christians by kinship, the powerful Saracen nobility to the Narbonnais clan through her marriage to Willehalm. She is concurrently Willehalm's wife, Terramer's daughter, Tybalt's queen and Rennewart's sister, and she is acutely aware of this singular status. Her presence in the story attests to the importance of kinship in war, in revenge and in achieving peace, and her prolific appearances in *chansons de geste* demonstrate her popularity with the medieval audience. Gyburg's character also exemplifies Wolfram's inclination to juxtapose contradictory elements, implying the coexistence of both good and evil, love and hate, life and death. As a converted Saracen queen and Christian liege-lady, Gyburg is both the reason for the war and the figure for whom peace between the opposing sides might be won. In *Willehalm*, Wolfram allows her character to embrace the pivotal role she had in *Aliscans*, extending it to its fullest potential in influencing the outcome of the war through other characters, by means of her piety and spirituality as well as her strength and fortitude.

In the following chapter, we will become acquainted with the complex character of Gyburg in the contexts of the textual tradition of the character, her significance to the story as it relates to her status, and the significance that Wolfram attributes to her in *Willehalm*. The background of the character of Gyburg in the *chansons de geste*, with particular focus on *La Prise d'Orange*, will be presented here with an intertextual perspective, illustrating how other material affects her portrayal in *Aliscans* and *Willehalm*. A study of the function of the character of Gyburg will follow, focusing on the means by which she uses influence and how she is motivated in the role of Orange's queen. Finally, Gyburg's relationship with Willehalm and the significance and function of the love-service that binds them will be discussed, with particular attention to the role she plays in the preservation of Orange and how she comes to serve as an example of properly directed chivalry and spiritual strength.

The Image of Gyburg

Female characters in *Willehalm* are of noble birth; they occupy positions of power and act as mediators in conflict; and they are strong-minded and beautiful (whether old or young). Gyburg is no exception to this. Such traits were well-established and especially characteristic of Saracen women in the *chansons de geste*.[1] Kay asserts that the *chanson-de-geste* woman played an important role in the social space between lord and vassal, between brother and husband, and that, contrary to the women in romance texts whose social space was their identification as objects of desire[2] or even as 'objects

---

1   Matthew Bennett writes that Saracen women in the *chansons de geste* and French epic are 'usually royalty and they supply a certain glamour [...] they tend like Braminonde [sic.] and Orable to be strong-minded, and are often prepared to throw over their Saracen husbands in favour of a handsome Christian paladin' (Bennett, 106). Jacqueline de Weever, in a similar study on how the Saracen princesses of French epics almost always 'betray the kings their fathers and their countries in one way or another and marry the Frankish knight,' points out that 'seventeen of the twenty-one princesses who appear in the poems written between 1150 and 1300 fall into [that] category.' (De Weever, 5) These prominent Saracen princesses include Bramimonde, Galienne, Floripas, Rosamonde, Nubie, Malatrie and Mirabelle. See also Harrison, Ann Tukey, 'Aude and Bramimunde: Their Importance in the *Chanson de Roland*', *The French Review* LIV/5 (1981), 672–9.

2   Sarah Kay describes the dimensions of the place occupied by *chanson-de-geste* women, here Olive in *Doon de la Roche* ('La représentation de la féminité', esp. 227).

by means of which negotiations between men [...] can be conducted,'³ she had a voice. Lachet explores the female characters in *Aliscans* itself, revealing the important roles they play, and he writes that in the warrior's domain, 'la femme lui est supérieure dans la conduite de l'action par sa vitalité, son sens de mesure et son intelligence du cœur' [the woman is superior to him in driving the action by her vitality, her sense of moderation and her knowledge of the heart].⁴ Evidence suggests that these character traits in medieval fictional women were well-established before the *chansons de geste* were recorded in written form and reflected interest in contemporary events. Matthew Bennett mentions historical bases for such depictions of strong female characters in the *chansons de geste*, referring to Mora Zaida of Seville, who became the concubine of Alfonso VI. This supports the stance that these images of Saracens were formed before the contact of the first Crusades penetrated the European imagination.⁵ Likewise, the subject of female rule was made popular by the ascent to the throne of Matilda of England and Eleanor of Aquitaine, as well as by the women left behind to manage the affairs of their estates by Crusading husbands, well before Wolfram heard *La Bataille d'Aliscans*.⁶ Historically, also, Gyburg bears a resemblance to Khaunagunda, the wife of Guilhem of Nîmes, part of Septimania.⁷

3   Young, Christopher, 'The Construction of Gender in Willehalm' in Martin H. Jones and Timothy McFarland, eds, *Wolfram's 'Willehalm': Fifteen Essays*, 249–69 (Rochester, NY: Camden House, 2002), 252.

4   Lachet, Claude. 'Figures féminines dans *Aliscans*' in *Mourir aux Aliscans: Aliscans et la légende de Guillaume d'Orange*, ed. Jean Dufournet, 101–19 (Paris: Honoré Champion, 1993), 119.

5   Bennett, 106. See also Chapter 2 section: 'Ethics of chivalry put to the test: the Crusades'.

6   See Ramey, 'Role Models?', 132.

7   Guiborc is an amalgamation of historical figures. Guilhem was married to Khaunagunda, or Cunégonde, daughter of the king Akhila II, the last sovereign Visigoth. She represents the importance to Theodoric and his dynasty's legitimacy to have a Gothic line in Septimania. However, Guilhem's situation changed when Khauna, an exceptional woman and ruler who had assumed authority over Nîmes, was assassinated during her command in 756. Her death enabled Guilhem to envisage

In the *chansons de geste*, female figures, both Christian and Saracen, bearing resemblance to historical figures, also display fantastical elements from other genres. In *Doon de la Roche*, Doon's wife Olive is tricked with a sleeping potion by a traitor and in *Les Enfances Guillaume*, Orable evades her obligation on her wedding night with Tiébaut by magically turning him into a gold ball.[8] The absence of such fantastical elements in *Willehalm* might well support Matthew Bennett's suggestion that contact with the Islamic world during the Crusades led to a different, more objective depiction of Saracens,[9] although only as far as *Willehalm*'s female characters are concerned, for Wolfram seems to enjoy describing the male Saracen adversaries on the battlefield, who have horned skin akin to armour and other fantastical traits, and come from exotic lands at the world's end.[10] The absence of the fantastical and grotesque in Saracen women adversaries on the battlefield in *Willehalm* is conspicuous,[11] and attests to Wolfram's image of women as the inspiration for Christian love, salvation, chivalry and spirituality, as well as his desire to exploit the reconciliatory, balancing role of the self-possessed women of *Aliscans* whom Lachet finds to be 'le réconfort et l'espérance de l'homme' [the comfort and hope of men].[12] The female characters in *Willehalm*, unlike the overprotective mothers, seductresses or objects of desire of *Parzival* (such as Herzeloyde, Jeschute, Condwiramurs or the ladies with whom Gawan has relations, such as Orgeleuse), tend more

---

a matrimonial alliance with the Franks. By some accounts, Guillaume's second wife, Guiborc, had a Frankish name, yet by some accounts it is a Catalan Visigothic name, Guitburg, but the need for an alliance with the Kingdom of Pepin would suggest she was of Frankish origin.

8   See: Kay, 'La représentation de la féminité', 226; and Ramey, 'Role Models?', 137. Ferrante also mentions a strong tradition of Gyburg being portrayed as a sorceress in the earlier *Chanson de Guillaume* and *Enfances Guillaume* (44).

9   See Bennett.

10   *Wh.* 35, 11–20; 395–6.

11   There are none of the gigantic and grotesque yet formidable Saracen warrior women of *Aliscans* in *Willehalm*, such as Flohart, who fights a momentous combat against Rainouart in the second battle (*Alisc.* CL–CLII). Women seem to serve a more courtly purpose for Wolfram. See Hathaway, 'Women at Montlaon'.

12   Lachet, 'Figures féminines', 119.

to reflect those characteristics of their *Aliscans* counterparts, offering to a bleak world 'un rayon de lumière, de beauté, de douceur, d'amour et de vie' [a ray of light, of beauty, of sweetness, of love and of life][13] as well as inspiration to the author to expand upon the image of women, so through her character 'faith, love, and knighthood become inseparable.'[14] The central female character in both texts is the Saracen queen Guiborc / Gyburg, whose character exemplifies this feminine image and unites the enamored queen and seductress, the powerful liege-lady and the faithful partner who serves as an inspiration to chivalry and service.

The character on which Wolfram drew, Guiborc in *Aliscans*, is a well-developed heroine, representative of the Saracen princess in the *chansons de geste*. She is so popular a figure that she features frequently in the *Petit Cycle de Guillaume*, in later poems about characters that became popular in *Aliscans*, and is the heroine of Ulrich von dem Türlin's thirteenth-century *Arabel*.[15] As a Saracen and as the queen of Orange and Gloriette (the exotic palace that Guillaume conquered in the *Prise d'Orange*), she is free from the expectations and requirements of French society,[16] free to oversee her city, Guillaume's march, and to effect its protection by any means open to her. Guiborc is the one who reminds Guillaume that he can appeal to his family and liege-lord, King Louis, at the court in Montlaon to protect Orange and it is she who is left behind to oversee the defence and survival of

---

13 Lachet, 'Figures féminines', 119.

14 Wolf, 381.

15 Joan Ferrante lists the *chansons de geste* of the *Petit Cycle de Guillaume: Enfances Guillaume, Couronnement de Louis, Charroi de Nîmes, Prise d'Orange, Aliscans* and *Moniage Guillaume*, and dates them in the mid-late twelfth century. The later poems about characters from *Aliscans* are listed as follows: *Enfances Vivien, Chevalerie Vivien, Bataille Loquifer, Moniage Rainoart* and *Foucon de Candie*, and date from the late twelfth to early thirteenth century (Ferrante, 9–10). It is a testament to the popularity of the characters in *Aliscans*, like Vivien, Rainouart and Guiborc, that so many later poems featured them, continuing and expanding their roles.

16 Ramey identifies the characteristic Saracen princess in the *chansons de geste* as free from societal expectations and thus able to take charge of her own destiny without suffering the consequences with which a Christian lady would be confronted. See Ramey, 'Role Models?', esp. 131, 133, 138.

Orange under siege, which she does with armour and sword. Guiborc's characteristics are consistent with those identified as archetypal of the Saracen princess: beautiful, of royal lineage, strong-minded, with a propensity to release the hero, in this case Guillaume in *La Prise d'Orange*, from imprisonment. Being part of both the Christian and Saracen worlds, Guiborc also occupies quintessential feminine spaces around the heroes and plots, functioning as the adulterous amour in *La Prise d'Orange*, the disobedient daughter of Desramé and the mother of Esmeré. She remains disobedient to her father, having brought about the conquest of Orange and its palace by releasing Guillaume, falling in love with him, converting to Christianity and refusing to yield to Desramé's forces during the siege in which Tiébaut hopes to regain his territory, Guiborc's dowry. Equally, as liege-lady and central feminine figure, her love inspires Guillaume and Rainouart in their endeavours towards victory as well as in their individual development and chivalry. Guiborc insists that Guillaume take a vow to remember her on his trip to Montlaon and that he return with help to save Orange. Her role in the reconciliation between Rainouart and Guillaume after the second battle (because Rainouart is left out of the victory celebrations) sustains her significance, though it does not feature in the *Willehalm* fragment; this breaks off before the celebrations (if, indeed, it was Wolfram's intention to continue the story as it was in *Aliscans*). Guiborc is the link between clans and between conflicting cultures, directing service through love and the example she sets in her commitment.

Though the influence of the pivotal women in the texts, Irmschart, Blancheflor and Alyze, is evident in the support of their clan, in the mercenary troops they raise, in the knights they inspire to their service, and in the ongoing hope of a greater reconciliation in the support of Willehalm by the imperial crown, their presence in the texts remains confined to Montlaon and Orleans, within the empire itself. However, the story, even the confrontation at Montlaon, centres on events in Orange, which lies outside the borders of the empire in a territory disputed by the Saracens and the Narbonnais. Orange is Gyburg's own city where she remains queen, though it has been conquered by Willehalm, who is its lord by marriage to her. It is her realm and, doing justice to the many *chansons de geste* that include her popular figure, she presides over Orange, at the edge of the

Christian world, as the exotic, converted Saracen queen and as a liege-lady in the Narbonnais clan. Her image in *Willehalm* corresponds to and at times exceeds that in *Aliscans*, combining the formulaic self-possessed Saracen princess character with spiritual chivalry and service to love. Even as a Saracen and a woman, and perhaps because of this, Gyburg's role is second in importance only to that of Willehalm. In *Willehalm*, she is the cause of the conflict and the object of the Saracen invasion; concurrently, she provides the motivation for the defence of Orange and is the agent securing Christian victory. She is exemplary in dedication and spiritual fortitude and inspires faithfulness, devotion and commitment. Here we will see how Gyburg's image is taken up by Wolfram from *Aliscans* and merged with his ideal of Christian chivalry, salvation and unity.

Wolfram saw the potential to exploit Gyburg's distinctly *chanson-de-geste* female role to demonstrate and expand themes prevalent in *Parzival*: service to love, unity, redemption, salvation and spiritual chivalry. Like her *Aliscans* counterpart, Gyburg is strong-minded, determined and capable as well as beautiful, and her love inspires those around her to her service. Gyburg takes an active role beside Willehalm when he returns from defeat in the first battle and continues to do so after the support troops have arrived, overseeing provisions and banquet preparations, and speaking at the war council before the second battle. Her involvement and influence in Rennewart's individual development and chivalry proves instrumental to the Christian victory.[17] As well as the strength and fortitude drawn from her *chanson-de-geste* background, Gyburg exercises an influence over those around her that is courtly in nature, such as the attention given to her appearance and clothing, and how it influences those at the banquet, inspiring them to service. She even accomplishes this by influencing Willehalm's own appearance at Montlaon. In addition. Wolfram adds two intimate scenes with Willehalm; after the first, Gyburg delivers a silent prayer for

---

17 Upon realizing his nobility and chivalry, and upon his achieving knighthood, Rennewart is able to turn back the fleeing French troops whose presence in the battle is vital and to emerge as the most formidable warrior on the battlefield, freeing the Narbonnais princes captured during the first battle.

Orange and her Narbonnais kinsmen. The effect of her presence is sooth-
ing and inspiring, though the exoticism of her status and setting lends a
sense of supremacy to Gyburg's character in *Willehalm* that builds upon
the established and popular figure from the *chansons de geste*.

Wolfram's 'reine Minne'

That the exploration and investigation of love, its service and its motivation
is important to Wolfram is already established in his works by the time
of the composition of *Willehalm*, where the female characters take on a
central and active role in its depiction and Gyburg proves exemplary. The
pure form that love takes, the *reine Minne* in *Parzival* as the deciding factor
in Feirefiz's conversion to Christianity, is arrived at through repeated trial
and introspection, and it is a love that Willehalm and Gyburg already share
when *Willehalm* begins. Wolfram underscores the role of Gyburg's love
for Willehalm in her conversion despite its remaining outside the timeframe in which *Willehalm* takes place,[18] and the purity of this Christian
love proves justification for Gyburg's disloyalty to her Saracen kin. This
justification of Gyburg's shift in loyalties and the motivation for her conversion to Christianity is, however, not exclusive to *Willehalm*: these are
themes that were treated often in the *Cycle de Guillaume* in the character
of Gyburg.[19] Wolfram uses his concept of a pure love between Gyburg and
Willehalm as a focal point and example of spiritual chivalry in society; its
power and influence is illustrated in the ability of the couple to rally forces
in the defence of their march.[20] Wessel-Fleinghaus's assertion that the outcome of the battle resides in this love between Gyburg and Willehalm is
consistent with this view.[21] To the Saracens who come to take back Orange
out of revenge, the war is motivated by vengeance and the all-important
acquisition of land. To Willehalm, Gyburg and the Narbonnais who come

18   *Wh.* 7, 27–30.
19   See Ramey, 'Role Models?', 137.
20   See Clifton-Everest, 'Wolframs Parzival und die chanson de geste', 713.
21   Wessel-Fleinghaus, 44.

to their aid, it is the defence of spiritual chivalry and indeed Wolfram's *reine Minne*, itself the embodiment of divine communion, that exemplifies an ideal Christian society.

The driving force of knighthood can be said to be *Minnedienst, fin' amors*. This complex service for love, as well as love governed by the rules of courtly etiquette, serves not only to motivate a knight to take action and, on a spiritual level, to search within himself for the divine love which will grant him communion with God, it also serves to unite opposing clans and cultures. Wolfram refined this brand of chivalry and *Minne*, fusing them in *Parzival* and exemplifying them in *Willehalm*. Huby-Marly writes of the chivalry in *Willehalm* as a universal chivalry of Wolfram's construction that functioned according to the same code and values as that of the early Feudal Age: courage, family and honour that exalted the place of the lady in chivalric life.[22] Love-service then takes on a more spiritual meaning and women are of greater significance to spiritual chivalry. Their active roles in the salvation and preservation of clan and land in the *chansons de geste* is complemented by their significance to chivalry in Wolfram's chivalric code. It is not only the dominating theme of a *reine Minne* that drives the action in *Willehalm* but also that this love-service is an integral part of spiritual chivalry in Christian feudal society. Wolfram's code of chivalry combines the strength of the Saracen queen of the *chanson de geste* with the motivation of love-service to her and accomplishes salvation, redemption and restitution through the key role played by Gyburg.

Wolfram uses love impartially with reference to heathens and Christians alike, and love's divine force is seen as perfection in spirituality and chivalry, embodying a duality of joy and sorrow. For Wolfram, it is clear that in chivalry, success lay in harmony: the completeness of happiness and misery together which could be accomplished only in service to love.

> wan urliuge und minne
> bedurfen beidiu sinne.
> einz hât semfte unde leit,
> daz ander gar unsemftekeit.

---

22   Huby-Marly, 'Willehalm', 406.

swer wîbe lôn ze reht erholt,
eteswenne er grôzen kumber dolt:
ob denne der minne süeze
sölhen kumber büeze,
swâ der site wirt begangen,
dâ ist der minne solt enphangen.
                    (*Wh.* 385, 3–12)

[for battle and love both demand understanding. The one comprises comfort and
suffering, the other nothing but discomfort. If a man strives properly for the reward
of women he must from time to time endure great pain: if then the sweetness of
love makes compensation for such pain, the reward of love will be received wherever
this occurs.][23]

Wolfram describes here the dual nature of *Minnedienst* in chivalry
and how going into battle without proper motivation in the service of love
brings only discomfort and reveals incomplete chivalry. He also makes
clear the invaluable role of women. Though many of the Saracens fight in
the name of love, they are not victorious because they have not embraced
love as a divine and Christian incarnation for which women are the inspiration; their service is not only misdirected but squandered, their chivalry
lacking. Though this love does not play as prominent a role in the *chansons
de geste*, nor does it feature in the motivations of the Saracen warriors of
Aliscans, it is reflected in the character of Guiborc. One of the most revealing passages to this effect can be found in the 'S' manuscript of *Aliscans*,[24]
in which Guiborc consoles Guillaume when he despairs of the losses after
the second battle:

Pleure Guillames, Guibors le conforta.
'Gentiex quens, sire, ne vos esmaiés ja!
Teus a perdu ki regaaignera,

23   Wolfram von Eschenbach. *Willehalm*, 190.
24   This *laisse* is exclusive to the Oxford/Halle 'S' manuscript, one believed to be more
      representative of a later, extended version with which Wolfram was less likely to
      have been familiar. It does, however, demonstrate the increased significance of the
      Guiborc character for Guillaume's personal chivalry.

Et teus est povres qui riches devenra.
Teus rit au main, au vespre ploërra.
Ne se doit plaindre li hom ki sauté a.
[...]
Molt a duré et encor duërra,
Molt a gent morte et encor en morra;
Ja de la mort uns seus n'escapera.
Tant com au siecle cascuns demouerra,
Si se contigne au miex ke il porra.
Se il sert dieu, a bone fin venra.
Molt doit liés estre hom qui bone feme a;
Et, s'il vaut auques, de bon cuer l'amera.
Le bon conseil, se li done, crera,
Et je sui cele qui bon le vos donra:
Refai Orengel A grant pris tornera.
(*Alisc.* CXCVIII, 8393–8, 8403–13)[25]

[William weeps and Guiborc comforts him: 'Noble count, sire, do not be distressed! Those who have lost will win again, and he who is poor will some day be rich. Who laughs in the morning will weep at night; a man of good health should not complain [... The world] has endured much and will endure more; many have died and many will die still; no one can escape from death. But as long as one remains in this world, he must carry on as best he can. If he serves God, his end will be good. A man who has a good wife should rejoice; and if he is worthy, love her with good heart. Good counsel, when given, should be followed, and I am one who will give some to you: Rebuild Orange. It will lead to great glory.][26]

This passage reveals the spiritual fortitude and hope of redemption and restitution that motivates Christian chivalry through love-service, and includes the idea of a divine communion guaranteed to him who can live in the world, where both joy and sorrow exist, without compromising his spiritual resolution. These ideas emerge in the final lines of *Parzival*[27] and are carried through in the character of the Saracen queen in *Willehalm*, where they remain important features which Wolfram was happy to exploit.

25   Wienbeck, Hartnacke, Rasch, ed. *Aliscans*.
26   Ferrante, 277–8.
27   See introduction to Chapter 2.

Kinship, Duty and Influence

Gyburg's familial status and her relations form a means by which she can influence events as well as providing motivation for her actions. She is bound by duty to kin and clan, but these groups are dictated by the oath she took in baptism, an oath of loyalty to the Christian fold entailing the protection of her new Narbonnais clan. Saracen family ties are still influential, however, as her relations with Terramer and Rennewart have shown and she is able to exercise her will to hold Orange against her father's forces and to encourage Rennewart to develop into the warrior who will defend Orange. Kinship is not Gyburg's only means of influencing and motivating characters and events; Wolfram also draws on the effects of her clothing and appearance, as well as the gestures, timing and staging in her communication with other characters and the audience.

Marriage and politics

With the exception of Alyze, whose fate remains incomplete in the *Willehalm* fragment, each of the women in the texts is involved in a marriage that is central to their influence upon the plot and upon other characters, as well as being subject to the loyalties and duties that a marriage implies for them, their families, their political environment and the social structure surrounding it. Marriage in the *chansons de geste* implies more than a contract between two people; it is an accord between families, an important institution for the regulation of property and office with the additional incentive of the possibility of territorial conquest.[28] This is focal in both *Aliscans* and *Willehalm*, as the bonds of marriage between Irmschart and Heimrich, Gyburg and Willehalm, and Blancheflor and Loys affect loyalties, victory, survival and honour of clan – and, in essence, the social fabric of Christian chivalry.

28   See Koss, 189–90.

Marriage bonds often function as double-edged swords in the *chansons de geste*. Koss observes that 'despite the many unifying properties of kinship, the very forces that are introduced to solidify society more than occasionally exert a disruptive force on it. Marriage [...] acts against its own basic function of forming alliances by sometimes creating situations of divided loyalty, as a spouse is forced to choose between the interests of her natal kin group and that which she has acquired by marriage.'[29] This dividing aspect of marriage with a conflict of loyalties falls upon the female rather than the male in *Aliscans* and *Willehalm*, and holds true for the Roman queen just as for the Saracen princess. Just as Blancheflor must support her Narbonnais kinsmen to whom the Roman Empire of her marital bond owes its strength and power by territory and loyal vassalage, Gyburg must decide against loyalty to her Saracen kinsmen in support of her Narbonnais husband and the Christian society to which she now belongs. That this deciding factor is placed upon the females increases their potential and political power. The decision to support Willehalm in his campaign to conquer and hold Orange rests upon the loyalties of Blancheflor and Gyburg. The importance of a queen to the display of the king's sovereignty must also be taken into account, as well as the power of a queen over court affairs, her duty to exert this power which rests in her own financial control, her influence over her husband through sexual intimacy and affection, and her status as mother.[30] It is the queen's duty to intercede between the king and his subordinates either on their behalf or on her own behalf, for mostly clan-oriented interests.[31] It is this upon which Gyburg relies when she sends Willehalm to Montlaon, anticipating in Blancheflor, the queen, the influence and sway that she herself exerts upon her own husband, Willehalm.

The shift of Gyburg's loyalty to the Narbonnais clan by her marriage to Willehalm and the seal on it with her conversion is pivotal to the political

---

29   Koss, 200.
30   See McCracken, Peggy, *The Romance of Adultery: Queenship and Sexual Transgression in Old French Literature*, ed. Ruth Mazo Karras, The Middle Ages Series (Philadelphia: University of Pennsylvania Press, 1998), 2–3.
31   McCracken, 7.

ambitions of both her Saracen kinsmen, the powerful king Terramer and his vassals, and Loys and his empire, ambitions that can be seen in terms of the break-up of the 'Saracen ruling family' and a change to the social order.[32] Even if it cannot be evidenced that Wolfram knew *Prise*, Gyburg's decision to convert to Christianity for Willehalm was of great interest to Wolfram and he treats the subject in the prologue as well as during the siege. The importance of Gyburg's conversion and marriage to Willehalm is noted, together with the fact that it is this marriage which enables Willehalm to hold land and power. As a convert, Gyburg's new loyalty is now unquestionable. Moreover, Orange remains hers, where she presides as queen, and her duty to safeguard her city and its defences follows naturally.

Guiborc enjoys a more developed past in *Aliscans*'s cyclic tradition and shares a marriage with Guillaume that, though having its origins in erotic love, functions with the duty of love-service by which both gain in security and loyalty; it is a marriage upon which Wolfram is happy to expand. Wolfram perceives the potential to portray the deeper sense of union that forms the essence of divine love, his *reine Minne*, between Gyburg and Willehalm. Of Wolfram's depiction of marriage in *Parzival* and *Willehalm*, Richey writes: 'Marriage remains the one complete symbol of love's true mating, […] it means a perfect sharing; a standing together in the world's sight, recognized and honoured; a privacy deeper than that of more casual ties; […] it means the giving of life to a new generation.'[33] For Wolfram, the ideal of marriage, like complete chivalry, is evidence of divine love and in *Willehalm*, it is the marriage between Gyburg and Willehalm that serves as an example. In this marriage, there is a visible unity between conflicting sides in the battle, between cultures and families; it symbolizes a mutual respect between husband and wife, queen and conqueror, Christian and convert, man and woman, and through it honour and loyalty are exemplified. It is within this institution that the young knights of the Narbonnais clan, Berthram and Vivianz, were nurtured and educated by aunt and uncle.

32   Daniel, *Heroes and Saracens*, 91.
33   Richey, 117.

Aunt and sister

From *Chanson de Roland* to the *Geste de Garin de Monglane*, the uncle-nephew relationship features prominently; sons were often sent to their maternal uncles who educated them in chivalric practice. Fosterage between kinsmen was a widespread medieval practice and the nephew is often seen in the *chansons de geste* as being the son of a sister – in *Willehalm*, the *swestersun* – representing an increasingly archaic significance in matrilineal descent.[34] Even in the *Cycle de Guillaume*, Guillaume is often accompanied by his sisters' sons, Bertrand, Guielin, Gui, Girard and Vivien, for whose tutelage in chivalry and warfare he is responsible, but who are also his companions in peace and in battle.[35] Koss observes that the nephews serve also as advisors, confidants and even squires to their uncle, with whom strong emotional ties are formed.[36] This avuncular theme carries through to *Willehalm* and the role that the aunt, in this case Gyburg, plays in the relationship is enhanced – particularly in the character of Vivianz, the young knight who was brought up at Glorjet by Gyburg. Gyburg functions as a partner to Willehalm in his duty as uncle, sharing the responsibility of the education of her husband's nephews, and it is her influence that is most important.

> gein dem kom Vivianz
> Des marcgrâven swester suon:
> der kunde ouch werdekeit wol tuon.
> sus was bewart sîn clâriu jugent:
> dehein ort an sîner tugent
> was ninder mosec noch murc,
> wand in diu künegîn Gyburc
> von kinde zôch und im sô riet
> daz sîn herze nie geschiet
> von durhliuhtigem prîse.
> der junge und der wîse

---

34 Koss, 184.
35 Koss, 198–200.
36 Koss, 184–5.

sah gein im stolzlîche komn
von des tjoste wart vernomn
jâmer unde herzen nôt.
            (*Wh.* 22, 30 – 23, 13)

[Riding towards him came Vivianz, the son of the Margrave's sister. He knew how
to acquit himself with honour, too. His pure youth was preserved in such a way that
his virtue was not the least bit blotched or blighted, for Queen Giburc had brought
him up from childhood and had given him her counsel in such a way that his heart
never turned away from resplendent fame.][37]

Here it is emphasized that Gyburg, not Willehalm, has raised Vivianz,
probably because Wolfram's audience is unlikely to have been familiar with
Vivien's story in either *Aliscans, Enfances Vivien* or *Chevalerie Vivien*. In
Aliscans, Vivien thinks of Guiborc before dying, long enough to voice his
farewell. In *Willehalm*, Gyburg is mentioned alongside descriptions of
Vivianz's courage during the battle and his bond to her can even be seen
in his equipage: 'in het durh sippe minne / Gyburc diu küneginne / ouch
wol gezimieret' [Giburc the Queen, out of love for him as her kinsman,
had equipped him lavishly] (*Wh.* 24, 13–15).[38] She has furnished him with
a jewelled helmet and shield, and at his investiture she funded two suits of
clothing for each of his hundred companions as well as special woollens
and silks for Vivianz himself. These symbols of patronage and favour mark
a distinctive relationship between aunt and nephew, and that his thoughts
are of his aunt as he dies attests to the great influence Gyburg has over the
young Narbonnais knight, as well as to her merit as Christian liege-lady.
Upon finding him dying, Willehalm laments, recalling Vivianz's youth: how
caringly Gyburg brought him up in her arms and how she loved him more
than her own children.[39] Vivianz recalls Gyburg's generosity as he dies:

der küneginne Gyburc
ir helfe an mir was wol sô kurc,
die man erkennen mohte,

37   Gibbs and Johnson, 27.
38   Gibbs and Johnson, 27.
39   *Wh.* 62–3.

diu baz ir wirde tohte
denne mînem armen prîse:
ich weiz wol, ist got wîse,
er lônt es ir mit güete,
hât er sîn alt gemüete.
oeheim, nu getrûwe ich dir
durh sippe die du hâst ze mir,
du habst si durch mich deste baz.
nu wirt des willen nimmer laz.

(*Wh.* 66, 13–24)

[The help which Queen Giburc gave to me was plain for everyone to see, and it was more fitting to her nobility than to my own meagre attainment. I know for sure that, if God is wise, He will graciously reward her for it, if He is as He has always been. Uncle, I depend on you, for the sake of our kinship, to cherish her all the more for my sake: never tire of doing so.][40]

This passage is significant in that it calls attention to and reinforces Gyburg's image: her status as queen, *riche dame*, is emphasized and her generosity and compassion is praised; she can expect divine reward for her noble character, we are assured in the dying martyr's words. Vivianz owes his upbringing to his uncle, Willehalm, but he credits Gyburg with his nurturing and education in his chivalry, which is impeccable. After his death, Vivianz is mourned by the Narbonnais clan; his death, as well as the capture of his cousins, serves as a principal motivation for the Narbonnais to support their brother, Willehalm, at Orange and for Blancheflor to convince Loys to send imperial troops with them.

The sibling relationship between Gyburg and Rennewart is another significant familial tie in play, despite the two not realizing that they are brother and sister in *Willehalm* and only realizing much later on in the story in *Aliscans*. In both texts, there is an implied recognition before Rainouart reveals his family history to Guiborc (and their connection is revealed) and this affinity permeates their relationship, leading up to the second battle.[41]

---

40   Gibbs and Johnson, 46–7.
41   See Chapter 4, section: 'Rennewart.'

Guiborc fu sage de la loi sarrazine.
'Renoart frere, dist ele, or adevine
S'onques eüs fresre, suer ne cosine.'
Dist Renoart: 'Oïl, vers la marine,
Je ei un roi et une suer roïne,
Onc n'ot si sage jusqu'as porz de Tabrine,
et s'est plus bele que fee ne serine.'
(*Alisc.* LXXXIX, 4630–6)

[Gyburg knows well the Saracen manner. 'Rainouart, brother,' she says, 'Do you remember if you ever had a brother, sister or cousin?' Rainouart says, 'Yes, beyond the seas, I had a brother, a king, and a sister, a queen; as far as the gates of Tabrine, no lady is as wise as she, and she is more beautiful than a fairy or a siren.']⁴²

Gyburg consoles Rennewart in his old place of respite, the kitchen; she shares her cloak with him and gives him arms and armour. She even shows her respect and admiration for this Saracen giant before an uneasy assembly of reinforcements at the banquet in Glorjet. In *Aliscans*, it is Rainouart's sister, Guiborc, who persuades him to accept Guillaume's apology for not having been included in the victory celebrations. Guiborc also secures Rainouart's future spouse, Princess Aélis, as Guillaume's ally and Rainouart becomes the hero of the *Geste Rainouart*, in which he is defender of the southern marches that Guillaume gives to him as a fief upon his baptism and marriage to Aélis. In a scene resembling that in Montlaon where Aélis achieves reconciliation by kneeling to plead before her uncle to forgive Blancheflor, Guiborc kneels before Rainouart, pleading with him to forgive Guillaume in return for the arms and armour she gave him before

---

42   Wolfram, true to form, allows Rennewart to embellish the description of his sister somewhat: 'man gap etswâ ze swester mir / ob aller clârheit lobes kranz, ein maget, diu nam der sunne ir glanz, sô man si bêde des morgens sach / und diu sunne durh die wolken brach' [I had a sister at one time who surpassed all others in beauty, a maiden who took away the radiance of the sun when people saw them both together in the morning, when the sun was breaking through the clouds] (*Wh*. 292, 10–14). Gibbs and Johnson, 148–9.

the battle; it is then, when he pledges his service to her, that he reveals the name of Desramé as his father.[43]

In both texts, the decisive imperial support that is needed rests in part on the influence via marriage that Gyburg and also Blancheflor exercise. In marriages that threaten to divide rather than to unite, Blancheflor and Gyburg realize and use the status that is theirs to exercise significant influence over political events. The underlying sense of a perfect union is expressed by Wolfram in his depiction of the marriage between Willehalm and Gyburg. Closer family bonds between Gyburg and her nephew and brother succeed in influencing the wider action as well as reinforcing the underlying themes of love and clan solidarity in the face of a common enemy. That kinship is an important feature in these texts is already evident, but the significant undertones of solidarity, redemption, restitution, service and salvation that are exemplified in the character of Gyburg form an integral part of *Willehalm*.

Dress and appearance

The description of characters, their clothes, skin and appearance, important and symbolically expressive in romance, is one means by which their influences on other characters are effected. In *Aliscans* and *Willehalm*, Guiborc / Gyburg motivates action and loyalty through her appearance. She is also aware of and orchestrates the appearances of those characters with whom she associates, to motivate them and influence events. By the time of the composition of *Willehalm*, the symbolic and even metaphoric significance of physical appearance in these texts was well-established and even the symbolic nature of skin and various elements of clothing and armour finds its way into Wolfram's retelling of *Aliscans*.

---

43 *Alisc.* CLXXVI–CLXXVII.

Covering the skin

We shall first consider Gyburg's influence with regard to Willehalm's appearance, which is demonstrated already in *Prise*, when Guiborc gives Guillaume armour and weapons so that he may conquer Orange.[44] Wolfram's own words emphasize the role that clothing and appearance play in inspiration and motivation, when Gyburg tells her ladies to dress beautifully, arranging their hair and faces to inspire good cheer and loyalty in the arriving reinforcements.[45]

The importance of the appearance of the human body in courtly relations is emphasized in E. Jane Burns's work on clothing in romance, when she affirms the connection of clothing and appearance with personal character identity, writing that 'scholars have most often understood the ostentatious display of luxury dress in courtly literature as a means of self-identification for members of the ruling elite.'[46] Burns continues, describing 'literary representations of courtly attire as a visible show of wealth and a public record status' and the conferring and exchange of

---

44   *Prise*, XXX. Guiborc gives Guillaume a shirt of mail, shield, sword and helmet to defeat her stepson and husband and to conquer Orange. It is also worth mentioning that clothing proves one of Wolfram's characteristically indulgent subjects. The remark by Wolfram about Chrétien de Troyes's dressing Willehalm in old dimity at Montlaon is treated by Volfing in terms of Wolfram's narrative ability when she comments, 'The particular formulation in line 125, 20–21 [...] suggests that, on one level, we are dealing with dressing or clothing as a metaphor for writing: the *Willehalm* narrator is not just picking up on a point of fact regarding the hero's apparel, but is asserting his own superior skill in terms of "dressing" the characters, and even "dressing" the tale.' Volfing, 49–50.

45   *Wh.* 247.

46   Burns, E. Jane, *Courtly Love Undressed*, ed. Ruth Mazzo Karras, The Middle Ages Series (Philadelphia: University of Pennsylvania Press, 2002), 2. Miklautsch studies and establishes the importance of clothing and bodily appearance in *Willehalm*; see: Miklautsch, Lydia, 'Glänzende Rüstung – rostige Haut, Körper- und Kleiderkontraste in den Dichtungen Wolframs von Eschenbach' in Gerhard Jaritz, ed., *Kontraste im Alltag des Mittelalters: internationaler Kongress, Krems an der Donau, 29. September bis 2. Oktober 1998* (Vienna: Verlag der Österreichischen Akademie der Wissenschaften, 2000), 61–74.

clothing between characters as a 'subtle means of redefining political and personal identity [...] and as an incipient attempt to enforce social order between status groups,' suggesting a dialogue as it is represented in clothing and appearance, and that the female character can thereby demonstrate her desire and will publicly.[47] These observations certainly hold some legitimacy when seen in an historical context, too, as Jesús D. Rodríguez-Velasco points out in his description of the function of chivalric display. Rodríguez-Velasco shows how the military and political function of the tournament in Castile, the rules of which are outlined in the *Book of the Order of the Sash*, was secondary to the display and that tournaments were mainly a cultural device to demonstrate the relationships of groups or individuals with power. Similarly, he refers to passages in the *Gran Crónica de Alfonso XI* and in the *Cantar de mio Cid* that demonstrate the function of knights' accoutrements as symbols of vassalage and royal power seen at a tournament or at court when contrasted to their appearance in a more practical military use.[48]

The demonstration and display of power is done with subtlety in *Willehalm* and in *Aliscans* when Willehalm's appearance on his way to Montlaon is dictated by his vow to remember Gyburg's peril: he declines the bath and fresh clothes offered by his brother Arnalt in Orleans[49] and refuses the same from the merchant Wimar the night before his confrontation at court.[50] He prefers the dirty and battle-weary armour he took from Arofel to the proper clothing at court, this acting both as a reminder to rescue Gyburg and Orange, and also to exhibit this duty to the assembled nobles and his liege-lord, the king.

> sîn wâpenroc, sîn kursît,
> an den beiden kôs man strît:
> die wârn verhowen, etswâ verhurt.
> sîn swert daz umb in was gegurt,

47 Burns, 2; also see 7–10.
48 See Rodríguez-Velasco.
49 *Wh.* 121.
50 *Wh.* 137–8.

dem wasz gehilze guldîn:
sîn harnasch gap nâh roste schîn.
(*Wh*. 140, 13–18)

[On both his surcoat and his fur cloak you could see evidence of fighting, for they had been slashed, in places pierced. His sword, girded round him, had a golden hilt. His armour looked rusty.][51]

He chooses to keep his appearance in Montlaon as it was when he parted from Gyburg, to remind himself not to forget the peril that surrounded Orange. It was out of loyalty, too, that Willehalm pledged not to kiss anyone until his return to Gyburg. This affects the way he is seen and received by others. Not only is his armour out-of-place at court, it is dirty as well, provoking a cool reception from the assembled nobles at Montlaon, and his refusal to approach his relatives is seen as an affront.[52] Philipowski reasons this to be a show of actuality, contrasting the urgent situation in Orange with the fantasy-world of the court.[53] This view is consistent with the importance to the genre of physical appearance and demonstrates the silent dialogue that, by his outlandish appearance, Willehalm initiates with the royal couple and the nobles coming to Montlaon. His final decision to confront the royal couple in his armour instead of courtly dress, made the morning after the night spent at Wimar's, is possibly due to his strategy of asking for support from the imperial crown. He has been refused a welcome and shelter by the nobility, princes and the royal couple, and he must now demand aid rather than be offered it. The ultimate result is that, after negotiations, he receives garments from the queen in a show of proper and reciprocal service and loyalty.[54]

An element largely absent in *Aliscans* but employed by Wolfram in *Willehalm* is the description of the feminine appearance in clothing and

---

51   Gibbs and Johnson, 79.
52   *Wh.* 127–8. This is paralleled with *Alisc.* LXI–LXII.
53   Philipowski, Silke, 'Geste und Inszenierung: Wahrheit und Lesbarkeit von Körpern im höfischen Epos', *Beiträge zur Geschichte der deutschen Sprache und Literatur (PBB)* 122 (2000), 455–77, 472.
54   *Wh.* 174–5.

body, illustrating inner integrity and inspiring loyalty and service from the warriors with whom the ladies interact. The shining example in these texts is Loys's daughter, Alyze. Alyze's appearance has a profound effect on the conflict taking place at court; this is credited to her beauty, which Wolfram underscores with descriptions of her clothing and body. Her hair is decorated with jewels; her belt is from London, long and narrow, and clasped with a ruby.[55] Wolfram sums up her clothing in the words: 'noch baz denne ichs gedenke / lât si getubieret sîn' [think of her as being better dressed than I can imagine] (*Wh*. 155, 2–3).[56] Her shape is perceptible too and inspires admiration and reassurance:

> ir brust ze nider noch ze hôch.
> der werlde vîentschaft si vlôch.
> ir lîp was wunsch des gernden
> und ein trôst des vreuden wernden.
> swem ir munt ein grüezen bôt,
> der brâhte saelde unz an den tôt.
> (*Wh*. 155, 7 – 155, 12)

[Her breast was neither too low nor too high. The whole world loved her. Her body was all that one could desire and a guarantor of that which brings joy. Anyone who received a greeting from her lips had happiness all his life long.][57]

Here Wolfram's expression of beauty goes beyond the illustration of a feminine commodity and his ideal of service to love and of an almost spiritual inspiration is embodied in beauty as it appears in the finely dressed Alyze.

---

55   The significance of Wolfram's details of description here is to emphasize the value of the princess and particular symbolism can be attached to the ruby, a stone featuring often in medieval literature. It is especially interesting, paralleling Alyze's ruby belt clasp, to note the significance of the ruby in Chaucer's *Troilus and Criseyde*, a stone that 'in addition to giving honor among men, [...] is said by the lapidaries to make any beholder who loves God forget his adversity by the virtue God has given this stone.' Bass, Eben, 'The Jewels of Troilus', *College English* 23/2 (1961), 145–7, 147. Floripas's magic belt that was used to protect the Twelve Paladins is also called to mind.

56   Gibbs and Johnson, 85.

57   Gibbs and Johnson, 85–6.

Having set this precedent in the princess's appearance, Wolfram shows Gyburg to surpass it, symbolizing her spiritual integrity and power of influence. The description of Gyburg's dress as she appears at the banquet in Glorjet outshines any woman the princes have yet seen, doing credit to her reputation. Her clothing is described as exotic and costly, and her belt, a favourite of romance texts because of its symbolic significance,[58] is emphasized more than once:

> ir aller kleider wâren guot,
> die ze sehen heten muot
> de künegîn, des wirtes wîp.
> ouch funden si ir süezen lîp
> gein in claerlîch aldâ.
> von pfell von Alamansurâ
> si beidiu roc und mandel truoc,
> spaehe und tiure alsô genuoc,
> het in Secundille Feirefîz
> gegebn, niht kosteclîcher vlîz
> möht an den bilden sîn gelegn.
> [...]
> ir gürtl man hôher koste jach,
> edel steine drûf verwieret,
> daz er noch bêdiu zieret
> ir hüffel unde ir sîten.
>   (*Wh.* 248, 21 – 249, 1; 249, 8–11)

[All those came in fine clothing who had in mind to see the Queen. And they found her in her sweet beauty, standing there resplendently before them. Both the gown and the cloak that she wore were of silk from Alamansura, so skilfully worked and costly that no more expensive effort could have been put into embroidering it, if Sekundille had given it to Feirefiz [...] They declared that her belt was extremely expensive, adorned with jewels, so that it flattered both her hips and her sides.][59]

---

58   The belt of a lady often symbolised her chastity or integrity, as in *Nibelungenlied*, *Parzival*, *Le Conte du Graal* and the *Prose Launcelot*. Similarly, a man's belt could symbolise his personal honour and dignity, as in *Le Moniage Guillaume*.
59   Gibbs and Johnson, 128–9.

Wolfram delights in the description of Willehalm's Saracen queen, including the intimation of her own exotic allure in the mention of those who dress well to be in her presence and their curiosity in seeing her is emphasized with a reference to the author's own *Parzival*.[60] They are her succour, the reinforcements who will save Orange and quash the Saracen threat upon her soil, and she displays her charm skilfully, donning beautiful clothing and revealing just enough of her shape to inspire admiration and loyal service:

> der mantl muos offener snüere pflegn.
> Si truoc geschickede unt gelâz,
> ich waen deis iemen kunde baz
> erdenken ân die gotes kunst.
> [...]
> ze etlîchen zîten
> des mantels si ein teil ûf swanc:
> swes ouge denne drunder dranc,
> der sah den blic von pardîs.
>   (*Wh.* 249, 2–5, 12–15)

[The cloak hung open with laces untied. She was beautifully formed and proportioned. I don't think anyone without God's artistry could have designed her better [...] Now and then she opened her cloak a little, and if any eye peeked in under there, it had a view of Paradise itself.][61]

This is a passage that, beautifully written by Wolfram, bears striking resemblance to the appearance of Gyburg as Orable, when Guillaume first sees and falls in love with her in *La Prise d'Orange*, adding to the enigma of Wolfram's familiarity with this *chanson de geste*:

60 Volfing examines the references to *Parzival* in *Willehalm*, giving special attention to the continued allusions to Sekundille when describing Gyburg's actions. She finds that in such descriptions of 'the opulence of [Gyburg's] dress is to be read against the background of Giburc's new life of physical hardship and mental anguish. It is precisely this backdrop which distinguishes Giburc from Secundille, whose loving largesse nevertheless lacked this particular dimension of sacrifice and commitment.' Volfing, 57.

61 Gibbs and Johnson, 128–9.

La sist Orable, la dame o le cler vis;
Ele est vestue d'un peliçon hermin
Et par desoz, d'un bliaut de samit,
Estroit a laz par le cors qui bien sist.
Voit la Guillelmes, tot le cors li fremist.
'Dex, dist Guillelmes, ceanz est paradis!'
                              (*Prise* XXII, 683–8)

[There sits Orable, fair of face, wearing an ermine fur pelisse, and underneath a samite
tunic tightened with laces that suited her shape. When Guillaume sees her, his whole
body trembles. 'God,' says Guillaume, 'herein is Paradise!']

If indeed Wolfram knew about the content of or had heard performed
the romance epic *Prise d'Orange*, the popular character of Orable / Guiborc
certainly intrigued him, and her clothing and beautiful shape are given their
due in *Willehalm*. It becomes clear, however, that Gyburg's appearance is
deliberate, increasing her influence on the arriving warriors and inspiring
them to fight for Orange.

Exposing the skin

Another aspect of appearance is the exposure and covering of skin that
female characters might or might not control is the exposure and covering of skin, which, though of sufficient symbolic and erotic significance
to the audience of Wolfram's *Willehalm*, is also discernible as having some
significance in *Aliscans*. Exposed flesh in romances can be seen to be the
quintessential sign of femininity – white flesh is something that is often
identified as feminine, or signifies low social status,[62] or purity. If this metaphoric treatment of skin exposure is indeed established in romance, then
the inclusion of it can certainly be seen in the exposure of Aérofle's thigh.[63]
Just as white flesh is feminine, the visible flesh of a warrior invites wounding and marks a knight's formal defeat.[64] When Aérofle's leg is exposed to

62   Burns, 136, 140.
63   See Chapter 4, section 'Arofel.'
64   Burns, 136.

Guillaume's blade in *Aliscans*, it is expressed by the somewhat ambiguous 'toute la cuisse del cors li dessevra' [severed his entire thigh [covering] from the body][65] in which *cuisse*, or *coisse* could mean either 'thigh' or the chain mail that covers the leg and which Wolfram's version in *Willehalm* expresses as an exposed thigh by a broken cuisse that has slid down the leg. Whether *Willehalm*'s author embellished the scene here or whether he saw a deeper significance in the battle, his description is more detailed: Wolfram adds the adjective *blanke*: 'des wart sin blankez bein verlorn.' [thus his exposed thigh was lost] (*Wh.* 79, 2).[66] This equally ambiguous word, *blanke*, is translated into modern German as 'nackt',[67] bare or naked, and into English as 'white',[68] the latter being possibly an interpretation of Wolfram's *blank* as a cognate of the French *blanc* and furthering the case for a symbolic function, as indeed it is the final exposure of this flesh that signifies Arofel's defeat, inviting the decisive blow from Willehalm's *Schoieuse*, his sword, Joyeuse, given him by Charlemagne.[69] This exposure of skin in battle as well as the description of the skin of the dying Vivianz both serve as examples for later descriptions of Gyburg's skin and the symbolic function of its covering and exposure.

The symbolic significance of exposure of skin in *Willehalm* seems to take its cue from instances of notable skin exposure in *Aliscans*. White, soft skin can be representative of youth and beauty, and symbolizes purity, as in the description of Vivien's hands during the first battle and of Aélis's skin at Montlaon. The symbolic significance of exposed skin is again apparent in the scene in which Aélis falls in love with Rainouart as he washes the dung from his club in the stream, removing his clothes and kissing his *tinel*.[70] Wolfram extends this significance to Gyburg and Willehalm as well as to

---

65 *Alisc.* XXXVIII, 1595.
66 My translation; Gibbs and Johnson translate this as 'unprotected' (52).
67 Wolfram von Eschenbach, *Willehalm*. 51.
68 Gibbs and Johnson, 52.
69 The question must remain as to whether this feminises the Saracen, for it does not seem to signify a lower social status of this character for Wolfram.
70 *Alisc.* LXXIX, 4049–65.

Vivianz, Alyze and Rennewart to symbolize purity and nobility, and also to illustrate contrast and conflict.[71]

Gyburg's hands are described as white and her skin soft as she removes Willehalm's armour after the first battle.[72] Later, Willehalm's skin is exposed and rusty from his armour in Montlaon, as is Gyburg's skin when she removes her armour upon Willehalm's return to Orange.

> dô wârens ungelîche lieht.
> der marcrâve engerte nieht
> daz sîn bart vel oder hâr
> iht waere wan nâch îser var
> [...]
> Gyburc was noch harnaschvar:
> er nams durch liebe kleine war
>   (*Wh.* 175, 9–12; 243, 29–30)

[Then his beauty was very different from hers, for the Margrave desired that his beard, his skin and his hair should all retain the colour of his armour.[73]
[...]
Giburc was still dirty from her armour, but in his love he didn't notice at all.][74]

Where in *Aliscans* the exposure of skin serves a symbolic purpose, in *Willehalm* it also, like clothing, inspires loyalty and service, and motivates action.

Gesture and staging

Just as clothing, skin and appearance serve as motivation to service in romance texts, the descriptions of them in *Willehalm* are employed to the same end: to motivate and inspire loyalty and to gain support to save

---

71   See Chapter 4, section 'Rennewart.'
72   *Wh.* 99–100.
73   Willehalm refuses to wash at Montlaon, fulfilling his vow to remember Gyburg's plight and stands in stark contrast to the assembled court and nobility.
74   Gibbs and Johnson, 95, 126.

Orange. Moreover, the revealing, exposing and dressing of the person remains predominantly the privilege of the female. The discourse between characters via clothing and appearance is not inconsistent with the medieval world view in which, as Reinhardt writes, 'all natural and human life is symbolical and analogical: it points beyond itself to its eternal source and cause [...] everything receives significance in view of the momentous decisions that precede and determine the end.'[75] He describes the significance of symbolism in medieval life and explains that 'this symbolical character of reality adds weight and meaning to the seemingly most indifferent things, words, thoughts, and deeds [...] this explains the important part that gestures, attitudes [and] formal social etiquette [...] play.'[76] The expression of emotion was part of the expression of the medieval mind as well as of the state and status of the individual in an age when that individual was seen as existing only as a part of a collective whole. Wolfram's works reflect this attitude and the clothes and bodily appearance of *Willehalm*'s characters and the expression of emotion, inspiration and motive through gesture and staging lies largely, if not exclusively, in the woman's domain.

Though expression in gesture and staging is apparent in *Aliscans*,[77] it appears as a more refined literary element in *Willehalm* and is employed by Wolfram through the calculated show of emotion, bodily gestures and the element of staging or through the presentation of these expressions in a calculated manner, place and time. The show of emotion is a public expression of power and negotiation of authority in *Willehalm*, exercised according to a recognized code of symbolic behaviour understood as communication in the hierarchical social structure and, in this instance, expressly for the purpose of the defence and preservation of Orange. Willehalm displays tears, anger and sadness at Montlaon in addition to words to accomplish

---

75   Reinhardt, 76.
76   Reinhardt, 76.
77   Starkey observes that communication in the *chansons de geste* remains primarily verbal, in contrast to the later *Willehalm* (335). However, there are a number of gestures that embellish expressions of emotion in *Aliscans*, such as touching, twisting and raising one's moustache, as well as weeping and bowing of one's head.

his negotiations with Loys[78] and Gyburg employs the same calculated and public display of emotion to accomplish the tasks at hand. Her tears are not merely *symbolic* of sadness; they are the means by which sadness expresses itself.[79] Gyburg and Alyze shed well-timed tears when delivering an address, which complements their words and also expresses sadness; a recognized provocation, an assertion of power and a charge to be obeyed.[80] Gyburg's tears at Glorjet and her account of what has occurred during the siege earn her and her ladies commendation for their efforts, as well as respect from the clan and admiration and adoration from the princes. These tears are an important motivating feature.[81]

If the body of a literary character defines its appearance through the display of emotion, it also acquires appearance and identity by means of gestures.[82] Whilst the primary function of gesture is to refer to something, it can also articulate a state of being.[83] The gestures implemented by Gyburg and Willehalm communicate their state of being or their position or status relative to other characters, which they might wish to accentuate and impose in order to influence a situation. That gesture and appearance are calculated to be in public view is understandably important. Gyburg directs her gestures when in front of the French nobles and reinforcements at Orange, revealing belt and shift effectively, and sheds tears to express her emotion at the end of her speech at the war council. It is the execution in public view that shows these gestures as more than symbolic and a means

---

78 Starkey.
79 See Philipowski, 463. That tears are the means of expression of sadness, rather than just a symbol of it, is apparent in *Aliscans* in the same way it is in *Willehalm*: for example, 'L'eve del cuer li est as elz montee, Aval la face li est chaude colee' [his heart forced up [inside] and hot tears were on his face] (*Alisc.* L 2198–9); 'ir herze durh diu ougen ructe / vil wazzers an diu wangen' [her heart flowed through her eyes with many tears on her cheeks] (*Wh.* 311, 4–5). Both passages describe tears as flowing from the intense sadness of the heart up to the eyes and face where the misery is visibly seen.
80 *Wh.* 157, 2–3; 310, 30.
81 *Wh.* 264.
82 See Philipowski, 463.
83 Philipowski, 477.

of expression; they are also a means by which characters, especially those in *Willehalm*, influence the action of the story and negotiate, exerting power over their circumstances.

The task in *Willehalm*, as in *Aliscans*, is to secure support for Orange, thereby avenging fallen Narbonnais kinsmen and saving it from the Saracen threat, an action that ultimately rescues Christian chivalry in the story. The realm in which Gyburg serves is that of inspiring, motivating and influencing the action, and the vehicle is that which is seen: clothing, skin, gesture and display of feudal authority. This power to influence and inspire is achieved adeptly by means of calculated appearance, by the covering and uncovering of the body, by displays of emotion, and by the staging and timing of these 'implements'. Gyburg's influence also resides in her clan and familial ties and the duty to which those ties bind her as well as those who are her kinsmen. It is evident that she exerts a significant power over the action in *Aliscans* and in *Willehalm*, purposefully serving to motivate specific actions as well as to illustrate the importance of themes such as loyalty and kinship.

The Queen and Her Knight

Arabeln Willalm erwarp,
dar umbe unschuldic volc erstarp.
diu minne im leiste und ê gehiez,
Gyburc si sich toufen liez.
Waz hers des mit tôde engalt!
    (*Wh.* 7, 27 – 8, 1)

[Willehalm won the love of Arabel, and because of this innocent people died. She who gave him her love and pledged herself to him in marriage was baptized and took the name Giburc. What a host of men paid for that with their lives!][84]

---

84 Gibbs and Johnson, 21.

Without a doubt, Gyburg, the link between the Saracen and Christian ruling families, Willehalm's loyal wife, a convert, a woman, and the motivation for both sides going to war, is the most pivotal figure in *Willehalm*. She is a figure popular already in *Aliscans*, with a distinctive identity and an established tradition upon which Wolfram built. Guiborc's character represents the sovereignty of Orange, Guillaume's past and heroic conquest, and she is an exceptional partner of the hero in battle and in peace in *Aliscans*. In *Willehalm*, Gyburg exemplifies the ideal of the converted Saracen Queen and Willehalm's liege-lady and symbolizes also the hope of reconciliation and salvation through loyalty, service and Christian love in her relationship to him.

Gyburg's impact with respect to her relationship with Willehalm is illuminated by first examining her character's background and history with Willehalm and the significance of her sovereignty over Orange. Taking into consideration the nature of the love-service that binds the couple and how it functions in the story shows us how Wolfram intended his audience to view her. Gyburg's motive is to preserve her city and we will see how she capably and calculatingly exercises her influence as Willehalm's wife in two arenas: the public sphere and her private domain,[85] with particular focus on two major innovations to the source by Wolfram: firstly, that Gyburg herself is made the objective in the Saracen attack; secondly, her address at the war council. Gyburg also serves as an example of Christian spiritual fortitude as she honours her vow of baptism, remaining loyal to her Narbonnais clan and husband. This intricate relationship seems to have special significance to Wolfram, as will be seen when we discuss how Gyburg's direction of chivalry and service corresponds to the ideals illustrated in *Parzival*, in particular Wolfram's Grail. It is through the investigation of this relationship between Gyburg and Willehalm, its history

---

85   Christopher Young alludes to public and private spheres of control in terms of
      Gyburg's influence upon events in the arena of sexual politics (266–7). This divi-
      sion of the spheres in which Gyburg's influences are discussed here is not meant to
      correspond to the confining categories of the political and the domestic with regard
      to female literary characters in recent scholarship, a view that Sarah Kay critiques in
      her study. See Kay, *The Chansons de geste in the Age of Romance*, esp. 31–2.

and function, and its focal significance in *Willehalm*, that the meaning of conversion in epic romance begins to emerge.

The treasure of Orange

The background story of Gyburg and Willehalm seems to derive its material from the story in *La Prise d'Orange*, even though Wolfram has left us scant evidence that he was familiar with this *chanson de geste*. The case can be made that the thematic background of Wolfram's portrayal of the couple takes its direction from the material in *Prise*. This story presents the character of Orable, who, through her marriage to Guillaume, becomes more than a Saracen queen, but also Guiborc, Marquise of Orange, committed in her loyalty to Guillaume and to Christianity. The story of how her heart was won by Guillaume, who with her help conquered the city with its opulent palace, Gloriette, is related in *Willehalm* and provides a strong image of a female protagonist upon whose abilities to influence characters and plot so much rests. This background sustains the significance of Gyburg to Willehalm and to Orange. It is not merely the land that holds value for Willehalm; it is Gyburg herself. She is the greatest treasure of his past conquest of Orange and its palace, and he is determined to protect and preserve her.[86]

There are four major themes surrounding Guiborc in *Prise* that feature prominently in Wolfram's *Willehalm*: the indivisibility of love and war; the identification of Guiborc with her city; the ongoing purpose of Guillaume's and Guiborc's adultery; and the legitimization of conquest and betrayal. In many ways, *Aliscans* is a continuation of the actions and roles in *Prise* and Wolfram shows this continuation in the presence of this thematic material in *Willehalm*. We have seen how Wolfram's love and

---

86 Wolfram alludes to this background story: 'ir habt ouch ê wol vernomen/ (es endarf iu nu niht maere komen)' [You have surely heard before – you do not need to hear that tale again.] (*Wh.* 7, 23–4). Gibbs and Johnson, 20–1. Gyburg also relates parts of this story at different times in *Willehalm*, once when conversing with Terramer (*Wh.* 220, 14–29) and again when talking with Rennewart (*Wh.* 293–4).

chivalry comprise both joy and sorrow (in *Willehalm* the sorrow is from battle losses) in order to be complete, but also to assure proper direction of chivalry and service. Similarly, *Prise* opens at the beginning of spring, 'the same spring thaw that inspires the lover's passion also signals the season of military campaigns,' showing love's desire and conquest to be congruent activities.[87] That Gyburg remains in Orange as its queen throughout these stories underpins how she and her city are inseparable; that she is identified with Orange in conquest has precedence in *Prise d'Orange*.[88] Gyburg's importance to Willehalm is almost eclipsed by her importance to the fabric of the plot in terms of the legitimacy of Willehalm's sovereignty over Orange, the survival of the feudal social structure and the confirmation of Frankish Christianity in the conquest of the southern march. In *Prise*, Orable's adultery with Guillaume is seen as an ideological victory, because it leads to her conversion and because it re-establishes the feudal dignity that Guillaume risked in attempting to conquer Orange. Also, as Kinoshita points out, Guillaume's adultery, unlike that of Tristan or Lancelot, 'does not violate his faith to his feudal lord but preserves it, by winning him the fief that helps compensate for his sovereign's neglect.'[89]

Guillaume's commitment to Orable begins in *Prise*, marked by the scene in which Orable supplies Guillaume with armaments and armour, and his commitment to her protection facilitates the social stability needed for the endurance of France. This element is reflected in Willehalm's loyal

---

87   Kinoshita, 267.
88   Orable is metonymically identified with her city, Orange, and after Guillaume's conquest her Christian name, Guiborc, identifies her as part of the Narbonnais clan along with Guillaume and his nephews who were with him, Guïelin and Guibert (Kinoshita, 270, 282–3). Philip Bennett also points out that the city belongs to Guiborc in *Prise*: Bennett, 'The Storming of the Other World', 2. The identification of the body, especially the feminine body, with a castle in conquest, siege and defence was a common concept in medieval literature; see Sinclair, Finn, 'Defending the Castle: Didactic Literature and the Containment of Female Sexuality', *Reading Medieval Studies* 22 (1996), 5–19, 3; and Cowling, David, *Building the Text: Architecture as Metaphor in Late Medieval and Early Modern France* (Oxford: Clarendon Press, 1998), 27, 39–40.
89   Kinoshita, 278; see also 266, 281.

service to Gyburg in *Willehalm*, when it is for her that he struggles to keep his march, for without Gyburg as its queen, Orange ceases to be a sovereign province for him and his influence over the crown of France will be diminished. A military victory in *Prise* would be incomplete without the winning of Orable, the achievement of her conversion to Christianity and her marriage to Guillaume, a triumph that legitimizes Guillaume's sovereignty over Orange along with the title over the city that is openly recognized as hers, for only then can it be passed to her new husband.[90] This is a title and sovereignty that Willehalm strives to defend and recognizes, perhaps even more so than does Guillaume in *Aliscans*, that it will only continue to be legitimate with the preservation of Gyburg and his loyal service to her. Gyburg upholds these values for the sake of both her husband and her city, and her motivation to keep Willehalm in her loyal service features prominently throughout *Willehalm*, recalling those commitments of *Prise*. Willehalm's power and legitimacy as a feudal lord rests with Gyburg, her city and their continuing survival.

The image of Guiborc in *Aliscans* is consistent with that of the exotic Saracen queen symbolized in *Prise*, but it is what she does with her Narbonnais status, as well as her importance to Guillaume, that makes her one of the most enduring and popular female figures in the *chansons de geste*. The fascination with the opulence of the East seems well-established in the courtly genre. It is juxtaposed with the threat to Christian lands both on the European continent and in the Levant, and is demonstrated in the representation of Eastern luxury in French courts; this is seen in Orable, her clothes and her palace, Gloriette.[91] Guillaume's conquest of Orange and Orable, and her conversion to Christianity out of love for him, can be described as a type of hybrid terrain between Saracen Orient and Christian Occident; so, too, can the character of Guiborc herself, who as we have

---

90   See Kinoshita, 284.

91   Burns discusses the impact of the luxury fabrics, which came from the Orient and had a great impact upon the courtly attire described in medieval French narrative. Burns, 197.

seen occupies the unique status of Queen of Orange and loyal Narbonnais liege-lady in *Aliscans*.

> 'Il n'a si bele en la crestïenté
> N'en paienie qu'en i sache trover:
> Bel a le cors, eschevi ey mollé,
> Et vairs les eulz comme faucon müé.
> Tant mar i fu la seue grant beauté,
> Quant Deu ne croit et la seue bonté!
> Uns gentils hom s'en peüst deporter;
> Bien i fust sauve sel vosist creanter.'
> Et dist Guillelmes: 'Foi que doi saint Omer,
> Amis, beau frere, bien la savez loër;
> Mes, par celui qui tot a a sauver,
> Ja ne quier mes lance n'escu porter
> Se ge nen ai la dame et la cité.'
>   (*Prise* IX, 254–66)

['There is none so beautiful to be found in all Christendom, nor among pagans. Her body is beautiful, slender and soft, and her eyes the colours of a moulted falcon [in the full splendour of its plumage], but of what use is her great beauty and goodness when she does not believe in God! A noble man could enjoy himself with her. She could be saved if she were willing to believe.' And Guillaume says, 'By my faith in St Omer, friend, brother, you know how to praise her. But by our Saviour I will not carry lance or shield again if I do not win both the lady and the city.']

Here Guibert, a baron who has escaped from Saracen captivity in Orange, tells Guillaume about the city of Orange and the exotic and unattainable Saracen queen Orable, whose conversion to the Christian faith is the challenge that motivates Guillaume's attempt to conquer the city and the lady. Her riches, palace and city form only part of the motivation for Guillaume to win her over in *Prise*, however, and the significance of a Saracen conversion to Christianity out of love is an element upon which Wolfram also capitalizes in both *Parzival* and *Willehalm*.[92]

---

92   Kinoshita remarks on the endurance of the theme of love as a means of converting someone, showing its prominence in *Prise* and *Roland* (273). In *Parzival*, it is love that leads Feirefiz to conversion.

Besides the description of Guiborc's opulent palace and city, her character exhibits the archetypal attributes of the Saracen princess of many *chansons de geste*, which in Kay's opinion does not originate in the romance genre and is fairly standard: the princess 'always converts to Christianity, the attachment [...] always leads to marriage, and there is nearly always explicit conflict between her and other members of her community: her father (as in the *Prise de Cordres*), a rival suitor, or a husband who then has to be scripted out (as in *Les Saisnes*).'[93] If this stereotypical Saracen-princess image can be said to be well-established and widespread, then it is evidenced in the *romanceros* of post-thirteenth-century Spain, where, among many *chanson-de-geste* elements, poets exploited depictions of *la belle Sarrasine*, princesses that were 'in real life remote, and if [they were] Muslims they were, as Spaniards very well knew even if the French did not, rigorously protected and enclosed, so that in such cases to the element of ordinary sexual fantasy there is added a dimension of power being secured over what is unattainable and forbidden.'[94] The forbidden lady is one of the driving elements of courtly romances, a theme that was popular in literature long before the Middle Ages and remains so long after. Likewise, the conquering of the forbidden, in Orable's case the conversion to Christianity of the Saracen queen and her marriage to Guillaume, and the power that it implies for the man who accomplishes this task is an attractive and motivating element for the hero of *La Prise d'Orange*[95] and it follows that he will use every possible resource to protect his treasure in *Aliscans*.

In *Aliscans*, descriptions of Guiborc are somewhat less extravagant than in *Prise*, depicting her as a loyal spouse and a *riche dame*. Ferrante remarks on how the Guiborc of *Aliscans* complements Guillaume in partnership;

93   Kay, *The Chansons de geste in the Age of Romance*, 31.
94   Smith, Colin, 'On Spanish Ballads and French Epics' in Philip E. Bennett, Marianne Ailes and Karen Pratt, eds, *Reading Around the Epic: A Festschrift in Honour of Professor Wolfgang van Emden* (London: King's College London Centre for Late Antique & Medieval Studies, 1998), 297–311, 308.
95   Kinoshita points out the significance in *Prise* of the political, cultural, religious and physical obstacles to winning Orable and her city (270).

'conversion to Christianity follows naturally from her commitment to [him ... and] she encourages William when he loses heart. She forces him to live up to the highest standards.'[96] Their partnership is exemplified in that Guiborc always tailors her words to Guillaume's mood; in fact, it is she who suggests rebuilding Orange when Guillaume's weariness after the second battle threatens to consume him.[97] This is apparent also in the effect she has on Guillaume, as Ferrante observes: 'in the worst moment of the battle he worries about *her* distress.'[98] Characteristic of converted Saracens in the *chansons de geste*, she is a model for Christian faith and not only reminds Guillaume of salvation but symbolizes through her faith the promise of divine redemption. When Guillaume recounts to her the last words of Vivien, she responds with sovereign authority ('a loi d'empereriz'), telling him to remember his nobility and control, and 'Damedeu Jhesucrist / Reçoive s'ame en son saint paradis! Mout est granz dels que si tost est feniz' [May Jesus Christ receive his soul into His divine paradise. It is most sad that he is killed so young] (*Alisc.* LII, 2299; 2296–8) Her courage and devotion, along with her determination to defend her city, stand out against and prove part of the remedy for the challenges facing Christianity as a result of the first battle: 'faiblesse et divisions. Mauvaise volonté de son chef temporel et de ses barons; découragement insinué au coeur des champions qui lui restent' [weakness and division. Enmity for the temporal leader and his barons; discouragement insinuated in the hearts of those champions [warriors] who stay with him].[99] It is the integrated image of the Guiborc of *Aliscans* whose commitment and encouragement serve Guillaume in saving Orange and the image of the exotic Saracen princess of *Prise* that drives the formation of the character of Gyburg in *Willehalm*.

96 Ferrante, 43.
97 This occurs in the 'S' manuscript, the most extensive of *Aliscans*, CXCVII–CXCVIII. See: Wienbeck and Ferrante. The presence of this scene in the manuscript representative of the expanded French traditional *Aliscans* shows the importance that the Guiborc character had gained in the life of the *chanson de geste*.
98 Ferrante, 43.
99 De Combarieu du Grès, 62.

The background of Gyburg's character is also important to Wolfram and he calls attention to it several times throughout the text.[100] The dual disposition of Gyburg's character – her bond to both Saracen and Christian cultures and clans, her sovereignty over Orange and her commitment to Willehalm – seems to intrigue Wolfram and he expands upon the idea that out of love for Willehalm, Gyburg converted to the Christian faith and changed her name, relinquishing her security as a queen who was supported by her vast and influential Saracen clan.

> [...] Arabeln, diu sich Gyburc
> nande, und diu mit toufe kurc
> was manegen ougen worden
> durch kristenlîchen orden.
> diu edel küniginne,
> durch liebes friwendes minne
> und durch minne von der hoehsten hant
> was kristen leben an ir bekant.
> (*Wh.* 9, 13–20)

> [[...] Arabel, who named herself Giburc and who, for the sake of the Christian faith, had become the focal point for many eyes through baptism. The noble Queen assumed the Christian way of life, for love of her dear friend and for love of the Almighty.][101]

Now Gyburg, as well as her city, is the object of the Saracen threat and the journey towards salvation for her is fraught with difficulty and grief; in converting and joining the Christian Narbonnais clan, she has become the inadvertent cause of many deaths in battle.

> Arabele Gyburc, ein wîp
> zwir genant, minne und dîn lîp
> sich nu mit jâmer flihtet:
> du hâst zem schaden gepflihtet.
> dîn minne den touf versnîdet:

---

100 Notable passages in *Willehalm* that allude to events in *Prise d'Orange* are *Wh.* 192, 6–9; 220, 14–29; and 293–4.

101 Gibbs and Johnson, 21.

des toufes wer ouch niht mîdet,
sine snîd von den du bist erborn.
der wirt ouch drumbe vil verlorn,
ez enwend der in diu herze siht.
mîn herze dir ungünste giht.
War umbe?
[...]
unschuldic was diu künegin.
                   (*Wh.* 30, 21 – 31, 4)

[Arabel-Giburc, one woman with two names, love and you have become intertwined with sorrow. You have pledged yourself to misfortune. Your love strikes at baptism, but those who are fighting for Christianity do not refrain from striking at the race of your birth either. Many of them will perish too, unless He who sees into the hearts of men prevents it. My heart accuses you. But why? [...] The Queen was innocent.][102]

In much the same way as the love for Repanse led to the conversion of Feirefiz and thereby his vision of the Grail in *Parzival*, the love between Gyburg and Willehalm is the motivation that illuminates the path towards salvation and divine communion, a path that is at best difficult, that entails as much sorrow as it does joy and is only for the faithful and devoted. Although Wolfram questions his own reaction to Gyburg's perhaps ill-considered decision to convert and marry Willehalm, he leaves no question as to her worthiness and value to both Willehalm and the story; she is spoken of by characters as well as the narrator throughout the first battle in terms of her inspiration to chivalry (even before she makes an appearance) and thereafter in tones of respect and admiration. Both Vivianz and Rennewart are more than perfunctorily devoted to her, as are Tybalt and Terramer who, despite their duty to avenge their losses, mourn their loss of her to Willehalm almost as much as they do the city and land. Willehalm is no less devoted to her and her ability to turn his sorrow into joy not only implies an impressive character in Gyburg, it is a mark of the impact she has upon the entire story.

102   Gibbs and Johnson, 30.

The audience of *Aliscans* can see the partnership of Guiborc and Guillaume as complementary and creditable in adversity, and the audience of *Willehalm* is shown what is essential in the difficulty of battle and siege, loss and sorrow, in the union of the Saracen queen and the knight who would become a saint. Hence Gyburg as a character is as important as the city and palace in terms of the motivation for the battles, for calling together kinsmen in their defence and for keeping alive the hope of salvation. Because of her status and background, Gyburg is of great significance to Willehalm in what she represents for him in material conquest, in temporal power and in spiritual fortitude. In *Willehalm*, Gyburg is the motivation for the defence of the city and the city is her motivation for acting in its defence; in that sense, Gyburg and her city are indivisible, just as they are in *Prise*. Equally important in her background story is the motivation by which she was won: the allure of Eastern opulence and exoticism, and the challenge to convert her to Christianity by winning her love. Finally, her character in *Willehalm* owes some of its development and formation to the tradition of the Saracen princess in the *chansons de geste* and the challenge of conquering the forbidden that drove Guillaume to her. Therefore, it is a well-developed character with an established tradition in the *chansons de geste* that is further portrayed by Wolfram as the real treasure of Orange.

Commitment and reward[103]

In both texts the relationship is clear that the relationship between Guillaume / Willehalm and Guiborc / Gyburg is above that of a conqueror and his prize. It is an intimate partnership in which loyalty and dedication proves the stronghold through the battles, the siege, the fallen kinsmen and the difficulties of weak leadership and despair. It is a relationship that endures, standing out as an example of Christian love and loyalty, of vows honoured and of dedication, consolation, restitution and salvation. It is a partnership of two complementary figures, each power-

---

103 Parts of this section are included within Hathaway, 'Women at Montlaon.'

ful in his and her own way: Willehalm is an accomplished knight who gained fame and vassalage in exploits in his youth; Gyburg remains the Queen of Orange and its famous palace, Gloriette, as well as a respected and admired Narbonnaise liege-lady, inspiring service and loyalty from all. Wiesmann-Wiedemann describes the relationship between Gyburg and Willehalm: 'Il y a entre eux une entente absolue. L'un ne vaut rien sans l'autre.'[104] [There is a perfect understanding between them. The one is nothing without the other.] Nothing could be more apt, for we have seen Gyburg's importance to Willehalm's power, wealth, spirituality and motivation. Gyburg gives courage to Willehalm when he despairs in both texts; she is his comfort and solace, and she influences his best chivalric qualities. In return, Willehalm has the means to provide protection for her city as well as to ensure her integration into the Christian fold through love, baptism and the title of Narbonnaise marquise. Without him, she would be less powerful in Orange; she would be subject to the will of her Saracen father and husband; and she would not receive the protection from the Roman crown she has gained through conversion to Christianity. This partnership retains its commanding presence through separation and reunion, Gyburg and Willehalm remaining unified in such a way that neither is ever without the other in thought, action and motive; they are both devoted and act in accordance to the requirements of love-service.

Separation

> [...] nu wirt vernomn
> alêrst wiez umbe triwe vert.
> bon âventiure in het ernert,
> und ouch Gyburge saelekeit.
> beide er bleip unde reit:
> in selben hin truoc Volatîn,
> Gyburc behielt daz herze sîn.
> ouch fuor ir herze ûf allen wegen
> mit im [...]
> (*Wh.* 109, 2–9)

---

104   Wiesmann-Wiedemann, 150.

[Now you will hear what loyalty is really like. Good fortune had protected [Willehalm], and the Grace of Giburc, too. He both stayed and rode away: Volatin bore his body away, but Giburc kept his heart there. Furthermore, her heart went with him on all the roads he travelled.][105]

When Willehalm and Gyburg are apart, their thoughts are for each other. This is the case even at the very beginning of narrative, during the first battle, when Willehalm suffers devastating losses on the field of Alischantz and Gyburg waits in Orange, the gates locked to any who seek entry. In *Aliscans*, Guillaume's defeat is great and he believes all is lost; he accepts the probability of death, but resolves to die fighting, lamenting the loss of their love in death.

> 'Dex, dist Guillelmes, dame sainte Marie,
> Or voi ge bienmout est corte ma vie.
> Dame Guiborc, douce suer, bele amie,
> La nostre amor sera hui departie,
> A torjorz mes nostre joie fenie.
> Mes, ainz que muire, voil fere une envaïe
> Que ja jugleres, s'il en chante, ne die
> Que je ai fete traïson ne boidie.'
> (*Alisc.* XVI, 497–504)

['God,' says Guillaume, 'Holy Lady Mary, I can see well that my life is short. Lady Guiborc, gentle wife, my fair beloved, our love will meet its end today, our joy will end forever. But before I die, I will launch an attack such that no jongleur, if he sings of it, will ever be able to say that I was treacherous or disloyal.']

Guillaume later asks for divine intervention that he might see Guiborc once again: '[...] s'aïde cest vassal / Qu'ancor revoie Guiborc au cuer leal' [help your vassal / so that he may again see Guiborc, the faithful of heart] (*Alisc.* XVIII, 617–18), demonstrating the priority Guiborc has, at a most desperate time in the battle. Wolfram expands upon this incident, elucidating the situation in Willehalm's reflection on the Saracen forces, as well as describing his strong love for Gyburg even in the face of his losses:

---

105   Gibbs and Johnson, 66.

'ey Gyburc, süeze âmîe,
wie tiwer ich dich vergolten hân!
soltez Tybalt hân getân
âne Terramêres kraft,
unser minneclîch geselleschaft
möhte noch wol lenger wern.
nu wil ich niht wan tôdes gern:
unde ist daz mîn ander tôt,
daz ich dich lâze in sölher nôt.'
er klagt daz minneclîche wîp
noch mêre dan sîn selbes lîp
und dan die flust sîns künnes.
(*Wh.* 39, 12–23)

['Ah, Giburc, sweet love, how dearly have I paid for you! If Tibalt had come without Terramer's forces, our loving union might now well last still longer. As it is, I want to seek nothing but death, and leaving you in such need will be a second death for me.' He lamented the loss of his lovely wife even more than the loss of his own life and the loss of his kinsmen.][106]

Wolfram's addition of Willehalm's reflection on the invading Saracen forces is significant here, as in it Willehalm realizes that it is not only Tybalt's forces but also those of Gyburg's father, Terramer, that have come to take back Orange and Gyburg. This is a combined force against which Willehalm's own is inferior and against which he has no hope of victory. That the Saracen forces have united against him is also significant in that the conflict has ceased to be a mere contest for conquest, but has now become a large-scale war between the Arab world and Christendom. Alone against this force, Willehalm has little chance of victory. Gyburg knows this too, and this will be reiterated in her reaction upon hearing this from Willehalm. Against such desperate odds, Willehalm reforms his knights for one last attack, calling upon the image of Gyburg for inspiration, demonstrating her powerful influence and honourable reputation:

106   Gibbs and Johnson, 34.

Gyburc diu küneginne,
diu mit helflîcher minne
uns dicke hât gerîchet,
swelch tugent sich ir gelîchet,
der waern gehêret drîzec lant.
dehein werlîchiu hant
ûf Oransche nu beleip.
(*Wh.* 52, 17–23)

[Giburc, the Queen, has often enriched us with her loving generosity. Virtue like hers would be sufficient to bring honour to thirty lands. Now there is not one hand left at Orange to defend her.][107]

When Willehalm tells Gyburg that he has lost the battle, they agree that Gyburg will stay in Orange and await Willehalm's return.[108] When they part, however, Gyburg insists that Willehalm remember her; he must not take any favours of French women, nor engage in their service, but return to save Gyburg and her city.[109] Rather than being merely a statement revealing jealousy, this entreaty is a profound expression of the importance of service and influence to Gyburg retaining her city as well as the love and service of Willehalm. Jones writes that 'it demonstrates that even where there is such a strong commitment, fears arising from awareness of human frailty are not entirely banished, and it enhances our sense of the act of faith that she makes here in urging Willehalm to leave Orange.'[110] Gyburg's faith in telling Willehalm to go is accentuated, true, but it is an act of faith from her because she, as well as Orange, is in jeopardy of falling into Saracen hands; her conversion and commitment to Christianity and to the Narbonnais clan will have been in vain. Not only is there the risk of losing Willehalm's love to another woman, but Gyburg's Christian faith will be tested. This speech seems to emphasize the importance of Willehalm to Gyburg in her determination to save Orange. There is no

---

107 Gibbs and Johnson, 39.
108 The decision for Willehalm to leave Gyburg in Orange to go to Montlaon to ask for reinforcements rests upon Gyburg and is discussed in detail below.
109 *Wh.* 104.
110 Jones, 'Giburc at Orange', 103.

question of their love, it binds Gyburg and Willehalm tightly throughout the narrative, and this plea comes directly after an intimate scene between the pair. Gyburg is more concerned about the service that love entails and that Willehalm's loyalty to her in service is not compromised by ladies at the French court seeking Willehalm's service for themselves. This is a reasonable concern, because Willehalm's past exploits imply that he might be given to capriciousness in conquest and service. The element of fancy is also perceptible in that Gyburg's conversion and hand in marriage were a challenge to Willehalm and now that he has accomplished both, his interest might be sparked elsewhere. This is underscored more explicitly in *Aliscans* when Guiborc tells Guillaume:

> 'Sire Guillelmes, dist Guiborc la senee,
> Vos irez en France la loee,
> Si me leras dolente et esgaree
> Entre tel gent dont point ne sui amee,
> Dendez Orenge enclose et enseree;
> Et vos irez en la terre asazee.
> Mainte pucele i verras coloree
> Et mainte dame par noblesse acesmee;
> Je sai tres bien tost m'avras oublïee;
> Lués i sera vostre amor atornee,
> Ariere doss serai mise et boutee;
> Mout tost avras ceste terre oublïee.'
>   (*Alisc.* LV, 2369–80)

[‘Lord Guillaume,’ says wise Guiborc, ‘You will go to renowned France and leave me sorrowful and troubled, among people who do not love me, enclosed and trapped in Orange; and you will go to an opulent country [where] you will see blushing maidens and luxuriously clad ladies. I know well you will soon have forgotten me, then your love will change; you will turn your back and reject me. You will very quickly forget this land.’]

This is less of a protest than it is a reminder of what she will be suffering and what trials await him when he is away from her. In *Willehalm*, Gyburg suggests that as an example to any who might prove cowards, Willehalm command those who will fight; she reminds him of the sacrifices she has made for him and finishes by promising him more of her love if he can save her:

> dennoch was ich in der schouwe,
> daz man mir clârheite jach,
> friunt und vîent, swer mich sach.
> du möhts mich noch wol lîden,
> und solt uns kumber mîden.
>
> (*Wh.* 104, 26–30)

[In those days I was considered beautiful, or so people said who saw me, friend and foe alike. You may still find me pleasing to you, if only we can get out of this trouble.][111]

In this last comment is the suggestion of a formal charge of service, a spoken contract for the relief and preservation of herself and Orange, between Gyburg and her knight in service. It is not, then, a fear of human frailty in infidelity alone that drives this plea; foremost in Gyburg's mind is the deliverance of her city and this is why she entreats Willehalm.

Willehalm knows that the softness of the French court will be more desirable to him, as well as to those from whom he seeks assistance, than the harshness of a lost battle and a beleaguered city, the relief of which would only come against great odds, and he makes a vow to Gyburg to assure both himself and her that he will not forget his duty to return to Gyburg and to save Orange. Willehalm gives his word of honour that his heart will ache until Gyburg is saved and goes even further by vowing to refuse all food other than bread and water.[112] Guillaume's vow in *Aliscans*, though, is much more descriptive and explains the details of Willehalm's restraint in *Willehalm*.[113] The audience can see his resolve throughout his

---

111 Gibbs and Johnson, 63.
112 *Wh.* 105.
113 *Alisc.* LV, 2390–405. Guillaume describes what clothes he will not remove, how he will not wash, that he will partake of neither meat nor pepper, nor wine nor spiced drink from any kind of goblet, nor kneaded bread; he will refrain from sleeping on mattresses under linen sheets and his lips will touch none other than Guiborc's until his return to Orange.

journey, at Orleans and at Montlaon, when he not only refuses food but also does not kiss anyone, including his family, and declines a comfortable bed. Thus Gyburg's image, plight and influence remain constantly with Willehalm and keep his mind on the dire task at hand. This visible commitment from Willehalm is also a reminder to those from whom he seeks aid, serving as an extension of Gyburg's influence upon the loyalty and service of those who have the power to save Orange:

> der wehsel rehte was gefrumt:
> ir herze hin ze friwenden kumt,
> sîn herze sol sich vînden wern,
> Gyburge vor untrôste nern.
>   (*Wh.* 109, 11–14)

[The exchange was accomplished properly, for her heart is heading towards friends, his heart shall fend off enemies and save Giburc from despair.][114]

Though she is absent from the court at Montlaon, Gyburg's presence is exercised in the appearance and actions of her spouse and knight, Willehalm. Her name is mentioned many times with reverence and admiration to inspire service and support from the Narbonnais clan and because Willehalm desires to remember his partner himself. Wolfram recounts how it is the inspiration of her love that keeps Willehalm faithful in his vow and gives him the courage to confront Loys: 'ir minne gebôt unde riet / daz sîn gelübde ân allen kranc/ gein ir stuont und âne wanc.' [her love counselled and commanded him to keep his oath to her intact and without fail] (*Wh.* 176, 28–30).[115] When Loys finally grants his support with imperial reinforcements for Orange, Gyburg's city is effectively saved and that these imperial troops are needed for this task, in addition to the Narbonnais forces, is confirmed by Wolfram's remark that 'der von Karle was erborn, der begienc dâ Karles tücke. daz was Gyburge gelücke' [he who had been born of Charles now behaved in the manner of Charles, and that

---

114   Gibbs and Johnson, 66.
115   Gibbs and Johnson, 96.

was Giburc's gain] (*Wh.* 184, 28–30).[116] Gyburg's entreaty to Willehalm has paid off in her absence: Willehalm shows his love and commitment to Gyburg outwardly in his appearance, which serves to remind him of his task as well as show the court the power of his commitment to Gyburg and her city; it also allows the audience to look towards their reunion.

Reunion

Although Willehalm thinks of Gyburg and their love first and foremost when Orange is in jeopardy and although Gyburg, whilst remaining his devoted and adoring wife, thinks mainly of the safety of her city, their commitment and love for one another is illustrated by Wolfram's embellishment of the two scenes in which Gyburg and Willehalm reunite after battle: the first after devastating losses; the second when he returns with reinforcements to relieve the beleaguered city and save its queen. Here, we continue to see how the image of Gyburg and of her relationship with Willehalm seem to take much of their precedent from that depicted in both *Prise* and *Aliscans* rather than from *Aliscans* alone. These scenes in *Willehalm* seem to elaborate upon the adoration of Willehalm for Gyburg, her significance and attraction to him and his duty to her in *Prise*, and their devotion and commitment to each other in *Aliscans*.

In both *Aliscans* and *Willehalm*, when Willehalm returns to Orange in retreat from the first battle, Gyburg refuses him entry into the city, displaying courage and fortitude, but also serving as an example of loyalty and chivalry, forcing Willehalm to live up to the same standards. Wearing Arofel's armour and riding the Saracen horse Volatin, Willehalm is not recognized by those inside the gates who take him for the enemy. When Guiborc is called to the gates in *Aliscans*, she does not believe that it is Guillaume. She tells him that she is alone, there are only other women and her child, and says that he doesn't sound like her husband, suggesting

---

116   Gibbs and Johnson, 99.

instead that he is a coward escaping from the enemy. Finally, she asks him to remove his visor, so that she can see him properly.[117]

> Dist a Guillelme: 'Or puis je bien prover
> Que tu n'iés mie dan Guillelmes le ber,
> La Fiere Brace qu'en soloit tant loër.
> Ja n'enlessasses paiens noz genz mener
> Ne a tel honte batre ne devorer;
> Ja nes sofrisses si pres de toi aller!'
> (*Alisc.* XLVIII, 2071–6)

[She says to Guillaume, 'Now I am sure that if you were the noble Guillaume Fierabras whose praises are sung everywhere, you would not let pagans take our people or beat them or mistreat them so badly. You would not suffer them to go so close to you!']

At first, she does not recognize him. Then, after he removes his visor, she is angered that he has come without his nephews, namely Bertrand and Vivien, who have been entrusted to their care.[118] It is clear that Guiborc recognizes Guillaume, but she forces him to prove his mettle and retain his respect and authority as lord of Orange, and she sends him out after a band of a hundred Saracens who have taken Christian prisoners.

In *Willehalm*, Wolfram follows the same course of events with some characteristically subtle modifications, such as elaborations to the dialogue and the sequence of events, revealing Gyburg's depth of character. Gyburg notices the Saracen armour and horse that Willehalm has when he is refused entry to Orange by the chaplain at the gate; taking Willehalm for a Saracen, she scolds him boldly for insulting the margrave's courage and boasts falsely that she has many knights inside the city to defend her:

> si sprach 'ir sît ein heidensch man.
> wen waent ir hie betriegen,
> daz ir sus kunnet liegen
> von dem marcrâven âne nôt?
> sîn manheit im ie gebôt

---

117   The scene at the gates is in *Alisc.* XLVI–XLVIII.
118   *Alisc.* XLVII–XLIX.

daz er bî den sînen streit
und flühtec nie von in gereit
durch deheiner slahte herte.
maneger iu daz werte,
iwer halden hie sus nâhen,
wan daz ez kan versmâhen
hie inne al mîner rîterschaft.'
dô was ir werlîchiu kraft
gedigen et an den kapelân:
dort inne was kein ander man.

(*Wh.* 89, 16–30)

['You are a heathen,' she said, 'Whom do you think you can fool here by telling these stupid lies about the margrave? His courage has always urged him to fight alongside his men and never flee from them on account of any trouble. Many a man would fight with you for venturing so close, if it were not for the fact that it is beneath the dignity of all my knights here.' Yet all the time her defence was reduced to the chaplain: there was no other man inside.][119]

Wolfram reveals a boldness in Gyburg's character to deceive any perceived attacker in the interest of the defence of herself and her city. She lies, telling of the many warriors inside who are above chasing away the knight at the gate. But her words about Willehalm's courage suggest that she does recognize Willehalm and also that she and her city would be dishonoured if the margrave were to flee into the city in defeat, leaving his comrades behind. Willehalm's appearance must strike fear into Gyburg, who knows her husband's mettle well enough, because she realizes that the battle is lost and that Orange is in real danger; hence the ruse of the defending knights.[120] Willehalm pleads with her, asking for the comfort of her love. Determined, Gyburg tells him that she is unaccustomed to seeing the margrave return alone, undoubtedly thinking of her nephews Vivianz and Berthram, and

---

119   Gibbs and Johnson, 57.
120   Though there is no description of Willehalm's own armour in *Willehalm*, audiences of *Aliscans* might have remembered that Guillaume's armour was given him by Guiborc in *Prise* and now lies on the battlefield, exchanged for Aérofle's by Guillaume himself, a symbolically significant act that might be interpreted by Guiborc as declining service to her under adverse circumstances.

tells him flatly that she will not suffer such unchivalrous behaviour: 'iwers haldens ich iu hie niht gan' [I shall not let you stay here any longer] (*Wh.* 90, 11).[121] She also says that stones will be thrown at him, a deed marking the scorn that she has for his behaviour. Before asking that Willehalm remove his helmet so that she can see whether it is him, as in *Aliscans*, Gyburg sends him out to rescue a group of Christian prisoners from some Saracen knights to prove his mettle. When he has accomplished this task, Wolfram says that now 'mit eren er do mohte komen vür die porten sin' [thus he could honourably come before his gates] (*Wh.* 91, 18–19).[122] When he has regained his honour in the eyes of the people of Orange, especially in the eyes of Gyburg, he can then reveal his identity by being asked to remove the helmet; this demonstrates the emphasis on the importance of honour and of protection of women and the weak in the chivalry of *Willehalm.*

Gyburg's reactions appear to be more than mere threats to a Saracen seeking entrance; if this had been the case, she could not have wasted time talking about courage and honour, and would have been more aggressive towards the intruder. Gyburg gives the impression that she recognizes her husband and she expresses her disapproval of the manner in which he returns to the city he is sworn to defend. This forces the margrave to modify the appearance of his chivalry, to keep up the appearance of the defence of Orange even though it is in imminent danger.[123]

The following scenes, when Willehalm and Gyburg are together, demonstrate their devotion to each other and also their mutual devotion to their nephews and kinsmen as they mourn them, taking comfort in each other. In *Aliscans*, intimacy takes the form of kisses and embraces, together with the words spoken before Guillaume's departure, when she worries that his loyalty might turn towards other ladies and when he vows to remember her plight by suffering himself until his return. In *Willehalm*, however, Gyburg's duty to comfort her husband goes beyond mere embraces and

---

121   Gibbs and Johnson, 57.
122   Gibbs and Johnson, 58.
123   However, Wolfram casts a shadow of doubt upon this suggestion by stating that, even after he had freed the prisoners, Gyburg was still afraid that he was a deceitful Saracen, perhaps as a pretext for her to then ask him to remove his helmet.

can be seen as a demonstration of the love to which Willehalm's service entitles him and which Gyburg delivers to Willehalm in fulfilment of her vow, as well as an expression of the intimacy of the couple:

> wan ob si wolden grîfen zuo
> ze bêder sîte ir frîheit,
> da engein si niht ze lange streit.
> wand er was ir und si was sîn:
> [...]
> si vielen sanfte ân allen haz
> von palmât ûf ein matraz.
> als senft was ouch diu künegîn,
> reht als ein jungez gänselîn
> an dem angriffe linde.
> mit Terramêres kinde
> wart lîhte ein schimpfen dâ bezalt,
> swie zornic er und Tybalt
> dort ûz ietweder waere.
> ich waen dô ninder swaere
> den marcrâven schuz noch slac.
>
> (*Wh.* 100, 4–19)

[If they both wished to do that which they were free to do, then she did not offer resistance long, for he was hers and she was his [...] Lovingly they dropped onto a soft, silk mattress, and the Queen herself was just as soft – like a young gosling, gentle to the touch. A tender battle was being waged inside there against the child of Terramer, no matter how angry Terramer himself, or Tibalt, might be outside. I can imagine that no shot nor blow caused Willehalm pain any longer!][124]

Whilst the Saracen forces are moving into siege positions around Orange, Willehalm and Gyburg take time for love, but Wolfram's words make clear that the significance of this is different to each of them. Willehalm requires the comfort of Gyburg's intimacy and is entitled to it as her knight; but even as he takes what is his and she offers little resistance, the 'battle' being waged is her concern for the immediacy of the threat to Orange and the time she must allow for giving solace to her husband in

124 Gibbs and Johnson, 61–2.

return for his service. Though Guillaume / Willehalm is the warrior, it is Guiborc / Gyburg who appears the more practical of the couple: she reminds him of the help he can expect from his family and liege-lord, King Loys in Montlaon; and she fulfils her duty to her husband as liege-lady whilst maintaining her focus on the defence of her city and how it is to be effected (including the importance of the margrave being seen entering the city as a strong and capable defender rather than fleeing and defeated). Gyburg's determination and commitment to the defence of her city is demonstrated in her parting words to Willehalm:

> ich belîb in disen pînen
> sô daz ich halde wol ze wer
> Oransch vor der heiden her
> unz an der Franzoysaere komn,
> oder daz ich hân den tôt genomn,
> ob noch groezer waere ir maht.
> (*Wh.* 103, 16–21)

[I shall remain behind in these dire straits and defend Orange against the heathen army, until the French arrive, or, if the heathen power should prove still greater, until I die.][125]

Love seems secondary to the Saracen queen, who sends Willehalm, who is in her service, on his way with a strong reminder to return with imperial support; she is ready to die rather than surrender her city or her faith. However, after his long absence during which Orange is besieged and Gyburg, threatened with death, employs every tactic at her disposal to hold out against the attackers, Willehalm returns to a grateful and devoted wife who gives him again that to which his service entitles him, but never recedes from her strong persistence in ridding Orange of the Saracen threat.

Again, he is refused entry to Orange, but this time it is not to serve honour so much as it is due to the constant threat under which the inhabitants of the city have been and their readiness to defend it at all costs. In *Aliscans*, Guillaume's appearance at the gates in Aérofle's armour and with

---

125   Gibbs and Johnson, 63.

Rainouart in tow strikes fear into those guarding the city; Guiborc hears his voice and demands that he remove his helmet so that she can identify him. He responds respectfully, doing just as she asks, and, his identity ascertained, he is let into the city where he embraces Guiborc and they share kisses and tears.[126] They ascend to the palace arm in arm, as equals, the lord and lady restoring safety to Orange.[127] When Willehalm and Rennewart cut fearsome figures at the gate of Orange in *Willehalm*, Gyburg is at the battlement with raised sword; clearly, only the defence of the city is on her mind and she addresses Willehalm in a Saracen language (*heidnisch*): 'hêrre, wer sît ir, daz ir sus nâhe haldet mir, unt daz âne vride tuot? ir habt alze hôhen muot: ir mugets wol schaden enphâhen' [sir, who are you, that you dare to stop so close to my palace and do so giving no assurance that you come in peace? You are too bold and can find a fight here as a result] (*Wh.* 228, 13–17).[128] When Willehalm asks after Gyburg, his voice is enough to establish his identity for Gyburg as well as for those at the gate.

Their reunion parallels that in *Aliscans*, with embraces and tears, even as they watch from a window recess as the reinforcements arrive, but after they have removed their armour, after Heimrich and the arriving troops have been greeted and fed, Wolfram includes another intimate and meaningful scene between lord and lady. This time Willehalm's service has been accomplished; he has returned as promised with reinforcements and the French imperial contingent to save Gyburg and Orange from the Saracen horde and Gyburg's unreserved love is his reward. Gyburg's beauty, love, devotion and of course her city are more than a reward for Willehalm, however; her love is his consolation and in this relationship Willehalm's service and love are Gyburg's salvation:

> des landes herre [...]
> kom wider ûf, der niht verbirt
> ern neme ouch die gesellekeit
> dâ von er liep unde leit

---

126 *Alisc.* LXXXI.
127 *Alisc.* LXXXII.
128 Gibbs and Johnson, 119.

ê dicke het enpfangen.
an ein bette wart gegangen,
dâ er und diu künginne
pflâgen sölher minne,
daz vergolten wart ze bêder sît
daz in ûf Alyschanz der strît
hete getân an mâgen:
sô geltic si lâgen.
                    (*Wh.* 279, 2–12)

[[Willehalm] came up again and did not fail to take advantage of that companionship from which previously he had often derived both joy and pain. He and the Queen went to a bed and made love so tenderly that for both of them there was recompense for what the battle had inflicted on them at Alischantz through the loss of their kinsmen, so mutual was their compensation as they lay there.][129]

Through mutual respect, love and devotion, both have gained in service, land and protection as well as in power and position. More than this, their love grants Willehalm hope and confidence, the very reward promised a knight in the service of a lady, and this love, a manifestation of divine mercy, is Gyburg's comfort. Wolfram emphasizes the value of Gyburg's love to Willehalm and of this love to both of them in their situation, underscoring the benefits of properly conducted and guided chivalry to both practicality and spirituality.

an sînem arm ein swankel rîs
Uz der süezen minne reblüete.
Gyburc mit kiuscher güete
sô nâhe an sîne brust sich want,
daz im nu gelten wart bekant:
allez daz er ie verlôs,
dâ für er si ze gelte kôs.
ir minne im sölhe helfe tuot,
daz des marcgrâven trûric muot
wart mit vreuden undersnitn.

129   Gibbs and Johnson, 142–3.

diu sorge im was sô verre entritn,
si möhte erreichen niht ein sper.
Gyburc was sîner freuden wer.
(*Wh.* 279, 30 – 280, 12)

[In his arm now a slender shoot was blossoming forth from sweet love. In her pure tenderness Giburc snuggled so close against his chest that he was recompensed: he claimed her as his compensation for everything that he had ever lost. Her love afforded him such aid that the Margrave's sadness was streaked with joy. Sorrow had ridden away from him so far that no spear could have reached it. Giburc was the guarantor of his joy.][130]

In these scenes of intimacy, which Wolfram adds to the *Aliscans* material, the spiritual, motivational and practical benefits of a partnership are illustrated in the fulfilment of the courtly paradigm. Wolfram cannot help but idealize love-serice by underscoring the value of loyalty and commitment from Gyburg, whose first concern is for her city but who proves an inspiration and motivation for the hero's actions, attesting to the proper application of chivalry and how it should be directed. Gyburg's direction of Willehalm's service in saving Orange from the Saracens is an act of devotion, reward and commitment through love and conversion that exemplifies the very fibre of Wolfram's code of chivalry; for in so doing, both benefit as one, presiding together over a Christian Orange.

In the public arena

Far from being relegated or limited to the domestic world that her gender might suggest, Gyburg is a mistress of influence in both her private as well as her public environment. As we have seen, her character's function in *Willehalm* is similar to that of Rennewart, which is to secure the Christian victory, thereby inspiring hope of reconciliation and harmony. Her influence over the action and other characters extends to her conversion to Christianity out of love for Willehalm. The means by which she can

---

130 Gibbs and Johnson, 143.

accomplish this goal is subtly different from that of her brother because of her status, her relation to Willehalm and the Narbonnais clan, and also because of her gender. Her relations and gender are not impediments; on the contrary, they are assets to her role. She is not excluded from her position in the Saracen hierarchy either, because her title of queen is retained throughout the narrative, and her loyalties to the Narbonnais clan as well as her personal values and integrity are clear when she boldly expresses her concerns during the war council.

Kinship and obligation

The penetrating theme of kinship and the obligations it implies in *Willehalm* has resulted in different suggestions regarding structures of tension within the story, such as the struggle for dominance between familial and Christian kinship,[131] or the dynamics of an undermined patriarchy.[132] Kay uses the idea of 'the poetics of the gift' or the way in which female characters use their position as articles of trade to their own advantage, to illustrate the battle for dominance of patriarchy in the *chansons de geste*, suggesting that the function of women as commodities was also a source for the disruption of male dominance.[133] In fact, all of these tensions within the circle of kinship and obligation interrelate, together exercising a dynamic influence upon the action in *Willehalm*, and Gyburg's familial ties are of central importance.

If we were to focus only upon the tension created when Gyburg must exercise obligation to her Christian kinship (gained through baptism) over the kinship binding her to the Saracen ruling house, the interplay of her peripheral relationships would be diminished. Although Gyburg is by birth the daughter of the most powerful Saracen king, she has also, because of her marriage to Tybalt, been made Queen of Todjerne, and thus occupies the position of ruling lady of a great Saracen power. Likewise,

---

131   See McFarland.
132   See Young.
133   See Kay, *Chansons de geste in the Age of Romance*, esp. 229; and Young, 251–2.

by her baptism, Gyburg is part of the Christian fold, inheritor of divine mercy and salvation. Through her marriage to Willehalm she is also now Narbonnaise nobility as well as Marquise of Orange. Thus Gyburg can exercise Christian duty over Saracen kinship and clan loyalty over obligation to her inherited Saracen kingdom.

The imbalance of clan obligation and loyalty is a source for tension, but it also allows Gyburg to employ leverage and exercise power over her environment and over the action of the protagonists in the story during the siege in Willehalm's absence. Kay writes that in the *chansons de geste*, there is a contradiction in the way Saracen princesses were regarded, as female persons or as sexual inferiors, and this would lie in the fact that these characters tend to 'assume control over their own persons rather than subordinating them to the control of their families, and thus cut across racial divisions which their relatives seek to enforce.'[134] This image can certainly be applied to the character of Gyburg in *Willehalm*, where she makes her own decisions rather than follow her father's commands and where her status as both subject of the Saracen attack and object of Tybalt's fealty to Terramer functions as narrative and social critique.[135] During a parley with Terramer, Gyburg's father, who holds Orange under siege, she makes her intentions clear as she defies his commands to return to the Saracen clan and take up her position as Queen of Todjerne. She declines her obligation to her Saracen blood ties and her inherited feudal dominions:

> Tybald ich Todjerne
> lâz, dâ du mich krôntes.
> dannoch du, vater, schôntes
> dîner triwe, dô daz selbe lant
> ze heimstiwer mir gap dîn hant.
> wilt du Tybalde volgen,
> du muost mir sîn erbolgen.
> nâch sîm erbeteile
> er füert dîn êre veile.
> (*Wh.* 221, 2–10)

---

134   Kay, *Chansons de geste in the Age of Romance*, 36.
135   See Young, 252–3; and Kay, *Chansons de geste in the Age of Romance*, 229.

[To Tibalt I leave Todjerne, where you crowned me Queen. At that time, father, you still preserved your loyalty when you yourself gave me that land as a dowry. If you are going to side with Tibalt, then you will have to be angry with me. He is selling out your honour for his inherited territorial rights.][136]

As Willehalm threatens Loys with the withdrawal of his fealty in Montlaon, Gyburg, on the wall of Termis, renounces her claim to the Saracen lands over which she is queen. The leverage of feudal vassalage is exercised and its importance is crucial to understanding the power which Gyburg now asserts. Without Gyburg and her inheritance, Terramer is without a powerful ally and without this inheritance of land and title, Tybalt is without influence, an army or a politically secure future. Gyburg reminds Terramer of Tybalt's claims to Frankish territory and that it is Terramer's military resources and allies that Tybalt seeks to use to win them for himself. Gyburg is thus exercising her power as a metaphoric commodity over Terramer, for she was given by him, along with land as a dowry, to Tybalt, circumstances that were related in *La Prise d'Orange*. Tybalt's motive, the protection of his marital inheritance (as it was in *Aliscans*), is evidenced by his reaction to Gyburg's suggestion:

> mahtu Todjern, mîn erbeteil,
> Tybalde und Ehmereize gebn,
> und lâz mich mit armuot lebn.
> [...]
> der künec Tybalt hin zer wide
> Arabelen dicke dreute.
>   (*Wh.* 221, 24–9)

[Go ahead and give Todjerne, my property by right, to Tibalt and Ehmereiz, and let me live in poverty. [...] King Tibalt repeatedly threatened Arabel with hanging.][137]

---

136   Gibbs and Johnson, 116.
137   Gibbs and Johnson, 116–17. Wolfram conveys Tybalt's motive at the beginning: 'er klagete êre unde wîp, dar zuo bürge unde lant' [He mourned his honour and his wife, his cities and his lands as well] (*Wh.* 8, 6–7). Gibbs and Johnson, 21.

Gyburg conveys the weight of her obligation to the Narbonnais clan, Orange and Willehalm, and to her father by renouncing her right to her inheritance, renouncing her status as the representation of fealty between Terramer and Tybalt,[138] and declaring that she will live in poverty, i.e., without the Saracen lands to which she holds title. Audiences know that in converting to Christianity, Gyburg is guaranteed a place in a desirable society and protection by Christian France, as well as an assurance in the afterlife; therefore, her position is preferable as liege-lady over a Christian Orange. She will defend Orange and fulfil her obligation as liege-lady of Willehalm's domains rather than capitulate to Terramer; she has chosen her obligation to her Narbonnais clan over the obligation resulting from her status as Queen of Todjerne.

It was not only Tybalt and Terramer who sought to have Gyburg returned to the Saracen clan. Ehmereiz, her son,[139] and Halzebier, her nephew,[140] both sought to bargain with her during the siege for her return to their family and to convince her that her Saracen kinship should take precedence over her ties to the Narbonnais clan. Where father and husband could not succeed with orders and obligation, the younger kinsmen in their positions of son and nephew seek to convince Gyburg by less threatening means. She has refused to honour her obligation to father and husband, remaining loyal to her baptismal vow as she would to a vow of fealty, and she must thereby decline to fulfil her familial obligation to her son and nephew by reminding her Saracen family of her commitment: 'zem marcrâven hân ich muot: niemen mac geleisten sölch guot daz mich von im gescheide' [I have committed myself to the Margrave, and no one can offer such wealth as to separate me from him] (*Wh.* 257, 27–9).[141]

Gyburg's decision not to yield to the demands and desires of her Saracen kinsmen is clearly influenced by her Christian spirituality; she has committed herself not only to Willehalm but also to Christianity and in doing so,

---

138   See Young, 252–3.
139   *Wh.* 256, 18 – 257, 10.
140   *Wh.* 258, 5–8.
141   Gibbs and Johnson, 132.

she must fulfil the obligation of fortitude, for what else could one expect of the wife of a future saint? When the reinforcements arrive, she demonstrates her loyalty to the Narbonnais clan by recounting the threats that she resisted and including the information she gathered from Halzebier: that the eight Christian princes taken prisoner during the first battle are still alive:

> die gevangen ich iu nenne.
> ez ist Gaudiers und Gaudin,
> Hûes und Gybalîn,
> Berhtram und Gêrhart,
> Hûnas 'von Sanctes; und Witschart.
> (*Wh.* 258, 22–6)

[Let me tell you [the prisoners'] names. They are Gaudiers and Gaudin, Huwes and Kibelin, Berthram and Gerart, Hunas of Saintes and Witschart.][142]

These princes, especially the Count Palatine, Berthram, son of Bernart of Brabant, are beloved kinsmen of the Narbonnais clan and news of their survival is instrumental in improving the morale of the relieving forces. In refusing the demands and bargains of her Saracen kinsmen, Gyburg has preserved her status as Christian liege-lady and thereby the preservation of her sovereignty over Orange, as well as displaying her concern for the Christian prisoners who are now part of her new family. Her decision is commended:

> Heimrîch und al die süne sîn
> dancten dô der künegîn
> daz si ir vater rât übergienc
> und von mâgen noh von sune enpfienc
> dehein ir sunder urbot:
> und si hete den hoehsten got
> und ir vil werden minne
> mit wîplîchem sinne
> an dem marcrâven gêret
> und ir saelekeit gemêret.
> (*Wh.* 260, 1–10)

---

142   Gibbs and Johnson, 132.

[Heimrich and all his sons thanked the Queen for having rejected her father's advice and for not having accepted the separate offers of her kinsmen or her son. They said that she had done honour to God Almighty and to the Margrave in her noble love as a proper woman should and had increased her claims to salvation.][143]

That Wolfram allows Gyburg to use the leverage she possesses via kinship ties and obligations that she can honour or renounce can be seen as necessary, not merely as a source for tension. Gyburg can exercise her choice in the influences she has because of her familial ties to both sides in the conflict; she must make decisions based upon the obligations that a liege-lady's kinship to both clans entails and upon the fortitude that her conversion to Christianity and marriage vow requires. As obligation and kinship were tied to feudal necessity, these decisions were in public view, demonstrating Gyburg's strength and determination despite her desperate situation during the siege of Orange, securing the way for a Christian victory.

Defender of Orange

Gyburc Oransch und ouch ir lebn
ir vater sô niht wolde gebn,
daz er si selben tôte
und drab die kristen nôte
den ungelouben mêren.
          (*Wh.* 109, 17–21)

[Giburc did not want to give up Orange and her life as well to her father, so that he might kill her himself and thereupon force the Christians to join the ranks of the unbelievers.][144]

Wolfram's detail of the siege of Orange is greater than that of *Aliscans* in the description of military strategy, fortification, siege engines, the place-

---

143 Gibbs and Johnson, 133.
144 Gibbs and Johnson, 66.

ment of attacking troops and their garrisons, and parley,[145] but perhaps his greatest contribution to the siege of Orange in *Willehalm* is the significance of Gyburg's character. Gyburg represents the strength in her city under attack in Willehalm's absence and her determination exemplifies courage as well as chivalric values. She is a woman whose ties to her Saracen family and whose husband's absence are a source of great strain, but whose commitment to the defence of Orange and whose devotion to Willehalm are demonstrated in the tactics she employs to hold the city.

Wolfram's innovation to Gyburg's character during the siege results in a significant change of perspective, underscoring the importance of Gyburg's character to the plot. In both *Aliscans* and *Willehalm*, Gyburg dons armour and defends the city alongside her ladies during the siege, but only in *Willehalm* is it related how Gyburg props corpses up on the battlements, putting helmets on their heads, to give the attackers the impression of a well-defended city.[146] Her account of the siege to Heimrich only underpins her role in holding out in beleaguered Orange, withstanding the threat of capture, and it emphasizes the strength and importance of her character to the Saracens and to the story.[147]

Wolfram also emphasizes the Saracen focus upon the capture of Gyburg rather than her husband, in addition to the dissent amongst the Saracens regarding their objective in attacking the city.[148] In *Aliscans*, Guiborc's

---

145   Martin Jones remarks that whilst Wolfram's narrative of the siege's progress is not continuous as is that of the battles, 'he supplies enough information about it to create a strong impression of this form of military engagement and to make it a feature of significance in the literary evaluation of the work' ('Giburc at Orange', 97). Jones attributes Wolfram's knowledge of sieges to his experience in Eisenach after the siege battle of Erfurt, 1203, and compares siege passages in *Parzival* (98). See also: Richey, 30–1; and Gibbs and Johnson, 229.

146   *Wh.* 111 and 230.

147   *Wh.* 250–63. Also see above section on *Kinship and Obligation*.

148   See *Wh.* 260, 23–5, and the above sections on Terramer and Ehmereiz. Also, Martin Jones writes of the innovations to the Saracen disposition as well as of two separate narrative strands concerning the siege, a 'Willehalm strand' and an 'Orange strand', which separate upon Willehalm's departure, and converge again upon his return ('Giburc at Orange', 99–100). See also Bumke, *Wolfram von Eschenbach*, 389–90.

strength and commanding presence are shown when she refuses to let Guillaume in through the gates after the first battle. Because the Saracens are pursuing Guillaume in *Aliscans*,[149] her act at the gate has no wider immediate consequence for her other than keeping Guillaume out, albeit thereby increasing the possibility of his capture. However, in *Willehalm* the Saracens have come to capture Gyburg and her ability to resist their attack will keep them from accomplishing this task. Consistent with her ruse with the corpses, Gyburg's tactic when confronting Willehalm before the gate of Orange is to boast to him that there are many knights inside to protect her when, in fact, there is no-one but her chaplain and her ladies.[150] Her ingenuity and determination, due to the threat which she is under from the Saracens, are again evident when Wolfram describes how she guarded the city under siege against penetration by means of a mutinous act:

> diu was mit slôze alsô behuot,
> ob iemen wolde wenken
> dort inne unt überdenken
> sîne triwe durch miete,
> swelch vîent daz geriete,
> dazz im vrumte niht ein hâr.
> Gyburc für den selben vâr
> der bürge slüzzel selbe truoc.
>
> (*Wh.* 229, 6–13)

[[The gate] was fastened so securely with locks that if someone inside should be tempted by an enemy to reconsider his loyalty for the sake of a bribe, it would not do him a bit of good. To guard against precisely such a danger, Giburc herself kept the keys to the fortress.][151]

The effect of the Saracen threat to Gyburg is underscored again when, upon Willehalm's return, she immediately relates the position of Terramer's

149 This intention is alluded to at the beginning of *Aliscans* (II–III), during Guillaume's combat with Aérofle (XXXIV–XL), and again as he makes his way toward Orange (XLI–XLVI).

150 *Wh.* 89.

151 Gibbs and Johnson, 120.

army and advises Willehalm how to dispose his forces in the interest of defence.[152] These precautions are the acts of a strong and astute margravine whose life is the focus of the attack and who takes her position in Willehalm's family, as well as her salvation as a Christian, seriously to ensure the protection of her city and her survival as its sovereign.[153]

Although there are subtle differences between *Aliscans* and *Willehalm* as to who makes the decision for Guillaume / Willehalm to go to Montlaon for reinforcements, there is sense of a determination in the character of Gyburg to safeguard Orange in Willehalm's absence. Though it has been emphasized in scholarship that it is ultimately Gyburg's decision for Willehalm to go away to Montlaon to ask for assistance,[154] significant elements of this decision have been neglected. The lines in which Gyburg tells Willehalm to go[155] occur only after the initial suggestion which is then followed by a love scene and Gyburg's private prayer and reflection. It is in fact Willehalm who suggests the trip to Montlaon and the prospect of assistance from his clan before the love and prayer scenes, after deliberating with Gyburg about their position. When Gyburg learns from Willehalm that her father, Terramer, has come with Tybalt, she then knows that Orange is under real threat and her determination to hold Orange is intensified.

> do ez Gyburc het alsus vernomn,
> daz ir vater selbe waere komn
> ûf Alischanz von über mer,
> si sprach 'al kristenlîchiu wer
> mag im niht widerrîten.'
> (*Wh.* 94, 5–9)

---

152   *Wh.* 233.
153   Here, again, it would be difficult for the student of Septimanian history not to question how much, if anything, Wolfram knew about the Visigothic queen Khaunagunda and her strength in holding a city besieged by Moors, much less Wolfram's reference to the castle Termis, which is located along the Spanish border with France and was the focus of Guilhem d'Aquitaine's actions on the river Orbieu.
154   See Bumke, *Wolfram von Eschenbach*, 286–7; and Jones, 'Giburc at Orange', 101–3.
155   *Wh.* 103, 9–21.

[When Giburc heard from what [Willehalm] had said that her father himself had come across the sea to Alischantz, she said: 'All the armies of Christendom cannot withstand him.']¹⁵⁶

She continues with an assessment of Terramer's power and his army's ability to besiege Orange and concludes that they must hold out inside Orange to the death. Willehalm has formulated from her words a plan, however, and it is he who first voices the suggestion:

> wer möht ouch haben den gewin,
> als ich von dir berâten bin
> an hôher minne teile,
> sîn lebn waer drumbe veile,
> und allez daz er ie gewan?
> guoten trôst ich vor mir hân,
> mahtu behalten dise stat:
> manec fürste, diechs noh nie gebat,
> durch mich rîtent in diz lant.
> mit swerten loes ich dîniu bant,
> swaz si dir mit gesezze tuont.
> mîner mâge triwe ist mir wol kuont.
> dar zuo der Roemisch künec ouch hât
> mîne swester, der mich nu niht lât.
>
> (*Wh.* 95, 11–24)

[Who might possess the advantage that I have, in that you have bestowed noble love upon me, and not risk his life, and everything he ever owned for it? I can see some real hope in prospect if you can defend this city. Many princes whom I have never yet asked to do so will ride into this country for my sake. I shall loose your bonds with swords, no matter how they may besiege you. I am well acquainted with the loyalty of my kinsmen, and, what is more, the Roman King is married to my sister and will not let me down now.]¹⁵⁷

Gyburg's love has encouraged Willehalm after his defeat and he can see that she is capable of defending Orange in his absence; this being so,

---

156 Gibbs and Johnson, 59.
157 Gibbs and Johnson 59.

he thinks of the obligation owed him by his liege-lord and kinsmen. He is confident that he can depend upon his kinsmen and king to lend him their assistance against the Saracen threat to Orange; the bulk of Saracen power must be answered by that of Christian Rome. It is then that he asks her if it will grieve her for him to leave her, for they now have separate yet complementary roles to play in the liberation of Orange and the defeat of the Saracens. Although the final decision for Willehalm to go remains Gyburg's, it is Willehalm who thinks of his kinsmen and first suggests going to Montlaon, a practical plan requiring devotion, commitment and fortitude from both in fulfilment of his vow of service to Gyburg. The couple are bound together in service and they continue to honour their vows.

It is significant that in *Aliscans* it is Guiborc who reminds Guillaume of the loyalty that he should expect from his kin and clan, and it is she who suggests that he go to Montlaon to ask for it. The *jongleur* devotes three *laisses* to Guiborc's suggestion of a trip to Montlaon, and to the mention of Guillaume's kinsmen who should be ready to come to his aid.[158] Because it is Guillaume who is the focus of the Saracen threat initially, not Guiborc as in *Willehalm*, the threat to Guiborc is not as immediate as that to the fortress of Orange, which perhaps facilitates her suggesting the trip as opposed to Guillaume, who leaves behind not only his wife but his fiefdom, his right to power gained in conquest.[159]

Despite this difference between *Aliscans* and *Willehalm*, neither Guiborc nor Gyburg appears a weak character; they are strong and capable defenders of the city in the absence of the hero. The element of encouragement and consolation of the discouraged hero remains consistent and is representative of the vow of service between them. Their strength, however, carries a subtly different emphasis. Guiborc's strength lies in her ability to

---

158   *Alisc.* LII–LIV. Wiesmann-Wiedemann writes that Guiborc's urging Guillaume to seek help from his family is due to her ability in human relations. (75)

159   This perspective changes during the course of Guillaume's absence in *Aliscans*, as is demonstrated when Guillaume returns from Montlaon and Guiborc thinks he is an enemy and that all is lost, lamenting the death that surely awaits her at the hands of the Saracens. (*Alisc.* LXXX, 4192–201). This follows the oath of Desramé, withdrawing with his army, that he will return to see her killed. (*Alisc.* LXXX, 4159–62)

remind Guillaume of salvation through God and his kinsmen's loyalty at a time of defeat and despair; she spurs him on to the duty that he must carry out, for his march now stands on the front line of conflict between the pagan world and Christendom. Gyburg's strength is an underlying quiet confidence in Willehalm's loyal service, in her faith in God, with whom she communicates through prayer, in fulfilment of her commitment to her vow of baptism, and in her determination before the enemy. In *Willehalm*, it is she, not her husband, who is the focus of the Saracen threat and her resilience is more crucial. It is this fortitude that sees her through the pressure from Terramer to submit under siege and that allows her to welcome and inspire the arriving Narbonnais clan at Glorjet before the second battle.

Addressing the nobles

Gyburg's role as defender of Orange continues after the siege itself; once Willehalm and the reinforcements arrive, her actions and words are all the more important and influential because it is their service that is essential for the success of Orange's defence. She has held out against the pressure of the besiegers and kept Glorjet from assault, earning respect and commendation from Willehalm's clan. When they arrive, Gyburg does not forget her duty as liege-lady, nor does she neglect her role in the Christian victory.

> Gyburc diu triwen rîche
> stuont dennoch werlîche,
> si unt ir juncfrouwen.
> der wirt wol mohte schouwen
> harnasch daz er an in vant.
> (*Wh.* 231, 19–23)

[Giburc, the ever-faithful woman, was standing there, with her maidens, still prepared to fight, and Willehalm could not fail to see the armour that they were wearing.][160]

---

160 Gibbs and Johnson, 121.

When Willehalm arrives at Glorjet, he finds Gyburg waiting loyally, albeit dirty from her armour and only slightly distressed from the strain of the siege; she is a leader who has fulfilled her duty in keeping the city that Willehalm won in conquest, just as she helped him to gain it in *Prise*. She removes her armour after leading Willehalm to his chamber, knowing that there would be no pressing battle because the Saracens have withdrawn to the harbour. The immediate threat having passed, she is already considering her role as Willehalm's liege-lady rather than as military defender and she makes the transition seamlessly to reward his service. In *Aliscans*, where there is no detailed account of the siege, Guiborc's strength of character lies in her support of Guillaume. In contrast to the strength she showed before Guillaume's departure in first suggesting the trip, there is no indication of her need to assume a commanding role when the Narbonnais clan arrives. It is Guillaume who naturally resumes charge of Orange, billeting his arriving troops and identifying them to Guiborc.[161] For Guiborc, the importance of her influence now lies in her personal relationship with Rainouart. In *Willehalm*, Gyburg's interest in Rennewart will come later, however, when he is presented to her in the hall, as Wolfram's intention seems to be to underscore her capability, motivation and importance to the arriving reinforcements and ultimately to the Christian victory.

Largesse

In *Aliscans*, unlike in *Willehalm*, a banquet occurs without any direct orders for its preparation, they being assumed. In *Willehalm*, Gyburg's role in the public eye is exercised in the event of the banquets and during the war council after mass the next day. Willehalm makes the suggestion that the arriving nobles be entertained in the palace, to which Gyburg replies as if she had expected it all along and was only waiting for a suggestion from the margrave:

> (mir ist liep daz es dîn munt gewuoc)
> von trinkn und spîse alsölhe kraft:
> al mînes vater rîterschaft,

op wirz in niht wolden wern,
sine möhtens wochen lanc verzern.'
(*Wh.* 234, 24–8)

[I am glad that you mentioned it. We have such quantities of food and drink that all my father's knights, if we did not want to stop them, could not consume it in weeks.][162]

She is not only ready and willing to entertain the Narbonnais, she has the means by which to do it, as if she had been anticipating the arrival of reinforcements. Had she really been saving provisions for an army during a devastating siege? Whether or no, she tells her husband that the warriors can axpect nothing less from her in her palace. Then Willehalm mentions further entertainment preparations:

die soltu schône enphâhen.
nu heiz des balde gâhen,
daz der palas an allen sîten
mit semften phlûmîten
sî beleit, und teppich vil derfür,
ûf diu phlûmît kultern von der kür
daz man ir tiure müeze jehen,
swer si hie ûf ruoche sehen,
von phelln die geben liehten schîn.
(*Wh.* 244, 9–17)

[[...] you should receive [the princes] graciously. Now see to it that soft pillows are quickly laid out all about in the great hall with rugs in front of them, and on the pillows quilted coverlets made of brilliant silks which people can see are expensive, if anyone chances to notice them.][163]

Willehalm is not taking over the duties of the lady of the palace nor is it to be assumed that Gyburg could not have implemented these tasks without his instruction; rather, it is to be perceived as an indication of

---

162 Gibbs and Johnson, 122.
163 Gibbs and Johnson, 126.

Willehalm's concern for the loyalty of his army and for the necessity to assert his sovereignty in Orange and thereby his strength of command.[164]

This seems also to be the concern of his father, Heimrich of Narbonne, who takes it upon himself to act as a sort of master of ceremonies at the banquet, making a point of adhering to propriety and etiquette from his first meeting Gyburg.[165] He foregoes formal greeting with her to present first each prince to her individually and Wolfram notes that 'er vuorte iegeslichen mit der hant' [he led each one by the hand] (*Wh.* 250, 24).[166] This, while proper, might also be seen as superfluous, but Heimrich does this for a reason, which he intimates to Gyburg upon sitting down next to her:

> [....]wan daz iu gebôt
> iwer triwe iu noch gebiutet
> daz iwer prîs bediutet.
> swes sich vriunt ze vriunden sol versehen,
> des mac mîn sun der markîs jehen,
> Unt sîne mâge über al.
> ir habt den tôtlîchen val
> unseres künnes wol vergolten.
> op wir nu niht gerne wolten
> dienn umb iwer hulde,
> diu unverkorne schulde
> solt immer unser sîn vor gote.
> wir sulen mit triwen iwerm gebote
> immer blîben, hab wir sinne.
>   (*Wh.* 251, 24 – 252, 7)

[But your loyalty directed you, and still does, to do that which demonstrates your renown. My son, the Marquis, and his kinsmen everywhere can say what a friend should expect from friends. You have made ample compensation for the deaths of our kinsmen. If we did not now gladly wish to serve for your favour, it would be an

---

164 E.J. Burns mentions how courtly social status was marked in romance by foreign opulence in Western courts (187). This would seem to indicate that a show of Willehalm's superior social status would be facilitated by the show of luxury in the banquet at Glorjet, the once-Saracen palace at Orange renowned for its magnificence in the *Cycle de Guillaume.*

165 *Wh.* 250, esp. 5–10; and 263–4.

166 Gibbs and Johnson, 129.

unforgivable sin on our part in the sight of God. We shall remain for ever faithfully in your service, if we have any sense at all.][167]

Heimrich's words commend Gyburg's loyalty; more than that, he is letting her know what he would like her to accomplish to ensure the loyalty and devotion of the knights who have come with the imperial army, speaking in the conditional construction that Wolfram seems to favour in such passages.[168] He then suggests to her in no uncertain terms that her role as liege-lady is to inspire loyalty from those friends from whom Willehalm should expect it; he reiterates the sentiment that men should want to seek her favour in service and that not to do so would be the act of fools and sinners. He also advises Gyburg to hide her tears and sorrow from the princes out of propriety,[169] adding a further explanation.

> der zage unt der quecke
> eteswenne bî ein ander sint.
> ich geloube wol daz mîniu kint
> dem ellen niht entwîchen.
> dar mag ich niht gelîchen.
> die man mir für genôze zelt,
> etslîch fürste ist niht erwelt
> ze der scharpfen rîterlîchen tât.
> wir sulen hôhmuotes rât
> den liuten künden unde sagn.
> guot trôst erküenet mangen zagn.
> (*Wh.* 268, 20–30)

---

167 Gibbs and Johnson, 130.

168 McFarland notes that this conditional clause construction in the lines of Gyburg's speech indicates significance and compares them to the prologue and epilogue lines in *Parzival*, 1, 1–2; 837, 1–4 and 25–30. See McFarland, 137. The use of the conditional in Heimrich's words, *Wh.* 252, 3f, are certainly congruent with descriptions of a significant passage. Michael Curschmann also notes the reason for Heimrich's words to Gyburg. (551)

169 *Wh.* 252, 20–4; 268, 7–9 and 17–19. The calculation of the show of emotion is evident when Wolfram adds as narrator: 'si wârn mit sorgen banden verstricket. merket wie dem sî: ir gebaerden was doch freude bî' [They were ensnared in the bonds of sorrow. Even so – take note of this – they acted as though they were happy] (*Wh.* 275, 10–12). Gibbs and Johnson, 141.

[The coward and the bold man are sometimes one and the same person. I am confident indeed that my sons will not lose their courage, but I cannot always say the same for those who are considered my equals. Some princes are just not made for fierce knightly combat. We should show the people high [chivalric] spirits and encourage them. Good encouragement has made many a coward bold.][170]

Heimrich's intentions are now evident: he will use every device at his disposal to encourage good morale from those who have come to relieve Orange. To this end, he does not underestimate the significance of Gyburg in her unique status as converted Saracen lady, for she is well-respected in the Narbonnais clan and is the symbol of Willehalm's authority and power, queen of Orange, who can inspire service.[171] Another element of this passage that should not be overlooked is Heimrich's concern for the loyalty of his *genozen*, his equals in rank, i.e., the princes in the service of the empire. This is significant, and the emphasis is not lost on Gyburg, for it will become evident in her address to the princes at the war council the next day.

War council

Gyburg's speech to the assembled army the following day has been much discussed, and its implications debated; this is because it is one of Wolfram's characteristic passages in which ambiguity seems prevalent and also because it has no parallel in *Aliscans*. Scholarship has focused on the most obvious and, incidentally, the most ambiguous element of her speech: that of religious metaphor and its meaning as expressed by Gyburg. Her appeal to the Christian army to show mercy to the heathens they will defeat is

170   Gibbs and Johnson, 137.
171   Michael Curschmann points out the necessity for Wolfram to emphasize King Louis as *rex inutilis* [the incompetent king] for the German audience, who would not as readily have recognized this theme, common to the *chansons de geste*, as would the French public and he emphasizes how the thus characteristic disloyalty in the Frenchmen is linked in *Willehalm* to the deeds and purpose of the character of Rennewart. (550–1)

charged with underlying meaning and interpretations, particularly her words regarding unbaptized heathens:

> wir wârn doch alle heidnisch ê.
> dem saeldehaften tuot vil wê,
> ob von dem vater sîniu kint
> hin zer flust benennet sint:
> (*Wh.* 307, 25–8)

[After all, we were all of us heathens once. It pains the person in a state of Grace if the Father has condemned his children to perdition.][172]

Themes of kinship, salvation and baptism all come into play within Gyburg's speech, if not in these short lines themselves.[173] Questions are

---

172 Gibbs and Johnson, 156.

173 Gibbs and Johnson have translated this passage reflecting the most widely accepted view of the meaning of *vater* and *kint* [father and child]: as God the Father and humanity as His children. As the Middle High German MSS do not employ capitalization and as the construction does not indicate any specific elucidation, these words in this passage could easily imply a father other than God, or even other than Christian. The subject for recent debate has been the question of whether Wolfram meant unbaptized heathens as God's children or children of a Christian or heathen father. The argument, spurred by Walter Johannes Schröder in a 1975 article, was taken up in 1989 by Carl Lofmark and enjoyed a lively presence over the next decade as scholars debated the plausibility of Wolfram's calling the heathens God's children and what implications such words might have. Fritz Peter Knapp and Joachim Heinzle formed the hub of the dispute, disagreeing upon who it was that Wolfram meant by *vater* and *kint*, God and humans or the Christian father and his unbaptized baby, around which swirled differing opinions. See: Schröder, Walter Johannes, 'Der Toleranzgedanke und der Begriff der "Gotteskindschaft" in Wolframs Willehalm' in G. Bellman, ed., *Festschrift für Karl Bischoff zum 70en Geburtstag* (Cologne: Böhlau, 1975), 400–15; Lofmark, Carl, 'Das Problem des Unglaubens in Willehalm' in Joachim Heinzle and Kurt Gärtner, eds, *Wolfram von Eschenbach: Festschrift für Werner Schröder* (Tübingen: Niemeyer, 1989), 399–413; Heinzle, Joachim, 'Die Heiden als Kinder Gottes, Notiz zum "Willehalm"', *ZfdA* 123 (1994), 301–8; Knapp, Fritz Peter, 'Die Heiden und ihr Vater in den Versen 307,27f, des Willehalm', *ZfdA* 122 (1993), 202–7; Heinzle, Joachim, 'Noch einmal: Die Heiden als Kinder Gottes in Wolframs "Willehalm"', *Zeitschrift für deutsche Philologie* 117 (1998),

raised as to what different interpretations might indicate about Wolfram's message and why he uses Gyburg's character to convey it. However, these issues must be considered as themes and not as the focus of the address, which is the duty Gyburg has to safeguard her city for Willehalm, fulfilling her vow to him in return for his service, and her oath in conversion to Christianity in preserving a Christian Orange. It is to this purpose that Gyburg's address is calculated and directed.

Among those scholars debating exactly what Wolfram intended with the words *vater* and *kint* [father and child] in the context of Gyburg's speech, Burghart Wachinger[174] and Joachim Bumke[175] concentrated their analysis on the religious elements and contributed to a diminishing of Gyburg's character in this scene, interpreting her words as those of a distressed and emotional woman. Rüdiger Schnell examines her speech in terms of a spiritual message that Wolfram is trying to convey to his audience, placing utmost importance upon her plea to show mercy to the Saracens and upon the placement of heathens and Christians in the same category.[176] Schnell makes a compelling investigation but misses the point entirely. In overlooking some significant elements of the text (namely Gyburg's

75–80; Knapp, Fritz Peter, 'Und Noch Einmal: Die Heiden als Kinder Gottes', *ZfdA* 129 (2000), 296–302; Steinmetz, Ralf-Henning, 'Die ungetauften Christenkinder in den 'Willehalm'-Versen 307, 26–30', *ZfdA* 124 (1995), 151–62; Przybilski, Martin, 'Giburgs Bitten: Politik und Verwandtschaft', *ZfdA* 133/1 (2004), 49–60.

174   Though Wachinger makes the valid point that for scholarship to concentrate so heavily on this speech lessens the understanding of the text, he also succeeds in reducing Gyburg to a less sharp-witted character than she actually is, commenting on her appeal for mercy that 'dieser Gedanke ist nicht als Programm geäußert, sondern als Nebengedanke in einer klagend fragenden Erwägung einer im Konflikt fast zerbrechenden Frau' [this thought is not expressed as a scheme, but as a secondary consideration in the lamenting, questioning reflection of a woman almost shattered by conflict]. Wachinger, 50.

175   Bumke concentrates his commentary on Gyburg's speech regarding the juxtaposition of Christianity and heathendom, of the saved and the damned, implying that through Gyburg's words come Wolfram's religious views (*Wolfram von Eschenbach*, 368–70).

176   See: Schnell, 'Die Christen und die "Anderen"', 193–8.

knowledge that the questionable loyalty of the imperial contingent poses an obstacle to victory, and the context of her speech), these conclusions reduce Gyburg's character from the astute and active individual she is and detract greatly from the real significance of her words. These key elements must be considered when analysing Gyburg's speech, but because of the ambiguity of the religious and spiritual metaphors in her address, they have gone overlooked, their significance unnoticed. These elements, and not the religious ambiguity, indicate a clear account of the importance of this speech in *Willehalm*: its placement as the last of the speeches during the war council; the content and orators of the speeches made *prior* to Gyburg's; the knowledge the characters and the audience have before the council occurs; the importance of the underlying themes of kinship and loyalty; and the goal towards which Willehalm and his family work – victory over the Saracens in Orange.

The obstacle to victory over the Saracens in Willehalm's march is the service of the troops sent by Loys. Willehalm has the unquestionable loyalty of his clan, but such loyalty is not assumed from the imperial troops, as can be seen by Willehalm's attention to his show of authority and by Heimrich's concern for their lack of courage in battle. Doubt about the reliability of the French troops comes down to two major factors, both well-known to Willehalm and his Narbonnais family: that the call to arms of these troops by Loys was not exactly an order, but a royal summons; and that their oath to him does not bind them to follow Willehalm unquestioningly.[177] Those troops attending out of duty as vassals, the Narbonnais princes and their armies, or those mercenaries purchased by the funds of Irmschart of Pavia and Queen Blancheflor,[178] are under direct orders and have thereby a specific structure of chain of command and clarity of duty.[179] The French imperial troops lack both direct orders and a clear chain of command. However, it

---

177 Bumke observes that their feelings of fear and thoughts of desertion at the first sight of the Saracen adversaries is proof that the promise of fiefs and money carries little enough weight with the French troops. See Bumke, *Ritterbegriff*, 43–4.

178 *Wh.* 161; 195–6; 199, 25–7. The loyalty of these mercenary troops is attested by Wolfram's words at the beginning of the second battle, *Wh.* 323, 1–11.

179 See Bumke, *Ritterbegriff*, 45.

is vitally important for Willehalm to have them present in force (as is indicated by his behaviour at Montlaon to secure Loys's support) not merely
because of their numbers, but also because the presence of the imperial
military contingent will be seen by the Saracens as the core of the military
power of the Christians, signalling and guaranteeing victory.[180]

It is important that Gyburg has been present in both instances in
which these concerns were expressed by Heimrich and Willehalm, and that
it is she to whom they were articulated. Far from cryptic suspicions, these
expressions of concern about the loyalty of the French princes are directed
towards Gyburg precisely because she has shown herself to be capable and
perspicacious, and with a confidence in her loyalty and ability to exert what
powers she possesses as liege-lady alongside the Narbonnais princes. She
already knows how important the imperial presence is and by articulating
to Gyburg the concerns for their reliability, the Narbonnais include her as
a visible instrument in the Christian victory.

The context of Gyburg's speech includes her recognition of these
challenges preceding the second battle, not least of which is her concern
for the presence of the imperial French contingent and her astuteness in
playing her part as a woman, as a Saracen and as liege-lady. The power held
by Gyburg's character derives from her unique status and Wolfram seems
to have been loyal to his source in her depiction. Of self-possessed Saracen
liege-ladies in the *chansons de geste*, Lynn Tarte Ramey writes:

> Leaving husbands and saving enemy troops are achievements that the Christian
> woman had little opportunity to accomplish in the *chansons de geste*. As a literary
> figure, the Saracen woman therefore had a freedom from societal expectations that

---

180 Bumke, *Ritterbegriff*, 43. See also: *Wh*. 434, 8–15: 'hôch mit hôher ahte/hât roemisch
krôn vor ûz den strît, daz ir niht ebenhiuze gît: sô scharpf ist roemisch krône ervorht.
swaz anderr krône sint geworht, die ûf getouften houbten sint, ir aller kraft gein dirre
ein wint/ist: sine mugens et niht getuon.' [The Roman crown ranks high in respect
so that it has nothing equal to it, so acute is the fear of the Roman crown. Whatever
other crowns are made and worn on Christian heads, all their power is nothing compared to that and they have no power at all] (Gibbs and Johnson, 211–12).

the Christian woman did not have. She could be a powerful woman in a text precisely because she was in reality already on the margins of society.[181]

Building on the remarkable strength of Guiborc in *Aliscans*, Wolfram allows his Saracen queen to address the assembled nobles as part of the war council, speaking daring words to parallel those of her husband at the court in Montlaon. Her actions are unquestioned and accepted because of her dual status as Saracen queen and Narbonnais liege-lady; she moves between two worlds, exercising her sovereignty in Orange and her Christian duty to her new clan. This status is recognized wholly by Willehalm and Heimrich as well as by Gyburg herself and she cleverly uses it to the advantage of Willehalm, his family and her city of Orange.

The speeches are made after mass in the council of war that precedes the second and decisive battle. The Narbonnais princes speak and behave as a cohesive clan unit, valuing clan loyalty highly since the reconciliatory scene at Montlaon where Heimrich, Irmschart and eventually Blancheflor rally their family behind Willehalm, achieving the support of his liege-lord and king, Loys. That the war council occurs *after* mass was sung further emphasizes the importance of clan and loyalty over the almost perfunctory Christian ceremony of which Wolfram makes only a passing mention.[182]

What is said by the five Narbonnais orators, given what they know about the shaky oath of the imperial troops and the need for their presence, and by Wolfram as narrator preceding Gyburg's address, is just as significant to the content of her speech.[183] Willehalm, the commander,

---

181 Ramey, 'Role Models?', 138.
182 *Wh.* 296, 19–25. Wolfram seems to enjoy narrating ceremonies, but almost pointedly leaves out the description of this mass.
183 Timothy McFarland emphasizes the idea of the context of Gyburg's speech with regard to the *kint* question, referring to Bertram's words and focusing upon the juxtaposition of the damned and the saved, the heathens and the Christians, which, while significant, overlooks the importance that Wolfram seems so determinedly to place upon clan loyalty and oaths of vassalage, as well as the strength and cleverness of Gyburg's character. He is right in asserting that scholars' emphasis on the Biblical conception of children of God in her speech is flawed, but his conclusion that 'one should see Giburc's words as representing her attempt to come to terms with her

speaks first, recalling the oath that the French nobles took at Montlaon and again at Orleans, before Loys, that they would serve under Willehalm to free Orange, calling them 'die des riches herre hat gesant' [Those whom the Lord of the Empire has sent here] (*Wh.* 297, 10).[184] His speech is rousing, making mention of the fallen princes and kinsmen, and the brutality of the occupying Saracens against Christian women and children; he then reminds the Frenchmen of their oaths to Loys and to the Empire several times, as well as of their obligation to him. The Crusade ideal of the juxtaposition of Christian and heathen features prominently when addressing these French nobles and is used as a motivating element replete with calls to defend the Empire from the infidel.[185] With all of the elements that excite lust for battle, Willehalm calls upon his army to help him avenge the deaths of his kinsmen and, as a final tribute to kinship and solidarity, he invites his father and brothers to speak.

The speeches that follow, given by Heimrich, Bernart *le fleuri*, Bertram of Berbester and Buov of Commercy, all reiterate the importance of fulfilling oaths and of remaining loyal to Willehalm who has earned great renown for the Empire; they call for the exacting of revenge for fallen kinsmen and contain the same motivational, encouraging words as did Willehalm's. The juxtaposition of Christian and heathen in these speeches attests to the strong draw of Crusade ideals in inspiring warriors (especially those fighting for the Holy Roman Empire) to battle, rather than reflecting a desire to engage in ecumenical dialectic or religious rumination.

Uncertain if inspirational tactics are enough to motivate loyalty in the imperial troops, Bernart, whose beloved son Berthram was taken prisoner in the first battle, goes so far as to challenge the Frenchmen:

---

anguish and her pain' falls short of the mark, given the textual evidence demonstrating Wolfram's message about clan loyalty. McFarland, 141.

184   Gibbs and Johnson, 151.

185   The mention of Crusade ideals here supports the idea that this is what motivates the French imperial troops and nothing more, and is further underscored by the contrast in the way Wolfram depicts Saracen adversaries with the way they are described in *Aliscans*.

Franzoyser, nuo sprechet ir
wes wir uns hin ziu sülen versehen,
und lât uns iwer ellen spehen.
(Wh. 301, 28–30)

[You, Frenchmen, speak up now and tell us what we can expect from you, and let us have a look at your courage.][186]

As if to impress this message further, each subsequent address stresses the punishment that awaits those who do not honour their oaths and Bertram reiterates:

dem werden nie gezam
daz ûz prîse traete:
swer in dar umbe baete,
dem solt er nimmer werden holt.
nu denket, helde, ir habt gedolt
in Francrîche mangen prîs:
ob ir nu den markîs
liezet in sus grôzer nôt,
iwer keines vriundîn daz gebôt.
iuch hazzt ouch drumbe (deist mir kunt)
(Wh. 303, 2–11)

[It was never right for a noble man to retreat from fame, and if anyone urged him to do so he should never again treat that man with favour. Now, heroes, remember that you have endured suffering to gain much fame in France. If you forsake the Marquis now, when he is in such dire straits, this will not match the intention of the lady of any one of you. I know, too, that [Jesus] will hate you for this.][187]

Wolfram interposes as the narrator between the last speeches, further underscoring the message about loyalty by foreshadowing the flight of the French troops at Petit Punt, an act so reprehensible to him that he never once mentions them by name in his story.

---

186   Gibbs and Johnson, 153.
187   Gibbs and Johnson, 154.

Der dis âventiur bescheiden hât,
der tuot iu kunt, durh waz man lât
daz die fürsten niht sint benant,
die der roemisch künec dar hât gesant.
wan etslîch wider wanden,
die ir fürstîe schanden,
si enphiengns mit zepter odr mit vanen.
swer si des lasters noch wil manen,
da geschach iedoch ein widervart:
die wante der junge Rennewart
an der enge ze Pytît punt,
fünfzehen tûsent zeiner stunt,
zwischen Oransche und Alyschans.
(*Wh.* 302, 1–13)

[He who is telling this tale will now explain to you why the princes whom the Roman King had sent there are not mentioned by name. This is because some of them turned back and brought shame upon their princely rank, whether they had received this through the sceptre or the flag. If anyone wants to remind them even now of their ignominy, let it be said that, after all, they did return. Young Rennewart turned them back at the narrow pass at Pitit Punt, fifteen thousand of them in one go, between Orange and Alischantz.][188]

These words recall vividly Heimrich's observation to Gyburg that some princes are not meant for battle, his concern about their courage and Willehalm's preoccupation with giving a sufficient impression of power and inducing knightly obligation by displaying the wealth and power of his opulent palace. Wolfram's message about loyalty seems clear, just as does his emphasis on the reliability of clan loyalty over imperial service. Those who exemplify loyalty to their clan and to their oath and who show courage when called upon are worthy in the spiritual chivalry that sets the tone of *Willehalm* and only by this chivalry can the day be won.

It is telling that Wolfram gives an account of those who are listening to the speeches made at the council. The Narbonnais princes are there as commanders, but they do not command the French imperial contingent.

188   Gibbs and Johnson, 153.

The reaction of the French to the Crusade ideals used to motivate them seems to be effective, for they eagerly declare all Saracens the enemy of the Roman Protector.[189] In striking contrast, the Narbonnais army are busy preparing themselves and their equipment for battle. Their absence as well as their activity would seem to indicate that the words were pointedly meant for the French nobles, whose oath is not reliable, and that the religious ceremony is seen by Wolfram only as symbolic of French imperial duty to the protection of the pontificate in Rome, a motivational element that the Narbonnais and their mercenaries do not share.

The queen of Orange takes the floor. When Gyburg speaks before the council, her words are not those of a rambling and emotionally distraught woman, a Saracen convert whom Christianity now influences explicitly; rather, her words and gestures are well-timed, just as Willehalm's were when he spoke before Loys and his court at Montlaon to secure imperial support.[190] In fact, Gyburg's speech can be seen as an extension of that action. Her speech is longer than those preceding it and, because of the content of those speeches and the knowledge of the Narbonnais regarding the reliability of the imperial troops, it can be seen in terms of an appeal to the French contingent to honour their oath to follow Willehalm into battle and free Orange. She opens by appealing to their sense of chivalry: 'swer zuht mit triwen hinne hât, der ruoche hoeren mîniu wort. got weiz wol daz ich jâmers hort / sô vil inz herze hân geleit, daz in der lîp unsamfte treit' [if any man present is loyal and chivalrous, [...] then let it please him to listen to what I say. God knows that I have laid up in my heart such a store of grief that my body is hardly able to bear it] (*Wh*. 306, 4–8).[191] She asks of men who are as courtly as they are loyal to listen and invites their

---

189 *Wh*. 304. McFarland remarks that 'the initially enthusiastic response which [the spiritual reference in the speeches] evokes in the French leaders must be seen as called somewhat into question by their subsequent failure to honour their oaths and their cross-taking' (132).

190 Starkey writes about the significance of Willehalm's words and gestures, and his timing of them in Montlaon, and asserts that his actions indicate planning and calculation. Mark Chinca has similar ideas. See Starkey and Chinca.

191 Gibbs and Johnson, 155.

compassion in her grief. She employs the device here of elevating the lis-
teners to meet her description of chivalrous knights. She then relates their
service to the Holy Roman Empire and the duty to avenge fallen knights
such as Vivianz: 'die roemschen fürsten ich hie man, daz ir kristenlîch
êre mêrt, ob iuch got sô verre gêrt, daz ir mit strîte ûf Alischanz rechet
den jungen Vivîanz an mînen mâgn und an ir her' [I hereby remind you
princes of the Roman Empire that you will be increasing the honour of
Christendom if God so honours you as to allow you to avenge the death
of Vivianz in battle against my kinsmen and their army on the field of
Alischantz] (*Wh.* 306, 18–23).[192]

The next and most lengthy appeal is that which has been the focus
of most of the scholarly criticism on Gyburg's speech: Gyburg's appeal
to show Christian mercy to the Saracens in defeat. She employs Biblical
imagery and references to baptism, salvation and to the chivalrous qualities of pity and compassion for the weak. While strong, her words are not
only focused on the mercy that should be shown to those members of her
Saracen family who will be defeated by the forces she has helped to assemble; they also demonstrate before the imperial troops her confidence in a
Christian victory and threaten them by appealing to their sense of sin and
punishment. Taking her cues from the words of the Narbonnais princes
who spoke before her, she refers to mankind's sin in turning from his duty
to God and the eternal punishment that incurs.[193] Death, damnation and
punishment were the message of the Church that the imperial French
would have recognized from mass; these were the words that governed
their lives and Gyburg builds on the speeches of her Narbonnais kinsmen,
driving the point further. The Saracens are referred to as heathens in order
to appeal to the Christian imperial mentality and the Crusade ideals that
motivate them to battle[194] for she, above anyone else, needs these troops
to defend Orange.

---

192   Gibbs and Johnson, 155.
193   *Wh.* 308, 1–15.
194   Koss observes that in the artificial kinship of the brotherhood of Christianity, 'the
        emphasis is not on the unquestioning solidarity of kin, but on the obligations of
        such relationships.' (188)

Gyburg then appeals directly to the French princes, whose thoughts she must know include fleeing before battle, by offering them encouraging words of salvation, of absolution from such thoughts if only they turn and fight for Orange: 'daz mennisch wart durch rât verlorn' [humans were betrayed by bad advice] (*Wh.* 308, 19) and:

die varent noch hiute dem mensche bî,
als op der kôr ir erbe sî,
der den ist ze erbe lâzen
die sich des kunnen mâzen
daz gotes zorn erwirbet,
des saelde niht verdirbet
(*Wh.* 308, 25–30)

[To this very day, these wicked angels pursue mankind, as though the choir were their inheritance, whereas it is in fact bequeathed to those who know how to avoid incurring the anger of God who grants eternal bliss.][195]

The following verse, more so than any other words of Gyburg in her speech, shows the emotion that her part in bringing the army of Christendom against her Saracen kinsmen has evoked: she makes a direct appeal to the knights to show pity on the defeated when they are victorious. Her words, this time less threatening, reveal a sense of hope in this time of crisis:

sîn werdeclîchez leben bôt
für die schuldehaften an den tôt
unser vater Tetragramatôn.
sus gab er sînen kinden lôn
ir vergezzenlîchen sinne.
sîn erbarmede rîchiu minne
elliu wunder gar besliuzet,
des triwe niht verdriuzet,
sine trage die helfeclîche hant
diu bêde wazzer unde lant

195   Gibbs and Johnson, 156.

vil künsteclîch alrêrst entwarf,
und des al diu crêatiure bedarf
die der himel umbesweifet hât.
                    (*Wh.* 309, 7–19)

[Our Father [Jahwe] offered up His virtuous life for the guilty ones and so rewarded His children for their forgetfulness. His love which is so full of mercy embraces all miracles and in His loving loyalty He will not cease to hold out the helping Hand which first brought into being both land and water: all creatures contained beneath the heavens have need of this.][196]

The emphasis on God's children is consistent with the references in the speeches prior to Gyburg's, especially Bertram's of Berbester.[197] It can also be interpreted in terms of Gyburg's sense of guilt over her present position against her Saracen father and kinsmen, for her actions have precipitated more than a mere feud of conquest; her conversion has resulted in a clash between Islam and Christendom. Her guilt also shows in passing reference to heathens being creatures of God, as is all mankind, and therefore worthy of the Christian chivalrous standard of mercy. This seems to be a consistent feature in Wolfram's narrative, underscoring the problematic relationship between God and man.[198]

However, her final words remain calculated, indicating less an emotionally overwrought woman than a sharp-witted, determined queen whose goal is the defence of her city and the assurance of its safety, which necessitates the presence of the French imperial contingent. She reasserts her loyalty to Christianity, recounting briefly her conversion and marriage to Willehalm, mentioned here to reaffirm her position: she is liege-lady of a Christian Orange in need of protection from the empire. In a final, clinching gesture, she expresses her sorrow at the loss of the Narbonnais kinsmen who fought with Willehalm for Orange. Her show of emotion and sorrow

---

196 Gibbs and Johnson, 156.
197 *Wh.* 303, 16.
198 See Toepfer, Regina, 'Enterbung und Gotteskindschaft: Zur Problematik der Handlungsmotivierung inm "Willehalm" Wolframs von Eschenbach', *Zeitschrift für deutsche Philologie*, 129/1 (2010), 63–81.

is calculated and timed, for it is a demonstration of provocation, just as it was used by Willehalm in Montlaon.[199] She weeps, and is taken into the arms of her brother-in-law, Gibert, her role in the Christian victory played out to its fullest extent; this is her last appearance in *Willehalm*.

Before Gyburg's role culminates in her speech to the assembled nobles, several features have been made evident: Wolfram's emphasis on Christian chivalry, loyalty playing a major part; his repeated foreshadowing of the desertion of the French imperial troops and his disapproval of their disloyalty; the absolute need for an imperial presence in Orange, this demonstrated by the necessity of Willehalm to secure Loys's support in Montlaon; the intimations made to Gyburg by both Willehalm and Heimrich; and the content of the Narbonnais speeches preceding Gyburg's. The interpretation of Gyburg's role in delivering her speech depends upon the reader's understanding of these features. Gyburg's address must then be seen as a continuation of the action undertaken after the first battle of Alischantz: to appeal to the seat of the Christian Empire for a show of support against the Saracen threat to Orange.

This address is, unfortunately, by no means the end of that action, as none of these appeals by Heimrich, Willehalm, Gyburg and the Narbonnais princes succeeds in securing the absolute loyalty of the French imperial contingent or their presence in the battle, for they flee at first sight of the Saracens.[200] Willehalm knows that their oath is not to him, rather to Loys, and he has therefore little power to make them stay, so there on the field before battle he offers them the chance to leave ignominiously, which they take.[201] It remains for Rennewart to turn them back at Petit

---

199   See Starkey, 339; and Philipowski. More scholarship has focused on the significance of the show of emotion and gestures for understanding medieval texts, which should be seen as a major component of the texts, as well as such visual components as illuminations that appear in many German and French manuscripts, and are the subject of current research. As the *chansons de geste* were first performed and written down only later, it can be understood that such gestures and shows of emotion were presented by the *jongleurs* as an integral part of the stories they told.

200   *Wh.* 321.

201   *Wh.* 320, 8–15.

Punt, forming the pinnacle of his character's development and attesting
to his unique status as a 'Christian' Saracen who can wield physical force
as power without humiliation and who becomes the instrument of the
Christian victory.[202]

Through Gyburg's address to the Narbonnais nobles, Wolfram conveys as clear a message about clan loyalty as in the scene at Montlaon with
Willehalm and Blancheflor[203] that is not without parallel in *Aliscans*.
Though there is no address in *Aliscans*, this does not indicate that Wolfram
went so far from his source as to create as new a character in Gyburg as
he did with many of the Saracen protagonists. Guiborc's strength and
influence as a Saracen queen is seen keenly with regard to these themes of
kinship and loyalty, and she is just as instrumental in the Christian victory
in Orange. Just as Guiborc's strength lies in her motivating Guillaume,
giving him the courage to count on the loyalty of his clan, Gyburg's function pivots on her comprehension of the suggestions of Willehalm and
Heimrich, in holding Orange while Willehalm is away and in continuing
the task of securing the loyalty of the French troops.

In the character of Gyburg, there is a meeting of opposing forces in both
Aliscans and *Willehalm*. While Wolfram's Gyburg exhibits a consciousness
of her situation through words and actions, and a capacity to employ her wit
and status to the advantage of her city, her husband and their Narbonnais
clan, her *Aliscans* counterpart has by no small means set the standard for her
importance and strength. Lachet writes that among the epic heroines, the
jongleur of *Aliscans* 'privilégie Guibourc qui, par ses qualités, la conscience
de sa responsabilité, sa foi profonde, sa charité, est d'une certaine manière
le reflet épique de la "nouvelle Eve"' [favoured Guiborc who, through
her qualities, the consciousness of her responsibility, her profound faith,
her compassion, is in a way the epic reflection of a contemporary Eve].[204]

---

202 See the Chapter 4, section 'Rennewart'.
203 Blancheflor's indifference to Willehalm's plight and her refusal to come to his aid
     with imperial support earns her a violent reprimand from Willehalm, demonstrating
     the importance of the duty of and obligation within clan. (*Wh.* 147; 152)
204 Lachet, 'Figures féminines', 119.

These qualities as well as the unique status of the converted Saracen queen were appreciated by Wolfram as in his depiction of Gyburg. Taking up this model, he imbued Gyburg with a more immediate importance to the action and characters of *Willehalm* by presenting her as the focus of the siege of Orange and expanding upon her status as liege-lady such that she attends the war council and speaks in words that demonstrate her loyalties, her commitment and her perspicacity.

The private sphere

Gyburg's actions in the public eye are only part of her influence in the story and indeed only a fraction of the manifestation of her character and its development. Gyburg's character is exemplary in more private ways, too. Among these are: her relationship with God and her personal spirituality; the chivalric qualities she possesses; and the influence she exercises behind the scenes. In addition to the establishment of her character as exemplary, Gyburg's activity in the private sphere proves most significant in her relationship and interaction with Rennewart. In this way, Gyburg plays an important part in the outcome of the attack on Orange even behind the scenes, complementing her role in the public arena and confirming her reputation as liege-lady *par excellence* and as Willehalm's natural partner.

Spirituality

Just as the converted Saracens in the *chansons de geste* prove themselves many times over as the best of Christians, Guiborc's character reveals time and again how her commitment to both Christianity and the survival of the Christian empire remains steadfast and her faith in the Christian God constant. She refers to her conversion when she needs to encourage

Guillaume in his despair, reminding him and the audience of the hope and salvation that follows suffering for Christians.[205]

> 'Sire, dist ele, je sui vostre juree,
> En l'anor Deu lëaument esposee,
> Et ensainz fonz bauptizee et levee;
> D'uile et de cresme fumes regeneree.'[206]
> (*Alisc.* L 2201–4)

['My Lord,' says [Guiborc], 'I am your sworn lady, by God's law I married you faithfully and was baptized and raised in the sacred fountain; and was reborn with holy oil.']

For Guiborc, as for her Narbonnais clan, Christianity and salvation are linked to loyalty. In this passage, her reaffirmation of her faith and loyalty to her marriage to Guillaume precedes her persuading him to relate the disasters of the first battle and her reminding him that he can expect loyal support from his kinsmen.

Guiborc's strength in her faith is transferred to Wolfram's Gyburg with an emphasis on her personal spirituality and relationship with God through prayer. Gyburg exemplifies faith in spirituality at times of impending disaster, serving a similar function to that of Guiborc in encouraging Willehalm. When Willehalm returns to Orange after the defeat of the first battle, she

---

205 Lachet describes one of the roles of the female character in the *chansons de geste* as reconciliatory: 'le trouvère semble conclure que le rôle de la femme consiste à adoucir la colère des hommes et à ramener l'harmonie entre eux' [the troubadour seems to conclude that the role of the woman consists in assuaging men's anger and in restoring harmony between them] ('Figures féminines', 114). Gyburg's role in *Willehalm* is similar: a balancing and comforting influence upon the male interaction, demonstrating that the importance of Guiborc was transferred to the Gyburg of *Willehalm*.

206 These lines correspond to L 2031–5 in the 'M' manuscript, where *juree* [sworn lady] is replaced by *sposee* [wife] and line 2204/2035 differs: 'D'uyle e de crisme en deu regeneree' [with holy oil in God reborn]. Also present in the 'M' manuscript is the line missing in Régnier's 'A' edition, 2033: 'Por vos su je crestïane clamee' [For you I proclaimed [converted to] Christianity]. These subtle variations show what is likely to have been in the examplar known to Wolfram when he retold the story, especially as these lines correspond in content to *Wh.* 7, 29–30; 9, 13–17.

comforts him with her companionship by removing his armour and tending to his wounds, and also in the intimacy that they share in the subsequent love scene.[207] Afterwards, Willehalm falls asleep and Gyburg reflects in sorrow on the defeat and losses suffered, her tears having been saved for a time when she is alone.[208] She then addresses God directly, something of which Guiborc has no need because of the different emphasis in her role. Alone and away from the ears of any other character, Gyburg expresses her remorse through prayer at the loss of Vivianz, at what Willehalm has suffered, at her plight in Orange with her Saracen family threatening invasion and capture, and at having to face this alone whilst Willehalm goes to Montlaon. This prayer is her own consolation after she has consoled Willehalm in accordance with her duty as his liege-lady. She appears the stronger afterwards, when she decides that he must go and sends him on his way, reassured by his vow of fidelity and that he will return to rescue her.

In the warrior's domain

In the scenes in which Gyburg is absent, such as in battle and in the scenes describing Willehalm's trip to Montlaon, her influence is evident in that she is in the thoughts and prayers of the protagonists, serving as a motivation and the object of their service, a symbol of Orange and *Minnedienst*, just like her counterpart in *Aliscans*. Lachet remarks that in the *chanson de geste* 'Guibourc occupe les prières, les souvenirs et les réflexions de son conjoint, comme elle hante l'esprit de Vivien jusqu'à son dernier souffle et la pensée de Rainouart avant qu'il ne rêve d'Aélis' [Guiborc occupies the prayers, the memories and the thoughts of her partner, just as she haunts the spirit of Vivien until his last breath, and Rainouart's thoughts before his

---

207 *Wh.* 100.
208 By contrast, Guiborc's tears are shed in front of Guillaume upon hearing his report of the death of Vivien and the nephews taken prisoner, in *Alisc.* L 2225–37. This contrast shows not only Gyburg's private activity, but also how, far from a simple display of internal emotion to be expected from a female, tears were employed with precise calculation; in Guiborc's case, she is persuading Guillaume to go to Montlaon. See Philipowski, esp. 463.

dreams are consumed with Aélis].[209] Indeed, as soon as Guillaume has left for
Montlaon, 'Souvent regrete Guiborc au cler visage' [He thinks always with
sadness on the fair face of Guiborc] (*Alisc.* LVI, 2474). Wolfram remains
true to his source in this respect, for this kind of influence and presence
in the minds of the warriors is the realm of the liege-lady. Not only is she
the single most important presence in Willehalm's thoughts while he is
away from her, proving his love by abstinence from both food and affection, Gyburg is foremost in the minds of his brothers in their reaction to
Willehalm's reports of Orange under threat.[210] Her reputation and her status
render her an important motivation for the undertaking of the liberation
of Orange among the kinsmen of Willehalm, which is evidenced first when
Willehalm meets his brother in Orleans. Arnalt shows his concern for her
even before the situation is fully recounted to him:

> ouwê hêrre bruoder mîn,
> lâz hoeren unde schouwen,
> mîner swester, mîner frouwen,
> waz wirret Gyburge der süezen?
> mac mîn helfe daz gebüezen?
> daz hât si wol verschuldet her,
> daz ieslîch werder Franzoys wer
> sînes dienstes zir gebote:
> man mac an ir gedienen gote
> und unseres landes êre;
> und durch die überkêre
> die si tet gein dem toufe.
> du hâst mit tiurem koufe
> ir minne etswenne errungen.
> mîne mâg die jungen,
> die si hât ûzen schalen erzogen
> und die Francrîche sint entflogen,
> sint die bî ir in der nôt?
>   (*Wh.* 119, 30 – 120, 17)

---

209 Lachet, 'Figures féminines', 116.
210 Buov of Commercy resolves to accompany his brothers to relieve Gyburg in Orange.
     (*Wh.* 172, 20–3) Irmschart mentions Gyburg in asking the support of Loys. (*Wh.*
     183, 16–20)

[Alas, my lord, my brother, let me hear and see what is troubling sweet Giburc, my sister, my lady? Can my help recompense her? She has well deserved to have every noble Frenchman's strength in service at her command. One can serve both God and the honour of our land in serving her, and this for the sake of her conversion to Christianity through baptism. You once paid dearly in gaining her love. My young kinsmen, whom she raised as fledglings and who have now flown away from France, are they with her in her distress?][211]

Arnalt's first response when he recognizes his brother and hears that Willehalm has met with trouble in Orange is to ask after the safety of Gyburg. Additionally, he mentions how she cared for Willehalm's nephews, a further testament to her worthiness for their service, and seems concerned about their duty to protect her (that is, until he learns from Willehalm what has transpired in Orange and that these young kinsmen have been either killed or taken prisoner). Then Arnalt's devotion to his sister-in-law becomes an even stronger motive:

> ode wie hâstu des gedâht
> daz wir Gyburg ze helfe komn,
> sît wir den schaden hân genomn,
> daz unser flust niht wahse baz?
> al den ich diens nie vergaz,
> die werdent drumbe nu gemant.
> al unser art waere geschant,
> ob Gyburc wurde enphüeret dir.
> (*Wh.* 121, 4–14)

[Or what did you think we might do to help Giburc and, in view of the losses we have suffered, to keep our losses from even increasing? All those to whom I have ever rendered service will be reminded of their debt to me now. Our entire lineage would be disgraced, if Giburc were taken away from you.][212]

Gyburg's importance to the Narbonnais clan is underscored here, for she was the object of Willehalm's past conquest of Orange and increased her value by converting to Christianity, marrying Willehalm. Willehalm's

211 Gibbs and Johnson, 71.
212 Gibbs and Johnson, 71.

position in Orange is due to Gyburg (recall that it was Gyburg who freed him from prison there, allowing him to take it). For this land and queen to be taken from Willehalm now would signal disfunctionality in the solidarity and loyalty of the Narbonnais, a loss of honour for the entire clan. Only by retaining his conquest can Willehalm keep his honour and a Christian Orange be legitimized. Without being present and by virtue of her image and status, Gyburg exercises an important influence over the rallying of Willehalm's family to relieve Orange in Montlaon.

Gyburg defends her city in Willehalm's absence by becoming its commander, but when the warriors are present, she moves behind the scenes, exercising her influence to secure victory and save Orange. She is the embodiment of Wolfram's chivalric standard and many times it is by her example that chivalry is encouraged in the steps towards a victory in Orange. Gyburg exemplifies the chivalrous ideals of loyalty (*triuwe*), generosity (*milte*), and compassion (*güete*) by entertaining and providing for the arriving army. This largesse is most marked in its extension towards Rennewart at the banquet when his arrival alarms the assembled nobles, conspicuous because it is an attribute that has not been shown him by his own Saracen kinsmen.[213] In this way, Gyburg's display of these values are as calculated as her speech and actions when she is the centre of attention.

> Et Guiborc ovre son mantel de porprine,
> Si l'afubla, quar li cuers li devine
> Qu'il est son frere, mes n'en fet nule sine.
> (*Alisc.* LXXXIX, 4638–40)

[And Guiborc opens her purple cloak, wraps him up in it, because her heart tells her that he is her brother, but she gives no outward sign.][214]

---

213   See Lofmark, *Rennewart*, 129.

214   Much significance has been given this cloak scene, especially in that, while the *jongleur* of *Aliscans* does not specify whether Guiborc was still wearing the cloak when she wrapped it around her brother, Wolfram's Gyburg 'swanc si umbe in ein teil' [tucked part of it around him; or, tucked it around him a little]. There is sufficient consistency in this scene between *Aliscans* and *Willehalm*, however, to suggest that Wolfram's Gyburg has the same feelings and motivations as does Guiborc. Lofmark

The interaction between Gyburg and Rennewart is significant in its intricacy and implications. They are siblings, though they do not find this out until later (in *Willehalm* not at all), and they have bonded with the Christian kinsmen: Rennewart to Alyze and to Willehalm, his liege-lord; and Gyburg to Willehalm and his family. Both of these pivotal characters have been influenced by their Saracen past and their Christian present, and Gyburg's astuteness and encouragement regarding the young Saracen giant in her husband's service demonstrates her considerable impact upon events.

The qualities of compassion and generosity, as well as the recognition of nobility in Rennewart, are present in the character of Gyburg, just as they are in her *Aliscans* counterpart. Recognizing his nobility and, in the case of Guiborc, that he is her brother, Desramé's son, Gyburg recognizes Rennewart's importance in securing victory and fulfils her role in supporting and encouraging his participation and success.[215] He cannot be a complete Christian knight without proper arms and accoutrements and he cannot be a complete member of the Christian fold without having the support of family. As he is orphaned from his Saracen family, Willehalm and Gyburg take on the role of an Aquitainian aunt and uncle, fitting him out with armour and a horse (possessions symbolizing his allegiance to her) as well as teaching him the ways of warriors, supporting him spiritually and supporting his integration into the greater clan.[216] As a high-ranking lady, Gyburg's role in Rennewart's fulfilment of his function in the story is all-important for the Christian victory.

---

sees no indication that the significance of the cloak was exploited in *Aliscans* as it seems to have been by Wolfram in *Willehalm*, but he lists many other examples of the significance of the cloak in medieval literature and the origins of the symbolism, including a comparison to a scene in *Parzival*. See Lofmark, *Rennewart*, 174–81. That this was a gesture replete with symbolism is evidenced by its occurrence in romance, especially in the *Prose Lancelot*, as described elaborately by Burns (141–2).

215   Lofmark writes that Rennewart's 'Quick sensitivity and responsiveness to Gyburg's *güete* [compassion] enable her to direct his energies with ease.' Lofmark, *Rennewart*, 167.

216   See McFarland, 129.

The idea of investiture and favours in romance texts is evident in both the *chanson de geste* and *Willehalm* in the context of Rennewart's interaction with Gyburg. Though Rennewart's horse is given him by Willehalm, his armour and weapons are gifts of Gyburg, to whom he is now bound in loyalty. In *Aliscans*, Guillaume recognizes that a feminine touch is necessary when he fails to control Rainouart's temper and he sends Guiborc to him.[217] After a conversation about his family, kinship is recognized; Guiborc gives Rainouart armour and a sword, after which he vows that he will protect Guillaume and serve Guiborc:

> Dist Renoart: 'Dame, lessiez ester,
> Que, par la foi que je vos doi porter,
> Ne vos estuet de Guillelme douter
> Tant com antiers puist mon tinel durer.'
> [...]
> 'Mes or vos voill par amors commander
> Que tu me sofres ton cors a adouber;
> A torjorz mes t'en voudrai plus amer.'
> Dist Renoart: 'Ne le vos quier veer.'
>   (*Alisc.* XCI, 4713–16, 4721–4)

> [Rainouart says, 'My lady, do not worry, because, by the loyalty that I have for you, you need have no fear for Guillaume, as long as my *tinel* is intact.' [...] But, for love allow me to dub you [my knight]; may my great affection always be with you.' Rainouart says, 'Do not [doubt] it.']

The sword is the most significant item that is given to Rennewart by Gyburg; it can be linked to the service of a lady in the romances. It is after Gyburg insists that he take the sword even if he does not intend to use it that he can be said to be in her service, to have become Gyburg's knight; he remains in her service to protect Willehalm and to save Orange.[218] In *Willehalm*, the symbolism is less direct:

---

217   *Alisc.* LXXXIX.
218   From references to Roland's legendary *Durendal* and Charlemagne's *Joieuse*, which is in Willehalm's possession, it is clear that swords have a greater, often metaphoric significance to the identity of a knight in *Aliscans* and *Willehalm* than just an elite

nu sî ouch mîn geverte
diz swert: daz sol her umbe mich.
der margrâf mac wol troesten sich
mîn, swaz i'm gedienen mac,
gefüeget er mir strîtes tac.

(*Wh.* 296, 10–14)

['Now may this sword be my comrade,' he said. 'Let me put it on. The Margrave can absolutely depend on me to serve him as well as I am able, if only he will give me the chance to fight.']²¹⁹

Wolfram's Rennewart needs his sword not only to fight the battle but to advance his personal development as a knight worthy of turning the tide of the battle and winning the day for the Christians, which is possibly why the emphasis in his vow is not that of service to Gyburg, in addition to his love for Alyze. Nevertheless, that it is she who equips him, especially with a sword, should be seen as significant, if only in that Gyburg, both in *Aliscans* and in *Willehalm*, exerts conscious influence over those whom she recognizes as instrumental in providing succour for her city, her husband and his kinsmen. In supplying and encouraging Rennewart, Gyburg gains loyalty from him and the certainty of the vow that he will serve Willehalm. This is a significant step considering the explicit suspicions of the unreliability of those troops sent from Loys and that Rennewart himself comes to Willehalm from Loys's service. Rennewart keeps his vow, however, and saves the day at Petit Punt.

Far from the fragile woman dismissed as emotional and vulnerable, Gyburg shines as a strong and intelligent ruler, capable of holding her own both spiritually and temporally, and playing her role in the Christian victory with conscious precision. Her character should not be investigated without

---

weapon. Perhaps the most notorious example of the significance of a sword given a knight by a lady in romance is that of the one given to Lancelot by Guinevere in the *Prose Lancelot*, which effectively puts Lancelot in the service of Guinevere, not Arthur.

219 Gibbs and Johnson, 150.

taking into account the profound circumstance of her position in Orange as liege-lady and queen, as Willehalm's devoted wife and thereby as an important member of the Narbonnais clan. As Orange's liege-lady, she motivates the men of the Narbonnais clan and acts to the very best of her abilities to ensure the loyalty of those warriors whose presence is vital to the security and deliverance of Orange, including her brother, Rennewart. As a converted Saracen, Gyburg possesses an inner strength; this stems from her spiritual fortitude and her confidence in Christian salvation, which her character exemplifies in word and deed, and it is through her that Wolfram's most significant thoughts emerge.

Wolfram's Grail ideal in 'Willehalm'

> Ei Gyburc, heilic vrouwe,
> din sælde mir die schouwe
> noch vüege, daz ich dich gesehe
> alda min sele ruowe jehe.
> durh dinen pris den süezen
> wil ich noch vürbaz grüezen
> dich selben und die dich werten
> so daz si wol ernerten
> ir sele vors tiuvels banden
> mit ellenhaften handen.
>   (*Wh.* 403, 1–10)

[Alas, Giburc, saintly lady, may you in your blessedness afford me the chance to see you with my own eyes there, where my soul will find repose! Because of your sweet renown I shall continue to call upon you yourself and those who defended you and thereby saved their souls from the Devil's bonds with their courageous hands.][220]

The question of continuity between Wolfram's major works, *Willehalm* and *Parzival*, has emerged from time to time in analyses of these texts,[221]

---

220 Gibbs and Johnson, 199.
221 Amongst the critical works addressing the ideal of the Grail in the context of continuity between *Parzival* and *Willehalm*, and which will be considered in this section,

and it rarely does so without reference to the Grail and the ideals that it symbolizes. Wolfram's Grail in *Parzival* is marked by a uniqueness of symbolism through humans' concept of God, spiritual chivalry and service, expanded by richness in narrative description, and has in more recent scholarship been viewed in terms of its relationship in the text to Saracen characters.[222] Whether out of translational inaccuracy or creative licence, Wolfram's Grail does not take the form of a chalice; rather, it is a mystical stone that fell from the Heavens, that yields food and drink, and also a healing salve, and allows divine communication. The key to the power of the Grail in *Parzival* lies in overcoming self-doubt and in the realization of one's spiritual calling through pure love that will alleviate suffering. There is clearly no Grail in *Willehalm*, nor is there a Grail castle; there is only chivalry in the midst of conflict; honour, love and loyalty contrasted with the consequences of duty. If there is a continuity between *Parzival* and *Willehalm*, then it must be sought out within the ideals that Wolfram's Grail signifies: love or *reine Minne*, service and excellence in spiritual chivalry, and there is no question that the relationship between Gyburg and Willehalm exemplifies these qualities.

The fabric of the plot of *Willehalm* revolves around the relationship between Willehalm and Gyburg and the ideals that function within it. Wolfram makes many references to *Parzival* in *Willehalm* when illustrating the relationship between Gyburg and Willehalm, a phenomenon that demonstrates the familiarity that he would have expected his audience to have with his previous work and one that generates a richness of narrative symbolism by recollection of the *Parzival* story.[223] The ideal of

---

are: Ortmann; Miklautsch, 'Minne-flust'; Volfing; and Clifton-Everest, *Wolframs Parzival und die chanson de geste.*

222   See Schotte, Manuela, *Christen, Heiden und der Gral: Die Heidendarstellung in den mittelhochdeutschen Gralromanen des 13. Jahrhunderts* (Frankfurt am Main: Peter Lang, 2005).

223   Volfing points out that one of the possible reasons that Wolfram alludes to events in *Parzival* during his narration of *Willehalm* is to polish and complete narrative threads that were not entirely finished, such as that of Anfortas and his affair with Sekundille. (50, 53) However, here I will focus on the reference to the Grail and its

Minne, love-service, as a universal aspect of chivalry in *Willehalm* takes on a spiritual quality, demonstrating that chivalric ethics are related to the *reine Minne* discussed above and even driven by it, an idea that was set up in *Parzival*: the fantastical Arthurian ideal was projected onto the Grail society that takes its chivalry directly from God.[224] Though it cannot be said that, as in *Parzival*, the power to free humanity from suffering lies in love in *Willehalm*,[225] the power of the marital love between Gyburg and Willehalm, observable in the service aspect of their love in *Aliscans* as well as in *La Prise d'Oange*, is established in the rewards of their dedication to each other. This steady commitment and affection is attested by the way they address each other (beloved, dear friend, spouse)[226] and in the comfort they take in the fulfilment of each other's reward in love. The physical love expressed between the couple in *Willehalm* has the power of restoration and consolation for both and is related to the element of spirituality and faith in God. Young also observes that this 'love-making leads to religious thought' and the significance of the two love scenes in *Willehalm* is that they 'contain two central elements: the healing, protecting and rejuvenating power of physical love and the religious context into which it flows.'[227] The love expressed between husband and wife then symbolizes how love leads to spiritual hope and salvation, and how spiritual fortitude is rewarded in marital love, but the love between Gyburg and *Willehalm* is also tied to spiritual chivalry and its ideals, very much like that of *Parzival*'s Grail. In *Parzival*, a knight must learn how to direct his love-service; in *Willehalm*, love-service inspires fortitude, courage, and a chivalric spirit. To serve without compromising one's spiritual chivalry is accomplished by both Gyburg

---

ideals as pertaining specifically to the relationship between Gyburg and Willehalm and what it signifies.

224 Ortmann, 116.

225 Miklautsch disputes the suggestion of Ortmann that *Minne* is the salvation of humanity. See 'Minne-flust', 232.

226 For some examples, see *Wh.* 9, 18; and 229, 18: 'liebe vriunde; besten vriunt' [dear friend, best friend] and *Alisc.* XVI, 499: 'Dame Guiborc, douce suer, bele ami' [Lady Guiborc, gentle sister, dear friend].

227 Young, 267.

and Willehalm, and their devotion to one another and to their chivalric ideals is the strength that leads to the preservation of Orange.

Wolfram's portrayal of the love between Gyburg and Willehalm as a tangible manifestation of what the Grail symbolizes in *Parzival*[228] is underscored by the references to Sekundille's gifts, a trend that reaches its peak in the passage during the love scene when Willehalm has returned from Montlaon:

> dô der milte Anfortas
> in Orgelûsen dienste was,
> ê daz er von freuden schiet,
> und der grâl im sîn volc beriet,
> dô diu künegîn Secundille
> (daz riet ir herzen wille)
> mit minne an in ernante
> und im Kundrîen sante
> mit einem alsô tiwerem krâm,
> den er von ir durch minne nam
> und in fürbaz gap durch minne,
> aller krôn gewinne
> und al Secundillen rîche
> diene möhten sicherlîche
> mit des grâles stiur niht widerwegn
> der grôzen flust der muose pflegn
> ûf Alischanz der markîs
>   (*Wh.* 279, 13–29)

[When the generous Anfortas was in the service of Orgeluse before he parted company with joy and the Grail provided for his people, and Queen Sekundille ventured to offer him love and sent Cundrie to him with such precious wares, which he accepted from her out of love and out of love passed to another, the acquisition of all the crowns and all the lands of Sekundille, with the bequest of the Grail itself, could surely not have compensated for the enormous losses sustained by Willehalm at Alischantz.][229]

---

228 See Volfing, 58.
229 Gibbs and Johnson, 143.

Wolfram's reference to the Grail here attests to 'the exceptional quality and significance of the love relationship of Willehalm and Giburc,'[230] by comparing its value in addition to the riches of Sekundille to the solace Gyburg's love offers Willehalm. Volfing asserts that Wolfram's comparison can be seen as 'the Grail context of the absolute value of Willehalm's and Giburc's love for each other.'[231] The power of such love, service and devotion as Gyburg and Willehalm share dwarfs the solace that would be offered by the Grail combined with Sekundille's treasures. This is also a profound reflection on the value of Gyburg's love for Willehalm, who gains from it not only solace but hope and an inspiration to excellence in chivalry that enables him to gain victory, saving Orange as well as ensuring the survival of the illustrious Narbonnais lineage. It also demonstrates the innate bond of love, spirituality and chivalric ideals which Wolfram seeks to exemplify and which is represented in *Parzival* by the Grail: 'in *Willehalm*, however, the function of the Grail as a tangible manifestation of *triuwe* [loyalty] has to a certain extent been replaced by the Willehalm-Giburc relationship itself: it is in pursuing this relationship that the protagonists express not only their loyalty to each other, but also their obedience to God and their trust in his support.'[232]

Hence, it is the love relationship between Gyburg and Willehalm that takes on the ideals that the Grail held in *Parzival*, leading towards excellence in service and chivalry and towards salvation, and making possible the devotion and fortitude necessary to hold out until victory is achieved in Orange. It is not the *Minne* itself in either text that achieves this nor is suffering relieved from humanity in either text. It is a goal that remains outside the scope of the stories, nevertheless embedded in the chivalry that Wolfram describes. That he has chosen to exemplify these ideals in *Willehalm* in the relationship between Gyburg and Willehalm, and especially in the inspiration and reward of Gyburg's love, speaks much for her character. Gyburg's love is the only fitting reward for properly directed

230   Volfing, 59.
231   Volfing, 51.
232   Volfing, 58.

service and proper direction of service by Gyburg forms an integral part of Wolfram's chivalry as it is developed in *Parzival*.

As we have seen, when comparing *Aliscans* and *Willehalm*, especially with regard to Gyburg's character, the impression is that the audience must have been expected to be familiar with some of the detail of *Aliscans* that was left out of Wolfram's work, but it is detail that nevertheless affects both actions and characters in *Willehalm* profoundly. Volfing makes a study of this phenomenon when comparing references to *Parzival* in *Willehalm* and notes that such references, despite the perceived generic differences of the materials, are consistent with references in many romance texts that 'play on common knowledge of other romances [...] when specific events from one romance are shown to constitute part of the factual background of another.'[233] It follows that Wolfram would treat *Aliscans* similarly to the way he did the *Parzival* material in *Willehalm*, alluding to it in places where he expects his audience to have some knowledge of the material, such as the particulars of Willehalm's vow to Gyburg before parting. It is also evident that Wolfram's allusions to his own *Parzival* are intended to emphasize not only his original ideals in the Grail story but to underscore the significance of these ideals in the context of *Willehalm*. This way, Wolfram shows the potency of Gyburg's love and how the relationship between Gyburg and Willehalm is exemplary of the service and chivalry that is required in order to succeed.

By examining the relationship between Gyburg and Willehalm in the context of service and reward rather than of conquest and prize alone and by taking into account the development of the character of Gyburg from the archetypal Saracen princess of *chanson-de-geste* tradition to the exemplary liege-lady of a knight of outstanding chivalry and spiritual steadfastness, a more complete picture of this couple's significance emerges. As the queen of Orange, Gyburg possesses great importance for Willehalm; through her conversion to Christianity and marriage to him, he becomes lord over a sovereign Christian march, securing his wealth and title as Margrave,

233 Volfing, 46.

remaining influential to the French monarch and fulfilling his duty to his illustrious lineage. In both *Aliscans* and *Willehalm*, it is this marital relationship that he must defend in order to preserve his conquest, but it is also this relationship that enables the success of saving Orange. Gyburg and Willehalm function together to achieve their city's deliverance from the Saracens. Willehalm remains in loyal service to Gyburg, returning to her to save her city, and she renders him his due reward, her love and devotion, for his fidelity and service. Her role is even more decisive in *Willehalm* due to the two alterations of Wolfram: changing the focus of the Saracen threat from Guillaume as in *Aliscans* to Gyburg herself; and allowing her to deliver a speech to the French troops at the war council. Privately, this relationship is deeper than the service-and-reward driving the action: Gyburg's spiritual fortitude helps them both to endure the adversity of their situation, and her encouragement of properly directed chivalry enables Willehalm to fulfil his duty both to her and to his integrity as a Christian knight. Although Gyburg's motive is to preserve her city and thereby her salvation in belonging to the Christian fold, her function is more than that of securing the service that will save Orange; it is also that of demonstrating how love, bestowed through properly directed chivalry, proves the greatest reward for the service of a knight.

Building upon the already established and popular character of Guiborc, the Saracen queen of Guillaume's youthful exploits and the *riche dame* who won his heart, Wolfram creates a character who proves to be the most pivotal figure in *Willehalm*. Gyburg's character draws much of its background from the material of *La Prise d'Orange* and is imbued with the traits of spiritual chivalry, devotion and the power to inspire service and loyalty, whilst symbolizing the city of Orange to whose defence she is entirely committed. Guiborc is the strong liege-lady whose illustrious lineage and courageous deeds have earned her the unswerving loyalty of Guillaume's family and she plays her part with a feminine strength and determination. Likewise, Gyburg displays intelligence and deliberation in bringing about the defence and liberation of Orange, with the innovations of an even more active role in the persuasion of the French reinforcements. Gyburg's actions are calculated and deliberate and she employs the advantages of her status, familial ties, dress and appearance, gesture and emotion in her interaction with other characters, motivating and directing service that leads to the preservation of Orange, as well as the typification of Wolfram's chivalry and representation of the reconciliation implicit in vows of conversion.

The relationship between Gyburg and Willehalm, already exemplary in *Aliscans*, is held up by Wolfram as a model of chivalry, devotion, service and commitment in *Willehalm*, suggesting a continuity in the ideals associated with the Grail of Wolfram's earlier *Parzival*. Gyburg inspires Willehalm never to waver from his duty or his loyalty; so powerful is her love and influence that it provides enough strength for both of them to endure their separation when Willehalm goes to Montlaon and to succeed both in defending Orange against the Saracen threat and in securing reinforcements from the French imperial crown for its deliverance. It is apparent from previous texts that Gyburg's love for Willehalm sprang from attraction and led to conversion. She is the model of how loyalty, service and chivalry should be directed by a lady and Wolfram elevates her for it. Through service and faith, combined with divinely directed chivalry, the love between Willehalm and Gyburg is more valuable than either temporal riches or the Grail itself. This love comprises the hope of reconciliation and gives strength and meaning to chivalry, and its driving force is Gyburg, the Saracen queen of Orange.

Conclusion

Saracens feature centrally throughout the many versions of the story of the battle at Aliscans. Their actions and relationships are important mirrors of their perception by authors and audiences. When presented together, as a progression of exploring and rewriting familiar material, *Willehalm* and its more-prominent sources (*La Prise d'Orange* and *Aliscans*) reveal how the themes of conquest, loyalty, solidarity, an integrated spiritual chivalry and love-service achieve their most profound expression through the actions and portrayal of the Saracens. A detailed study of those pivotal Saracen characters in *Prise d'Orange*, *Aliscans* and *Willehalm* puts forward an integrated reading of *Willehalm* and its sources, in terms of retelling the story for the purpose of exploring and refining these themes. The most important moral value to Wolfram is the practice and direction of chivalry and it is demonstrated by his treatment of themes from *chansons de geste* and romance sources, especially in his portrayal of the Saracens.

Diplomatic letters and canon law, as well as what is known about twelfth-century German, French and Aquitainian court practice and inter-relations, reveal how information, ideas and literature, as well as the people that propagated them, were more mobile than has been previously understood. A route from Umayyad Spain through Aquitaine and Champagne to Thuringia can be seen as a highway for the courtly ideals and poetry that pervaded the *chanson-de-geste* material, requiring expression and inspection from the new knightly class. Thus the framework for Wolfram's sources of material for *Willehalm* includes more than just *La Bataille d'Aliscans* and indicates how time, geography and the development of ideas influenced the portrayal of Saracens. The Crusades, too, had great impact upon the literature of what is now France and Germany. The image of the Saracens and their practice of chivalry was to reflect in literature the change in perspective that time and recurrent interrelations brought. This impact can be seen in how chivalry itself is depicted in *Aliscans*, *La Prise d'Orange* and *Willehalm*.

The ideal of chivalry opened up new parameters by which to gauge the integrity of a character. In *Willehalm*, chivalry forms a cornerstone of salvation and survival, conquest and legitimacy, and justifies Christian rule. Through chivalry, the characters can transcend worldly imperfection. We have seen how the portrayal of Saracens depicts the flaw in their practice of chivalry: that to practise perfect chivalry involves communion with God and that this is only fully achieved by conversion vows of baptism, which they lack. The audience is shown how the Saracen knights are capable of exemplary chivalry and love-service and how this allows them, after they convert, to practise a more complete chivalry than some of the Christian knights themselves, such as the cowardly French princes or King Louis. Striving towards perfect chivalry leads Wolfram's characters towards Christianity, spiritual enlightenment and the integration of contradictory elements. Coming to Christianity through love, in terms of vows and loyalty, is most profoundly expressed in the figure of Gyburg, the Saracen Queen, in whom chivalry and spirituality are joined and whose development throughout *Prise* and *Aliscans* is built upon and surpassed by Wolfram.

Converted out of love for Guillaume in *Prise*, great importance rests upon Gyburg for Willehalm's legitimacy as a knight and as sovereign marquis over Orange. She stands as an example of the proper motivation, influence and practice of chivalry. It is her character, its background and its development in *Willehalm* that presents one of the strongest cases for Wolfram having been familiar with and taken up themes from *La Prise d'Orange*. Gyburg's speech at the war council is one of Wolfram's most significant innovations to his sources. Its inclusion underscores the importance of chivalry and clan loyalty in securing Christian victory. Wolfram's variations to Gyburg's actions, including her speech in *Willehalm*, are consistent with rather than divergent from that of her character's motivations in *Aliscans* and *Prise*. Critics have reduced Gyburg's speech to the outcry of an emotionally distraught woman, but this speech is something altogether different: Gyburg's oration epitomizes her significance as Queen of Orange and her purpose as Narbonnaise liege-lady, taking an active role to influence Loys's unreliable reinforcements and in the outcome of the war between Islam and Christendom. At the same time, she functions as liege-lady to her Saracen brother, Rennewart. In her service and by realizing the full potential of his nobility, Rennewart succeeds in turning back the fleeing French princes, releasing the Christian prisoners from the Saracen ships and making possible the victory in Orange. Only when the texts are considered together as interconnected, rewritten explorations of chivalry and its practice is the true function of the Saracen Queen evident to the reader.

La Prise d'Orange, *Aliscans* and *Willehalm* should be perceived together as the products of stories retold in varying geographic, political and cultural environments, partly because of the popularity of the subject matter and partly as a way to explore themes such as chivalry and love-service. The legitimacy of conquest is developed, defined by honour and loyalty to vows in the *chansons de geste* and emphasized by way of a refined ideal of chivalry in *Willehalm*. Although the medieval German audience would have had varying degrees of familiarity with the *Guillaume d'Orange* material, this integrated reading of *Willehalm* with the texts comprising its source material takes into account the development of each retelling, considering *Willehalm* as a product of multi-faceted rewriting, just as the text itself seems to demand. Thus a more complete understanding of how the *Guillaume* material was proliferated and developed across cultural and political boundaries is achieved and *Willehalm* can be seen as a continuation of the rewriting process that played a major part in the composition of its sources.

Bibliography

Primary Material

Middle High German texts

Wolfram von Eschenbach, *Parzival*, Albert Leitzmann, ed., 7th edn, 3 vols (Tübingen: Altdeutsche Textbibliothek, 1961).

——, *Parzival*, trans., Arthur Thomas Hatto (London: Penguin, 2004).

——, *Willehalm*, Ms codex sang, 857G (Stiftsbibliothek St Gallen, ca, 1260).

——, *Willehalm*, Ms cod, Ser, nova 2643 (Austrian National Library, Vienna).

——, *Willehalm*, Werner Schröder, ed. (Berlin: Walter de Gruyter, 1978).

——, *Willehalm*, Werner Schröder, ed., trans. (Dieter Kartschoke, Berlin: Walter de Gruyter, 1989).

——, *Willehalm*, Marion E. Gibbs and Sidney M. Johnson, trans. (London: Penguin, 1984).

Old French texts

Chrétien de Troyes, *Four Arthurian Romances by Chrétien De Troyes – Erec et Enide, Cligés, Yvain, Lancelot*, trans., William Wistar Comfort, reprint edition (London: J.M. Dent & Sons, 1958).

Dufournet, Jean, ed., *La Chanson de Roland* (Paris: Flammarion, 1993).

——, ed., *Le Charroi de Nîmes, Chanson de Geste Anonyme du XIIe Siècle*, trans., Fabienne Gégou, *Traductions des Classiques français du Moyen Age* vol. XI (Paris: Honoré Champion, 1984).

Ferrante, Joan M., ed. and trans., *Guillaume d'Orange: Four Twelfth-Century Epics* (New York: Columbia University Press, 2001).

Guibert d'Andrenas, chanson de geste, ed. J. Melander (Paris: Edouard Champion, 1922).

Holtus, Günter, ed., *La versione franco-italiana della 'Bataille d'Aliscans': Codex Marcianus fr, VIII[=252]*, Kurt Baldinger, series ed., Beihefte zur Zeitschrift für romanische Philologie, vol. 205 (Tübingen: Max Niemeyer Verlag, 1985).

Les Narbonnais, chanson de geste, ed. H. Suchier (Paris: SATF, 1898).

Régnier, Claude, ed., *Aliscans*, 2 vols, Les Classiques français du Moyen Age (Paris: Honoré Champion, 1990).

——, ed., *La prise d'Orange: Chanson de geste de la fin du XII siècle / Editée d'après la rédaction AB*, 4th edn (Paris: Klincksieck, 1972).

Wienbeck, E., Hartnacke, W., and Rasch, P., eds, *Aliscans*, Halle, 1903, Reprint (Geneva: Slatkine Reprints, 1974).

Other primary texts

Alighieri, Dante, *La Divina Commedia* (Florence: Accademia della Crusca, 2000).

Andreas Capellanus, *The Art of Courtly Love*, John Jay Parry, trans., W.T.H. Jackson, ed., Records of Civilization, Sources and Studies (New York: W.W. Norton, 1969).

Arnold von Lübeck, *Chronicle, Monumenta Germaniae Historica*, George Henry Pertz, ed., Scriptores XXI, 100–250 (Anton Hiersemann, 1869).

De Vitae & miraculorum Actis. Willelmus, Duce Aquitaniae et Monachus Gellonensis, Ordinis S, Benedicti (S.), Acta Sanctorum, Société des Bollandistes (Antwerp, Brussels: 1643, Col, 0809A ff, *Vita Sancti Willelmi*).

Gregory of Tours, *The History of the Franks*, trans., Lewis Thorpe (London: Penguin, 1974).

Huchet, Jean-Charles, ed., *Flamenca: Roman occitan du XIIIe siècle* (Paris: Union Générale d'Editions, 1988).

Loth, Agnete, ed., *Karlamagnús saga: Branches I, III, VII et IX / edition bilingue projetée par Knud Togeby et Pierre Halleux* (Copenhagen: Société pour L'étude de la langue et de la littérature danoises, 1980).

Migne, Jacques-Paul, *Patrologia Latina 1844*, <http://pld.chadwyck.co.uk/> accessed 3 February 2012.

Pertz, George Henry, ed., *Chronicon Moissiacense, Monumenta Germaniae Historica*, Series Scriptores I (Stuttgart: Anton Hiersemann, 1963), 280–313.

Bibliographic Works

Bumke, Joachim, *Die Wolfram von Eschenbach Forschung seit 1945* (München: W. Fink, 1970).

——, *Wolfram von Eschenbach*, 8th edn, vol. 36, Sammlung Metzler (Stuttgart: Verlag J.B. Metzler, 2004).

Germanistik (Tübigen: Niemeyer, 1960–2007).

Klapp, Otto, *Bibliographie der französischen Literaturwissenschaft* (Frankfurt am Main: V. Klostermann, 1960–2007).

Olzien, Otto Heinrich, *Bibliographie zur deutschen Literaturgeschichte* (Stuttgart: Metzler, 1953).

Pérennec, René, *Wolfram von Eschenbach* (Paris: Belin, 2005).

Romanische Bibliographie (Tübingen: Max Niemeyer, 1965–2007).

Vielliard, Françoise, *Manuel bibliographique de la littérature française du Moyen âge de Robert Bossuat* (Paris: CNRS, 1986–2007).

Secondary Literature

Willehalm

Ashcroft, Jeffrey, '"Dicke Karel wart genant:" Konrad's *Rolandslied* and the Transmission of Authority and Legitimacy in Wolfram's *Willehalm*', in Martin H. Jones and Timothy McFarland, eds, *Wolfram's 'Willehalm': Fifteen Essays* (Rochester: Camden House, 2002), 21–43.

Bertau, Karl, 'Das Recht des Andern, Über den Ursprung der Vorstellung von einer Schonung der Irrgläubigen bei Wolfram von Eschenbach' in Karl Bertau, ed., *Wolfram von Eschenbach: Neun Versuche über Subjektivität und Ursprünglichkeit in der Geschichte* (Munich: C.H. Beck, 1983), 241–58.

——, 'Versuch Über Wolfram' in Karl Bertau, ed., *Wolfram von Eschenbach: Neun Versuche über Subjektivität und Ursprünglichkeit in der Geschichte* (Munich: C.H. Beck, 1983), 145–65.

Bumke, Joachim, *Wolframs Willehalm, Studien zur Epenstruktur und zum Heiligkeitsbegriff der ausgehenden Blütezeit* (Heidelberg: Carl Winter, 1959).

Chinca, Mark, 'Willehalm at Laon' in Martin H. Jones and Timothy McFarland, eds, *Wolfram's 'Willehalm': Fifteen Essays* (Rochester: Camden House, 2002), 75–94.

Classen, Albrecht, 'Emergence of Tolerance: An Unsuspected Medieval Phenomenon', *Neophilologus* 76/4 (1992): 586–99.

Curschmann, Michael, 'The French, the Audience, and the Narrator in Wolfram's "Willehalm"', *Neophilologus* 59/4 (1975): 548–62.

Edwards, Cyril, 'Wolfram von Eschenbach, Islam, and the Crusades' in James R. Hodkinson and Jeffrey Morrison, eds, *Encounters with Islam in German Literature and Culture* (Columbia, S.C.: Camden House, 2009), 36–54.

Fasbender, Christoph, '*Willehalm* als Programmschrift gegen die "Kreuzzugsideologie" und "Dokumen der Menschlichkeit"', *Zeitschrift für deutsche Philologie* 116 (1997), 16–31.

Gerok-Reiter, Annette, 'Die Hölle auf Erden: Überlegungen zum Verhältnis von Weltlichem und Geistlichem in Wolframs "Willehalm"' in Burghart Wachinger, Hans-Joachim Ziegeler, and Christoph Huber, eds, *Geistliches in weltlicher und Weltliches in geistlicher Literatur des Mittelalters* (Tübingen: Niemeyer, 2000), 171–94.

Greenfield, John, '"ir sît durh triuwe in dirre nôt:" The Role of *triuwe* in Wolfram's *Willehalm*' in Martin H. Jones and Timothy McFarland, eds, *Wolfram's 'Willehalm': Fifteen Essays* (Rochester: Camden House, 2002), 61–75.

——, 'Vivien und Vivianz', *Wolfram-Studien* XI (1989), 47–64.

——, 'Willehalm's Fall from Grace', *Neophilologus* 73/2 (1989), 243–53.

Heinzle, Joachim, 'Die Heiden als Kinder Gottes, Notiz zum "Willehalm"', *ZfdA* 123 (1994), 301–8.

——, 'Noch einmal: Die Heiden als Kinder Gottes in Wolframs "Willehalm"', *Zeitschrift für deutsche Philologie* 117 (1998), 75–80.

Jones, Martin H. 'Giburc at Orange: The Siege as Military Event and Literary Theme' in Martin H. Jones and Timothy McFarland, eds, *Wolfram's 'Willehalm': Fifteen Essays* (Rochester: Camden House, 2002), 97–120.

Kiening, Christian, 'Umgang mit dem Fremden, Die Erfahrung des "Französischen" in Wolframs "Willehalm"', *Wolfram-Studien* XI (1989), 65–85.

Kirchert, Klaus, 'Heidenkrieg und christliche Schonung des Feindes, Widersprüchliches im Willehalm Wolframs von Eschenbach', *Archiv für das Studium der neueren Sprachen und Literaturen* 231 (1994), 258–70.

Knapp, Fritz Peter, 'Die Heiden und ihr Vater in den Versen 307,27f, des Willehalm', *ZfdA* 122 (1993), 202–7.

——, 'Heilsgewißheit Oder Resignation? Rennewart's Schicksal und der Schluß des Willehalm', *Deutsches Vierteljahrsschrift für Literaturwissenschaft und Geistesgeschichte* 57 (1983), 593–612.

——, 'Leien munt nie baz gesprach, Zur angeblichen lateinischen Buchgelehrsamkeit und zum Islambild Wolframs von Eschenbach.' *ZfdA* 138 (2009), 173–84.

——, *Rennewart: Studien zu Gehalt und Gestalt des 'Willehalm' Wolframs von Eschenbach* (Wien: Verlag Notring, 1970).

——, 'Review of: Carl Lofmark, Rennewart in Wolfram's "Willehalm" (Anglica Germanica Series vol. 2), Cambridge 1972' in *Anzeiger für deutsches Altertum und deutsche Literatur* 85 (1974), 179–92.

——, 'Und Noch Einmal: Die Heiden als Kinder Gottes', *ZfdA* 129 (2000), 296–302.

Lofmark, Carl, 'Das Problem des Unglaubens in Willehalm' in Joachim Heinzle and Kurt Gärtner, eds, *Wolfram von Eschenbach: Festschrift für Werner Schröder* (Tübingen: Niemeyer, 1989), 399–413.

——, *Rennewart in Wolfram's 'Willehalm' A Study of Wolfram von Eschenbach and his Sources*, Cambridge: Cambridge University Press, 1972.

Martin, John D., 'Christen und Andersgläubige in Wolframs "Willehalm"', *ZfdA* 133 (2004), 45–8.

McFarland, Timothy, 'Giburc's Dilemma: Parents and Children, Baptism and Salvation' in Martin H. Jones and Timothy McFarland, eds, *Wolfram's 'Willehalm': Fifteen Essays* (Rochester: Camden House, 2002), 121–42.

Miklautsch, Lydia, 'Glänzende Rüstung – rostige Haut, Körper- und Kleiderkontraste in den Dichtungen Wolframs von Eschenbach' in Gerhard Jaritz, ed., *Kontraste im Alltag des Mittelalters: internationaler Kongress, Krems an der Donau, 29. September bis 2. Oktober 1998* (Vienna: Verlag der Österreichischen Akademie der Wissenschaften, 2000), 61–74.

——, 'Minne-flust: zur Rolle des Minnerittertums in Wolframs *Willehalm*', *Beiträge zur Geschichte der deutschen Sprache und Literatur (PBB)* 117 (1995), 218–34.

Naumann, Hans, 'Der Wilde und der Edle Heide: Versuch über die höfische Toleranz' in Paul Merker and Wolfgang Stammler, eds, *Vom Werden des deutschen Geistes, Festgabe Gustav Ehrismann zum 8. Oktober 1925* (Berlin: Walter de Gruyter, 1925), 80–101.

Ortmann, Christa, 'Der utopische Gehalt der Minne, Strukturelle Bedingungen der Gattungsreflexion in Wolframs *Willehalm*', *Beiträge zur Geschichte der deutschen Sprache und Literatur (PBB)* 115 (1993), 86–117.

Pastré, Jean-Marc, 'Étranges Sarrasins: le luxe et l'exotisme dans le Willehalm de Wolfram' in *De l'Etranger à l'étrange ou la conjointure de la merveille, En hom-*

mage à Marguerite Rossi et Paul Bancourt (Aix-en-Provence: Sénefiance, 1988), 329–39.

Pérennec, René, 'Histoire, géographie et écriture dans le Willehalm de Wolfram von Eschenbach', *Littérales*, 14 *La Chanson de geste, Écriture, intertextualités, translations, Textes présentés par François Suard* (1994), 173–201.

Przybilski, Martin, 'Giburgs Bitten: Politik und Verwandtschaft', *ZfdA* 133 (2004), 49–60.

Reichel, Jörn, 'Willehalm und die höfische Welt', *Euphorion Zeitschrift für Literaturgeschichte* 69 (1975), 388–409.

Richey, Margaret Fitzgerald, *Studies of Wolfram von Eschenbach* (Edinburgh: Oliver and Boyd, 1957).

Richter, Julius, 'Zur Ritterlichen Frömmigkeit der Stauferzeit: Die Kreuzzugsidee in Wolframs Willehalm', *Wolfram Jahrbuch* (1956), 23–33.

Rushing, James A., 'Arofel's Death and the Question of Willehalm's Guilt', *Journal of English and Germanic Philology*, October (1995), 469–82.

——, '*Er liez en wage iewedern tot*, A Reconsideration of "Willehalm" 3,4f', *ZfdA*, 120 (1991), 304–14.

Schellenberg, Kurt, 'Humanität und Toleranz bei Wolfram von Eschenbach', *Wolfram Jahrbuch* (1952), 9–27.

Scheule, Rupert M., 'Um Gottes Willen Schonung: Ein geschichtsethischer Blick auf Christen, Muslime und Gottes barmherzige Unberechenbarkeit im Willehalm des Wolfram von Eschenbach' in Klaus Kienzler et al. eds, *Islam und Christentum, Religion im Gespräch* (Münster: Augsburger Schriften zur Theologie und Philosophie, 2001), 153–70.

Schmid, Elisabeth, 'Enterbung, Ritterethos, Unrecht: Zu Wolframs "Willehalm"', *ZfdA* 107 (1978), 259–75.

Schnell, Rüdiger, 'Die Christen und die "Anderen": Mittelalterliche Positionen und germanische Perspektiven' in Peter Schreiner and Odilo Engles, eds, *Die Begegnung des Westens mit dem Osten, Kongreßakten des 4. Symposions des Mediävistenverbandes in Köln 1991 aus Anlaß des 1000. Todesjahres der kaiserin Theophanu* (Cologne: Jan Thorbecke, 1991), 185–202.

Schröder, Walter Johannes, 'Der Toleranzgedanke und der Begriff der "Gotteskindschaft" in Wolframs Willehalm' in G. Bellman, ed., *Festschrift für Karl Bischoff zum 70en Geburtstag* (Cologne: Böhlau, 1975), 400–15.

Schröder, Werner, 'Der Markgraf Und Die Gefallenen Heidenkönige in Wolframs "Willehalm"' in Christian Gellinek, ed., *Festschrift Für Konstantin Reichardt* (Munich: Francke Verlag, 1969), 135–67.

——, 'Willehalms Pferde' in Ingrid Kühn and Gotthard Lerchner, eds, *Von wyßheit würt der mensch geert, Festschrift für Manfred Lemmer zum 65. Geburtstag* (Frankfurt am Main: Peter Lang, 1993), 105–15.

Starkey, Kathryn, 'Die Androhung der Unordnung: Inszenierung, Macht und Verhandlung in Wolframs Willehalm', *Zeitschrift für deutsche Philologie* 121/3 (2002), 321–41.

Steinmetz, Ralf-Henning, 'Die ungetauften Christenkinder in den 'Willehalm'-Versen 307, 26–30', *ZfdA* 124 (1995), 151–62.

Toepfer, Regina, 'Enterbung und Gotteskindschaft: Zur Problematik der Handlungs-motivierung inm "Willehalm" Wolframs von Eschenbach', *Zeitschrift für deutsche Philologie*, 129/1 (2010), 63–81.

Volfing, Annette, '*Parzival* and *Willehalm*: Narrative Continuity?' in Martin H. Jones and Timothy McFarland, eds, *Wolfram's 'Willehalm': Fifteen Essays* (Rochester: Camden House, 2002), 45–59.

Wachinger, Burghart, 'Schichten der Ethik in Wolframs Willehalm' in Michael S. Batts, ed., *Alte Welten, neue Welten: Akten des IX. Kongresses der Internationalen Vereinigung für Germanische Sprach- und Literaturwissenschaft* (Vancouver, BC/ Tübingen: Niemeyer, 1995), 49–59.

Wessel-Fleinghaus, Franziska, 'Gotes hantgetat, Zur Deutung von Wolframs Willehalm unter dem Aspekt der Gattungsfrage', *Literaturwissenschaftliches Jahrbuch* 33 (1992), 29–100.

Yeandle, David N., 'Rennewart's "Shame": An Aspect of the Characterization of Wolfram's Ambivalent Hero' in Martin H. Jones and Timothy McFarland, eds, *Wolfram's 'Willehalm': Fifteen Essays* (Rochester, NY: Camden House, 2002), 167–90.

Young, Christopher, 'The Construction of Gender in *Willehalm*' in Martin H. Jones and Timothy McFarland, eds, *Wolfram's 'Willehalm': Fifteen Essays* (Rochester: Camden House, 2002), 249–69.

The 'Cycle de Guillaume'

Bennett, Philip E., 'Heroism and Sanctity in the *Cycle de Guillaume*' in Martin H. Jones and Timothy McFarland, eds, *Wolfram's 'Willehalm': Fifteen Essays* (Rochester: Camden House, 2002), 1–19.

——, 'The Storming of the Other World, the Enamoured Muslim Princess and the Evolution of the Legend of Guillaume d'Orange' in Duncan McMillan, Wolfgang van Emden, Philip E. Bennett and Alexander Kerr, eds, *Guillaume d'Orange and* the *'Chanson de Geste': essays presented to Duncan McMillan in celebration of his seventieth birthday by his friends and colleagues of the Société Rencesvals* (Reading: University of Reading, 1984), 1–14.

Buschinger, Danielle, 'Les Relations entre epopée française et epopée germanique: Essai de position des problèmes', *Xe Congrès International de la Société Rencesvals pour l'Étude des Épopées Romanes: Au Carrefour des routes d'europe: la chanson de geste, Strasbourg 1985,* series Senefiance 20–21 (Aix-en-Provence: CUER MA, 1987), 77–101.

De Combarieu du Grès, Micheline, 'Aliscans ou la victoire des "nouveaux" chrétiens (étude sur Guibourc et Rainouart)' in Jean Dufournet, ed., *Mourir aux Aliscans: Aliscans et la légende de Guillaume d'Orange* (Paris: Honoré Champion, 1993), 55–77.

Flori, Jean, 'L'idée de croisade dans quelques chansons de geste du cycle de Guillaume d'Orange', *Medioevo Romanzo* 21/2–3 (1997), 496–506.

Frappier, Jean, *Les Chansons de geste du cycle de Guillaume d'Orange,* 2nd edn, vol. II (Paris: SEDES, 1967).

Hathaway, Stephanie, 'Chivalry and Spirituality: Chivalry in the *chanson de geste* Material from Aquitaine to Germany' in Stephanie Hathaway and David W. Kim, eds, *Intercultural Transmission Throughout the Medieval Mediterranean* (London: Continuum, forthcoming).

Huby-Marly, Marie-Noël, 'Willehalm de Wolfram von Eschenbach et la chanson des Aliscans', *Études germaniques,* 39 (1984), 388–411.

Koss, Ronald G., *Family, Kinship and Lineage in the Cycle de Guillaume d'Orange,* vol. 5, Studies in Mediaeval Literature (Lewiston: The Edwin Mellen Press, 1990).

Labbé, Alain, 'De la cuisine à la salle: la topographie palatine d'*Aliscans* et l'évolution du personnage de Renouart' in Jean Dufournet, ed., *Mourir aux Aliscans: Aliscans et la légende de Guillaume d'Orange* (Paris: Honoré Champion, 1993), 207–25.

Lachet, Claude, 'Echos significatifs dans la composition d'*Aliscans*' in J. Claude Faucon, Alain Labbé and Danielle Quéruel, eds, *Miscellanea Mediævalia: Mélanges offerts à Philippe Ménard* (Paris: Honoré Champion, 1998), 783–97.

——, 'Figures féminines dans *Aliscans*' in Jean Dufournet, ed., *Mourir aux Aliscans: Aliscans et la légende de Guillaume d'Orange* (Paris: Honoré Champion, 1993), 101–19.

——, *La Prise d'Orange ou la parodie courtoise d'une épopée,* Editions Slatkine, vol. 10, Nouvelle bibliothèque du Moyen Age (Genève: Libr, H. Champion, 1986).

Martin, Jean-Pierre, 'D'où viennent les Sarrasins? A propos de l'imaginaire épique d'*Aliscans*' in Jean Dufournet, ed., *Mourir aux Aliscans: Aliscans et la légende de Guillaume d'Orange* (Paris: Honoré Champion, 1993), 121–36.

Monteverdi, Angelo, 'La laisse épique', *La Technique littéraire des chansons de geste: actes du colloque de Liège Septembre 1957* (Paris: Société d'Édition Les Belles Lettres, 1959), 127–40.

Pastré, Jean-Marc, 'Un avatar courtois de la Bataille d'Aliscans, le Willehalm de Wolfram von Eschenbach' in *Essor et fortune de la chanson de geste dans l'Europe et l'Orient latin: actes du IXe congrès international de la Société Rencesvals pour l'étude des épopées romanes, Padoue-Venise, 29 août–4 septembre 1982* (Modena: Mucchi, 1983), 333–47.

Price, Glanville, ed., *William, Count of Orange: Four Old French Epics* (London: Dent, 1975).

Rocher, Daniel, 'Wolfram von Eschenbach, Adapteur de la chanson d'Aliscans', *Xe Congrès International de la Société Rencesvals pour l'Étude des Épopées Romanes: Au Carrefour des routes d'europe: la chanson de geste, Strasbourg 1985*, series Senefiance 20–21 (Aix-en-Provence: CUER MA, 1987), 959–73.

Ruiz-Domènec, José Enrique, 'La Chanson de Guillaume: Relato de frontera.' *Medioevo Romanzo* 21/2–3 (1997), 496–506.

Saxer, Victor, 'Le Culte et la légende hagiographique de Saint Guillaume de Gellone' in *La chanson de geste et le mythe carolingien: Mélanges René Louis*, vol. 2 (Saint-Père-sous-Vézelay: Musée archéologique national, 1982), 565–89.

Vallecalle, Jean-Claude, 'Aspects du héros dans *Aliscans*' in Jean Dufournet, ed., *Mourir aux Aliscans: Aliscans et la légende de Guillaume d'Orange* (Paris: Honoré Champion, 1993), 177–95.

Wathelet-Willem, Jeanne, 'Les Refrains dans la chanson de Guillaume', *La Technique littéraire des chansons de geste: Actes du colloque de Liège Septembre 1957* (Paris: Société d'Édition Les Belles Lettres, 1959), 457–83.

——, 'Sur la chanson de Guillaume' in *La chanson de geste et le mythe carolingien: Mélanges René Louis*, vol. 2 (Saint-Père-sous-Vézelay: Musée archéologique national, 1982), 607–21.

Weeks, Raymond, 'The "Chancun de Willame": A French Manuscript Preserved in England', *Library* VI, 2/22 (1905), 113–36.

Wiesmann-Wiedemann, Friederike, *Le Roman du Willehalm de Wolfram d'Eschenbach et l'épopée d'Aliscans: Étude de la transformation de l'épopée en roman*, Göppinger Arbeiten zur Germanistik, ed., F.H.a.C.S, Ulrich Müller, vol. 190 (Göppingen: Alfred Kümmerle, 1976).

Chansons de geste

Besnardeau, Wilfrid. *Représentations littéraires de l'étranger au XIIe siècle: des chansons de geste aux premières mises en roman*. Jean Dufournet, ed. Nouvelle Bibliothèque du Moyen Âge (Paris: Honoré Champion, 2007).

Bezzola, Reto R., 'A Propos De La Valeur Littéraire Des Chansons Féodales', *La Technique littéraire des chansons de geste: Actes du colloque de Liège Septembre 1957* (Paris: Société d'Édition Les Belles Lettres, 1959), 183–95.

Buschinger, Danielle, 'Rezeption der Chanson de Geste im Spätmittelalter', *Wolfram-Studien* 11 (1988), 86–106.

Daniel, Norman, *Heroes and Saracens: An Interpretation of the Chansons de Geste* (Edinburgh: Edinburgh University Press, 1984).

De Riquer, Martín, *Les Chansons de geste françaises*, Irénéee Cluzel, trans. Spanish-French, 2nd edn (Paris: Librairie Nizet, 1968).

——, 'Epopée jongleuresque à écouter et épopée romanesque à lire', *La technique littéraire des chansons de geste: Actes du colloque de Liège Septembre 1957* (Paris: Société d'Édition Les Belles Lettres, 1959), 75–84.

De Weever, Jacqueline, *Sheba's Daughters: Whitening and Demonizing the Saracen Woman in Medieval French Epic* (New York: Garland, 1998).

Delbouille, Maurice, 'Les chansons de geste et le livre', *La technique littéraire des chansons de geste: Actes du colloque de Liège Septembre 1957* (Paris: Société d'Édition Les Belles Lettres, 1959), 295–407.

Diaz, José Miguel Lamalfa, 'La culture musicale dans les chansons de geste', *Essor et fortune de la chanson de geste dans L'Europe et L'Orient latin: Actes du IXe Congrès International de la Société Rencesvals pour L'étude des épopées romanes Padoue-Venise, 29 août–4 septembre 1982*, vol. I (Modena: Mucchi, 1982), 111–30.

Du Bellay, ed., *The Oxford Book of French Verse* (Oxford: Clarendon 1908).

Harrison, Ann Tukey, 'Aude and Bramimunde: Their Importance in the *Chanson de Roland*', *The French Review* LIV/5 (1981), 672–9.

Kay, Sarah, *The Chansons de geste in the Age of Romance: Political Fictions* (Oxford: Clarendon Press, 1995).

——, 'La représentation de la féminité dans les chansons de geste', *Charlemagne in the North: Proceedings of the Twelfth International Conference of the Société Rencesvals Edinburgh 4th to 11th August 1991* (Edinburgh: Société Rencesvals British Branch, 1993), 223–40.

Kibler, William W., 'From Epic to Romance: The Case of *Lion de Bourges*' in Douglas Kelly, ed., *The Medieval Opus: Imitation, Rewriting, and Transmission in the French Tradition* (Amsterdam: Rodopi, 1996), 327–55.

Kinoshita, Sharon, 'The Politics of Courtly Love: "La Prise d'Orange" and the Conversion of the Saracen Queen', *Romanic Review* 86/2 (1995), 265–87.

Ménard, Philippe, 'Les jongleurs et les chansons de geste', *La Chanson de geste et le mythe carolingien: mélanges René Louis publiés par ses collègues, ses amis et ses élèves à l'occasion de son 75e anniversaire* (Saint-Père-sous-Vézelay: Musée archéologique régional, 1982), 33–50.

Micha, Alexandre, ed., 'De la chanson de geste au roman: études de littérature médiévale offertes par ses amis, élèves et collègues', vol. 139, *Publications romanes et françaises* (Genève: Droz, 1976).

Poe, Elizabeth W., '*E potz seguir las rimas contrasemblantz*: Imitators of the Master Troubadour Giraut de Bornelh' in Douglas Kelly, ed., *The Medieval Opus: Imitation, Rewriting, and Transmission in the French Tradition* (Amsterdam: Rodopi, 1996), 279–97.

Ramey, Lynne Tarte, 'Role Models? Saracen Women in Medieval French Epic', *Romance Notes* 41/2 (2001), 131–41.

Rychner, Jean, *La Chanson de geste: essai sur l'art épique des jongleurs*, Mario Roques, ed., vol. LIII, Société de publications romanes et françaises (Geneva: Librairie E. Droz, 1955).

Serper, Arié, 'Sarrasins et chansons de geste' in *Essor et fortune de la chanson de geste dans l'Europe et l'Orient latin: actes du IXe congrès international de la Société Rencesvals pour l'étude des épopées romanes, Padoue-Venise, 29 août–4 septembre 1982* (Modena: Mucchi, 1983), 179–83.

Suard, François, *La chanson de geste*, Paul Angoulvent, ed., 1st edn, vol. 2808, Que sais-je? (Paris: PUF, 1993).

——, *Chanson de geste et tradition épique en France au moyen âge* (Caen: Paradigme, 1994).

——, ed., *Plaist vos oïr bone cançon vallant? Mélanges offerts à François Suard: études recueillies par Dominique Boutet, Marie-Madeleine Castellani, Françoise Ferrand et Aimé Petit*, series eds, Marie-Madeleine Castellani Dominique Boutet, Françoise Ferrand, Aimé Petit, 2 vols, Collection Travaux et recherches, UL3 (Lille: Villeneuve d'Ascq: Université Charles de Gaulle-Lille 3, 1999).

Wolf, Alois, 'Rewriting Chansons de geste for a Middle High German public' in Douglas Kelly, ed., *The Medieval Opus: Imitation, Rewriting, and Transmission in the French Tradition* (Amsterdam: Rodopi, 1996), 369–86.

Literary history and criticism

Adams, Jeremy duQuesnay, 'Modern Views of Medieval Chivalry, 1884–1984' in Howell Chickering and Thomas H. Seiler, eds, *The Study of Chivalry: Resources and Approaches* (Kalamazoo: Medieval Institute Publications, 1988), 41–89.

Althoff, Gerd, 'Wolfram von Eschenbach und die Spielregeln der mittelalterlichen Gesellschaft', *Wolfram-Studien* 16 (2000), 102–20.

Bass, Eben, 'The Jewels of Troilus', *College English* 23/2 (1961), 145–7.

Batts, Michael, 'National Perspectives on Originality and Translation: Chrétien de Troyes and Hartmann von Aue' in Martin H. Jones and Roy Wisbey, eds, *Chrétien de Troyes and the German Middle Ages, Papers from an International Symposium* (Cambridge: D.S. Brewer, 1993), 9–18.

Bednar, John, *La Spiritualité et le symbolisme dans les oeuvres de Chrétien de Troyes* (Paris: Libraire A.-G. Nizet, 1974).

Bertau, Karl, 'Versuch Über den Späten Chrestien und die Anfänge Wolframs' in Karl Bertau, ed., *Wolfram von Eschenbach: neun Versuche über Subjektivität und Ursprünglichkeit in der Geschichte* (Munich: C.H. Beck, 1983), 24–59.

Bumke, Joachim, *Höfische Kultur: Literatur und Gesellschaft im hohen Mittelalter* (Munich: Deutscher Taschenbuch Verlag, 2002).

——, *Mäzene im Mittelalter: die Gönner und Auftraggeber der höfischen Literatur in Deutschland 1150–1300* (Munich: C.H. Beck, 1979).

Burns, E. Jane, *Courtly Love Undressed*, Ruth Mazzo Karras, ed., The Middle Ages Series (Philadelphia: University of Pennsylvania Press, 2002).

Campbell, Mary B., *The Witness and the Other World: Exotic European Travel Writing 400–1600* (Ithaca: Cornell University Press, 1988).

Chejne, Anwar, 'The Role of al-Andalus in the Movement of Ideas Between Islam and the West' in Khalil I. Semaan, ed., *Islam and the Medieval West: Aspects of Intercultural Relations* (Albany: State University of New York Press, 1980), 110–33.

Clifton-Everest, John, 'Knights-Servitor and Rapist Knights: A Contribution to the Parzival/Gawan Question', *ZfdA* 119 (1990), 290–317.

——, 'Wolframs Parzival und die chanson de geste' in Ulrike Hirhager Christa Tuczay and Karin Lichtblau, eds, *Ir sult sprechen willekomen: Grenzenlose Mediävistik: Festschrift für Helmut Birkhan zum 60. Geburtstag* (Bern: Peter Lang, 1998), 693–713.

Clouard, Henri, Le Moyen Age, *Des origines à la fin du dix-huitième siècle*, vol. 1 of *Anthologie de la littérature française* (New York: Oxford University Press, 1975).

Cooper, Helen, *The English Romance in Time: Transforming motifs from Geoffrey of Monmouth to the death of Shakespeare* (Oxford: Oxford University Press, 2004).

Cowling, David, *Building the Text: Architecture as Metaphor in Late Medieval and Early Modaern France* (Oxford: Clarendon Press, 1998).

Doss-Quinby, Eglal, 'Rolan, de ceu ke m'avez/parti dirai mon samblant: The Feminine Voice in the Old French jeu-parti', *Neophilologus* 83/4 (1999), 497–516.

Fahrner, Rudolf, *West-Östliches Rittertum: Das ritterliche Menschenbild in der Dichtung des Europäischen Mittelalters und der islamischen Welt*, Stefano Bianca, ed. (Graz: Akademische Druck- und Verlagsanstalt, 1994).

Ferrand, Françoise, 'La Réception de la littérature française médiévale en Allemagne au XIXe siècle: l'exemple de Richard Wagner' in J. Claude Faucon, Alain Labbé and Danielle Quéruel, eds, *Miscellanea Mediavalia: Mélanges offerts à Philippe Ménard* (Paris: Honoré Champion, 1998), 529–46.

Ferroul, Yves, 'Le Mythe du courage individuel et l'exploit singulier' in François Suard, ed., *Plaist vos oïr bone cançon vallant? mélanges offerts à François Suard: études recueillies par Dominique Boutet, Marie-Madeleine Castellani, Françoise Ferrand et Aimé Petit* (Lille 3: Villeneuve d'Ascq, 1999), 251–60.

Flori, Jean, 'La Croix, la crosse et l'épée, La Conversion des infidèles dans la Chanson de Roland et les chroniques de croisade' in François Suard, ed., *Plaist vos oïr bone cançon vallant? mélanges offerts à François Suard: études recueillies par Dominique Boutet, Marie-Madeleine Castellani, Françoise Ferrand et Aimé Petit* (Lille 3: Villeneuve d'Ascq, 1999), 261–72.

Hanning, Robert W., 'The Criticism of Chivalric Epic and Romance' in Howell Chickering and Thomas H. Seiler, eds, *The Study of Chivalry: Resources and Approaches* (Kalamazoo: Medieval Institute Publications, 1988), 91–113.

Hathaway, Stephanie L., 'Women at Montlaon: The Influential Roles of the Female Characters in Court Negotiations in *Aliscans* and Wolfram's *Willehalm*', *Neophilologus* 93/1 (2009), 103–21.

Jackson, W.T.H., *Chivalry in Twelfth-Century Germany: The Works of Hartmann von Aue*, Arthurian Studies XXXIV (Cambridge: D.S. Brewer, 1994).

——, *The Challenge of the Medieval Text: Studies in Genre and Interpretation*, Joan M. Ferrante and Robert W. Hanning, ed. (New York: Columbia University Press, 1985).

Jones, Martin H. and Roy Wisbey, *Chrétien de Troyes and the German Middle Ages, Papers from an International Symposium* (Cambridge: D.S. Brewer, 1993).

Kartschoke, Dieter, *Geschichte der deutschen Literatur im frühen Mittelalter, vol. 1, Geschichte der deutschen Literatur im Mittelalter* (Munich: Deutscher Taschenbuch Verlag GmbH & Co., 1990).

Kern, Manfred, 'Krieg der Worte – Kreuzzug und Poesie bei Walther von der Vogelweide und Wolfram von Eschenbach' in *Orient und Okzident im Mittelalter – Kontakte und Konflikte* (University Salzburg: Salzburger Mittelalterstudien, 2002).

Knapp, Fritz Peter, 'Die grosse Schlacht zwischen Orient und Okzident in der abendländischen Epik: Ein antikes Thema in mittelalterlichem Gewand', *Germanisch-romanische Monatsschrift* 24/2 (1974), 129–52.

Lafitte-Houssat, Jacques, *Troubadours et cours d'amour*, 1st edn, vol. 422, Que sais-je? (Paris: Presses Universitaires de France, 1950).

Louis, René, 'Qu'est-ce que l'Épopée Vivante?', *La Table Ronde* 132 (1958), 9–17.

Maurer, Friedrich, *Dichtung und Sprache des Mittelalters: Gesammelte Aufsätze*, 2nd edn (Bern: Francke Verlag, 1971).

McCracken, Peggy, *The Romance of Adultery: Queenship and Sexual Transgression in Old French Literature*, Ruth Mazo Karras, ed., The Middle Ages Series (Philadelphia: University of Pennsylvania Press, 1998).

Minnis, Alastair J., *Medieval Theory of Authorship: Scholastic literary attitudes in the later Middle Ages*, 2nd edn (Aldershot: Scolar Press, 1988).

Owen, D.D.R., *Noble Lovers* (London: Phaidon, 1975).

Philipowski, Silke, 'Geste und Inszenierung: Wahrheit und Lesbarkeit von Körpern im höfischen Epos', *Beiträge zur Geschichte der deutschen Sprache und Literatur (PBB)* 122 (2000), 455–77.

Pidal, Ramón Menéndez, *La Chanson de Roland et la tradition épique des Francs*, Irénée-Marcel Cluzel, trans. Spanish-French, 2nd edn (Paris: J. Picard, 1960).

Ramey, Lynn Tarte, *Christian, Saracen and Genre in Medieval French Literature*, Francis G. Gentry, ed., Medieval History and Culture (New York: Routledge, 2001).

Schnell, Rüdiger, *Causa Amoris: Liebeskonzeption und Liebesdarstellung in der mittelalterlichen Literatur* (Bern: A. Francke AG Verlag, 1985).

Schotte, Manuela, *Christen, Heiden und der Gral: Die Heidendarstellung in den mittelhochdeutschen Gralromanen des 13. Jahrhunderts* (Frankfurt am Main: Peter Lang, 2005).

Sinclair, Finn, 'Defending the Castle: Didactic Literature and the Containment of Female Sexuality', *Reading Medieval Studies* 22 (1996), 5–19.

——, 'Reproductive Frameworks: Maternal Significance in *Berte as grans piés*' in Philip E. Bennett, Marianne Ailes and Karen Pratt, eds, *Reading Around the Epic: A Festschrift in Honour of Professor Wolfgang van Emden* (London: King's College London Centre for Late Antique & Medieval Studies, 1998), 269–95.

Smith, Colin, 'On Spanish Ballads and French Epics' in Philip E. Bennett, Marianne Ailes, Karen Pratt, eds, *Reading Around the Epic: A Festschrift in Honour of Professor Wolfgang van Emden* (London: King's College London Centre for Late Antique & Medieval Studies, 1998), 297–311.

Stolz, Michael, ed., 'Introduction' to *Sankt Galler Nibelungenhandschrift (Cod. Sang. 857)*, vol. 1, Codices Electronici Sangallenses, Basler Parzival-Projekt (St Gallen: Stiftsbibliothek St Gallen, 2003), CD booklet.

Switten, Margaret, 'Chevalier in Twelfth-Century French and Occitan Vernacular Literature' in Howell Chickering and Thomas H. Seiler, eds, *The Study of Chivalry: Resources and Approaches* (Kalamazoo: Medieval Institute Publications, 1988), 403–47.

Tobin, Frank, 'Middle High German' in Kim Vivian, ed., *A Concise History of German Literature to 1900* (Columbia, SC: Camden House, 1992), 34–9.

Williams, Andrea M.L., *The Adventures of the Holy Grail: a study of La Queste del Saint Graal* (Oxford: Peter Lang, 2001).

Political and cultural history

Bäuml, Franz H., *Medieval Civilisation in Germany 800–1273*, Dr Glyn Daniel, ed. (London: Thames and Hudson, 1969).

Bennett, Matthew, 'First Crusaders' Images of Muslims: the Influence of Vernacular Poetry?', *Forum for Modern Language Studies* 22/2 (1986), 101–22.

Bloch, Marc, *Mélanges historiques*, vol. I (Paris: S.E.V.P.E.N., 1963).

——, *La société féodale*, 2 vols (Paris: Albin Michel, 1939–40).

Bonath, Gesa, 'Reflets des croisades dans la littérature allemande' in Karl-Heinz Bender and Hermann Kleber, eds, *Les Épopées de la croisade* (Stuttgart: Franz Steiner Verlag Wiesbaden, 1987), 105–18.

Bosl, Karl, *Staat, Gesellschaft, Wirtschaft im deutschen Mittelalter*, 3rd edn, vol. 7, Gebhardt Handbuch der deutschen Geschichte (Munich: Deutscher Taschenbuch Verlag GmbH & Co, 1976).

Boyd, Douglas, *Eleanor April Queen of Aquitaine* (Stroud: Sutton, 2004).

Brooke, Christopher, *The Structure of Medieval Society*, Joan Evans and Prof. Christopher Brooke, eds, 1st edn, Library of Medieval Civilisation (London: Thames and Hudson, 1971).

Bumke, Joachim, *Studien zum Ritterbegriff im 12. und 13. Jahrhundert* (Heidelberg: Carl Winter, 1964), trans. W.T.H and Erika Jackson (New York: AMS Press Inc, 1977).

Cutler, Allan, 'The First Crusade and the Idea of Conversion', *Muslim World* 58 (1968), 57–71, 155–64.

Daniel, Norman, *The Arabs and Mediaeval Europe*, M.N.A. Ziadeh, ed., Arab Background Series (London: Longman, 1975).

Dennis, George T., 'Schism, Union, and the Crusades' in *The Meeting of Two Worlds: Cultural Exchange between East and West during the Period of the Crusades*, Vladimir P. Goss, ed. (Kalamazoo: Medieval Institute Publications, 1986), 181–7.

Dozy, Reinhart Pieter Anne, *Histoire des musulmans d'Espagne*, Francis Griffin Stokes, trans. (London: Frank Cass, 1972).

Duby, Georges, *Les trois ordres: ou l'imaginaire du féodalisme* (Paris: Gallimard, 1978).

Duffy, Eamon, *Saints and Sinners: A History of the Popes* (New Haven, CT: Yale University Press, 1997).

Duggan, Lawrence G. 'For Force Is Not of God? Compulsion and Conversion from Yahweh to Charlemagne' in James Muldoon, ed., *Varieties of Religious Conversion in the Middle Ages* (Gainesville: University Press of Florida, 1997), 49–62.

Elisséeff, Nikita, 'Les échanges culturels entre le monde musulman et les Croisés à l'époque de Nur ad-Din b, Zanki (m, 1174)' in Vladimir P. Goss, ed., *The Meeting of Two Worlds: Cultural Exchange between East and West during the Period of the Crusades* (Michigan: Medieval Institute Publications, 1986), 39–52.

——, *Nur ad-Din: un grand prince musulman de Syrie au temps des Croisades (511–569h, / 1118–1174)*, 3 vols (Damascus: Institut Francais de Damas, 1967).

——, *L'Orient musulman au Moyen Age 622–1260* (Paris: Armand Colin, 1977).

Flori, Jean, *L'Essor de la chevalerie XIᵉ–XIIᵉ siècles, Travaux d'histoire éthico-politique XLVI* (Geneva: Droz, 1986).

——, *L'Idéologie du glaive: préhistoire de la chevalerie* (Geneva: Droz, 1983).

Gauss, Julia, 'Toleranz und Intoleranz zwischen Christen und Muslimen in der Zeit vor den Kreuzzügen', *Saeculum* 19 (1968), 362–89.

Gautier, Léon, *Chivalry*, D.C. Dunning, trans., Jacques Levron, ed. (London: Phoenix House, 1965).

Ghali, Wacyf Boutros, *La Tradition chevaleresque des Arabes* (Paris: Plon-Nourrit, 1919).

Goss, Vladimir P., 'Introduction' to *The Meeting of Two Worlds: Cultural Exchange between East and West during the Period of the Crusades* (Kalamazoo, MI: Medieval Institute Publications, 1986), 3–14.

Grabar, Oleg, 'Patterns and Ways of Cultural Exchange' in Vladimir P. Goss, ed., *The Meeting of Two Worlds: Cultural Exchange between East and West during the Period of the Crusades* (Kalamazoo, MI: Medieval Institute Publications, 1986), 441–6.

Green, D.H., *The Beginnings of Medieval Romance: Fact and Fiction, 1150–1220*, Alastair Minnis, ed., Cambridge Studies in Medieval Literature (Cambridge: Cambridge University Press, 2002).

Hindley, Geoffrey, *Saladin* (London: Constable, 1976).

Houben, Hubert, 'Die Tolerierung Andergläubiger im normannisch-staufischen Süditalien' in Odilo Engels and Peter Schreiner, eds, *Die Begegnung des Westens mit dem Osten* (Sigmaringen: Thorbecke, 1993), 75–87.

Kedar, Benjamin Z, 'Muslim Conversion in Canon Law' in Benjamin Z. Kedar, ed., *The Franks in the Levant: 11th to 14th Centuries* (Brookfield, VT: Variorum, 1993), 321–32.

Keen, Maurice, *Chivalry* (New Haven: Yale University Press, 1984).

Knowles, David, *The Evolution of Medieval Thought*, D.E. Luscombe and C.N.L. Brooke, eds, 2nd edn (London: Longman, 1988).

Lane-Poole, Stanley, *Saladin and the Fall of Jerusalem* (New York: G.P. Putnam's Sons, 1898).

——, *The Story of Cairo*, 3rd edn (London: J.M. Dent, 1918).

Leonard, Frances, 'The Art of Chivalry: Portrait of an Elite Culture', *The Texas Humanist* 5/3 (1983), 4–6.

Makdisi, George, 'On the Origin and Development of the College in Islam and the West' in Khalil I. Semaan, ed., *Islam and the Medieval West: Aspects of Intercultural Relations* (Albany: State University of New York Press, 1980), 26–49.

McCash, June Hall Martin, 'Marie de Champagne and Eleanor of Aquitaine: A Relationship Reexamined', *Spéculum* LIV/4 (1979), 698–711.

Muldoon, James, *Popes, Lawyers, and Infidels*, Edward Peters, ed., The Middle Ages (University of Pennsylvania: University of Pennsylvania Press, 1979).

——, *Varieties of Religious Conversion in the Middle Ages* (Gainesville: University Press of Florida, 1997).

Newby, P.H., *Saladin in His Time* (London: Faber and Faber, 1983).

Nicol, Donald M., 'The Crusades and the unity of Christendom' in Vladimir P. Goss, ed., *The Meeting of Two Worlds: Cultural Exchange Between East and West During the Period of the Crusades* (Kalamazoo, MI: Medieval Institute Publications, 1986), 169–80.

Reinhardt, Kurt F., *Germany: 2000 Years*, vol. 1 (New York: Continuum, 1990).

Rodríguez-Velasco, Jesús D., *Order and Chivalry: Knighthood and Citizenship in Late Medieval Castile*, Eunice Rodriguez Ferguson, trans., The Middle Ages (Philadelphia: University of Pennsylvania Press, 2010).

Rossi, Marguerite, 'Rapport introductif: épopée française et épopée non française', *Essor et fortune de la chanson de geste dans l'Europe et l'Orient latin: actes du IXe congrès international de la Société Rencesvals pour l'étude des épopées romanes, Padoue-Venise, 29 août–4 septembre 1982* (Modena: Mucchi, 1983), 247–65.

Schwinges, Rainer Christoph, *Kreuzzugsideologie und Toleranz*, vol. 15, Karl Bosl, ed.,
    Monographien zur Geschichte des Mittelalters (Stuttgart: Anton Hiersemann,
    1977).
Sire, H.J.A., *The Knights of Malta* (New Haven, CT: Yale University Press, 1994).
Tolan, John V., *Saracens: Islam in the medieval European Imagination* (New York:
    Columbia University Press, 2002).
Ullmann, Walter, 'The Development of the Medieval Idea of Sovereignty', *The English
    Historical Review* 64/250 (1949), 1–33.
Vernet, Juan, *La Cultura Hisponoárabe en Oriente y Occidente* (Barcelona: Ariel,
    1978).
Weir, Alison, *Eleanor of Aquitaine: by the Wrath of God, Queen of England* (London:
    Jonathan Cape, 1999).
Wentzlaff-Eggebert, Friedrich-Wilhelm, 'Kreuzzugsidee und Mittelalterliches Welt-
    bild', *Deutsches Vierteljahrschrift für Literaturwissenschaft und Geistesgeschichte*
    30 (1956), 71–88.
Wolfzettel, Friedrich, 'Die Entdeckung des "Anderen" aus dem Geist der Kreuzzüge'
    in Peter Schreiner Odilo Engels, ed., *Die Begegnung des Westens mit dem Osten:
    Kongressakten des 4. Symposions des Mediävistenverbandes in Köln 1991 aus Anlass
    des 1000. Todesjahres der Kaiserin Theophanu* (Sigmaringen: Thorbecke Verlag,
    1991), 273–95.

Reference Works

Chandler, Frank W., Martin H. Jones, ed., *A Catalogue of Names of Persons in the
    German Court Epics*, vol. VIII, King's College London Medieval Studies (Exeter:
    Short Run Press, 1992).
Godefroy, Frédéric, *Lexique de l'ancien francais* (Paris: Welter, 1901).
Happold, F.C., *Mysticism: A Study and an Anthology*, 3rd rev. ed. (London: Penguin,
    1990).
Hennig, Beate, *Kleines Mittelhochdeutsches Wörterbuch* (Tübingen: Max Niemeyer
    Verlag, 1993).
Kinder, Hermann and Wilgemann, Werner, *The Anchor Atlas of World History*, 2 vols,
    Ernest A. Menze, trans. (New York: Anchor, 1974).

Mann, Horace K., *The Lives of the Popes in the Early Middle Ages: The Popes During the Carolingian Empire; Leo III to Formosus, 795–891*, 2nd edn, vol. II (London: K. Paul, Trench, Trubner, 1925).

Schimmel, Annemarie, 'Islam' in C. Jouco Bleeker and Geo Widengren, eds, *Historia Religionum: Handbook for the History of Religions* (Leiden: E.J. Brill, 1971), 125–210.

Thorne, J.O., and T.C. Collcott, eds, *Chambers Biographical Dictionary* (Cambridge: Cambridge University Press, 1984).

Other Works Consulted

Ali, Samer M., *Arabic Literary Salons in the Islamic Middle Ages: Poetry, Public Performance, and the Presentation of the Past* (Notre Dame, Indiana: University of Notre Dame, 2010).

Aroux, Eugène, *Les Mystères de la chevalerie et de l'amour platonique au Moyen Âge*, Georges Gondinet, ed., GALAAD (Puiseaux: Pardès, 1988).

Collier's Cyclopedia of Commercial and Social Information and Treasury of Useful and Entertaining Knowledge, Nugent Robinson, ed. (New York: P.F. Collier, 1882).

Gamer, Helena M., 'The Earliest Evidence of Chess in Western Literature: The Einsiedeln Verses', *Speculum* 29/4 (1954), 734–50.

Huda, Qamar-ul, 'The Light beyond the Shore in the Theology of Proper Sufi Moral Conduct (Adab)', *Journal of the American Academy of Religion* 72/2 (2004), 461–84.

Kashifi Sabzawari, Husayn Wa'iz, *The Royal Book of Spiritual Chivalry (Futuwat Namah Yi Sultani)*, Jay R. Crook, trans., Seyyed Hossein Nasr, ed. (Chicago: J.P. Kazi Publications and Great Books of the Islamic World, 2000).

Loewen, Arley, 'Proper Conduct (*Adab*) is Everything: The *Futuwwat-namah-i Sultani* of Husayn Wa'iz-i Kashifi', *Iranian Studies* 36/4 (2003), 543–70.

Milani, Milad, 'Cyclical history, gnosis, and memory: A study in the role and significance of Mystical Poetry as a medium of Popular Culture for Persian Sufism' in *The Buddha of Suburbia: Proceedings of the Eighth Australian and International Religion, Literature and the Arts Conference 2004* (University of Sydney: RLA Press, 2005).

———, 'Medieval Persian Chivalry and Mysticism' in Stephanie L. Hathaway and David W. Kim, eds, *Intercultural Transmission Throughout the Medieval Mediterranean* (London: Continuum, 2012).

———, *The Secret Persia*, Gnostica Series (London: Equinox Publishing: 2012).

Nasr, Seyyed Hossein, 'The Rise and Development of Persian Sufism' in Leonard Lewisohn, ed., *The Heritage of Sufism, Volume I: Classical Persian Sufism from its origins to Rumi (700–1300)* (Oxford: Oneworld, 1999), 1–18.

Shelton, Mahmud, 'Introduction' to Kashifi Sabzawari, Husayn Wa'iz, *The Royal Book of Spiritual Chivalry (Futuwat Namah Yi Sultani)*, Jay R. Crook, trans., Seyyed Hossein Nasr, ed. (Chicago: J.P. Kazi Publications and Great Books of the Islamic World, 2000), xxi–xxx.

Ward, John O, 'Some Principles of Rhetorical Historiography in the Twelfth Century' in Ernst Breisach, ed., *Classical Rhetoric & Medieval Historiography* (Kalamazoo: Medieval Institute Publications, 1985).

Wulff, David, 'Psychological Approaches' in Frank Whaling, ed., *Theory and Method in Religious Studies: Contemporary Approaches to the Study of Religion* (Berlin: Mouton de Gruyter, 1995), 253–320.

Index

Studies in Old Germanic Languages and Literatures

Series editor: Professor Irmengard Rauch

Vol. 1   Seiichi Suzuki
The Morphosyntax of Detransitive Suffixes -Þ- and -n- in Gothic:
A Synchronic and Diachronic Study
ISBN 978-0-8204-1032-6

Vol. 2   Anne A. Baade
Melchior Goldast von Haiminsfeld: Collector, Commentator and Editor
ISBN 978-0-8204-1835-3

Vol. 3   Joseph D. Wine
Figurative Language in Cynewulf: Defining Aspects of a Poetic Style
ISBN 978-0-8204-1936-7

Vol. 4   Colette van Kerckvoorde
A Descriptive Grammar of Jan Yperman's *Cyrurgie*
ISBN 978-0-8204-2149-0

Vol. 5   Paul W. Brosman, Jr.
The Rhine Franconian Element in Old French
ISBN 978-0-8204-4189-4

Vol. 6   Stephanie L. Hathaway
Saracens and Conversion: Chivalric Ideals in *Aliscans* and Wolfram's
Willehalm
ISBN 978-3-0343-0781-9